LETTERS TO REBECCA

Stories of Real Families Never End

William B. Moore, Jr.

*

HERITAGE BOOKS
2012

HERITAGE BOOKS
AN IMPRINT OF HERITAGE BOOKS, INC.

Books, CDs, and more—Worldwide

For our listing of thousands of titles see our website
at
www.HeritageBooks.com

Published 2012 by
HERITAGE BOOKS, INC.
Publishing Division
100 Railroad Ave. #104
Westminster, Maryland 21157

International Standard Book Numbers
Paperbound: 978-0-7884-0304-0
Clothbound: 978-0-7884-9417-8

I dedicate this book to my mother,

May Isom Whitten Moore,

who wanted me to learn about her family,

And to Arthur Reagan,

who taught me how.

TABLE OF CONTENTS

Silas Reagan Whitten
1794-1888
father of Rebecca,
head of household from which her letters were collected

FOREWORD

I am still not sure why Rebecca's letters grip me as they do, but I read each one with a growing sense of family, of love, and of gratitude that she allowed us an intimate look back more than one hundred and seventy-five years into the minds and hearts of her people. There were more than a hundred and fifty letters, stained, torn, and faded, but neatly folded and protected in clear plastic envelopes. I can almost see the writers laboring with the sharpened end of a large feather in the dim light of a fire, candle, or lantern. They were delivered by post, by hand, sometimes through the kindness of a traveler. The correspondents were Rebecca's Earles and Whittens, plus a few friends and acquaintances. Many of the original envelopes are intact and have been used for doodling, writing notes, and practicing penmanship. Spanning about a century, they involve four generations of her family. Most were written from South Carolina, Georgia, Alabama, Tennessee, and Mississippi. They speak of daily life, of war and worship, of birth and death. While telling of the Earles and Whittens, they depict typical southern families as they moved south and west to settle the vast wilderness that became these United States.

I suppose my fascination with Rebecca's letters stems from my being an Earle, a Whitten, and a child of the South.

Throughout my childhood my mother's family was all around me. Whittens seemed, somehow, different from my father's relatives, and those of my friends. They sang more and louder. Some of them wrote poetry, and some painted nice pictures. My Whitten uncles wrote me letters when something important happened in my life. When I received my naval commission during World War II, Uncle Les had his tailor make me a uniform, then took me for lunch to the Army/Navy Club in Washington, introducing me to captains and admirals as one of their peers.

His son, Les Whitten Jr., was an associate of columnist Jack Anderson and has written several books. Mother's brothers and sisters made me feel special when I was with them. They talked about things that sounded important, and held strong opinions, which they expressed without apology. They were more emotional than other people I knew, laughed a lot, and cried at times, even the men. Every one was unabashedly religious. They went to church, read the

Bible, talked about Jesus, and spoke of relatives I had never met and places I had never been, like the Mississippi communities of Chalybeate, Ripley, Jonesborough, Blue Mountain, Oxford, Burgess, and Coffeeville. Sometimes they argued, and often admonished.

I look like my father looked. Even a casual observer knows I possess the best and worst of Moore genes. However, often I am accused of being a Whitten by those who see those materials in my construction. But the inoculation of family history didn't take. The old people and places didn't interest me, despite mother's pouring stories and letters and records into me all her life. She prayed that I would become interested enough to learn about her family, and died believing I never would.

She was wrong. About the time I started drawing Social Security and got on the receiving end of Medicare, the bug bit. Dusting off all the stuff she sent, I became the fanatic I am today. After I discovered Rebecca's letters, mother's family became so real to me that I decided you should meet them as well.

The book contains little that is mine. It is the work of many researchers, and I will try to cite them here for most are not mentioned in the text.

Chapter Six of *Whitten and Allied Families*, second edition, published in 1984 by Virginia Wood Alexander and William C. Whitten, concerns Rebecca's Whittens. I have helped myself to large portions of it. Author William C. Whitten has encouraged, advised, and assisted me.

Much was learned about the Earles of the Carolinas and Virginia, the Rev. John Gill Landrum, and the history of Upper South Carolina from these books:

The Earles and The Birnies, by Joseph Earle Birnie, privately published in 1974.

History of Spartanburg County, Parts I & II, by Dr. J. B. O. Landrum, published in 1900 by the Franklin Printing and Publishing Co. of Atlanta, republished 1991 by Heritage Books, Inc., of Bowie, Maryland.

The Life And Times Of Reverend John Gill Landrum, by H. P. Griffith, published in 1885 by H. B. Garner of Philadelphia, reprinted in 1992 by SCMAR of Columbia, South Carolina.

Whitten friends and relatives have supplied information. They include these bearing the Whitten name: Walter Wood, Alfred Tennyson, Sarah Agnes Durham, Paula, Milton Clay Jr., Henry A., and Alice and Aubrey Dewitt. Whitten descendants with other last names whose assistance is much appreciated include: John Whitten Street, Karen McCann Hett, Mitch Vetusky, Shirley Ann Wilkinson, Dora Whitten Rice, Patrick Roten, and Penny McNair. Karen and Mitch gave me most of the information on the family of David and Elizabeth Whitten Barrett. My cousin, Jane Wilson Lauber, provided the illustrations.

Rebecca Berry Whitten died about twenty years before I was born. To her, heartfelt gratitude. She saved the letters for us to read.

Without Joanne Foster this manuscript would be a mess. She punctuated and spelled, and generally established order amid chaos. Joanne reintroduced me to English language and grammar after a hiatus of more than fifty years.

But it is to Arthur Reagan of Alexandria, Virginia, I am most indebted. Descended from James Reagan, father of Mary and Millicent Reagan Whitten, he spent more than forty years searching for descendants of Charles Whitten, pewter caster. Out of the blue, Arthur sent me his extensive files and challenged me to continue the search. He urged me on, cheering from the sidelines. Arthur knew of Rebecca's letters and provided the clues that led me to them. This book is, in large measure, an extension of his work.

Lillian Wells Moore, the southern belle with whom I share my life, has suffered through this ordeal with grace and compassion. My three children have put up with it with neither. Some day one of them will inherit the task of finishing what so many have begun. Each prays the cup will pass to another.

Now please let me tell you about the family and friends of Rebecca Berry Whitten.

William B. Moore Jr.
1995

CHAPTER ONE

The Letter Writers

Most of the letters Rebecca Berry Whitten saved were written by her brothers and sisters, aunts and uncles, nieces and nephews, parents, and cousins. Those on the side of her father, Silas Reagan, bore the surname Whitten; of her mother, Eleanor Kee, Earle. In the early 1840s teenage Rebecca began saving all the mail that came to her home, Pleasant Grove, near Gowensville, South Carolina. A steady flow dwindles down to a precious few by the late 1800s as most writers age and die, or are scattered over the South. There are glimpses as early as 1811, and late as 1936, through letters mailed before and after Rebecca lived. The families of her grandparents, John and Mary Reagan Whitten, and Col. John and Rebecca Berry Wood Earle, wrote, and Rebecca saved their letters. Various Earles lived nearby, and were closely associated with the Silas Reagan Whittens. Those children of Eleanor Kee's cousin, Theron Earle, who married Hannah Miller, must have been among the Whitten children's closest friends. They wrote, and were frequently mentioned.

That each letter be fully savored requires an introduction to the members of these families. In what is to follow, therefore, you will meet some of the descendants of John and Charles Jr., sons of Charles and Nancy Smith Whitten of Virginia and South Carolina, and Col. John and Judge Baylis, two sons of Maj. Samuel and Anna Sorrell Earle III of Westmoreland and Frederick counties of Virginia.

THE EARLIEST WHITTENS

Charles Whitten, a pewter caster, and the earliest of his line yet identified, was born about 1736; his wife, Nancy Smith, about 1740. They lived in Virginia during the latter half of the eighteenth century. Two sons moved with them to South Carolina about 1785, where Charles bought land on the Tiger River in Spartanburg District. Typical families of the time had many children, and this was likely their case as well. Unfortunately, we only know sons John and Charles Jr., born 12 April 1762 and 18 January 1769 in Virginia, who married sisters, Mary and Millicent Reagan, born 4 August 1766 and 1769 in

Stafford, Virginia. They were daughters of James Reagan, veteran of the Revolution, and his first wife, Elizabeth Hayes. When Mary and Millicent married the Whitten brothers, the Reagans lived in Rockingham, North Carolina, so it is easy to speculate that the Whittens were in a nearby Virginia county. Families bearing the names Southerland, Jernigan, and Graham were closely associated with the Charles Whittens and their descendants, and may have been those of married daughters. Charles died in Spartanburg District about 1798, after deeding land to James Southerland in 1797, and before 1800, when his wife was recorded living in the home of son Charles Jr. in Greenville District. She probably died in Greenville before the 1810 census, for she did not appear with her son's family in that year. ✳

CHAPTER TWO

John Whitten and Family

Whitten researchers have discovered much about the lives and descendants of John and Mary Reagan Whitten. Married about 1784 in Rockingham, North Carolina, John and Mary moved in that year to Spartanburg District, South Carolina, with his father, Charles. In 1795 they bought land on Morgan's Creek, a branch of the Tiger (current spelling) River, and moved to adjacent Greenville District. The new home was on the upper South Pacolet River, up against Hogback Mountain, near the site of present day Gowensville. It was to become Pleasant Grove, the home of Rebecca, whose father purchased it from his father 4 March 1832.

John and Mary were loyal Baptists, joining Tygar (old spelling) Baptist Church in 1802, two years after it was founded. Its records are liberally sprinkled with their names and those of members of their family. Cross Roads Baptist Church, about a mile from the Whitten home, was organized some years later, and John and Mary joined in May 1822. Much later Cross Roads was moved into the village and its name changed to Gowensville Baptist Church.

The following entries appear in the records of Tygar Baptist Church:

> The Tygar Church was established in 1800, as a branch of Reedy River Church.
>
> August 21 1802, John Whitten offered by experience.
>
> August 26th 1802, Sister Mary Whitten (joined).
>
> January the 22nd, Brother David Forrest, Brother Joseph Barrett, and brother Charles Whitten our messengers to hear the petitions to the sister churches.
>
> February 26th 1803, came Nancy Barrett and offered and was received. Respecting Brother John Stanford's getting drunk twice, therefore nominated our Brothers Nathaniel Jackson and Charles Whitten to go to him.
>
> April the 25th, then came forward David Barrett.
>
> 4 June 1803, nominated for Deacon, John Whitten.
>
> August 26 1803, was received by experience, Milly Whitten.

September 24th 1803, appointed Brethren Nathaniel Jackson, Abner Cass, and John Whitten as delegates to the association.

November 26 1803, ordained minister and three deacons, (including) John Whitten.

January 21st 1804, met in Church meeting. Also Brother Charles Whitten reported that Brother Stanford had been drunk and denied it, appointed Brothers Whitten and Dill to cite him to meeting and request those that saw him to come likewise.

March 24th 1804 also three other judges, appointed Charles Whitten.

August 24th 1804, (thinking Brother Charles Gosnell ripe for excommunication) nominated Brother John Whitten, et al., to go out and settle it.

March 23rd 1806, Brothers Jackson and John Whitten were appointed to search the church book and to instruct the clerk in his duty (David Barrett was clerk and needed training).

November 9 1805, called meeting, a matter brought forward against Brother John Tubb by Mrs Prince, a charge of uncleanness. Appointed Brothers Abner Center and Charles Whitten to cite her to our next meeting with all her friends, white and black, to authenticate her charges.

December the 21st 1805, also the matter of Brother David Barrett's riding into Littleberry Holcombe's house and denied it, and afterward acknowledged it, laid over till next meeting, nominated Brethren Nathaniel Jackson and Charles Whitten to cite him to next meeting.

September 27th 1806, rose up Brother Charles Whitten and confessed he had got angry and bore with, and rose up Sister Mary Whitten and confessed she had got angry and bore with, also appointed Brother Nathaniel and John Whitten as delegates to the association.

February the 20th 1807, application was made for letter of dismissal, also by Brother Charles Whitten and wife, also by David Barrett for Brother Joseph Barrett.

July the 25th 1807, rose up Brother Michel Pruet and lade in an allegation against Nicholas Gosnell for selling corn at one dollar per bushel, after some talk upon it the Church lade it off til third Saturday in August and appointed brethren to settle it, (nine appointed, including John Whitten), the majority of 7 or 5 to carry the pint (point).

August the 20th 1807, also took in consideration the gift of Brothers Abner Center and John Whitten.

September the 26 1807, delegates to the association, (including John Whitten).

June 24th 1808, Brothers John Whitten and A Senter came forward and made a report of Sister Hannah Bellows present circumstances.

April 21st 1810, nominated a Presbytery to go and act for the church and their satisfaction should be the churches satisfaction (John Whitten among 10).

January 26th 1811, also Brother David Barrett applied for a letter of dismissal.

February the 21 1812, then Brother Whitten made application to the Church to know what was to be done with Church members that neglect to pay their just debts, in answer says, deal with such members agreeable to the Gospel.

November the 20th 1812, Brother Rueben Barrett rose and unfellowshipt himself for drinking too much liquor and gave satisfaction for the same, (June 1813, Brother Rueben Barrett in identical condition).

April the 22 1814, David Barrett and wife (Elizabeth Whitten) came forward and gave themselves to the care of the Church.

March 21 1817, received Priscilla Southerland.

April the 27th 1822, met in Church meeting after prayer by Brother John Whitten, then chose Brother Whitten moderator.

May the 24th 1822, (plans made to ordain Brother Thomas Barton, messengers from other churches to assist) Brothers John and James Whitten from the Cross Roads Church were present to assist.

Oct 25 1823, proceeded to deal with Brother Page for believing and practicing the cure of witchcraft and excommunicated him for the same, then received a petition from the Cross Roads Church for the Eldership of our Church to assist them in the licencing of James Whitten.

November the 27th 1824, February 27 1825, and November 25 1825, received a petition from the Cross Roads Church for help to assist in the ordination of James Whitten if found ripe, and the Church granted the petition and sent the Eldership.

October the 22 1825, then came forward Nancy Southerland and joined by letter.

May the 15th 1831 Martha Southerland, joined by letter.

John, son of Charles and Nancy Smith Whitten, held the rank of matross in the Virginia Artillery during the Revolution (Service Record #5751 National Archives). He owned considerable land, and was justice of the quorum in the early 1800s. He and his family moved to Hall County, Georgia, between 1832 and 1834, probably to be near their eldest son, James. Following the trail of daughter Elizabeth and her husband, David Barrett, who told of their trip from South Carolina in a letter written in 1827, they moved to Fayette County, Tennessee. Sons Alfred and Ranson and daughter Nancy soon joined them. Both died and are buried there: John, 8 Feb. 1837; Mary, 29 July 1836. Their home was on the north fork of Wolf River. Having been among the early settlers of upper South Carolina, they became pioneers in the opening of western Tennessee.

John and Mary had nine children. They were: James, Charles, Elizabeth, Nancy, Silas Reagan, Alfred, Isaac Smith, Mariam, and Ranson. The following paragraphs describe them, their families, and descendants who lived during the time of Rebecca's letters.

A. Rev. James Whitten was born 26 Jan. 1785 in Spartanburg District, South Carolina. He married 5 Oct. 1809, Elizabeth Ann Thompson, who was born 24 Feb. 1788 in Greenville, South Carolina, and died 23 Feb. 1835 in Hall County, Georgia. Young James was a well-known surveyor, and in 1814, served in the 21st General Assembly of South Carolina. He joined Cross Roads Baptist Church in 1815, was licensed to preach in December 1825, and moved to Hall County, Georgia, the same year, becoming pastor of Yellow Creek Baptist Church. After the death of Elizabeth Ann, James Whitten moved to Whitesville, Harris, Georgia, and served for a time as pastor of Mount Creek Primitive Baptist Church. On 8 Sept. 1836 he married Sarah Little Hogan, who was born March 1797 and died 21 Feb. 1853. After her death he moved on to Columbus, Muskogee, Georgia, and lived with his daughter, Elizabeth Ann. He died there 16 Nov. 1859.

The ten children of James and Elizabeth Ann Thompson were:

1. Harriet Whitten, born 19 Oct. 1810, died 21 Aug. 1823.
2. Rev. Arphax Whitten was born 5 March 1812 in Greenville, District, South Carolina, and married 8 Jan. 1834 in Lee, Alabama, Matilda Allen Bennett, born 17 Nov. 1813. Both Arphax and Matilda died at Smith's Station, Lee, Alabama, and are buried in Mount Zion Cemetery: he, 15 Oct. 1872; she, 27 March 1848. The family lived in Whitesville, Harris, Georgia, and Heard, Georgia, settling in Chambers, Alabama.

Arphax was a Missionary Baptist preacher. After the death of Matilda, Arphax married 22 Feb. 1851, in Georgia, Aurelia Priddy, born 6 Nov. 1826. She moved, after his death, to Smith County, Texas, with his young children and died there 14 June1888.

The eight children of Arphax and Matilda Allen Whitten were:

a) Julia Ann Elizabeth Whitten was born 20 Feb. 1835. She died 1 Jan. 1867 in Alabama, and was buried in Mt. Zion Cemetery, Lee, Alabama.
b) Doleska Fitzallen (Dolly) Whitten was born 22 May 1837 in Georgia, died 13 Dec. 1900 in Alabama, and was buried in Mt. Zion Cemetery. She and Talitha Emily were twins.
c) Talitha Emily Whitten was born 22 May 1837 and married 1 Feb. 1872, E. Alonza Bell. They, then, moved to Texas. Their two children were:
    (1) Arthur Bell.
    (2) Mary Susan Bell.
d) Mary Didema Whitten was born 8 July 1840 in Georgia, and married William H. Tarver. She died 15 Dec. 1931 in Texas, where they lived.
e) Orpha Judson Whitten was born 7 March 1842 in Georgia, and married 16 July 1867, Alexander Lamb. She died 23 May 1870.
f) Sarah Mitchell Whitten was born 14 May 1843 in Georgia, and married 8 Jan. 1867, George Washington Lafayette Ard. She died 19 Nov. 1930; he, 1904. They lived in Stewart County, Georgia.
    Their nine children were:
    (1) Annie Ard, born 1 Oct. 1867, died 16 Dec. 1867.
    (2) Julia Clifford Ard, born 6 July 1869, died 30 May 1944.
    (3) Charles Edgar Ard, born 23 Jan. 1871, died 15 Jan. 1922.
    (4) Sarah Matilda Ard, born 17 Aug. 1872, died 26 Nov. 1951.
    (5) George Fitzallen Ard, born 24 April 1874, died 1876.
    (6) Mary Jane Ard, born 22 March 1876, died 21 Oct. 1924.
    (7) Georgia Agnes Ard, born 14 Nov. 1877, died 5 April 1907.

(8) Thomas Arphax Ard, born 15 April 1881, died 13 Oct. 1921.

(9) John Ard, born 22 March 1883, died 12 July 1923.

g) Matilda Allen Whitten was born 17 May 1845 in Georgia, and married 12 Dec. 1865, Ira Crowe. She died 19 Sept. 1927 in Lee, Alabama.
Their three children were:
(1) Jake Crowe.
(2) Will Crowe.
(3) Julia Crowe.

h) Georgia Ann Whitten was born 26 Feb. 1847 in Georgia, and married 12 Dec. 1871, John Duke Richardson. She died 17 May 1928 in Stewart County, Georgia.
Their child was:
(1) Mary Richardson.

The three children of Arphax and Aurelia Priddy Whitten were:

i) Joanna E. Whitten was born 20 Feb. 1852 in Georgia, and married 23 Feb. 1879, John W. McRae who was born 18 Nov. 1851, and died 31 Dec. 1881.
Their two children were:
(1) William Whitten McRae, born 18 April 1880, died 27 Feb. 1903.
(2) Johnnie S. McRae, born 1 Feb. 1882, died 31 Jan. 1884.

j) James E. Whitten, born 25 Feb. 1863, died 11 Jan. 1913.

k) Harriette V. Whitten was born 26 Dec. 1867 in Georgia, and married 27 July 1904, William H. Swann. She died 4 Dec. 1915.

3. Melicent Mazelle Whitten was born 1 Jan. 1814 in Spartanburg District, South Carolina. She married 10 Jan. 1828 in Hall County, Georgia, Nathaniel Harbin Goss, born 3 Sept. 1805, in Pendleton, South Carolina. The couple died in Phelps, Lawrence, Missouri, and are buried in Goss Cemetery there: she, 27 April 1900; he, 5 Sept. 1888.
Their sixteen children were:

a) Benjamin Franklin Goss was born 30 March 1829 in Hall, Georgia, and married 23 Jan. 1851, Louisa Perry. He was killed by a falling tree 7 Dec. 1894 in Arkansas.

b) Martha Elizabeth Goss was born 3 Feb. 1831 in Hall County, and married 2 Feb. 1847 in Dawson City, Georgia,

Nathaniel Jackson Ayres, who was born 5 Feb. 1823 in Greenville, North Carolina. Martha Elizabeth died 3 Sept. 1864 in Elijay, Gilmer, and Nathaniel Jackson, 12 April 1911 in Cartecay, Gilmer, Georgia.

Their child was:

(1) Nathaniel Jackson Ayres Jr., born 27 April 1855, died 26 Jan. 1916.

c) Malinda Eleanor Goss was born 21 Aug. 1832 in Georgia, and married 21 Aug. 1851, Evan Pierson Perry. She died 12 Dec. 1907 in Phelps, Lawrence, Missouri. This family had moved to Tennessee by 1864, then to Missouri about 1871.

d) James Whitten Goss was born 29 Jan. 1834 in Georgia, and married 3 March 1853, Eunice West, who died before 1870. James then married Malinda Caroline Payne 23 Dec. 1870. They moved to Missouri, then to Texas. He died September 1914 in Dallas, Texas, and was buried in Old Soldiers Cemetery.

e) Louisa Caroline Goss was born 5 Feb. 1836 in Georgia, and married 30 July 1854, the Rev. James M. West. She died 26 April 1864.

f) Calvin Benson Goss was born 9 Dec. 1837 in Georgia, and married 10 Oct. 1858, Mary Ann Densmore. He died in an army hospital from wounds received during the siege of Vicksburg 28 Feb. 1863, and was buried in the Confederate cemetery there. Calvin Benson served as private, Company I, 52d Regiment, Army of Tennessee. They lived in Dawson, Georgia.

g) Melicent Elvira Goss was born 14 July 1840 in Dawson, Georgia, and married 25 July 1858 there, Samuel Mercer Densmore, born 4 March 1838 in Dawson. Both died in Bluff Dale, Erath, Texas: she, 14 March 1912; he, 1 May 1921.

Their child was:

(1) Melicent Rhoda Densmore, born 26 Sept. 1859, died 12 Jan. 1930.

h) Nathaniel Jackson Goss was born 15 July 1842 in Georgia, and married 14 Feb. 1865, Mary Elizabeth Roe. He died 31 Jan. 1918 in Missouri, and was buried in the Goss family cemetery in Lawrence.

- i) Alfred Webb Goss was born 26 Sept. 1844 in Georgia. He died 5 March 1845 and was buried in Dawson, Georgia.
- j) Robert Lewis Goss was born 11 Dec. 1845 in Dawson and married there 28 Dec. 1873, Hannah Mancencella Roe. He died 19 March 1923 in Rogers, Benton, Arkansas.
- k) Silas Washington Goss was born 2 Feb. 1848 in Dawson and married 24 Nov. 1872 in Lawrence, Missouri, Catherine Ellen Shelton. He died 18 Nov. 1920 in Missouri, and was buried in Springfield.
- l) Wilson Lumpkin Goss was born 8 July 1850 in Dawson, married 19 Sept. 1867, Hulda Jane Wilkins, and died in Humble, Texas.
- m) Mary Irene Goss was born 20 Aug. 1852 in Dawson, and died 1 April 1893 in Phelps, Missouri. She was buried in the Goss family cemetery in Lawrence.
- n) Infant Goss was born 20 Aug. 1852 in Georgia, and died 3 Sept. 1854.
- o) Orpha Louisa Goss was born 18 Feb. 1856 in Georgia, and died 21 Sept. 1880.
- p) Juliann Melissa Goss was born 21 June 1858 in Dawson, Georgia, and married 30 Dec. 1877 in Phelps, Missouri, John Franklin Morgan. She died 18 June 1934 in Colfax, Whitman, Washington.

4. Emily Whitten, born 14 Jan. 1816, died 18 Dec. 1816.
5. Orpha Judson Whitten was born 21 Nov. 1817 in Spartanburg District, and married 7 Dec. 1837, in Harris, Georgia, Col. Thomas M. Hogan, born 1809 in Kershaw, South Carolina. Orpha Judson died 18 March 1878, Col. Thomas 23 Jan. 1886 in Smith's Station, Lee, Alabama.
   Their nine children were:
   - a) James Hogan was born 15 July 1844 in Georgia, and married 11 April 1868, Belle Wilson.
   - b) Thomas M. Hogan, born 10 Sept. 1845, died 13 April 1848.
   - c) John L. Hogan was born 1 Dec. 1847 in Georgia, and married Minnie Rhinehardt.
   - d) Eliza Hogan was born 3 Dec. 1850 in Georgia, and married Charles Yorston. They lived in Atlanta.
   - e) Susan E. Hogan was born 15 Feb. 1854 in Georgia, and married Peyton E. Moore. They lived in Atlanta. She

died in Norfolk, Virginia.

f) Rebecca Hogan, born 15 May 1856.

g) Mary E. Hogan was born 5 Oct. 1860. She lived in Atlanta.

h) Emily Hogan, infant.

i) Anne Hogan, infant.

6. Calvin Thompson Whitten was born 23 Jan. 1820 in Spartanburg District, South Carolina, and married 25 Nov. 1841 in Lumpkin, Georgia, Malinda Catherine Kinsey, born 23 Feb. 1819 in South Carolina. Calvin Thompson died 21 Feb. 1886, Malinda Catherine 4 Feb. 1893, both in Belton, Bell, Texas. They lived in Guntown, Lee, Mississippi, until the Civil War and moved to Texas thereafter.

   Their two children were:

   a) Mary Clifford Whitten was born 9 Oct. 1842 in Columbus, Georgia, and married 10 Jan. 1871 in Guntown, Lee, Mississippi, Capt. Rufus Young King, born in Lexington, Lee, Texas. They died in Belton, Bell, Texas: she, 6 Jan. 1892; he, 8 Feb. 1911.

      Their four children were:

      (1) Dr. Rufus Whitten King.

      (2) Sallie Florence King.

      (3) Hugh Clarence King.

      (4) Joseph Sayers King.

   b) Sarah Rebecca Whitten was born 23 July 1844 in Georgia, and married 15 Feb. 1872 in Guntown, Mississippi, Wilson Marion Richey, born 12 Dec. 1842. She died 20 May 1908; he, 1894. They lived in Guntown.

      Their three children were:

      (1) Jettie Clifford Richey.

      (2) Robert Calvin Richey, born February 1876, died July 1955.

      (3) Linda Rilla Richey.

7. Edgel Elvira Whitten was born 15 May 1822 in Spartanburg, and married 13 Dec. 1843 in Gilmer, Georgia, James Green Perry, born 17 Nov. 1820. They died in Dawson, Georgia, and are buried in Antioch Cemetery: she, 26 March 1891; he, 22 April 1892.

   Their ten children were:

   a) William Washington Perry was born 25 Feb. 1845 and

married 10 Feb. 1867, Louisa Lowman. He died 24 June 1905 in Missouri.

b) James Whitten Perry was born 6 Oct. 1846 and married 2 Jan. 1870, Leah Jane Fricks. He died 2 Aug. 1924. On 10 Oct. 1897 James married Nancy Jane Waters.

c) Millicent Louisa Malinda Perry was born 5 Feb. 1849 and married 14 Feb. 1873, John Stephen Holden, born 9 June 1831. She died 6 March 1916; he, 10 Feb. 1911.

d) Sarah Elvira Elizabeth Perry was born 14 Jan. 1851 and married 15 May 1880, Benjamin H. Mearse. She died 29 March 1897.

   Their six children were:

   (1) Emmet M. Mearse, born 1891, died 1938.
   (2) James Bascomb Mearse, born 1884, died 1965.
   (3) Homer Jackson Mearse, born 1885, died 1962.
   (4) William Luther Mearse, born 1889, died 1963.
   (5) Harley Dallas Mearse, born 1891, died 1966.
   (6) Albert H. Mearse, born 1894, died 1966.

e) Artimissa E. A. Perry, born 27 Feb. 1853, died 29 March 1887.

f) Nathaniel Lewis Perry was born 6 May 1855 and married 18 Oct. 1874, Cynthia Bryant, born 27 Nov. 1854. He died 9 March 1937; Cynthia, 12 July 1920. They lived in Marble Hill, Pickens, Georgia.

g) Orpha E. Perry, born 5 May 1857, died 20 Sept. 1857.

h) Benjamin Arphax Perry was born 4 Sept. 1858 and married 1883, Martha Darnell. They lived in Jasper, Pickens, Georgia. Martha died before 1909 and Benjamin Arphax married Avarilla Thoresa Dobbs in that year. He died 19 March 1927.

   The child of Benjamin Arphax and Martha Darnell was:

   (1) May Perry.

   The child of Benjamin Arphax and Avarilla Thoresa Dobbs was:

   (2) Amy Perry.

i) John Evans Green Perry was born 2 Sept. 1863 and married 3 Aug. 1884, Sadie Carmack. He later married Sis Cochran Thomas and died 11 Dec. 1917.

j) Thomas Jackson Perry was born 9 Nov. 1865 and married 29 Sept. 1887, Angeline Anderson, born 28 Nov. 1863.

Both died in Dawson, Georgia: he, 27 Feb. 1934; Angeline, 27 Aug. 1921. He married Rebecca Anderson after the death of Angeline.

The eight children of Thomas Jackson and Angeline Perry were:

(1) James Vance Perry, born 8 Feb. 1889, died 15 May 1971.
(2) Ina Ethel Perry, born 10 April 1891, died 26 March 1978.
(3) Millard Arphax Perry, born 18 Aug. 1893, died 10 March 1966.
(4) Henry Clay Perry, born 29 June 1895.
(5) Alma Edge Perry, born 27 June 1898.
(6) Beulah Mae Perry, born 3 May 1900.
(7) Emmett Stephens Perry, born 28 Jan. 1903.
(8) Clarence Bell Perry, born 5 Oct. 1905.

8. Unnamed infant Whitten, born and died December 1824.
9. Unnamed twins Whitten, born and died 22 May 1827.
10. Elizabeth Ann (Eliza) Whitten, was born 9 Aug. 1829 in Harris County, Georgia, and died 25 Sept. 1864 in Columbus, Georgia. Diphtheria was the cause of her early death.

B. Charles Whitten was born 7 April 1787 in Spartanburg District, and died 19 Sept. 1804 in Greenville District, South Carolina.

C. Elizabeth Whitten was born 8 May 1789 in Spartanburg District, South Carolina, and married 16 Aug. 1807 there, David Barrett, born 22 Feb. 1786 in Greenville District. After marriage, the Barretts moved to Fayette, Tennessee, migrating to Houston County, Texas, in about 1840. They settled in Mustang Prairie, between Crockett and Madisonville. After the death of David Barrett 10 April 1845, Elizabeth Whitten Barrett married Barton Clark, who was born 1800 in Vermont. She died in Houston County, Texas, in October 1855.

Their four children were:

1. Albert Gallatin Barrett was born 7 Oct. 1810 in Greenville District, South Carolina, and married 16 April 1832 in Hardeman County, Tennessee, Elizabeth Seaton, born 15 April 1812 in Fayette, Tennessee. Albert Gallatin died 8 March 1847; Elizabeth, 17 Nov. 1847 in Houston County, Texas.

Their eight children were:

a) Polly Caroline Barrett was born 12 April 1833 in Fayette, Tennessee, and died there 24 May 1833.

b) James Whitten Barrett was born 24 April 1834 in Fayette, Tennessee, and died 12 Nov. 1834 in Houston County, Texas.

c) David William Barrett was born 3 Jan. 1836 in Fayette, Tennessee, and married 12 May 1859 in Cherokee County, Texas, Elizabeth Hill, born 1840 in that state. He died 27 Jan. 1863 in South Bend, Arkansas, while serving as corporal, CSA.
Their child was:
(1) Mary Barrett, born April 1860.

d) Elizabeth Mariam Barrett was born 15 June 1837 in Fayette, Tennessee, and died 11 June 1841 in Houston County, Texas.

e) John George Barrett was born 11 July 1839 in Fayette, Tennessee, and married 11 Aug. 1859 in Cherokee, Texas, Mary Hill, born about 1843 there. John George died 10 May 1862 in Arkansas, while serving as private, Company I, 10th Texas Cavalry, CSA.
Their child was:
(1) Unnamed Barrett, born 1862.

f) Infant Barrett, born and died 1862.

g) Joseph Albert Barrett was born 17 May 1844 in Grimes County, Texas, and married 21 March 1867 in Walker, Texas, Elizabeth Skelton Edinburg Papera, who was born about 1848. He died before 1870 in Texas. Joseph Albert served as private in the 11th Texas Infantry, CSA.
Their child was:
(1) Sarah Barrett, born 1868.

h) Sally Jane Barrett was born 20 May 1846, and died 4 Aug. 1846 in Grimes, Texas.

2. John Whitten Barrett was born 20 May 1813 in Greenville District, South Carolina, and married 7 April 1837 in Mustang Prairie, Texas, Hulda Jane Reding, born 20 Aug. 1820 in Davidson County, Tennessee. They died in Madison, Texas, and were buried in the Barrett Cemetery there: he, 6 May 1877; she, 8 Jan. 1894. He traveled by wagon train from Fayette, Tennessee, to Crockett, Texas, in 1836 and was in

Montgomery County before 1840. He later became one of the first settlers of Madison County, Texas.

Their four children were:

a) Stephen Reding Barrett was born 8 Sept. 1840 in Montgomery County, Texas, and married 7 Sept. 1858 there, Sarah L. Larrison who was born 8 Nov. 1837 in Plantersville, Grimes, Texas. Stephen Reding died of typhoid fever 8 Dec. 1863 in Louisiana while serving with The Army of Tennessee, CSA. She died 1 Dec. 1895 in Madison, Texas.

   Their two children were:

   (1) John Daniel Barrett, born 21 March 1860, died 22 April 1945. He had six wives.

   (2) Steven Franklin Barrett, born 19 April 1863, died 17 March 1903.

b) William Robert Barrett was born 30 Dec. 1842 in Montgomery, Texas, and married 14 Feb. 1866 there, Elizabeth E. Walters, born 30 July 1849 in Mississippi. Both died and are buried in Madison County, Texas: he, 1 Jan. 1903; she, 19 March 1921.

   Their seven children were:

   (1) William Seymour Barrett, born 30 Jan. 1867, died 15 Sept. 1929.

   (2) John I. Barrett, born 8 Jan. 1870, died 1954.

   (3) Florence Barrett, born 6 Feb. 1873, died 2 Sept. 1896.

   (4) Johnston Tolephus Barrett, born 20 April 1875, died 24 April 1935.

   (5) Hugh Hayes Barrett, born 14 Dec. 1877, died 13 May 1950.

   (6) Henry Barrett, born 2 Dec. 1882, died 6 Sept. 1884.

   (7) Ima Osamae Barrett, born 6 Dec. 1887.

c) Nancy Elizabeth Barrett was born 6 Feb. 1845 in Montgomery County, Texas, and married 5 Dec. 1861 in Madison County, John Washington Jenkins, born 23 Jan. 1812 in South Carolina. She died 28 Feb. 1925 in Johnson, Texas. He also died in that state.

   Their six children were:

   (1) John Jenkins, born 2 Aug. 1864, died February 1865.

   (2) Thomas Milton Jenkins, born 17 Nov. 1866.

   (3) John W. Jenkins, born January 1870.

(4) Ophelia Jenkins, born 1873.
(5) Cyrena Jenkins, born 1875.
(6) Martie B. Jenkins, born 1879.

d) Martha Elizabeth Barrett was born 17 March 1847 in Montgomery, and married about 1869 in Madison, William F. Bobo, born 1848 in Bastrop, Morehouse, Louisiana, and died 3 Jan. 1888 in Madison County, Texas. In 1894 she married, in Brown County, Texas, Albert Morton, who was born in September 1859 in Illinois. Martha died after 1913 in Brown County, while Albert died 15 Sept. 1932.
The eight children of Martha and William Bobo were:
(1) Asie Bobo, born about 1869.
(2) Robert Bobo, born about 1871.
(3) Bill Dugan Bobo, born about 1873.
(4) Mattie Bobo, born about 1877.
(5) Lucy Bobo, born about 1877.
(6) Annette Bobo, born 25 Dec. 1879.
(7) Charles Bobo, born September 1884.
(8) Thomas Nathaniel Bobo, born 9 April 1887, died 6 July 1944.

e) Amanda Catherine Barrett was born 2 May 1849 in Montgomery, and married 20 Jan. 1869 in Madison, James Marion McCan, born 20 Oct. 1834 in Lawrence, Alabama. Both died in Madison, Texas: Amanda Catherine, 12 Jan. 1915; he, 31 July 1915.
Their ten children were:
(1) James Littleton McCan, born 27 May 1870, died 8 Nov. 1923.
(2) Hulda McCan, born 16 Nov. 1872, died 19 March 1966.
(3) Samuel Wooldridge McCan, born 11 Feb. 1875, died 9 March 1962.
(4) Kenneth Nathan McCan, born 17 March 1877, died 11 Jan. 1899.
(5) Minnie Ola McCan, born 22 Aug. 1879, died 26 Oct. 1880.
(6) Allie Angeline McCan, born 8 March 1881, died 27 Sept. 1962.
(7) William Walter McCan, born 6 Nov. 1884, died November 1967.

(8) John Reuben McCan, born 6 May 1886, died 6 April 1965.
(9) Benjamin Monroe McCan, born 29 Nov. 1889, died 1949.
(10) Hettie M. McCan, born 11 Aug. 1892, died 1918.

f) David Albert Barrett was born 2 May 1849 in Montgomery County, and married 7 Dec. 1876 in Madison County, Texas, Martha J. Tolbert, born about 1853 in Texas. He died 28 Dec. 1928; she, before 1900 in Madison, Texas. Their eight children were:
(1) William Anthony Barrett, born 14 Dec. 1877, died 17 Feb. 1941.
(2) Martha Elizabeth Barrett, born July 1879.
(3) Conrad Barrett, born September 1888.
(4) Robert K. Barrett, born November 1883, died 1953.
(5) Amanda Barrett, born February 1886.
(6) Roscoe Wiley Barrett, born August 1889.
(7) Ida Barrett, born March 1891.
(8) George Barrett.

g) Jonathon Collard Barrett was born 22 Nov. 1851 in Madison, and married about 1871 there, Martha Shepherd. He died in Harper Hill, Texas.
Their eight children were:
(1) Roy Franklin Barrett, born 4 April 1872.
(2) Ada Mae Barrett, born March 1876.
(3) James Walter Barrett, born 11 Dec. 1879.
(4) Walter Barrett, born 28 Sept. 1881.
(5) Samuel Shepard Barrett, born 28 Sept. 1881.
(6) Hubert Redding Barrett, born 19 Feb. 1884, died 26 March 1965.
(7) William Barrett, born about 1887.
(8) Guy Roland Barrett, born June 1889, died 24 Nov. 1938.

h) Thomas Barrett was born 4 Feb. 1854 in Madison, Texas, and died there 21 Oct. 1854.

i) Luther Monroe Barrett was born 26 July 1855 in Madison County, Texas, and married 8 Oct. 1874, Sarah L. Laney. On 26 June 1877, in Madison County, he married Sarah Louisa Adams, who was born 28 Nov. 1859 in Ellwood, Madison, Texas, and died 13 Sept. 1957 in Houston.

Luther Monroe died 10 Jan. 1894 in Madison, and was buried in Barrett Cemetery.

The eight children of Luther Monroe and Sarah Louisa were:

(1) Amanda Annis Barrett, born 1 July 1879, died 20 Sept. 1885.

(2) Minnie Ora Barrett, born 1 Jan. 1883.

(3) Maude Elizabeth Barrett, born 7 April 1885.

(4) William Joseph Barrett, born 26 May 1886.

(5) James David Barrett, born 24 March 1887, died 27 Nov. 1956.

(6) Mollie Connor Barrett, born 28 July 1889, died 23 Jan. 1972.

(7) Martha Alice Barrett, born 27 Dec. 1891, died 1927.

(8) George Barrett, born 28 Dec. 1893, died 3 Jan. 1894.

j) Sarah Alice Barrett was born 12 May 1858 in Madison, and married 3 July 1878 there, James Manning, born 30 Nov. 1856 in Texas. She died 18 March 1923 in Texas. James died 10 Jan. 1894 in Madison, and was buried in Midway Cemetery.

Their eight children were:

(1) John Ida Manning, born 21 Aug. 1879, died 23 Feb. 1961.

(2) Hulda Manning, born 1881.

(3) James B. Manning, born 8 Jan. 1884, died 17 Sept. 1884.

(4) Martha V. Manning, born 22 Sept. 1885, died 14 Oct. 1885.

(5) Lilla Manning, born January 1886.

(6) Benjamin F. Manning, born December 1890.

(7) Nugent B. Manning, born 12 June 1892, died 27 Jan. 1896.

(8) Exa Manning, born 22 Feb. 1894, died 29 March 1965.

k) James Silas D. Barrett was born 17 Nov. 1860 in Madison, and married 15 May 1882 there, Clara Viola Manning, born 1866. James Silas D. died 12 June 1889; Clara Viola, 18 April 1893 in Madison, Texas. They must have divorced, for he also married Mattie Adams, sister of Sarah Louisa Adams, wife of Luther Monroe.

The child of James Silas and Clara Viola was:

(1) Silas Clarence Barrett, born 13 April 1893, died 13 Nov. 1978.

l) James W. Barrett was born 9 May 1873 in Madison, and married 3 Jan. 1896 there, Rosa Vaughn. He was called Withers.

3. Mary (Polly) Barrett was born 30 Jan. 1819 in Greenville District, South Carolina, and married 13 Aug. 1838 in Fayette, Tennessee, Dean McCarley, who died 31 Aug. 1840 in Fayette County, Tennessee. Mary then married 13 Oct. 1841, in Fayette, John R. Parker, born 1815 in Virginia. He died about 1869 in Houston County. They were in Houston by 1846 and Mustang Prairie, Madison, Texas, by about 1854. Mary died 1860 in Madison, Texas.

The child of Dean McCarley and Mary Barrett was:

a) James McCarley was born 1839 in Fayette County, Tennessee, and died before 1865 in St. Louis, Missouri.

The ten children of Mary and John R. Parker, all born in Texas, were:

b) David Henry Parker was born 1842 in Houston County, and died 18 Feb. 1863 in St. Louis, Missouri.
c) Rebecca Elizabeth Parker, born 1844.
d) Marion Parker, born 1846.
e) James Parker, born about 1847.
f) Sarah Parker, born 1849.
g) Richard Parker, born 1853.
h) Mary Parker, born 1855.
i) Lavina Parker, born 1857.
j) Louise Parker, born 1857.
k) William Parker, born 1859.

4. Mariam Hannah Barrett was born 25 April 1821 in Greenville District, South Carolina, and married 18 July 1839 in Fayette, Tennessee, Hansell Coburn. They moved to Houston, Texas, after marriage, to Walker County, by 1848, and back to Prairie Community, Houston County, in 1860.

Their four children, all born in Texas, were:

a) Harriet D. Coburn was born 1847, and died 10 Sept. 1864 in Houston County, Texas.
b) Jane Coburn, born 1850.
c) Margaret Coburn, born 1857.
d) Willie Coburn, born 1860.

D. Nancy Whitten was born 10 Sept. 1791 in Spartanburg, South Carolina, and married John Bradley Dalton Jr. Nancy died 25 Sept. 1831, John before July 1847, in Fayette County, Tennessee. Their child was:

1. Mary E. Dalton was born about 1830 in Georgia, and married 25 May 1848 in Fayette, Tennessee, John J. Boyd, born 1825 in North Carolina.
   Their child was:
   (1) Martha E. Boyd, born about 1849 in Fayette County, Tennessee.

E. Silas Reagan Whitten was born 19 Feb. 1794 in Spartanburg District, South Carolina, and married 31 Oct. 1815 in Rutherford, North Carolina, Eleanor Kee Earle, born 6 Jan. 1792 in Earle's Fort, Rutherford, North Carolina. Silas Reagan and Eleanor died in Ripley, Tippah, Mississippi: he, 27 Oct. 1888; she, 18 Aug. 1857. They are buried in Ripley Cemetery. Silas served in the War of 1812 as ensign, and was elected to the 1832 Nullifying Convention of South Carolina. He favored the Union. He farmed, made fine whiskey, and held public office in South Carolina and Mississippi.
Their eight children were:

1. James Wood Whitten, born in Greenville District, South Carolina 27 Oct. 1816, died 15 Nov. 1816.
2. Joseph John Whitten was born 25 Sept. 1817 in Gowensville, Greenville, South Carolina, and married 3 Feb. 1842 there, Mesina Deborah Adams, born 1 May 1824 in Greenville. She died, in Tippah County, Mississippi, 17 Oct. 1851. He then married, 15 Dec. 1853 in Tippah, Mary Jane White, born 4 March 1830 in Mississippi. She died 11 Jan. 1864. After her death Joseph John married, 5 Oct. 1871, Maggie Davis Doyle, born 18 May 1841 in Mississippi. She died 12 Feb. 1873 in Tippah. Joseph John died 18 Nov. 1885 in Ripley, Tippah, Mississippi, and was buried with his three wives in the Ripley Cemetery. He had moved, with his family, in early 1850 to Mississippi, and lived on land adjoining that of his father the rest of his life.
   The five children of Joseph John and Mesina Deborah Whitten were:
   a) Mary Eleanor Whitten was born 17 Nov. 1842 in Gowensville, South Carolina, and married 10 March 1868

in Tippah County, Mississippi, Dr. Adrian Brown Caruth. She died 7 Dec. 1885 in Tippah, and was buried in Ripley. Their three children were:

(1) Albert Bedell Caruth.

(2) Rebecca Whitten Caruth, born 11 June 1877.

(3) Thomas Dick Caruth.

b) Harriett Earle Whitten was born 15 Dec. 1844 in Gowensville. She died 30 Oct. 1902 in Tippah, Mississippi, and was buried in Ripley.

c) Baylis Earle Whitten was born 31 Dec. 1846 in Gowensville. He died 23 May 1865, while serving with the Armies of the Confederacy.

d) Walter Wood Whitten was born 25 April 1849 in Gowensville. He died 15 June 1861 in Ripley, Mississippi, and was buried there.

e) Dr. Frank Adams Whitten was born 26 July 1851 in Tippah, and married there 27 April 1877, Mary Dora (Molly) Whitten, daughter of Alfred Washington and Elliott Ann Ray Whitten, who was born 7 June 1855 in Jonesborough, Tippah County. She was his first cousin. Both died in Poplar Springs, and were buried in Endville, Mississippi: he, 23 July 1903; she, 3 Jan. 1941. Their seven children were:

(1) Nathaniel Carter Whitten, born 14 June 1878, died 21 Dec. 1945.

(2) Mesina Elliott Whitten, born 12 March 1880, died 27 Oct. 1967.

(3) Frank Adams Whitten Jr., born 21 June 1882, died 5 Aug. 1957.

(4) Alfred Washington Whitten, born 26 Feb. 1885, died 19 July 1887.

(5) Walter Wood Whitten, born 21 Sept. 1887, died 2 Sept. 1973.

(6) William Holcomb Whitten, born 21 Aug. 1889, died 27 April 1893.

(7) Langston Agnew Whitten, born 3 Dec. 1890, died 25 June 1980.

The five children of Joseph John and Mary Jane White Whitten were:

f) Dr. William Andrew Whitten was born 25 Dec. 1854 in

Ripley, and married 8 Dec. 1887, May Ellen Tate, born 1 May 1862. He died 15 June 1924; she, 1948. They lived in Keownville, Mississippi, and he practiced medicine in Orizaba.

Their four children were:

(1) Harriet Beulah Whitten, born 4 Oct. 1888.
(2) Harvey Earle Whitten, born 12 March 1890.
(3) William Homer Whitten, born 9 Oct. 1892.
(4) Cora Mae Whitten, born 4 Sept. 1896.

g) Narcissa Amaryllis Whitten was born 8 May 1856 in Ripley, and married 8 Dec. 1897 there, Richard Allison Cox, born 30 Jan. 1849. They died and are buried in Ripley, Mississippi: she, 1936; he, 30 Oct. 1927.

h) Elliot Kee Whitten was born 27 Feb. 1858 in Ripley, and married 1 Sept. 1886 there, James Newton Belote, who was born 22 Dec. 1859. She died 24 May 1892 and was buried in Ripley; he, 7 March 1917.

Their two children were:

(1) Mary Ellen Belote, born 24 Aug. 1888.
(2) Thomas Earle Belote, born 24 April 1890.

i) John Dayton Whitten was born 30 March 1860, died 2 April 1905, and was buried in Ripley, Tippah, Mississippi.

j) Hester Virginia Whitten was born 7 April 1862, died 11 Feb. 1903, and was buried in Ripley.

The child of Joseph John and Maggie Davis Doyle Whitten was:

k) Maggie Medora Whitten was born 19 Jan. 1873 in Ripley and married 14 Dec. 1892 there, Mark McKinney Lowry, born 12 Oct. 1865 in Benton County, Mississippi. Maggie Medora died 20 Feb. 1955 in Tippah, and was buried in Ripley.

Their five children were:

(1) Ruth Lowry, born 7 May 1895, died 23 Dec. 1959.
(2) Mark Nathaniel Lowry, born 10 Jan. 1899, died 1965.
(3) Margaret Davis Lowry, born 18 April 1904.
(4) William Whitten Lowry, born 6 Nov. 1906.
(5) Paul Raymond Lowry, born 29 Jan. 1917.

3. Harriet Earle Whitten was born 4 Feb. 1820 in Gowensville, and married 4 Sept. 1845, there, Nathan Alexander Lankford, born 20 May 1819 in Greensboro, North Carolina. Harriet

Earle died 17 Oct. 1908 in Cameron, Texas, and was buried in Oakwood Cemetery, McLennan, Texas. He died 16 May 1872 in Lee County, Mississippi, and was buried there. This couple moved to Pontotoc County, Mississippi, in late 1845 and lived near Palmetto, in what was to become Lee County. She, with some of her children, settled near Waco, Texas, after Nathan Alexander died.

Their nine children were:

a) Rebecca Eugenia Lankford was born 11 June 1846 in Pontotoc, Mississippi, and married Dr. T. J. Allen, born 1846. Rebecca Eugenia died October 1910; he, 1923.

b) William Henry Lankford was born 18 Oct. 1847 in Lee, Mississippi, and married 4 Sept. 1872, Mollie F. Gatewood. She died and he married Sarah Katherine Lettie Gatewood. He died 1929. William Henry fought with the 11th Mississippi Cavalry, surrendered at Selma, Alabama, and moved to Sherman, Texas in 1869.
   The child of William Henry and Molly Gatewood Lankford was:
   (1) Henry Oswald Lankford, born 5 Nov. 1878.
   The three children of William Henry and Sarah Katherine Lankford were:
   (2) William Henry Lankford Jr., born 18 April 1889, died 26 Feb. 1929.
   (3) John Gunby Lankford, born 10 June 1892, died 15 July 1916.
   (4) Ann Consuelo Lankford, born 23 March 1895.

c) Anna C. Lankford was born 14 April 1849 in Pontotoc, Mississippi, and married 25 Jan. 1875, James Sample who was born 26 Jan. 1853. She died 26 Sept. 1883.
   Their five children were:
   (1) Mollie Juanita Sample, born 3 April 1875.
   (2) Maurine Earle Sample, born 26 Aug. 1877.
   (3) Fannie Lula Lynn Sample, born 24 Dec. 1878, died 29 Nov. 1929.
   (4) Jesse Dwight Sample, born 28 Feb. 1881.
   (5) Dora Eugenia Sample, born 7 Dec. 1882.

d) Thomas Earle Lankford was born 8 Jan. 1851 in Pontotoc, and married 6 Feb. 1870, Mary Adaline Frierson, born, in Maury, Tennessee, 30 April 1848. He died 15 Oct. 1887;

and she, 26 Oct. 1931.

Their child was:

(1) Mary Earle Lankford, born 2 March 1886.

e) Charles Alexander Lankford was born 29 June 1852 in Pontotoc, and married 11 Feb. 1918, Mary Rosanna Alexander, who died in 1933. He died 11 March 1915.

Their three children were:

(1) Ethel Pearl Lankford, born 3 Oct. 1881, died about 14 July 1905.

(2) Milton Alexander Lankford, born 1 Nov. 1882.

(3) Florence Kee Lankford, born 12 May 1884, died about 16 June 1905.

f) Sallie Florence Lankford was born 29 June 1852 in Pontotoc County, Mississippi, and married 22 Oct. 1876, James William Lee, who was born 7 June 1844, and died 1 March 1916.

Their six children were:

(1) William Ivon Lee, born 26 July 1877.

(2) James Lankford Lee, born 29 July 1879.

(3) John Charles Lee, born 31 May 1881, died 31 May 1881.

(4) Robert Earle Lee, born 15 April 1889, died 5 Feb. 1911.

(5) Idanita Lee, born 21 June 1896.

(6) Bertral Lee.

g) Mary Kee Lankford was born 22 Sept. 1855 in Pontotoc County, Mississippi, and married 26 Feb. 1879, Thomas Marion Dilworth, born 1832. She died 24 March 1924; he, 25 March 1932 in Waco, Texas. They were buried in Oakwood Cemetery.

Their three children were:

(1) Thomas Gordon Dilworth, born 5 Jan. 1880, died 18 Nov. 1944.

(2) Anna Lee Dilworth, born 26 Nov. 1886, died 9 April 1960.

(3) Marion Adair Dilworth, born 14 July 1897, died 17 Jan. 1977.

h) Dr. John Silas Lankford was born 27 Oct. 1858 in Pontotoc, and married 25 July 1882, Orienna Belle Gatewood, born 6 July 1860, and died 30 Nov. 1932. He died in San Antonio, Texas.

Their four children were:

(1) Lettie O'Barr Lankford, born 6 June 1883.

(2) Earle Miller Lankford, born 29 Oct. 1884, died 19 April 1918.

(3) Eugenia Franklin Lankford, born 22 Feb. 1886.

(4) Anna Lutie Lankford, born 17 July 1888, alive February 1993.

i) James Dwight Lankford was born 2 Oct. 1861 in Pontotoc, and died 6 Nov. 1923.

4. Dr. Alfred Washington Whitten was born 1 March 1822 in Gowensville, South Carolina, and married 26 Feb. 1853 in Chalybeate, Tippah, Mississippi, Elliott Ann Ray, daughter of Rev. Ambrose Ray II, and Mary Garrett Ray, who was born 22 Nov. 1834 in South Carolina. Alfred Washington died 9 March 1897 in Chalybeate, and was buried in Union Cemetery. Elliott Ann died 31 Aug. 1920 at the home of her daughter, Mattie Flynn, in Olive Branch, DeSoto, Mississippi, and was buried with Alfred. Alfred Washington studied medicine at Transylvania College, Lexington, Kentucky, and the University of Pennsylvania in Philadelphia. He practiced medicine in Gowensville, Pickensville, and Pendleton, South Carolina, and after moving in 1850 to Mississippi, in Chalybeate.

Their ten children were:

a) Mary Dora (Molly) Whitten was born 7 June 1855 in Jonesborough, Tippah, Mississippi, and married 27 April 1877 there, Dr. Frank Adams Whitten, her first cousin, son of Joseph John and Mesina Deborah Whitten. He was born 26 July 1851 in Ripley. Mary Dora (Molly) died 3 Jan. 1941; Frank Adams, 23 July 1903, in Poplar Springs, and were buried in Endville, Mississippi.

Their children are listed under Dr. Frank Adams Whitten.

b) Sarah (Sallie) Kee Whitten was born 14 Nov. 1856 in Jonesborough, and died July 1936 at the home of her sister, Mattie Flynn, in Olive Branch, Mississippi.

c) John Graves Whitten was born 9 Dec. 1858 in Jonesborough, and married 6 Dec. 1885, Sallie Griffin Worsham, who was born 21 Aug. 1865. She died 3 Sept. 1894 in Burgess, Lafayette, Mississippi, and was buried in Clear Creek Baptist Cemetery there. Then John Graves married 6 Jan. 1895, Annie Frances Eaves who was born 30 Jan. 1874. He died 14 April 1934.

The four children of John Graves and Sallie Griffin Worsham Whitten were:

(1) Artelia Clara Whitten, born 28 Oct. 1886.
(2) Alfred Washington Whitten, born 8 Dec. 1888, died 28 April 1940.
(3) Benjamin Franklin Whitten, born 7 Jan. 1891, died 1 Sept. 1971.
(4) Willie Griffin Whitten, born 2 July 1893, died 3 Oct. 1894.

The eight children of John Graves and Annie Frances Eaves Whitten were:

(5) Leonard Griffin Whitten, born 23 Oct. 1895.
(6) Della Kee Whitten, born 12 June 1897.
(7) Edward Earle Whitten, born 7 June 1899.
(8) Pearl Gladys Whitten, born 2 Sept. 1901.
(9) Hubert Fulton Whitten, born 28 Jan. 1904.
(10) John Graves Whitten Jr., born 15 May 1908.
(11) Bertha Alene Whitten, born 27 April 1910.
(12) Woodrow Wilson Whitten, born 16 Feb. 1913, died 17 Feb. 1913.

d) Silas Ray Whitten was born 10 Aug. 1860 in Jonesborough, and married 29 Nov. 1882 in Oxford, Ruth Sawyer Burt, daughter of Isaac Hunter and Sarah Margaret Carothers Burt, who was born 9 Nov. 1859 in Clear Creek, Lafayette, Mississippi. Silas Ray died 4 Feb. 1940, and Ruth Sawyer, 24 Oct. 1937 in Jackson, Hinds, Mississippi. They are buried together in Lakewood Memorial Cemetery.

Their eight children were:

(1) Lucille Burt Whitten, born 4 Oct. 1883, died 1973.
(2) Pauline Earle Whitten, born 8 Oct. 1885, died 20 June 1969.
(3) Lottie Helon Whitten, born 18 May 1887, died 15 Jan. 1958.
(4) Leslie Hunter Whitten, born 26 April 1889, died 26 Oct. 1959.
(5) Sherod Roscoe Whitten, born 29 Dec. 1890, died 1947.
(6) Ruth Christine Whitten, born 25 Dec. 1894, died 21

Feb. 1965.

(7) May Isom Whitten, born 17 Feb. 1897, died 14 July 1982.

(8) Margaret Elliott Whitten, born 7 June 1900, died 20 July 1983.

e) Hosea Ransom Whitten was born 10 April 1862 in Jonesborough, Tippah, Mississippi, and married 17 March 1892 in that county, Sarah Agnes Durham, born 18 March 1871 in Blue Mountain, Mississippi. He died 10 July 1944 in Olive Branch, Desoto, Mississippi. She died in Texas and lies with her husband in Olive Branch.
Their three children were:

(1) Mary Elliott Whitten, born 13 Oct. 1896, died 16 Jan. 1901.

(2) Paula Laeta Whitten, born 6 Oct. 1903.

(3) William Douglas Whitten, born 13 April 1911.

f) Rev. Bedford Forrest Whitten was born 20 April 1864 in Jonesborough, and married 17 Jan. 1886, Flora Lee Bennett, born 4 Nov. 1866 in Tippah County, Mississippi. Bedford Forrest died 26 May 1943; Flora Lee, 14 May 1951, in Coldwater, Tate, Mississippi. They were buried side by side in Memorial Park, Memphis, Tennessee. He was licensed as a Baptist preacher in 1894.
Their seven children were:

(1) Leon Theodore Whitten, born 21 Jan. 1886, died 2 March 1970.

(2) Lester Calhoun Whitten, born 12 Feb. 1888, died 27 July 1933.

(3) Lacy Roger Whitten, born 16 Jan. 1890.

(4) Laura Laeta Earle Whitten, born 27 Feb. 1892.

(5) Lorimer Steadman Whitten, born 13 April 1894.

(6) Loren Darnell Whitten, born 17 June 1895.

(7) Lou Anna Whitten, born 22 Feb. 1902, alive 1987.

g) Martha Earle (Mattie) Whitten was born 22 March 1866 in Jonesborough, and married 12 Jan. 1904 there, George Lewis Flinn, born 9 Aug. 1858. They died in Olive Branch, DeSoto, Mississippi: she, 1957; George Lewis, 23 Feb. 1922, and are buried there. Her marriage was a double ceremony with sister Maude.

h) Joseph Brooks Whitten was born 11 Aug. 1868 in

Jonesborough, and married 20 Nov. 1906 in Tate County, Mississippi, Aubra Burford, who was born 7 Nov. 1879. Joseph Brooks died 14 April 1937 in Memphis; Aubra, 12 July 1959 in Searcy, Arkansas. They were buried in Memorial Park, Memphis, Tennessee.

Their seven children were:

(1) Joseph Burford Whitten, born 7 April 1908, died 5 Sept. 1986.
(2) Corinne Whitten, born 28 Sept. 1910.
(3) Aubrey DeWitt Whitten, born 19 Jan. 1913.
(4) Woodrow Carlton Whitten, born 3 Jan. 1915, died 24 Dec. 1988.
(5) Howard Brooks Whitten, born 6 Jan. 1917, died 27 Jan. 1989.
(6) Lourelia Whitten, born 6 Feb. 1920.
(7) Marie Whitten, born 11 April 1922, died 30 April 1932.

i) Jesse June Whitten was born 13 June 1871 in Jonesborough, and married 29 Jan. 1896, Ora B. Anderson, born 28 June 1873 in Selmer, McNairy, Tennessee. She died 26 March 1918 and is buried in Henry Cemetery, Corinth, Mississippi. They lived in Iuka, Mississippi. Jesse June later married, 5 June 1919, Maggie Allen Harris, born 13 May 1874. She died 9 March 1948 and was buried in Oak Grove Cemetery, Iuka, Tishomingo, Mississippi. Jesse June died 11 Jan. 1949 in Corinth, and was buried with Ora Anderson.

The three children of Jesse June and Ora Anderson Whitten were:

(1) Irene Whitten, born 18 Nov. 1896, died 7 Dec. 1958.
(2) Logan Alfred Whitten, born 16 Feb. 1901, died 2 Jan. 1987.
(3) Jesse Julian Whitten, born 12 June 1904, died 1936.

j) Maude Elliott Whitten was born 12 Jan. 1875 in Jonesborough, and married 12 Jan. 1904 there, Frank Hudson Bradley, born 20 Aug. 1879 in Gonzales, Texas. Maude Elliott died 16 Jan. 1918, Frank Hudson, 7 Dec. 1948, in Memphis where they are buried.

Their five children were:

(1) Elliott Elizabeth Bradley, born 18 Oct. 1904, died 22

June 1919.

(2) Louise Elverta Bradley, born 19 Dec. 1905.

(3) Frank Herman Bradley, born 12 Jan. 1909.

(4) Naomi Bradley, born 14 Feb. 1911.

(5) Ed Farmer Bradley, born 14 Feb. 1911.

5. Narcissa Amaryllis Whitten was born 8 July 1824 in Gowensville, and married 15 Sept. 1842 in Rutherford, North Carolina, Elias Holcombe, born about 1821 in South Carolina. Narcissa Amaryllis died 22 Jan. 1852 in Charleston, South Carolina, and was buried in the churchyard of the First Baptist Church of Charleston.

   Their child was:

   a) Isabell Tominson (Bell) Holcombe was born 15 July 1843 in Greenville, District, South Carolina. She died 29 Aug. 1848 at the home of her uncle, Col. A. W. Holcombe, in Pickens District, South Carolina.

6. Rebecca Berry Whitten, collector of letters, was born 18 Aug. 1826 in Gowensville, Greenville, South Carolina, and died 2 May 1909 in Poplar Springs, Pontotoc, Mississippi. She is buried in the Baptist Cemetery in Endville, Mississippi. Rebecca lived her entire life with her father until 1883 when she moved to Poplar Springs, and lived with niece Mary Dora and nephew Frank Adams Whitten.

7. Silas Reagan Whitten Jr. was born 2 June 1830 in Gowensville, and married 12 Oct. 1855 in Union County, Mississippi, Francis Medora Ray, sister of Alfred Washington Whitten's wife, Elliott Ann. She was born 3 April 1837 in South Carolina. Silas Reagan Jr. died 22 July 1863 in an army hospital at Newton Station, Mississippi, and was buried there. Francis Medora died 29 June 1917 in Tippah, Mississippi, and was buried in the Ray Cemetery near Chalybeate. Silas Jr. served in Company G, 7th Mississippi Cavalry, and Company C, 23d Mississippi Infantry, CSA.

   Their four children were:

   a) Carrie Isabel Whitten was born 30 Aug. 1856 inTippah, Mississippi, and married 30 Nov. 1884 there, Mark P. Richardson, who was born 16 Aug. 1855 and died 23 Feb. 1947. She died 7 Sept. 1905, and is buried with him in Union Cemetery, Chalybeate, Tippah, Mississippi.
      Their four children were:

(1) Etta Berry Richardson, born 25 Sept. 1885, died 24 April 1911.
(2) Willie Gertrude Richardson, born 12 Dec. 1887, died 21 Dec. 1973.
(3) Alabama Lee Richardson, born 8 Feb. 1889, died 2 Feb. 1921.
(4) Mark Lowrey Richardson, born 29 Jan. 1890.

b) Effie Berry Whitten was born 29 July 1858 in Tippah, and married 10 Dec. 1895 there, John Caswell Perkins, born 20 Sept. 1840. They died in Tippah: she, 6 Nov. 1942; he, 12 Feb. 1924, and are buried in Union Cemetery.
Their child was:
(1) Estilla Perkins, born 22 Aug. 1900, died 13 Oct. 1900.

c) William Pendleton Whitten was born 30 April 1860 in Jonesborough. He died 15 May 1881 in Tippah, and was buried in the Garrett family cemetery.

d) Ranson Hosea Whitten was born 21 Jan. 1862 in Jonesborough and died 6 May 1888 in Tippah. He was buried in the Garrett cemetery.

8. Ranson Edwin Whitten was born 9 July 1832 in Gowensville, and married, in Tippah, 12 Dec. 1865, Pocahontas Medora Rogers, born 4 March 1849. She died 11 June 1878 in Tippah and was buried in the Ripley Cemetery. He married a second time, 17 April 1883, Sarah (Sally) Moran, born 9 Jan. 1844, in Benton County, Mississippi. She died 9 June 1905 in Tippah County, and was buried in the Moran family cemetery in Benton. Sally was a daughter of Willis Moran, husband of Harriet M., daughter of Uncle Ranson Whitten. Ranson E. enlisted in 1861 and served with The Army of Northern Virginia, Longstreet's Corps, CSA, until its surrender. He died 11 June 1906 in Blue Mountain, Mississippi, and was buried with Pocahontas Medora.
The four children of Ranson E. and Pocahontas Medora Whitten were:

a) Eleanor Kee Whitten was born 20 Jan. 1867 in Tippah, and married 2 Oct. 1887 there, Thomas Counseille Rucker, born 22 July 1861. They died and are buried in Ripley: she, 20 May 1933; he, 1935.
Their five children were:
(1) Emmaline Medora Rucker, born 1 Aug. 1888.

(2) Rupert Clyde Rucker, born 21 Aug. 1890.
(3) Joe Rogers Rucker, born 14 Sept. 1893, died 28 Feb. 1968.
(4) Ernest Rucker, born 5 June 1896.
(5) Evelyn Kee Rucker, born 24 May 1899.

b) Joseph Earle Whitten was born 15 May 1869 in Tippah, and married 29 Dec. 1898, Lula May Tate, born 22 May 1876.
Their child was:
(1) Hazel Marie Whitten, born 22 Feb. 1904.

c) Silas Reagan Whitten was born 6 Sept. 1872 in Tippah. He died 3 Oct. 1921, and was buried in Ripley.

d) Frank Alma Whitten was born 27 Dec. 1875 in Tippah, and married 1 Oct. 1896 there, Charles Edward Tate, who was born 26 May 1857. She died 1955; Charles Edward, 14 Jan. 1930.
Their two children were:
(1) Charles Edward Tate Jr., born 27 June 1897.
(2) William Irvin Tate, born 9 June 1899.

The child of Ranson E. and Sarah Moran Whitten was:

e) Alfred Tennyson Whitten was born 1 March 1884 in Tippah, and married 1 March 1917, Margaret Josephine Halsell, born 25 March 1882 in Chickasaw County, Mississippi. Alfred Tennyson died 22 Aug. 1959; she, 8 Dec. 1963, in Jackson, Hinds, Mississippi. They are buried in Lakewood Memorial Cemetery. He was a prominent educator. Jackson's Whitten Junior High School is named for him.
Their child was:
(1) Joseph Nathaniel Whitten, Ph.D., born 30 Nov. 1917, alive July 1994.

F. Alfred Whitten was born 8 June 1797 in Greenville, South Carolina, and married 4 Oct. 1825 in Rutherford, North Carolina, Caroline Matilda Prince, who was born 1809 in Greenville District, South Carolina. Caroline Matilda died 15 Nov. 1833 of scarlet fever in Gowensville, South Carolina. Next Alfred married Bridget Graham 5 Aug. 1834 in South Carolina. She was born about 1801 in that state. They moved to Fayette County, Tennessee, about 1834 and she died 10 Sept. 1841 there. He married a third time 25 April 1842 in Fayette County, Nancy Ann Malone, who was born 25 June 1821 there. The family left Fayette, Tennessee, for Montgomery County, Texas, in November 1849, settling shortly thereafter in Madison County. Nancy Ann died there 12 May 1898, and was buried in Park Cemetery. Alfred was executor of his father's will. He died 9 June1884 in Madison County, Texas, and is buried in Park Cemetery with Nancy Ann.

The two children of Alfred and Caroline Matilda Whitten were:

1. Rebecca Ann M. Whitten was born 7 Feb. 1829 in Greenville District, South Carolina, and married 13 Aug. 1844 in Fayette, Tennessee, Sam Lewis Desbough, who was born about 1819 in North Carolina.
   Their two children were:
   a) William Desbough was born about 1846 in Fayette, Tennessee, and died there in 1846.
   b) Martha Desbough was born about 1848 in Fayette, Tennessee.
2. Mary Jane Whitten was born 18 June 1832 in Greenville District, South Carolina, and married 12 Nov. 1846 in Fayette, Tennessee, Edward Americus Anderson, born 1 Feb. 1820 in Sumner, Tennessee. Mary Jane died about 1862; Edward Americus, 1 Dec. 1896, both in Willis, Montgomery, Texas. They were buried there. He was a cabinet maker, poet, musician, master mechanic, and inventor who first settled in Old Danville, Texas.

The four children of Alfred and Bridget Whitten were:

3. Sarah Eleanor Whitten was born 20 May 1835 in Fayette, Tennessee, and married 22 Dec. 1859, William P. King.
4. John D. G. Whitten was born 27 Oct. 1836 in Fayette, Tennessee, and married 7 March 1861 in Montgomery, Texas, Antonette Folk, born July 1844 in Texas. John D. G. died 20 Oct. 1894. They had ten children; only one is known.
   He was:
   (1) Johnnie Whitten was born 1885 in Texas, and married Myrtle Freeman. He died in Bryan, Texas, in 1962. Johnnie loved to sing.
5. James Frank Whitten was born 1838 in Fayette, Tennessee.
6. Martha Whitten was born 1840 in Fayette, Tennessee.

The eight children of Alfred and Nancy Ann Whitten were:

7. Harriett Louise Whitten was born 22 Aug. 1843 in Fayette

County, Tennessee, and married 15 Nov. 1866 in Madison, Texas, Augusta James Morgan, born 29 May 1839 in Alabama. She died 14 Nov. 1930; he, 6 April 1895 in Madison County, where they are buried.

Their eight children were:

a) Minnie J. Morgan was born 1867 in Texas. She died 1873 in Madison, Texas, and was buried there.

b) Annie E. Morgan was born 1870 in Texas. She died 1872 in Madison, and was buried there.

c) Lucy Irene Morgan was born 1873 in Texas, and died 1952.

d) Thomas Carrol Morgan was born 1876 in Texas. He died 1958 in Madison, and was buried there.

e) Oran Morgan was born 1878 in Texas. He died 1888 in Madison, and was buried in that county.

f) Lewis Irving Morgan was born 1880 in Texas, and died in 1954.

g) Benton H. Morgan was born 10 Nov. 1885, died 24 July 1963, and was buried in Madison, Texas. He was a twin of Banton.

h) Banton A. Morgan was born 10 Nov. 1885 in Madison. He died 24 July 1969.

8. Alice Anderson Whitten was born 10 Dec. 1845 in Fayette, Tennessee, and married 14 March 1866 in Madison, Texas, David Edward Roten, born 1 May 1834. David Edward died 10 Sept. 1917.

Their eight children were:

a) Howard Macon Roten was born 11 April 1868 in Texas, and married 28 Feb. 1894 in Cherokee County, Texas, Martha Ellen Evans, born 1874. Howard Macon died 29 July 1940 in Montgomery County, Texas. Martha Ellen died 1964 in Texas, and was buried with Howard in Oakwood Cemetery.

Their seven children were:

(1) Ruby Lee Roten, born 30 Sept. 1895.
(2) Anella Roten, born 15 Aug. 1897.
(3) Clara Roten, born 2 Nov. 1900.
(4) Ernest Roten, born 1903, died 1977.
(5) Leola Roten, born 22 March 1905.
(6) Nena Roten, born 23 Dec. 1909, died 18 June 1933.

(7) Elsie Roten, born 30 March 1914.

b) Edward Whitten Roten was born 30 June 1871 in Texas, and married 19 Dec. 1895 in Cherokee County, Texas, Lucy Odom. Edward Whitten died 27 Feb. 1949 in Hardin, Texas, and was buried in Resthaven Cemetery. Their five children were:
(1) Bertie Roten, born 1896.
(2) Neil Roten, born 1899.
(3) Luray Roten, born 1902.
(4) Pleasant Roten, born 6 Jan. 1904.
(5) Oran Roten, born 7 Jan. 1906.

c) Harriett Alice Roten was born 10 Dec. 1873 in Texas, and married 14 Sept. 1892 in Cherokee County, Charles Albert Vining. He was the twin of George Albert Vining, who married her sister, Ruba Lee Roten. She later married 22 June 1904, in Cherokee County, Texas, John Raper, who was born 1861 and died 1939.
The three children of Charles Albert and Harriett Alice Vining were:
(1) Lucy Vining, born 1894.
(2) Agnes Vining, born 1896.
(3) Charles Macon Vining, born 1898.
The two children of John and Harriett Alice Raper were:
(4) Edward Raper.
(5) John Raper Jr.

d) Ruba Lee Roten was born 26 April 1876 in Midway, Madison, Texas, and married 28 Feb. 1894 in Cherokee County, George Albert Vining. Ruba Lee married Lee Ross after 1905 and died 23 April 1966 in Rusk, Cherokee, and was buried in Cedar Hill Cemetery.
The two children of George Albert and Ruba Lee Vining were:
(1) William Macon Vining, born 20 Jan. 1896.
(2) Fitzhugh Vining, born 29 March 1898, died 21 Aug. 1902.

e) William Marvin Roten was born 9 Oct. 1878 in Texas, and married 1910, Callie Woodward, born 1889. She died in Cherokee County in 1930 and was buried in Cedar Hill Cemetery. After her death he married, in 1932, Alta Mae Sherman. William Marvin died 18 Nov. 1970 in Cherokee

County and is buried with his first wife.

The two children of William Marvin and Callie Woodward Roten were:

(1) Walter Roten.

(2) Marvinal Roten.

The child of William Marvin and Alta Mae Roten was:

(3) Travis Roten.

f) Irvin Tabor Roten was born 4 Jan. 1881 in Iola, Grimes, Texas, and married 30 Sept. 1903 in Rusk, Cherokee, Texas, Jesse McDowell, born 17 July 1885. Irvin Tabor died 12 Sept. 1966 in Corpus Christi, Texas, and was buried in Memory Gardens. Jesse died 9 Oct. 1956 also in Corpus Christi and was buried with him.

Their five children were:

(1) Wallace Wesley Roten, born 16 Nov. 1904.

(2) James Whitten Roten, born 4 May 1910.

(3) Lucy Victoria Roten, born 3 Nov. 1913.

(4) Helen Louise Roten, born 26 Nov. 1919.

(5) Jo Bess Roten, born 7 Oct. 1924.

g) Benny Oran Roten was born 25 Nov. 1883 and died 19 Aug. 1885 in Texas.

h) Annie Barnett Roten was born 14 Feb. 1886 in Madison County, Texas, and married 5 Jan. 1910 in Cherokee County, Claude L. Barley, born 1883. Claude died 1914, and, on 26 Dec. 1917, in Cherokee County, Texas, she married Arthur McIver. Annie died 7 Dec. 1972 in Texas, and was buried in Cedar Hill Cemetery, Cherokee County.

The two children of Claude and Annie Barley were:

(1) Thomas Luther Barley, born 21 Sept. 1910.

(2) Pauline Ross Barley, born 7 Dec. 1912.

The child of Arthur and Annie McIver was:

(3) George David McIver.

9. Helen Josephine Whitten was born 28 Dec. 1848 in Fayette, Tennessee, and married Dan Stewart Jr. She was, at birth, named Helen Pulleam. Her name was later changed to Josephine.

Their four children were:

a) Dan Stewart III.

b) Norman Stewart.

c) Jim Stewart.

- d) Molly Stewart, who married William Park.

10. Ervin Dunaway Whitten was born 27 Dec. 1851 in Madison, County, Texas, and died there 20 Dec. 1855.
11. Eugene Grimes Whitten, was born 1855 in Madison County, Texas.
12. Huldy Eugene Whitten was born 25 Jan. 1855 in Madison, and married 7 Jan. 1872 there, Warren Crabb Sr.
13. Alfred Whitten Jr. was born 19 March 1858 in Madison, and married 19 Feb. 1879 there Mattie E. Park who was born 1 April 1863. She died 21 Sept. 1887 in Madison, and was buried in Park Cemetery.
    Their four children were:
    - a) Levin H. Whitten was born 3 May 1881 in Madisonville, Texas, and married 14 Dec. 1903 there, Fannie Carter. Levin died 10 April 1959 in Madison County, and was buried in Park Cemetery.
    - b) Berry W. Whitten was born 5 Nov. 1882 in Madison, and married 8 May 1905 there, Ellen Floyd, born 5 Aug. 1885. Both died in Madison: he, 1 Oct. 1951; she, 25 Dec. 1970. They were buried in Park Cemetery.
    - c) Ruth Whitten was born 1883 in Madison, and married 23 Nov. 1905 there, H. Sanders. She died 1974.
    - d) Mada Alevia Whitten was born 1884 in Madison, and died 1968. She married William Leroy McGaughey.
      Their child was:
      - (1) Eska Lamar McGaughey, born 2 Aug. 1907.
14. Robert Lee Whitten was born 23 July 1861 in Madison, and married 25 July 1892 in that place, Cordia Savell, born 19 Oct. 1868. Robert Lee died 21 March 1902; she, 16 April 1902 in Madison. They were buried in Park Cemetery.
    Their three children were:
    - a) Sam Whitten was born 16 Sept. 1894 in Madison, and married Ruby, born 12 Feb. 1895. Sam died 13 May 1890; Ruby, 5 May 1981.
    - b) Edd Whitten was born 4 March 1896 in Madison, Texas, and married Emily C. who was born 25 Dec. 1868. Edd died 25 March 1968 in Madison County, and was buried in Park Cemetery. She died after 1973.
    - c) Abb Whitten was born 31 Jan. 1898 in Madison, and died 1979.

G. Dr. Isaac Smith Whitten was born 23 July 1800 in Greenville, South Carolina, and married 22 Nov. 1827 in Abbeville, South Carolina, Martha Jackson, born 5 Nov. 1805 there. She died 5 Oct. 1831 and was buried in the Calhoun family cemetery in Abbeville District. Dr. Whitten later married Martha F. Meriwether who was born about 1806 in South Carolina. Neither marriage produced children. Isaac Smith died about 1860 in Mt. Zion, Hancock, Georgia. He must have been wealthy. His home, called Mound Farm, was near Sparta, within two miles of Mt. Zion, Georgia. The house was large and well furnished. He had many slaves.

H. Mariam Whitten was born 16 Sept. 1802 in Greenville, South Carolina, and married David Mc. Davis there in 1825. He was born 10 April 1800. Mariam died 13 July 1887 in Texas, and was buried there. David died 21 Feb. 1862 and was buried in Zion Presbyterian Cemetery, Pontotoc County, Mississippi. The Davis family moved to Pontotoc about 1840, and lived near Palmetto. After her husband's death Mariam migrated with her family to Texas and lived near her brother, Alfred.
Their eight children were:

1. Isaac Alvin Davis was born 10 Feb. 1826 in Greenville District, South Carolina. He died 12 Aug. 1826 there.
2. James Addison Davis was born 26 Sept. 1827 in Greenville, and married 11 Aug. 1854 in Mississippi, Elizabeth C. Miller, born 6 June 1830 in Alabama. She died 14 April 1867 in Pontotoc County, Mississippi, and was buried in the Zion Presbyterian Cemetery there. James Addison Davis also married Olive, who was born 3 Oct. 1850. She died 23 March 1884 and was buried in Palmetto, Lee, Mississippi. He died 3 Aug. 1897 in Reagor Springs, Texas, and was buried in Boren, Texas.
   The four children of James Addison and Elizabeth Davis were:
   a) John Alexander Davis was born about 1855 in Pontotoc, Mississippi, and married first, Pally, and later an Indian woman from Oklahoma. John Alexander died 1940 in Oklahoma. There were no children.
   b) Nancy M. Davis was born about 1858 in Pontotoc County, Mississippi, and married Tom Dupree. She died during childbirth at Laredo, Texas.
   c) James Alvin Davis was born 26 March 1861 in Pontotoc,

and married 25 Feb. 1947 in Tupelo, Lee, Mississippi, Georgia Earl Helms, born 15 Nov. 1862 in Saltillo, Mississippi. James Alvin died 25 Feb. 1947 in Waxahachie, Texas. Georgia Earl died 3 Jan. 1936 in Reagor Springs, Texas. Both are buried in Ennis, Texas.

Their two children were:

(1) Addison Dupree Davis, born 1 July 1891, died 13 June 1958.

(2) Jewel Celeste Davis, born 7 Sept. 1897.

d) Thomas Davis was born about 1864 in Lee County, Mississippi, and married Florence Cunningham. He was buried in Reagor Springs, Texas.

Their three children were:

(1) Stanley Davis.

(2) Elizabeth Davis.

(3) Lucille Davis, born 1891, died 1981.

The child of James Addison and Olive Davis was:

e) David Oliver Davis was born in Lee County, Mississippi, and married Ruth. He died about 1965 in Texas. David had several other wives.

Their three children were:

(1) Ava Ruth Davis.

(2) Bernice Davis.

(3) Olive Davis.

3. Nancy Ellen Davis was born 11 Dec. 1829 in Greenville, and married 18 Oct. 1854 in Mississippi, S. Finis Handley, born 1828 in Alabama. Nancy Ellen died 18 July 1878 in Mississippi, and was buried in Tupelo, Lee County.

Their child was:

a) Robert D. Handley was born about 1858 in Cherry Creek, Pontotoc, Mississippi.

4. Mary Elizabeth Davis was born 8 Jan. 1833 in Greenville, and married 1 Feb. 1855 in Mississippi, Bunyan B. Barmore.

5. Martha Caroline Davis was born about 1835 in Greenville District, South Carolina, and married Hosea H. Porter, born 1830 in South Carolina, and died before 1900. He was a dentist.

Their two children were:

a) Mariam D. Porter was born about 1859 in Harrisburg, Lee, Mississippi.

b) Laura Porter was born about 1880 in Brownwood, Brown, Texas.

6. Harriet Whitten Davis was born 18 Oct. 1838 in Greenville District, South Carolina. She died 27 Oct. 1866 in Mississippi, and was buried in Zion Presbyterian Cemetery, Pontotoc County.
7. Joseph Alexander Davis was born 16 Jan. 1843 in Pontotoc, Mississippi, died 11 Dec. 1849, and was buried in Zion Presbyterian Cemetery, Pontotoc County. He was the twin of Josephine Rebecca.
8. Josephine Rebecca Davis was born 16 Jan. 1843 in Pontotoc County, Mississippi, and married 14 Dec. 1879 there, W. M. Cunningham, born 8 July 1827. She died in Brownwood, Brown, Texas, he, before 1900, also in Texas.
   Their three children, all born in Mississippi, were:
   a) William J. Cunningham.
   b) David E. Cunningham.
   c) George C. Cunningham.

I. Ranson Whitten was born 1 Nov. 1805 in Greenville District, South Carolina, and married 27 Feb. 1834 in the Hall County, Georgia, home of brother James Whitten, Elizabeth Sullivan, who was born 3 Oct. 1814 in South Carolina. They lived for a short time in Cherokee County, Alabama, near Uncle Charles Whitten Jr., and moved to Fayette County, Tennessee, before 1840. In the spring of 1856 the family moved to Tippah County, Mississippi, where Elizabeth died 17 Aug. 1857. She was buried in Ross Chapel Cemetery. Ranson lived with his brother Silas Reagan Whitten near Ripley, Mississippi, until 16 Dec. 1862, when, in Tippah County, he married Susan Elizabeth Morgan, who was born 2 Nov. 1831 in Tennessee. They settled in the nearby Shady Grove community. She died 24 July 1899 at the home of her daughter in Benton County, Mississippi, and was buried in Old Antioch Cemetery there. Ranson died after 1880 in Tippah or Benton County, Mississippi.
The seven children of Ranson and Elizabeth Sullivan Whitten were:

1. Edwin Whitten was born about 1835 in Cherokee County, Alabama.
2. Harriet M. Whitten was born about 1840 in Fayette, Tennessee, and married Luther White, born about 1825 in South Carolina.

Luther died 21 Jan. 1867 in Tippah County, Mississippi. Harriet M. then married Willis J. Moran who was born 1806 in North Carolina. His daughter, Sally, later married Ranson Edwin Whitten, son of Ranson's brother Silas Reagan. She must have died before 1870, for her children were living with her sister in that year.

The two children of Harriet Whitten and Luther White were:

a) M. E. White, daughter, born about 1858 in Tippah County.
b) William E. White was born about 1860 in Tippah, and died before 1932.

The three children of Harriet Whitten and Willis J. Moran were:

c) Hatty Moran was born about 1869 in Misissippi, and married a Mr. Gates. She lived with her daughter Bettie in Bartlett, Tennessee, in 1932.
   Their child was:
   (1) Bettie Gates.
d) Tom P. Moran was born about 1872 in Mississippi, and died before 1932.
e) Effie Moran was born about 1874 in Mississippi, and died before 1932.

3. Lewis Irvine Whitten was born about 1842 in Fayette County, Tennessee.
4. James Lawson Whitten was born about 1846 in Fayette County, Tennessee, and married 26 Jan. 1869 in Tippah, Mississippi, F. Bowdon E., born about 1848 in Mississippi. They died January 1907 in Florida and were buried in Benton County, Mississippi.
   Their three children were:
   a) R. Whitten, daughter, was born about 1871 in Mississippi.
   b) Carry Whitten was born about 1874 in Mississippi.
   c) J. J. Whitten was born about 1878 in Mississippi, and married 14 Jan. 1904 in Kemper County, Mississippi, Allie White, born in Kemper, who died 12 Dec. 1906 in Mississippi.
5. M. Fidelia Whitten was born Aug. 1848 in Fayette, and died after 1860. She was married, but her spouse is not known. M. Fidelia lived with sister Harriet M. in Tippah County, Mississippi, in 1860.
6. Sarah Elizabeth Whitten was born about 1851 in Fayette

County, Tennessee.

7. William R. Whitten was born about 1855 in Tippah, Mississippi.

The five children of Ranson and Susan Elizabeth Morgan Whitten were:

8. Rev. Henry Lee Whitten was born Oct. 1863 in Tippah County, Mississippi, and married 17 Nov. 1885 there Sarah Frances Hobson, born October 1866 in that state. Both were buried in Ashland, Benton, Mississippi. Henry Lee was a Hardshell Baptist preacher who lived most of his married life in Jackson, where he served for seventeen years in the Mississippi Legislature.

   Their eighteen children were:

   a) Luther M. Whitten was born December 1886 in Tippah County, Mississippi, and died 27 April 1974 in Tennessee. He was buried in Memorial Park, Memphis.
   b) Ethyl W. Whitten was born February 1888 in Tippah.
   c) Henry Earl Whitten was born March 1889 and married Ira. He died March 1909 in Jackson, Mississippi, and was buried in Shady Grove, Tippah, Mississippi.
   d) Willie Frankie Whitten, daughter, was born 13 March 1890 in Tippah, died 7 Oct. 1904 in Mississippi, and was buried in Shady Grove Methodist Cemetery, Tippah County.
   e) Lemuel Lawson Whitten was born 2 March 1891 in Tippah, died 17 Sept. 1891 there, and was buried in Shady Grove Methodist Cemetery.
   f) Albert Ray Whitten was born 26 April 1892 in Tippah, died 14 Sept. 1892 in Mississippi, and was buried in Shady Grove Methodist Cemetery.
   g) Allie P. Whitten, daughter, was born December 1893 in Tippah, and married Simon Childers who was alive in Ashland, Mississippi, May 1992.

      Their four children were:

      (1) Simon Earl Childers.
      (2) J. W. Childers.
      (3) Frank Childers.
      (4) Margaret Childers.
   h) Arthur Whitten was born September 1894 in Tippah County.
   i) Alfred L. Whitten was born 26 April 1895 in Tippah, died

9 March 1918 of pneumonia in an army camp in Louisiana, and was buried in Shady Grove Methodist Cemetery, Tippah County.

j) Ellis H. Whitten was born about 1897 in Mississippi, and married Nettie Mae Hand. He died before 1967. They lived in Raymond, Mississippi.
Their child was:
(1) Wanda Dale Whitten.

k) Elizabeth Whitten was born January 1898 in Tippah. She lived in New York.

l) Mary H. Whitten was born February 1899 in Tippah, died 1909, and was buried in Shady Grove, Tippah, Mississippi.

m) Howard Lee Whitten was born in 1901 in Tippah, Mississippi, and died in 1935.

n) Carl Grady Whitten was born 19 April 1903 in Tippah, died 17 Jan. 1904 there, and was buried in Shady Grove Methodist Cemetery.

o) Infant son Whitten was born 19 April 1903 in Tippah, died that year, and was buried in Shady Grove Methodist Cemetery.

p) Rev. Milton Clay Whitten was born 1905 and married 1926 in Ashland, Benton, Mississippi, Mallie Viola Bright, who was born 1904. Mallie Viola died 1958 in Desoto County, Mississippi, and was buried in Hernando cemetery. Reverend Whitten later married Nettie Mae Hand, widow of his brother Ellis H. Whitten. He attended Mississippi College and the Southern Baptist Seminary in Louisville, Kentucky, and later was pastor of Baptist churches in Elk Creek and Bloomfield, Kentucky, and Hernando, Eudora, Oak Grove, Senatobia, Looxahoma, Grays Creek, Byhalia, Raymond, and Terry, Mississippi. Milton Clay died 1967 in Jackson, Hinds, Mississippi, and was buried in Hernando, with Viola Bright, his first wife.
The five children of Milton Clay and Mallie Viola Whitten were:
(1) Milton Clay Whitten Jr., born 1927.
(2) Robert Bailey Whitten, born 1928.
(3) Edward Lee Whitten, born 1932.
(4) Shirley Ann Whitten, born 1934.
(5) James Allen Whitten, born 1935.

q) Henrietta Whitten was born 4 March 1909 in Jackson, Mississippi, died 4 March 1909 there, and was buried in Shady Grove, Tippah County.

r) Hugh Collins Whitten was born 16 Feb. 1910 in Mississippi, and married Ruby. He died 3 Oct. 1971 in Jackson, Mississippi, and was buried in Lakewood Memorial Park there.

9. Kate Whitten was born about 1868 in Tippah County, Mississippi, and married 28 Jan. 1892 W. A. C. Spencer there.
10. Sam Whitten was born about 1866 in Tippah County.
11. Laura L. (Tish) Whitten was born about 1869 in Tippah, and married there 23 Dec. 1884, William C. Graves, born 1862. He died 8 Nov. 1941 in Holly Springs, Mississippi, and was buried in Shady Grove Cemetery, Tippah.
12. Albert Whitten was born 6 June 1873 in Tippah, and married Ida S. Barber, born 17 Nov. 1870 in Mississippi. Ida S. died 14 Feb. 1898 in Tippah, and was buried in Ross Chapel Cemetery. Albert also married Nora Barber, born in Mt. Pleasant, Mississippi. She died 1961 in Memphis and was buried in Memorial Park. Albert died 19 Feb. 1948 in Memphis, Tennessee, and was buried in Memorial Park.
The two children of Albert and Ida Barber Whitten were:

a) Bama Whitten was born December 1892 in Tippah, and married Reuben W. Spencer. She died 25 Jan. 1992 in Memphis, and was buried in Memphis Memorial Park.

b) Effie Whitten was born July 1896 in Tippah, and married 14 July 1921 in Ripley, Vibrant L. Street, born 30 Oct. 1887 in Mississippi. She died 9 Oct. 1976 in Memphis and was buried in Ripley with her husband, who died 1966 in Memphis.
Their four children were:
(1) John Whitten Street, born 15 April 1925.
(2) Vernon Street, born 28 July 1928.
(3) Anita Street, born 15 April 1932.
(4) Robert Street, born 25 April 1939.

The five children of Albert and Nora Barber Whitten were:

c) Elton B. Whitten was born 1907 in Tippah, and married Ethel Duckworth. He died 1989 in Winston Salem, North Carolina, and was buried there.

Their child was:

(1) Betty Jo Whitten.

d) Hermie Lee Whitten, daughter, was born 1909 in Tippah, Mississippi, died 1989 in Memphis, and was buried in Memorial Park.

e) Elizabeth Whitten was born 1911 in Tippah. She lived in Memphis in 1992.

f) Albert Whitten Jr. was born 1913 in Tippah, and married Lucille Kane. He was living in Memphis in 1992.

Their two children were:

(1) William Albert Whitten.

(2) James Thomas Whitten, who died in 1990.

g) Henry A. Whitten was born in Tippah, and married Betty C. They lived in Memphis in January 1992.

Their child was:

(1) Wanda Whitten. ✳

CHAPTER THREE

Charles Whitten Jr. and Family

Little is known of John's brother, Charles Jr., and his wife, Millicent Reagan. Most of what is reliable is contained in letters saved by Rebecca. Charles Whitten Jr., born 18 Jan. 1769 in Virginia, settled first in Greenville District, South Carolina, buying land near his father on Beaverdam Creek, which flows into the Tyger (current spelling) River. Both he and Millicent Reagan, born about 1769 in Stafford, Virginia, whom he married about 1788 at her home in Rockingham, North Carolina, joined the Tygar (old spelling) River Baptist Church in 1803. In 1807, they requested letters of transfer, and the following year sold the Greenville land.

The North Carolina Genealogical Society Journal for November 1978, page 261, shows them living in Buncombe, North Carolina, in 1807. It is probable they moved from Greenville District to that place with cousins Eliakim and Anna Reagan Hamlin, who were known to have made a similar move in 1805. Before 1810, they transferred to Pendleton District, South Carolina, buying land in 1812. Charles Jr. appears, with a growing family, in Pendleton in 1810 and 1820, and in 1830 in Pickens District, which was carved out of Pendleton in 1826. The oldest female in 1820 was younger than Millicent, and did not appear in 1830. There is a son and a daughter in 1830 born after 1820. From this, one could conclude that Millicent died before 1820, Charles took a second wife before that year, she died before 1830, and at least a son and a daughter were hers. The *Pendleton Messenger* obituary of 10 Oct. 1827 stating that Mrs. Charles Whitten died on the 27th must refer to Charles Jr.'s second wife. We have further evidence of an early death for Millicent. She was not mentioned when her father wrote his will in 1821. Charles Jr. may well have married a third time.

In 1840 and 1850 Charles Jr. was in Cherokee County, Alabama, near Leesburg. Both Charles and daughter, Mariah S., bought land in Section 3 of Township 10, Range 8, East. Charles Jr. received the SE1/4 of NE1/4 1 Oct. 1844, the NE1/4 of SW1/4 13 Oct. 1845, and the SW1/4 of NE1/4 11 Aug. 1848, a total of 120 acres. Mariah S. obtained the NW1/4 of SE1/4 13 Oct. 1845, 40 acres. Charles Jr. was 81 years of age in 1850 and, as he did not appear in subsequent enumerations, probably died prior to 1860. Census listings indicate there were between seven and twelve children. The destruction by fire of the Cherokee County courthouse in May 1882 makes a full accounting of the Charles Whitten Jr. family virtually impossible.

Alexander and Whitten in *Whittens and Allied Families*, second edition, speculate that Zachariah, William, and Albert may have been among the children of Charles Jr.; Zachariah due to the close proximity of the Charles Whitten home in Pickens District to that of Zachariah's wife, Margaret Whitten; Albert, who was thrown from a horse and killed in Pendleton, and whose executor was Charles Whitten; and William S., who bought land in Pendleton in 1830 and was listed in 1850 and later censuses, close to Charles Jr., in Cherokee, Alabama.

But Rebecca's letters identify five children with certainty. On 5 Oct. 1849 daughter Mariah S. wrote to cousin Silas Reagan and gave the birth date of her father, Charles Whitten Jr. Eliza Whitten wrote 12 Oct. 1851 to Ranson E. Whitten, and mentioned cousin Alvin Earle, who can be connected to Charles Jr. by elimination. Writing, in 1863, from camp near Chattanooga, Ranson E. tells his father of meeting, in Marietta, Georgia, Nancy Thomason, Charles Jr.'s daughter, and learning of her brothers, John and Silas Reagan (b. 1815).

The following paragraph consists of excerpts of letters written during 1991 and 1992 by a Charles Jr. descendant, Penny Holsomback McNair of Meridian, Mississippi, to Arthur Reagan, William C. Whitten, and W. B. Moore Jr. In them she told what she knew of the life of her great-grandfather Silas Reagan Whitten (b. 1815), and his family:

> I am delighted to find someone with knowledge of my Whittens. I never heard my father mention him (Silas Reagan Whitten, b. 1815), as he died soon after they went to Texas. Of course Papa (George Everett Holsomback) was a grandson and Silas and Martha had teenagers. I am sending you our family information. In 1873 the Whittens and their daughter Mary Amelia and her two small children, one being my father, left Louisville, Winston, Mississippi, and went to Texas where Silas died. They were accompanied by lots of cousins, uncles, and aunts.
>
> What they did not know was that Silas and Martha's son Charles Everett Whitten was alive and well. He had left Mississippi when he was 17 years old and lived to be 95 or 96 and died in Houston, Texas after he had again met with my father in the 1940s. Charles had led quite a life as a prospector for gold in Mexico, a Texas Ranger, and many other things. He was bright, remarkably intelligent, with a startling memory. Charles Everett called my brother in Houston and asked to speak to George Holsomback. My brother said it was he.

Uncle Charlie asked how old he was and George said 35. Uncle Charlie said "No, the boy I'm looking for would be about 75." That was my father. Papa met him and still was not sure this was Mother's twin brother. He coyly asked if Uncle Charlie remembered the old dog they had in Mississippi 70 years before. Uncle Charlie said, "You mean old dog Blue? Fine dog."

Silas had lost a leg, I'm told. My oldest sister said he lost a leg in the War between the States. I don't believe this as he would have been near 50. (Silas did not serve in the CSA.) I was in Crippled Childrens Hospital in Memphis in 1932 or 1933 and met a child there named Pearl Whitten from Clarksdale, Mississippi. She had one leg that had never grown, a baby's leg really, and her middle finger was missing. They removed the leg and sewed the hand down to meet the other fingers. When I told my father about her, he said, "She is kin to you." Whether he recognized the name, or a genetic fault I don't know.

If you want my sisters and brothers and their children let me know. I am the youngest and last. I am a generation nearer my Silas (b. 1815) than Mr. Moore is to his. My father was 53 when I was born and my mother 42. They wanted a puppy. I was the 10th also.

Penny

Many descendants of this Silas Reagan and Alvin Earle are known, some living. Only one from the other children has, as yet, been positively identified.

These are five proven and three possible children of Charles Jr. and Millicent Reagan Whitten and their descendants who relate to Rebecca's letters:

A. Albert Whitten, possible son, was born about 1795 in Greenville District, South Carolina, and married Margaret. He was killed when thrown from a horse in 1825 in Anderson, South Carolina. Charles Whitten Jr. was his executor and Margaret a buyer at his estate sale.

   Their child was:

   1. Martha Ann Whitten, born in South Carolina; she was a minor in 1825.

B. Nancy H. Whitten, daughter, was born 7 May 1799 in Greenville District, South Carolina, and married James Thomason, also born there on 6 June 1796. He died in the Civil War 10 Jan. 1863, she

22 May 1878. In September 1863, she was living in Marietta, Georgia, with a married daughter and fifteen-year-old son. Nancy and James are buried in Citizens Cemetery, Marietta.

Two of their children were:

1. Female Thomason, married by 1863.
2. Judson J. Thomason, born about 1848 in Marietta, Georgia.

C. Alvin Earle Whitten, son, was born 1803 in Greenville District, South Carolina, and married 22 Feb. 1827 in Carnesville, Franklin, Georgia, Mary Catherine Whiting Jones, born in 1815 there. He died 2 July 1852, she, the same year in Wharton, Texas. Both are buried in that county. From Carneysville they moved to Holmes County, Mississippi, then, in 1847 to Matagorda, Texas, and finally, in 1849, to Wharton.

Their nine children were:

1. Julia F. Whitten was born about 1828 in Carnesville, Franklin, Georgia, and married, about 1850 in Wharton, Texas, William C. C. Foster, born in Alabama. She was robbed and murdered at her home near Wilson's Station, Shelby County, Tennessee, on 26 Jan. 1879, and is buried in Elmwood Cemetery in Memphis. He died about 1877. Julia F. and her husband, brother, and sister visited Dr. Isaac Smith Whitten and his brother, Reverend James, in Georgia in 1851.
2. Dudley J. Whitten was born about 1829 in Franklin, Georgia, and died 15 July 1859 of yellow fever in New Orleans. He became infected while traveling to Alabama attempting to settle his father's estate.
3. Judge Terrell J. Whitten was born 1832 in Franklin, Georgia, and married 4 Aug. 1881, in Wharton, Texas, Sarah F. Still Callaway. She was born in 1845 in Alabama. Both died in Wharton: he, 28 March 1899; she, about 1892.

   Their child, born in Wharton, Texas, was:

   a) Fannie Eugenie Whitten.
4. Maj. James Drayton Whitten was born 16 Jan. 1833 in Carnesville, Franklin, Georgia, and married 18 April 1855 in Wharton, Corinne Levinia Thomas, who was born 10 April 1836 in Mississippi. The couple died in Wharton: he, 11 April 1878; she, 19 Jan. 1907 and are buried in the East Ave. Cemetery in Wharton, Texas. He settled in Wharton in 1851. He

served in the first Texas Assembly after the war. James Drayton was listed as head of family in the 1880 census of Wharton, Texas, with wife, six children, and Banny Whitten born in Mississippi, age seventy. No Whitten of this line was in that state in 1810. For Banny to be a son of Charles Whitten Jr., he would have been born in South Carolina. Instead, he was a slave, left James Drayton in his father's will.

Their nine children, born in Wharton, most dying there, were:

a) Kathryn Marie Whitten, born 31 May 1856, died 8 Jan. 1940.
b) Corinne Eahi Whitten, born 1857, died before May 1866.
c) Dudley V. Whitten, born 1860, died before June 1900.
d) James Dudley Dee Whitten, born 19 Dec. 1864, died 8 Jan. 1936.
e) Corinne T. Whitten, born May 1866, died after 1918.
f) Lula A. Whitten, born about 1869, died about 1890.
g) William E. Whitten, born about 1871, died before 1920.
h) Julia F. Whitten, born about 1874, died after 1880.
i) Leona A. Whitten, born about 1877, died before 1899.

5. Isaac B. Whitten, born in Carnesville, Franklin, Georgia, about 1836, died in Wharton, Texas, about 1894.
6. Charles Henry Whitten was born 25 April 1837 in Carnesville, Franklin, Georgia, and married 12 June 1865 in Montgomery, Alabama, Christiana Turner, born 25 Nov. 1845 in Lowndes County, Alabama. Charles Henry died 16 Nov. 1901, while Christiana died 27 Sept. 1877 in Lowndes. Both are buried in Oakview Cemetery, Lowndesboro, Alabama.

   Their six children all born in Rugeley Place, Lowndes, Alabama, were:

   a) Infant female Whitten, born and died 23 Feb. 1866.
   b) Harriet Anna Whitten, born 18 April 1867, died 20 Aug. 1888.
   c) Charles Alvin Whitten, born 1 Sept. 1869, 16 March 1903.
   d) Julia Whitten, born 27 March 1872, died 29 Aug. 1953.
   e) Carlinne Whitten, born 23 April 1875, died 16 April 1952.
   f) Infant male Whitten, born and died 20 Sept. 1877.
7. Martha E. Whitten was born about 1840 in Carnesville, Franklin, Georgia, and married Oct. 1857 in Wharton, Texas, Dr. Bushrod W. Bell, who was born 20 April 1820 in Alabama. Martha E. died before 1894 in Texas; Dr. Bell, 3 Feb. 1883 in

Ft. Bend. He was buried in Richmond, Texas.
Their three children, all born in Texas, were:

a) Frank W. Bell, born in 1859, died 29 Jan. 1942.
b) Mattie E. Bell, born July 1870, died 15 June 1935.
c) Edward Dudley Bell, born in 1869, died in 1938.

8. Alice C. Whitten was born in Lexington, Mississippi, about 1844 and died 15 Aug. 1870 in Memphis, Tennessee.
9. William S. Whitten was born about 1846 in Lexington, Holmes, Mississippi, died 6 Nov. 1917 in Caldwell, Burleson, Texas, and was buried in Wharton, Texas.

Texas and Texans says William S. joined the Army of the Confederacy in Alabama at age thirteen. He served in Company C, 35th Alabama Infantry, Prestons Brigade, Breckenridge Division, as messenger boy to Jefferson Davis in Montgomery until the Confederate Capitol was moved to Richmond, Virginia. He had dropped out of LaGrange Military School in Franklin, Alabama, to join. William S. fought at Vicksburg as a sharpshooter and was captured during the battle of Iuka, Mississippi, on 19 Sept. 1862. He was held at Corinth and Hatchie, Mississippi, and forwarded to Columbus, Kentucky. From there he was shipped on the steamer *Dacotan* to near Vicksburg, where he was exchanged 18 Oct. 1862. On 27 April the following year William S. Whitten was discharged as a minor.

D. Mariah S. Whitten, daughter, was born about 1810 in Pendleton, South Carolina, and died in Cherokee County, Alabama, after 1850.

E. Zachariah Whitten, probable son, was born about 1810 in Pendleton and married, about 1830 in Pickens, Margaret Whitten, who was born about 1815 there. Both died after 1870 in Abbeville, South Carolina.
Their eight children, all born in South Carolina, were:

1. Malachi Whitten, born about 1836.
2. Margaret Whitten, born about 1844.
3. Austin Whitten, born about 1847.
4. Harriett Whitten, born about 1848.
5. John Whitten, born about 1849.
6. Baylis Whitten, born about 1849.
7. A. F. Whitten, born about 1853.
8. Zachariah Whitten, born about 1855.

F. William S. Whitten, probable son, was born about 1811 in Pendleton and married, about 1841 in Pickens, Harriett A., born about 1826 in North Carolina. William S. died in Cherokee, Alabama, after 1893, as did Harriett A. Both are buried in the Shiloh/Bothwell Cemetery in Cherokee, Alabama.
Their ten children, born in Cherokee, Alabama, were:

1. Mary M. E. Whitten, born about 1842, died after 1860.
2. Duett Gordon Whitten was born about 1848 in Cherokee, Alabama, married Georgia in 1871, and died before 1900 in Lamar, Texas. She was born May 1850 in Alabama, and died 30 May 1930 in Hidalgo, Texas.
   Their five children were:
   a) Lular Whitten, born about 1872.
   b) Lela Whitten, also born about 1874.
   c) Ora Whitten, born in 1877.
   d) John Lawrence Whitten, born September 1883, died 1931.
   e) Brode Hamilton Whitten, born 1884, died 24 June 1934.
3. Charles Mack Whitten was born December 1850 in Cherokee, Alabama, married, in 1874 Mary M. Allen, and died 25 May 1943 in Lamar, Texas. Mary was born 22 June 1855 in Alabama and died 31 Aug. 1896.
   Their six children were:
   a) Charles William Whitten, born 7 Feb. 1875, died 27 Oct. 1919.
   b) Nena Whitten, born February 1877.
   c) Luthur M. Whitten, born 5 Feb. 1881, died 18 Feb. 1955.
   d) Ernest Garrett Whitten born March 1855, died 26 Dec. 1943.
   e) Ukler W. Whitten, born 18 Oct. 1886, died 28 Dec. 1932.
   f) Carl Mack Whitten, born 3 Nov. 1892, died 17 March 1910.
4. George Whitten was born 5 Jan. 1852 in Cherokee, Alabama.
5. Silas L. Whitten was born January 1853 in Cherokee, Alabama, married Ruth in 1878, and died 17 April 1926 in Lamar, Texas. Ruth was born in Alabama in 1861 and died after 1892 there.
   Their seven children were:
   a) Dorothy Whitten, born 1879.
   b) Leota Whitten, born May 1881.
   c) Benjamin Washington Whitten, born 25 Nov. 1883, died

25 Feb. 1965.

d) Joe Garrett Whitten, born November 1885, died 26 Dec. 1943.
e) Jessie L. Whitten, born 28 Sept. 1890, died 7 Dec. 1918.
f) Cora Whitten, born 1890.
g) Mary Whitten, born May 1892.

6. William F. Whitten, born 1854, died before 1860.
7. Martha S. Whitten, born about 1856, died after 1870.
8. Permelia Laura Whitten was born February 1860 in Cherokee, Alabama, married Byram McHam in 1903, and died 29 April 1944 in Lamar, Texas.
9. Willie Ann Whitten, born about 1861, died after 1880.
10. Jessie Thomas Whitten was born 19 Feb. 1868 in Cherokee, Alabama, and married Alma Higgins about 1892 there. She was born 8 Aug. 1878. Alma and Jessie died in Cherokee: she, 26 March 1927; he, 17 March 1920. They are buried together in the Shiloh/Bothwell Cemetery.
    Their five children, all born in Cherokee County, Alabama, were:
    a) Erby Judson Whitten, born 5 July 1893, died 26 Sept. 1976.
    b) Nora A. Whitten, born June 1898, died before 1994.
    c) Mamie P. Whitten, born 1904, died before 1994.
    d) Homer Whitten, died 1981.
    e) Rev. John Clint Whitten, born 1915, died 1981.

G. Silas Reagan Whitten, son, was born 1815 in Pendleton, South Carolina, and married 20 Oct. 1851, in Louisville, Winston, Mississippi, Martha Caroline Yarbrough. She was born on 10 Feb. 1832 in South Carolina. Both died in Dallas, Texas: he, 16 Aug. 1889; she, 16 Nov. 1919. They are buried in Greenwood Cemetery. In the 1850 census Silas was living in the home of Dr. J. C. Hughes in Louisville, Mississippi. He moved to Ellis, Texas, in 1873 with wife, daughter Mary Amelia, and her two small children. He then moved to Dallas and was listed in the 1880 census there with spouse and children William S., Elizabeth, and Sarah N. Silas was missing, or had lost a leg. Penny McNair believes this was due to a genetic defect.
Their five children were:

1. Mary Amelia Whitten, born 7 Dec. 1852 in Louisville, Missis-

sippi, married 24 Dec. 1867, Henry William Holsomback, born May 1845 in South Carolina. She died 16 April 1910 in Dallas, Texas, and is buried in Greenwood Cemetery. Henry William died 1911 in Wills Point, Van Zandt, Texas, and was buried at White Rose Cemetery in Van Zandt. Mary Amelia was the twin of Charles Everette and moved to Texas with her parents and "many cousins, uncles, and aunts" in 1873. She divorced her husband that same year and married about 1875, in Dallas, Texas, Michael Greenlun. He was born in Ohio and died in Dallas.

The two children of Mary Amelia and Henry William Holsomback, born in Winston County, Mississippi, were:

a) John Henry Holsomback, born October 1868, died 22 Dec. 1916.

b) George Everette Holsomback, born 15 April 1870, died 3 April 1957.

Her two children by Michael Greenlun, born in Texas, were:

c) Tom S. Greenlun, born 1877.

d) Lillian Greenlun, born 1879.

2. Charles Everette Whitten, twin of Mary Amelia, was born 7 Dec. 1852 in Louisville, Winston, Mississippi. He died 14 Dec. 1945 in Houston, Texas and was buried in Rest Haven Cemetery there. Leaving home at age seventeen, he did not see or communicate with his family again until 1943. During this period he served as a Texas Ranger, mined for gold in California, and worked on a Mexican railroad. At some point he took the name of Charles White. Charles married Carrie about 1884. She was born January 1860 and died before 1945. They lived in El Paso in 1910; also, at various times in Dallas and Houston.

   Their two children were:

   a) Beatrice Whitten, born January 1888 in Texas.

   b) Male Whitten, name and birth not known.

3. Elizabeth M. Whitten was born December 1854 in Louisville, Winston, Mississippi. In 1879 she married Jesse James Whitten in Ellis County, Texas. He was also born in Winston, about 1857 and died in Waxahatchie, Texas, one year after the marriage. She died in Dallas 13 Feb. 1911 and was buried in Greenwood Cemetery there.

   Their child, born in Ellis County, Texas, was:

   a) Thomas Lee Whitten was born August 1880, died 1904, and was buried in Greenwood Cemetery, Dallas, Texas.

4. John William S. Whitten was born November 1858 in Louisville, Winston, Mississippi, and married about 1890, Lillie D. O'Brian, born May 1870 in Texas. She died 3 April 1920, he, after that date, both in Dallas, Texas. The couple was divorced 21 March 1904.

   Their two children, born in Dallas, were:

   a) Hattie Whitten, born March 1891.
   b) Earl R. Whitten, born January 1893, died after 1930.

5. Sarah Nanny Whitten was born 1861 in Louisville, Winston, Mississippi, married about 1884 in Dallas, and died there. Her husband's name has not been discovered. Their only known child was an infant, unnamed, who was born and died before 1900.

H. John Whitten, son, was born in South Carolina, and lived somewhere in Mississippi in 1863. ✳

CHAPTER FOUR

Earles of the Carolinas

The Earle family of Rebecca's mother is an old and distinguished one. Its members have served England, her Virginia colony, and the states of Virginia, the Carolinas, and Kentucky, with honor. John Earle, founder of the American line was born in Dorsett, England, around 1612, a son of Sir Richard Earle. He married Mary Symmonds, also born in England, about 1630. The Earles, with three children, came to America in about 1640, landing at St. Mary's in Maryland, and moving shortly thereafter across the Potomac River to Northumberland County, Virginia, in what was to become Westmoreland County. John Earle received extensive land grants from the English king, which the Earles retained for nearly one hundred and twenty years. The family then moved west to nearby Frederick County, from which many migrated to the Carolinas and Kentucky. Their history and genealogy have been well documented elsewhere.

The Whittens and the Earles were closely associated from the time that Charles Whitten Sr., Colonel John, and his brother, Judge Baylis Earle moved into close proximity along the North-South Carolina border well before 1800 until the 1850s when their members had spread over the South. In 1815, Silas Reagan Whitten married Eleanor Kee Earle, daughter of Col. John and his second wife, Rebecca Berry Wood.

The children of Colonel John and his brother, Judge Baylis, both sons of Samuel Earle III and his wife, Anna Sorrell, are listed in the paragraphs that follow. Members of a third generation of Earles who wrote or were mentioned in the letters are also identified.

A. Col. John Earle was born 5 June 1737 in Prince William County, Virginia. He died in 1800 and is buried at Earle's Fort, North Carolina. He married first about 1765 in Virginia, Thomasine Prince, who was born 1 Oct. 1746 in Frederick County, Virginia, and died in Rutherford County, North Carolina, about 1777. In 1787, he married Mrs. Rebecca Berry Wood, widow of John Wood who was murdered by Bloody Bill Cunningham and his Tories in November 1781.

The five children of Colonel John and Thomasine Prince, all born at Earle's Fort, were:

1. Gen. John Baylis Earle was born 23 Oct. 1766 and died February 1836. He married Sarah Taylor.
2. Anna Berry Earle, born 3 Aug. 1768.
3. Elizabeth Sorrell Earle, born 2 Aug. 1771.
4. Caroline Matilda Earle, born 25 Feb. 1774.
5. George V. Earle, born 22 Feb. 1777.

The seven children of Col. John Earle and Rebecca Berry Wood, all also born at Earle's Fort, were:

6. Dr. Joseph Berry Earle was born 29 Feb. 1788 and married Rebecca Sloan.
7. Lydia Maverick Earle was born 4 Jan. 1790 and married William Prince.
8. Eleanor Kee Earle was born 6 Jan. 1792 and married Silas Reagan Whitten.
9. Letitia Sorrell Earle was born 16 Jan. 1793. She married Laban Poole. They lived in Pontotoc, Mississippi, in 1846.
10. Amaryllis Earle was born 16 Feb. 1795. She married Elisha Bomar and had a daughter, Harriet, who married Judge Thomas O. P. Vernon.
11. Maj. John Earle remained in South Carolina.
12. Harriett Harrison Earle was born 27 Aug. 1797. She married Ephriam Roddy and moved to Texas before 1850. Their three daughters and two sons included: an unnamed daughter, who married a Mr. Woodlief; Eleanor Kee; Baylis; and Joseph.

B. Judge Baylis Earle was born 8 Aug. 1734 in Prince William, Virginia, and died at Earlesville, South Carolina, 6 Jan. 1825. On 16 April 1757 he married Mary Prince, born December 1744 in Charles City, Virginia, and died in 1807 in South Carolina. She was the sister of Thomasine, wife of Col. John Earle, and thirteen years old when she married.

Their first eight children, born in Frederick County, Virginia, were:

1. Sallie Earle was born 4 Jan. 1759 and married Edward Hampton.
2. Capt. Samuel Earle was born 28 Nov. 1760 and died 23 Dec. 1833. He married Harriet Harrison.
3. Jack Earle, born 1762, died 1767.
4. Anna Earle was born 24 Dec. 1764 and married Ephriam Reese.

5. John Earle was born 18 Sept. 1766 and married Nancy Holland Burns.
6. Baylis Earle Jr. was born 11 Sept. 1768 and married Anna Hewlett.
7. Demaris Earle was born 11 Jan. 1771 and died 8 March 1804. She married Michael Dillingham.
8. Rhoda Earle was born 25 May 1773 and married Benjamin Clark.

These six children were born in Earlesville, South Carolina:

9. Miriam Earle was born 4 Nov. 1775 and married John William Gowen.
10. Thomas Prince Earle was born 16 Sept. 1778 and married Mary Stallard.
11. Edward Hampton Earle was born 15 Oct. 1780 and married Susan Davis.
12. Theron Earle was born 13 March 1783 and died 3 Nov. 1841. He married Hannah Miller. Their children grew up with those of Silas Reagan and Eleanor Kee Whitten and appeared frequently in Rebecca's letters.
    Their ten children, all born near Earlesville, South Carolina, were:
    a) Samuel Earle.
    b) Dr. Michael Baylis Earle, who married Harriet Maxwell.
    c) Crawford Montgomery Earle.
    d) Thomas J. Earle, who wrote many of the letters, and later married Jane Kenedy of Georgia.
    e) Oliver Perry Earle, who married Catherine Davis.
    f) John Chevis Earle.
    g) Elizabeth Earle, who married Gen. Joel W. Miller.
    h) Nancy Miller Earle, a correspondent who became the second wife of Rev. John Gill Landrum.
    i) James Earle.
    j) Theron Earle Jr.
13. Aspasia Earle was born 21 Feb. 1785 and married Mary Montague.
14. Providence Earle was born 10 July 1788 and married John Lucas. ✳

CHAPTER FIVE

Rebecca's Letters

A good letter must be short and concise. No more than one page is the criteria. Americans don't have time to read! Before radio, television, telephones, and *The Readers Digest,* this wasn't true. People communicated by mail, in person, or not at all. Letter writing was an art form, good penmanship a source of pride. Letters, newspaper stories, and books were lengthy, language formal; even minute details were not omitted. Heartfelt sentiments were often expressed, poetic license was granted, verse was acceptable. Writers wrote to entertain as well as to inform.

More can be learned from old letters than from those we write today. The old ones were longer and covered a broader range of subjects. Aside from intimate personal contact, nothing reveals the thoughts and character of individuals with greater clarity than old letters written to friends and family. Always valuable for genealogical research, they let us peer into the hearts and minds of writer and recipient. It is sad that most old correspondence has long since been discarded, and with it, bits and pieces of our past.

Rebecca Berry Whitten saved her family's letters, and we are blessed for they reveal the lives of her Earles and Whittens, their times, their travels, their joy and sorrow, sickness and death.

Before Rebecca died, she entrusted her treasures to nephew Walter Wood Whitten, son of Frank Adams and Mary Dora Whitten. Becoming interested in family history, Walter transcribed a few letters and shared them with relatives. Among those was Arthur Reagan, a cousin, well known for his own collection of Whitten lore. Reagan later visited Walter in Macon, Mississippi, and spent an evening transcribing others.

When Walter Wood Whitten died, his wife, Mary Lillian, became custodian of the collection. She remarried and moved from Macon, after which researchers who knew of Rebecca's letters tried, in vain, to locate her, finally concluding that she had died and the letters were lost.

More than ten years later, because of his failing vision, I became heir to Arthur Reagan's matchless Whitten family records. References to the letters were scattered throughout his files. The few he had transcribed were there, and I became determined to find the rest. Through good fortune and AT&T directory assistance, I located Mrs. Walter Wood Whitten and found she had given the collection to Walter Wood's nephew, Nathaniel Murry Whitten, of Memphis, Tennessee. When I visited Mr. and Mrs. Murry Whitten in their home, I was a distant and unknown cousin and yet they allowed me to return to Virginia with Rebecca's letters. While spending nearly a year studying and transcribing them, I became convinced they should be shared with the families whose stories they told and with everyone interested in southern life during the nineteenth century.

A few letters from the files of Arthur Reagan; Alfred Tennyson Whitten and his son, Joseph Nathaniel; Elizabeth Ann and Doleska Fitzallen Whitten and G. W. Ward, descendants of James Whitten of Hall, Georgia; Alice and Aubrey DeWitt Whitten; Penny McNair; Mitch Vetusky; May Isom Whitten Moore; and the author have been added.

All were transcribed from handwritten originals, many damaged, some extensively. Editing was kept to a minimum, some spelling corrected, periods, commas, and paragraph separations added when it was thought helpful to clarify the writers' meaning. Individuals have been identified when known and not clearly described elsewhere in the book.

Presented in chronological order, the letters speak for themselves, although from time to time comment has been inserted to clarify or highlight some fact or family trait, and, on occasion, to indulge the author's bent to pontification.

These are Rebecca's letters. ✻

CHAPTER SIX

1811 to 1848

During these years America waged a second war with England. We Americans claimed victory. Historians call it a draw. The Baptists fought and split twice, first, over support of foreign missionaries, and then, because northern churches insisted that slave ownership was contrary to the teachings of Christ. A temperance movement was gaining support. Ties binding the nation were fraying and failing from the effects of acrimonious debate over the future of slavery and the right of states to chart their own courses. In 1836 the Alamo fell, Texans defeated a Mexican Army at San Jacinto, and a new republic was born. On the 29th of December, 1845, Texas became a state and soon thereafter, the United States invaded Mexico, acquiring vast areas of the West and Southwest, and opening it to eager settlers. Europe's poor and persecuted continued to arrive at eastern seaports, and the entire country seemed to be moving south and west as its citizens yielded to the lure of cheap land and new beginnings.

The subjects of our letters were in the thick of this great migration. By 1811 the Reagans, who had moved from North to South Carolina with the Whittens, had left for Kentucky and Tennessee; Charles Whitten Jr. and family were in Pendleton District, South Carolina; and many Earles had left for Kentucky.

By 1835 John and Mary Reagan Whitten and all but two of their children were no longer in South Carolina. They, with Elizabeth, Ranson, Alfred, and Nancy, were in Fayette, Tennessee, while James and Dr. Isaac Smith lived in Georgia. Charles Whitten Jr. and an, as yet, undetermined number of his children were in Cherokee County, Alabama, by about 1830.

Mariam, first to move to Mississippi, left South Carolina in 1840, leaving only Silas Reagan of that generation. His daughter Harriet Earle married and moved to Mississippi in 1845, first of his to succumb to the call of the wilderness.

Dr. Joseph Berry Earle to Eleanor Kee Earle—Greenville, South Carolina, to North Pacolet, North Carolina, 2 Aug. 1811

Dear Ellen,

Mr. Southern has just called on his way home. He has not seen

Brother James, nor can I prevail with him to return to see him.

I have not time to answer your letter by Doc McEntire more than to say your suspicions are entirely groundless with respect to Miss Taylor and myself, as I adjure. I have never had the most distant idea of anything of that kind.

Letty (Letitia Sorrell Earle) is out here. She came out here with Uncle Elias's family on Tuesday last. I expect I shall have to bring her in, in the course of two or three weeks, when I shall want to bring some one of you out with me.

I send three pairs of slippers, one for yourself, and a pair for Betsy (Elizabeth Sorrell Earle), the other pair for Ammy (Amaryllis Earle), or Harriet (Harriet Harrison Earle), whoever most needs them. (Letty, Ammy, and Harriet were Eleanor Kee Earle Whitten's sisters, and Betsy, her half sister.)

Give my love to Mother and sisters and receive the affectionate regard of,

J. B. Earle

In this earliest letter, Dr. Joseph Berry Earle, Eleanor Kee's brother, or Gen. John Baylis Earle, her half brother, wrote to his unmarried sister, Eleanor Kee, who was living at home near Earle's Fort in Old Rutherford County, North Carolina. Her father, Col. John Earle, active in the Revolution and the affairs of Rutherford, with his first wife, Thomasine Prince, had come from Frederick County, Virginia, to the Carolinas shortly before 1766, where he founded Earlesville in South Carolina. After being joined there by his brother, Judge Baylis, in about 1774, John moved across the Pacolet River where he built Earle's Fort overlooking the river near Earle's Ford in North Carolina. It is today on what is called Prince Road, between Landrum, South Carolina, and Tryon, North Carolina. The fort was used during the war as a refuge from Indians and Tories.

There, Eleanor married Silas Reagan Whitten in 1815. If the letter was from brother Joseph Berry Earle, it must have come from Greenville where Dr. Earle made his home after marriage. That growing village would have provided a source for the slippers he sent, and was a more lucrative location for a young doctor. If half brother John Baylis Earle wrote it, the slippers may have come from Washington, where he served in Congress. His first wife was Sarah Taylor. She could be the Miss Taylor about whom Eleanor Kee had the suspicions that J. B. Earle denies in this letter. Gen. Earle was nearly forty-five years old when it was written, and Sarah Taylor was his first wife. He died at age seventy after two wives and ten children. If he was unmarried in 1811, he lived the remainder of his life on a fast track. Dr. Joseph Berry Earle is the most likely author of this first letter.

David Barrett to John Whitten—Gowensville, South Carolina, 29 April 1826 from Fayette County, Western District, State of Tennessee, North Fork of Wolf River, near the head, half way between Browns Ferry on the Tennessee River and Chickasaw Bluffs on the Mississippi. Distance from one to the other: 125 miles.

Dear Father,

We landed here on the 6th day of March last and are all in good health, Betsy (wife, Elizabeth Whitten) excepted, and I think she is feeling better than when she was in South Carolina, though she frets a good deal about you all and the distance she is from you all. Tho as to the country, I think we are all as well pleased as I expected to be. To be sure this country is not without failings. They are these in my view. I do not like the general chance of water, i.e., I do not like the common creeks. They sink too much, tho I think the cause is from the vast looseness of the earth. As a proof of my opinion, wells will not do without walling immediately after, or before, done digging for caving in. Also the surface of the earth is so loose you may track any animal where the woods is burnt. Springs also are tolerable scarce and they are all boiling ones, though good water and freestone also in places, timber and rock very scarce. I think these are the principle faults I have to this country.

And as to the advantages are these. Good land is tolerable plenty, prairies thought to be best as to summer range. I cannot make you sensible of the appearance of that, except you had been acquainted with such countries. The grass, now a great deal of it, and weeds are half too high. I do not know how high it will get. I am told people can save as much hay as they please. Anywhere in the woods the common land, I am bound to believe, is good for 1000 lbs of cotton an acre. My reasons are the sight of the old stalks and the peoples word. Corn from 8 to 13 barrels an acre. There have been small experiments on small grain and they are promising. Markets are plenty and convenient. Steamboats run almost all around us and keel boats come within 12 miles on two directions and I have settled as far from market as I could get on the dividing ridge and within 7 or 8 miles of the Indian line on the south, the beautifulest country I ever saw.

I will now give you some of our difficulties in getting here. We took water in East Tennessee on the 18th day of Dec last and left Browns Ferry on the 24th of Feb. following. I believe I can safely say

I was never well one day (after the first week) until we landed here, and In fact Betsy was down most of the time and always some of the children. Lucy (slave), I believe, stood it best of all, I worst of all. We had very disagreeable companions in the boat with us. They were of this new sect called Cumberland Presbyterians, and I must confess, I got tired of them and their religion. When we landed we had then to come by land 65 miles and that took us till 6th of March, all sick and traveled slow but thank the Lord I never saw my family as hearty since I have had one, tho bad colds are very prevalent in this and the adjoining countries.

There is another misfortune attends this country at the present tho I hope it will not last very long. Corn is scarce at one dollar per bushel and cash, also the mills plenty near us. Bacon plenty at the Chickasaw Bluffs at 6 cents, flour at $4, corn at 50 cs CB, which, as before stated, is about 60 miles from us. Gallatin (son, Albert Gallatin) has been there since we landed here with my wagon and brought me what bacon I wanted and a barrel of flour. I also bought a cow at Browns Ferry and drove her here and when we landed the grass was so good we never fed her anymore and she now gives as much milk as we all can eat, say three gallons a day besides sporting her calf.

The time for speculation for land is about over in this country i.e., to make a fortune quick as a heap has done, tho vast quantity of vacant land here. Yet there is a great stir among new settlers about occupant claims. The occupant is entitled to 200 acres of land if he is living on it the first day of May, or any quantity under, at 50 cents an acre and has till the first of July to pay and have his land run out. Others has, after July, to give $1 an acre for all the vacant land he takes up. I have bought, and am living on occupant claim, which, if I can save I shall be, I think, well satisfied. I think I have on it 40 or 50 acres of as good land is common. I do not expect to save more than about 75 acres tho cash is scarce as well as corn and I do not know how it will be.

There is no person except by experience knows the expense, the trouble, attending so great a journey with a family and to be scarce of money. The poor people has always to labor under disadvantages.

The religion of this country appears to be going on by forces of arms. Cumberland Presbyterians and Methodists are vying which can be most powerful and I fear popularity is what most of them are after. There is also a new kind of Baptist called United Baptist. I am not acquainted with them and I believe I do not want to be. Then there is

Regular Baptists enough in this purchase to form an association called the Forked Deer Association, tho none about us. There is but one man and his wife that are Regular Baptists anywhere in my acquaintance and they live in sight of us. We both bring water out of one spring and I would not risk them in a swap for any strangers tho we appear to have wonderful good neighbors. Esquire John Reagan lives in about one mile of us and his children are settled all about him. He is a son of old Charles Reagan. He is well settled.

Betsy wants me to write something about the children and in particular the little girls. I cannot tell what to write. They are as hearty as you ever saw them and are full of gab and grows like little pigs. While we was at Browns Ferry lying there was 6 steam boats past us at Waterloo. Betsy went in and explored it (one). I was not able to go in with her. She gives a great account of the inside. The children was mightily pleased at the sight and motion of them.

We got our dog, Taylor, drowned while coming down the river by the fool conduct of the man in command.

I expect to get in about 8 acres of corn cleared. Since I come here I have begun to plow and have got about half rails to fence it. No chance of hiring, done it all myself as Gallatin has been gone 2 trips. I had to send him to Browns Ferry for part of our things. Him and his mother went. Me and John (son, John Whitten Barrett) stayed at home and worked as we have to make every edge cut that can. I expect to take up a school the first of July for 8 months. Necessity drew me to it as I could do better to improve my place.

We are living in a 14 foot cabin on the dirt without any chimney, cook out of doors, no time to get pencheons to lay the floor and the house is too small for to have chimney. Excuse my flying about on so many subjects. If I could see you I could tell you what I think for a month and if a quire of paper was in one piece I could fill it. When you write direct your letter to Summerville in Fayette.

D Barrett and E Barrett

David and Elizabeth Whitten Barrett's letter to her father describing the trip from South Carolina to Fayette, Tennessee, is a classic account of a pioneer journey westward into newly opened wilderness seven or eight miles from the Indian line on the south, the present Tennessee-Mississippi border.

Chickasaw Bluffs was yet to be renamed Memphis, and "we are living on dirt." David's comments about Cumberland Presbyterians may have come back to haunt him when brother Alfred and family joined that group in 1845.

Nancy Miller Earle to Harriet Whitten—Earlesville to Gowensville, South Carolina, 1835

My Dear Cousin,

I regretted, very much, that I could not join the party to the gold mine. I should have been much pleased to have gone had it been convenient, but it was not at the time. I regret it the more as I partly promised you I would go. I hope you had a pleasant party, and that you were compensated for the ride. Dear Cousin, I feel very grateful indeed to you for the many kind expressions of affection and esteem in your last, and indeed in all your notes to me. I am truly thankful. I am truly blessed in having so dear and kind a friend as you have ever shown yourself to be, and I earnestly desire that I may merit your esteem.

You say you fear that you appeared melancholy and unsocial when you were last here. I did not think so at all. You are never unsocial. If you were not so cheerful as usual, you had a sufficient reason for it. One could hardly expect you to be so under the circumstances. We cannot, I think, avoid such feelings at times. I know that I am apt to have them myself often and without being able to assign a cause. And I will certainly truly forgive you when there is anything to forgive. I know I have much more reason to ask you forgiveness on many occasions.

I know I cannot always appear as sociable as I would wish when with my friends, but I fear we can not always do as we wish, or I think I would do very differently often times.

You asked me if I have seen somebody since the party. Now I can't tell you unless I knew who somebody was. Neither do I know what you mean by committing yourself and all this. When shall I see you again? Will you visit us soon? I hope you will.

May every blessing and happiness be yours is the sincere wish of your devoted friend. Love to all,

N E

Nancy Miller Earle to Harriet Whitten—Earlesville to Gowensville, South Carolina, about 1840

My Dear Cousin,

I take the opportunity of answering your very kind note for which I feel very thankful indeed. It always delights me very much to receive a letter from you and know that you regard me as one of your dear friends. It is a very great pleasure to me I assure you. It is a great blessing to have a really sincere friend. I have ever regarded you as such a one and I earnestly wish that I were more worthy of your esteem.

You seem to think my situation a very happy one and I certainly have no reason to complain of it but I don't know why you should not be equally as much so for you are blest with friends and affectionate family relatives more so that we often meet with. I have often heard it remarked what an affectionate family. I think it one of the chief requisites of happiness is to be happy in the domestic relation.

I am very glad to find that you have been writing for the Social Fellows. I think the ladies ought to aid them if they can. I would willingly do so if I could.

We had a pleasant trip to the mountains though it was very fatiguing. I was disappointed in my expectations. I expected to see a good deal more than I did. I was very sorry you could not be with us for I believe it is thought that it is the last party of the kind for some time, at least.

Thomas (brother Thomas J.) said that you spoke of going to the Muster on next Saturday. You and Rebecca must come and go. I should like very much to go if I had company and I believe a good many girls speak of going.

I shall expect you to come over Friday evening. I have sent you a pamphlet which I found rather interesting and I thought perhaps you would like to read it. I have heard that Mr. Barton is to be at Cross Roads on Sunday. I hope he will not disappoint you again. I hope to see you soon.

My respects to the family. Oh my dear cousin, I sincerely wish that you may live happily and may the choicest of Heaven's favors be bestowed upon you is the wish of your friend,

Nancy E.

Contract from Deed Book A, Greenville County, South Carolina, recorded 6 Sept. 1841

Memorandum of a contract made and entered into between Guilford Cavet of the one part and Silas R. Whitten, president of the Gowensville Silk Company, of the other part, witnesseth. I, the above named Guilford Cavet agree to lease or rent to the above named Silas R. Whitten, for the use and purpose of the Gowensville Silk Company, for the lessor of ten years, or whatever term under ten years that the said company, through their proper officers, may desire; that lot of grounds now under fence and a part of it planted in numerous multicultured mulberry trees lying near my house and on the western side of the Greenville Road and so much thereof as the said Company may wish to occupy or cultivate, also to the same, for the same purpose, and for the same time, a small lot that is likewise near my house on the Eastern side of the said Greenville Road and on which a granary is now erected. I the said Silas R. Whitten for, and, in behalf of the above named Gowensville Silk Company, in consideration of the above lease, agree to pay to the above Guilford Cavet whatever sum or sums he, the said Silas, may be directed to do by the directors of said company. To the confirmation of which we have hereto set our hands this 20th July 1841 in presence of I. P. Carruth and John Lankford. signed Guilford Cavet and Silas R. Whitten.

Contract recorded 6 Sept. 1841

Our Silas Reagan was an entrepreneur. He signed this contract as president of a newly formed company that plans to produce silk from silkworms fed on mulberry leaves. Later we will find that he made and sold whiskey, farmed, and held public office. This venture was not successful. Virginia Farrar, daughter of John Farrer, treasurer of the Virginia Company, supported an effort to introduce silk production into the Jamestown colony in the early seventeenth century. The eighteenth and early nineteenth centuries saw similar enterprises end in failure. Silk production remains a mystery of the Orient.

Narcissa Amaryllis to Eleanor Kee Whitten—Gowensville, South Carolina, about 1842

Mother, I think proper to write these lines and hand them for your inspection and ask your advice. I have been persuaded by Mr. Barton and others that I have an experience et grave. If I have I would not conceal it from the world. I am solicited to join the church and perhaps by a higher power than any human. I have expressed my feelings to Mr. Barton and Mr. Walker. They both agree, if they have ever heard a Christian experience, mine is, which is certainly great encouragement.

My life was spent in sin and vanity until three or four years past. I mingled in all the scenes of gaiety and mirth that my circumstances would allow but often while participating in these awful joys, my conscience would check me and I would sometimes retire from the company and weep, fearing that I had done wrong. Thus did I spend my life until about four years past while attending a singing school at the Cross Roads. Our teacher would admonish us to come to God. He would tell us about the glories and advantages of religion in this world and the eternal happiness it would afford us in the world to come. He told us when we went home we should try to pray to God to have mercy on us accordingly. I did so but was a poor prayer. I prayed until I became weary. I thought it was nothing but hypocrisy and I would not try to pray. I would be several weeks and perhaps months that I did not care much what became of me. I was given over to hardness of heart. There again I would conclude that pray I must, or be forever lost and so I would try to pray.

I felt much distressed for a while. These impressions again would wear away. One year passed I attended a meeting at Mr. Prince's. Rev. B preached. He said I must be born again if ever Heaven I did obtain. He remarked that if there was any person there who wished christians to pray for them he wanted them to designate themselves and he would not only pray for them there but he would remember them when he went home. I tried to go but was not enabled to do it. When the meeting closed I went upstairs and wept bitterly. My friends tried to console me, but I told them there was nothing in this world could comfort me. I returned home very much distressed.

I remained so for several days when one day I was sitting in my room so much distressed that I thought I could not live, I felt that I was a wretched sinner, but I knew that God was all wise and had powers to do all things and I thought of His promises and I knew that He was true. He had said those who come unto Him He would in no wise cast out. Blessed are those who mourn for they shall be comforted and more than all. Those who seek Me early shall find Me.

I suddenly felt calm and composed, but I did not know what was the reason, yet I could not but believe that I had obtained a little hope in Heaven. These impressions in some measure wore away and I became rather confused until Mr. Barton and Uncle Billy were here about one past. You know Mr. B preached a good sermon that night. I felt that every word of it was applicable to my case. Next day he conversed with us and admonished us to our duty. For two days after that I felt a calm serenity and sweet composure that had heretofore been a stranger to my bosom. I loved everything around me and I loved christians dearly and I love religion. I sometimes feel that if death would come, he would be a welcome messenger, not that I wish to leave the world but that I feel drawn to the will of God, on Him do I put my trust. I seek your opinion and that of Father, then I will know my duty.

This was written about one month past.

Our Whittens and Earles had deep religious roots. Most were Baptists, active in their churches, dedicated to Christ. This letter describing the conversion of Narcissa Amaryllis is the first of several dealing with that subject. Each describes a view of the conversion experience different from that of most present-day Baptists, who accept Christ's simple statement recorded in John 3:16 "that whosoever believeth in Him shall have everlasting life." Narcissa and her fellow Baptists believed that only those predestined by God could receive salvation. It was typical for one who became convicted of sin and the need of a savior to develop a "hope" that they were among those selected for God's great gift. They longed and prayed for it, as Mary Dora later told of her husband, Frank, who hoped for eighteen years, until he became convinced that God had accepted him into His Kingdom. That realization was typically accompanied by deep emotion and great joy. This belief that God has preselected only a certain number of sinners to be saved and the rest of mankind has no chance for eternal life is the cornerstone of Calvinism, a doctrinal system attributed to sixteenth-century theologian John Calvin. Calvinists' influence waned during the hundred years after 1850, but is once more being debated within the ranks of present-day Southern Baptist Fundamentalists.

D. Metzger to Silas Reagan Whitten—to Gowensville, South Carolina, 28 July 1842

Dear Friends,

I agreed to write, and as Mrs. Whitten said, if no one would answer it Harriet would. Well, here we all are and one more. But first, as for business it is of but limited and that to a small account.

It has been, as now is, much sickness in this ville which is uncommon, and may be more so by early fall, a bilious fever. We expect soon to leave here, I reckon, for towards your region, can't now tell but shall know further when Wales returns. It may be in Rutherford Village or some 25 miles below. Have not seen any person from your way nor heard since W saw Ranson (Ranson E.) soon after we was here. I designed to have seen him and sent Nero (dog?) by him to Jo (Joseph John), as not my folks made so much fuss about him but was too late as R had left. So W took him off last week and he did not return. I have made no inquiries after him, If it will only please all the house I will be quiet. I was sorry I could not get him to Jo where he would be well treated. Sis has been at school till two weeks past. She has had the augue in her face the worst kind, suffered greatly and yet is but little better. It is common here.

Marie transgressed on the last Sabbath AM July 24th and now she has two children, gal and boy. They all say he is a perfect thing of the Lord, black hair and big eyes, very quiet and hardly cried a whimper yet. M is quite smart and could you but see her with him. As she has mourned so much over the boy she lost. And now her wishes are gratified in it being a son. She does nearly worship him with her natural fondness for children. As for me, shall say nothing about him at present but hope I shall be able to show him to you by fall and then leave it with you if he would not win the medal of all the young ones you ever see. So know I have done with the baby talk.

How are you all? I tell M I am going to this fall because I did not see the Esquire when there. Oh she, "You will drink whiskey if you go there." Don't you think her acting miserable when she sees or thinks I take a drink or so, so afraid one drink will ruin me, etc., have none here. There is next to none used in this place. I know but very few in the place. I stay at home way, go in to the street on business. I don't favor much the Dutch. They are a close, tight, pernicious people.

Has Jo (Joseph John) worked himself to death making a crop? I see Alf (Alfred Washington) going on as fast as a cheap watch is for time and Narcissa is thinking about the hereafter. I suppose Harriet's heart is all in flutter, Rebecca, happy as any earthly being and the two lesser lads living on, little thinking of the hard road before them. And last but not least in memories thought, how comes on Mr. and Mrs. W, they whose presences are a whole world and whose absence leaves an emptiness, and that you are moving on as usual in your wonderful sphere of happiness. And do you know of any person who has a yelloe dog, one of the finest dogs in the county and a hundred of Walkers Lawyer's books. Then give him my best respects.

Sis often asks where's Ellen. W is yet in the AM, and it is now late and I am tired and sleepy and got to be up 3 to 5 times before AM. Let me have a Nig, but they can't get long well with our way of feeding the cattles, so I do it myself as I had rather after serving and having learned the trade so well.

So good night. Fare you well one and all,

D. Metzger

W left Union day after Alf did. Did Esq call there? Write us a long, big, and full of news letter and tell us all that's happened and is to happen. Marie says, my love to you all, and as Sis is asleep can't say to Joe what she might say. She talks often about Joe and how kind Rebecca was to her when we was there. We got on here well and did not get wet. I now have made a body with a top so I can remedy the trouble I was at when with you lest M and things might all get wet. I got here in time yet Wales patience all gone by my absence so we was right off to the mill for the lumber which he said was all ready and when we got there the trees were in the woods.

A family friend tells us that Silas Reagan made, drank, and sold whiskey. From the early 1800s, drunkenness and the use of alcohol had been condemned by the churches. A great temperance movement was afoot, culminating some hundred years later in Prohibition. During colonial times, whiskey making had been an honorable profession, particularly in the Carolina mountains. It was one among several sources of income for Silas Reagan Whitten.

That he never joined the church was a matter of great concern for those who loved him. His family prayed he would make a public profession of faith. (Note the 5 Oct. 1849 letter from cousin Mariah, daughter of Charles Jr.) He never did. In his 8 Nov. 1888 obituary there was high praise, but also the odd statement: "Although not a professor of Christianity, he revered and honored it above all men."

We know from these letters that he raised funds for Cross Roads Church, sought new clergy and teachers for the area, was on the best of terms with local ministers, regularly read and studied scripture, and lived like a Christian, in remarkable harmony with a deeply religious wife and seven children. Other researchers appear puzzled by this seeming inconsistency in an otherwise exemplary life. After careful study of nearly two hundred letters from and to his family, I believe Silas Reagan Whitten acted boldly and from conviction. He openly made, sold, and drank whiskey. Churches condemned the practice. He was not a hypocrite.

O. H. Wells, search recorder to Silas Reagan Whitten—Greenville to Gowensville, South Carolina, by Dexter, 7 March 1843

My Dear Friend,

I have seen Maj. Perry, stated the whole case fully to him. He says there is no better chance than to let my niece remain a few days where she is, that it will not do to move her for a few days. It would be almost certain death. He says he will do everything in the case that is necessary. He says there is no danger of conviction and let the law take its course. He says a jury revolts at the idea of convicting a woman of felony and the evidence, which I stated to him in its worst form, would not condemn her. I shall relieve you of the awful burden of having her about your house in a day or two. The community sympathizes with you as well and myself and her brother.

My health is such that I can't go up to your house today and my wife is sick besides. I thought it my duty to go or send up immediately. Dexter bears affliction with better nerve than myself and I have sent him. God bless you and yours.

Yours truly and cordially,
O. H. Wells

Mr. Wells, Greenville District search recorder, must have worked with Silas Reagan, magistrate, tax collector, and census enumerator. The letter reveals an intriguing mystery. What did his niece do? Why was her life in danger?

Unknown to Harriet Whitten—before 1844

Harriet,

Forgive my assurance and confidence if in this epistle I express my sincere admiration and esteem for one whose sweet of disposition and amiable manners have enkindled a peculiar, painful yet pleasurable sentiment in my throbbing heart. With you, it may in truth be said that winning ways and pleasures sweet as love with sanctity and wisdom tempering, blend their soft allurement. But perhaps I should not encourage hope. Presenting simple flowers are the mysterious marks of affection, esteem, and love.

Perhaps I have said or disclosed more than I should have done. With the most fervent spirit, your admirer,

Friendship be yours
How seldom in this dreary vale,
congenial happenings we find.
Seldom, but friendships steady gale
Ruminates the dreaming mind.
Friendship be yours while life endures,
May happiness be your repast.
May joys increase. May sorrows cease,
Till heaven shall be your home at last.

Perhaps the anonymous admirer was Nathan Alexander Lankford, who

married Harriet in 1845. He proved to be an excellent husband, though, if this is his work, a bard of little merit.

Rebecca to Harriet Whitten—Greenville to Gowensville, South Carolina, 22 March 1844

My Dear Sister,

You perhaps are very anxious to hear from us and as I can not get to send a letter by hand I will send it by mail. How do you all do now? I hope you are all doing very well. I am getting homesick. Oh, none of you know how much I want to see you and were it not for Cissa's being here I could not stay at all, but she and Elias are so very kind, and Bell so sweet that I love to be with them, but I wish we were all at the mountains. When shall I ever hear from home? Oh, if I could only get one line from some of you I would be so glad. How are Mother and Papa, Jo, Mesina, and little Mary? I suppose Alfred is very busy in the field and Silas too. Does Rant feed the cow well?

I must give you the news of the town as far as I know. I attended a very large party last night at Mr. Long's. There were a great many persons there. I got a little acquainted with the Misses Earles and Misses Stones. Eugenie inquired about you, said she would call on us in a few days. Invited me to see them, and I would not have gone to the party but some of my friends persuaded me. I have not visited anywhere but Mr. Loveland's.

What have you done with Caesar? I hope you have not let any of the girls take him. Have you seen, or heard anything of my bay horse? I hope the Dr. has not forgotten his promise. I see a great many fine horses here but I do not like the ride. Hat, tell all of them that Bell is so sweet. She can hardly cry. She is very lively. She has not got any teeth yet, and little Mary as pretty and sweet as ever. I do want to see her. Does she think as much of Papa and Mother as she used to? Kiss her for me and all our folks and then tell them to kiss you. It is snowing very hard, the first snow I have seen this year. I'm afraid all the peaches are killed, I believe they are down here.

When is Papa going to come or send after me? I reckon you are trying to get your new dress made. You must have a very pretty stripe. When you see the Misses Goodletts, give them my love. I want to see the girls very much. We cannot find such girls as they are often. I saw their cousins at the party last night but did not get acquainted with them. The ladies were nearly all dressed in white and in fine style. We are all well. Bell was rather sick yesterday but much better today.

Now be sure and don't let any girl take my horse and I shall want him when I get home. Kiss Papa, Mother, Alfred, Pluck, Rant, Jo, Mesina, and little Mary for me and tell Mesina to kiss you for me.

Give my warmest love to all of them and receive a large share from your sister,

Rebecca

Note added by Narcissa:

It is almost my bedtime and I am very tired, but Rebecca has left a little room in her letter for me, and you know I am always glad to say a word to our folks at home. I have no news worth writing, only that we are well. Elias and the baby have both been a little sick but they are very well now.

Bell can almost talk, but it is nonsense for me to tell you all how smart she is for you know anyhow. Rebecca has attended two parties since she came down. She seems to enjoy herself very well and I am so happy to have her with me that I hardly know how to act.

Oh, I do wish I could see you all. I never wanted to see you half so bad in my life. Do come. Every one of you come and see us. Harriet, I shall expect you to stay with me when R goes home. Pa, you and Mother must come to see me, and Jo and Mesina, and Silas and Ranson. I want to see little Mary. Does she dance yet? I reckon she has forgotten her aunt Cis. I intend to go to see you in May, but I reckon it will be about the last.

I don't know whether you can read this or not. My paper is gone. Do receive the warmest love of your affectionate daughter,

sister Narcissa

This is our only letter penned by Rebecca. Writing from the home of sister Narcissa in Greenville to sister Harriet in Gowensville, she returned and saved it for us. Cissa added a note. Aside from establishing that Bell was then too young for her first teeth, the letter is typical of those written by the Whitten sisters. It reveals, as her entire life confirms, that Rebecca lived truly in the bosom of her family.

Narcissa to Rebecca Whitten—Pickensville to Greenville, South Carolina, 28 July 1844

My Dear Sister,

Having an opportunity I cannot neglect writing you a few lines to let you know how we all come on for it don't look like any of you are coming down. I looked for you every day last week and I shall look constantly until you come. We are all well and getting on pretty much as usual. Bell has got entirely well. She walks everywhere and tries very hard to talk. She is very lively. She thinks a great deal of her doll. She sits down in her little chair and rocks it to sleep very often, singing all the while. I know you would laugh to see her. Everyone notices her and she likes that.

Very well. Girls, I know you want to know how I come on doing all the things myself. Well, I can tell you, I get on first rate. I have lots of tomatoes but not a bean have I had since home. Somebody steals every one before they get large enough to eat. It won't be long before we will have plenty of potatoes. I have put me up a nice jar of whiskey pickles. My cow gives a fine chance of milk and so we have lots of buttermilk. But as you know we have plenty to eat. Everybody says I have got fat and feel very well, indeed. Now I am not joking, some of you come down. I do want to see you all very much. Do come.

It is very late and I must stop. Give my love to Jo and Sina and tell them I am looking for them. Good night it is very late. Elias joins me in love to you all. Silas, you and Ranson must come and stay with me. Alfred, come to see us. Harriet, you and Rebecca must come with Papa and Mother, you must come with Jo and Sena. Bell sends a kiss to Mary.

Your affectionate daughter and sister,
Narcissa.

Henrietta says tell all of you howdy.

Narcissa Amaryllis and husband, Elias Holcombe, lived several places in South Carolina. After marriage they were in Gowensville with her family, moved to Greenville, and on to Pickensville, where Elias tried to farm and teach school. Returning to Gowensville for a time, they transferred to Pendleton. Elias was subsequently employed by the firm of Betts and Marshall, for whom he traveled extensively. His headquarters was in Charleston, where Cissa joined him for spring, fall, and winter seasons, fleeing, in summer, to the safety of Pendleton in the cooler uplands, as she sought to avoid the annual epidemics of malaria, yellow fever, and broken bone fever (dengue). Henrietta must have been a family slave.

Narcissa to Harriet Whitten—Greenville to Pleasant Grove, South Carolina, 1844

My dear Sister,

Although I look for some of you this evening that cannot keep me from writing. Aunt thinks she will go home tomorrow and if some of you don't come today you will hear from us. I can't tell how I long to see my dear Father, Mother, Brothers, and Sisters and would give a great deal just to be with you all when you gather round that happy fireside at night.

Elias generally stays at the store till 7 or 9 O'clock and you know I am lonesome but sometime the ladies come in and sit with me till bedtime. We have very kind neighbors. Some of the ladies called on me this very day. Mrs. Perry called to say she was going to the lowlands. She seemed to think very strange that Alf did not go to see them when he came to town. Mrs. Jones and Mrs. Stone came to see me recently. I visit very little and I have not been to Church since I came to town. Bell won't stay with anybody but Elias and me.

Well, guess who went to the Sherman's wedding down at the paper mill. There were 20 or 30 there from the village. They had a very nice supper. I have saved some of the cake for you. Bell was universally admired. Oh girls, she has grown a great deal since you saw her and you would hardly know her if you saw her now.

Harriet, I received a letter from you last Sunday. Oh you don't know how glad I was to hear from you all. I have not heard from you since and the time seems very long. I should have answered your letter that evening but I had some ladies and gentlemen to tea and you know I had no time. I thought Sol was going up the next day and I did not know he stayed so long until he was gone but you know my dear sisters, I will write every chance for I know you are always happy to get a letter from Cissy. I am so anxious to have you come and stay with me. I would be delighted to have you spend all the time with me. What has become of my dear Father and Mother? I have been looking for them these two weeks and I think Mother is sick or Papa has the backache, then you know that makes me feel very bad.

Alfred, I thought you was going to write soon. I have not got one letter yet. Do come and see us. Bring Silas Jr. and Ranson. Oh, I want to see you all so much. Sometime I cry a half bushel because I cannot see you.

Give my love to Jo and Mesina. Tell them to come and see us. They don't know how glad I would be to see them. Rebecca and Harriet, you would come to see me first. I shall look for you every day until you come. You must all write to me. Do kiss sweet little Mary for me. Dear child, I want to see her very much, but I don't know when I will see her. Bell can get up by a chair. I think she will walk very soon. It is getting late and I want to close my letter.

Oh my dear Harriet, since I have written this letter Alfred and Rebecca have come. Oh you don't know how glad I am to see them. I hardly know what to do with myself. Oh I do wish you were all here. I could kiss you again and again and I know you would all be just as glad to see me. O Hat, I thank you very much for the cake you sent. It is very nice, and you know I think a great deal of it because Harriet baked it. I will send you some of my wedding cake. Rebecca says you must kiss them all for her and I say you must kiss them all for me and then they must kiss you. Tell Silas and Ranson they must write to me. It is very late. I cannot write much more.

Elias joins me in love to all.

Your sincere and affectionate sister,

Narcissa

I will send some seed pods.

G. A. Montague to Silas Reagan Whitten—New Haven, Connecticut, to Gowensville, South Carolina, 8 Sept. 1844

Silas Whitten, Esq. Dear Sir,

Knowing your friendly disposition toward Martha, I take the liberty to write you for some information about her situation. Upon my arrival from sea last June I received a letter from her in which she requested me to send funds for her to get home, which I immediately complied with. Since which we have received a few lines acknowledging the receipt of the money. The letter was postmarked Gowensville July 7. Since which we have heard nothing and we are very anxious to hear. It appears that Martha disappeared after the letter.

Will you be so kind as to call on Martha if she has not left and inform me the reason. It is now a week since my arrival from sea and I was disappointed in not seeing Martha on my return. We would be much in your debt if you would make us a visit. We would be glad to have as you expressed a wish to see the North when I was with you.

Mrs. Webster was with us in August and will write you.

Yours truly,

G. A. Montague

Inside this letter is another letter from a Montague daughter. It is not readable.

Robert McKay to Harriet Earle Whitten—Greenville, South Carolina, 30 Oct.

1844

Lines to Miss Whitten (soon to be Mrs. Nathaniel Alexander Lankford) in her album on her leaving Greenville.

Here's peace to thy heart, though anothers it be,
And health to thy cheek, though it bloom not for me.
May you live in this world free from care and from strife,
And joy and contentment attend thee through life.
May friends ne'er desert thee, no, never deceive,
And cause thee in anguish and sorrow to grieve.
Though many there be you know very well,
In whose bosom sincerity never can dwell.
Like the rose of the morn may your heart ever be,
Pure, spotless, and bright, from sorrow be free.
But not like the rose ere its blossoms have spread,
Be called in thy beauty to dwell with the dead.
Earth's flowers may bloom and die in a day,
Memory lose it's endearments and friendships decay.
More lasting than these thy memory shall be,
And long be remembered and cherished by me.
When this album's fair pages you hastily turn,
And the warmth of pure friendship your bosom shall burn,
As each piece you peruse from beginning to end,
Cast a glance o'er the lines of a far distant friend.
Then farewell my friend, it is sad we must part,
Rich blessings attend thee wherever thou art.
Here's peace to thy heart, though another's it be,
And health to thy cheek, though it bloom not for me.

Alfred Washington to Silas Reagan Whitten—Greenville to Gowensville, South Carolina, 16 June 1845

Dear Father,

We arrived here, quite snugly at 3 o'clock PM, found things pretty quiet, weather excessively hot, the folks well and cheerful according to my expectation. I have engaged boarding at Col. Coleman's, paying for the same $2.00 per week. I find Col. Coleman a gentle agreeable man, his wife a modest, unassuming lady I think I shall get along with very smoothly. I shall doubtless be much benefitted by going there, though I could have obtained boarding cheaper and equally as good for less money. Mrs. Thurston would have willingly fed me for $1.75 per week, but you know that the difference is not very considerable as my stay will be short in this place, and as living is distressingly dear anyhow I prefer stopping where I will be benefitted most. By calculation you will find that in the space of 4 months this would cost about $4.00 more at $2.00 than at $1.75. I'll grub that out.

The friends treat me kindly. Dr. Earle pays every attention to me that I could ask. I, at this time, sleep with Dr. Earle but will move to my room tomorrow. My situation will be a lot more comfortable.

I write in haste, without correcting. Respects to Drs. Mooney and Beauford. Respects to Major Eaves and family. At all times an affectionate remembrance to the families, etc.

In reality yours,
A. W. Whitten

NB I will write better when will get a desk to use, AWW

Alfred began his medical training in Gowensville by becoming an apprentice to Dr. Mooney, moving on to Greenville, where he sought to learn from his uncle, Dr. Joseph Berry Earle.

Narcissa to Rebecca Whitten—Pickensville to Gowensville, South Carolina, 14 Aug. 1845

My Dear Sister,

What in the world has become of you all? We have not heard one word from you since you left our house. Have you ever got home or are you still on the way? I think you promised to write to us when you got home. We are very anxious to hear from you all. You made such a short visit but, Oh I assure you, it was very sweet. There is nothing delights me more than to have such dear friends with me. I have been looking for some of you all this week and thought perhaps that was the reason you did not write.

Are you drying fruit at your house? We have dried some. We will have lots of ripe pears in about two weeks. They are getting ripe now. We have very fine weather for drying fruit but it is too dry for the corn.

Becker have you heard from Harriet? I have not heard anything from her since I saw you. How does Liz and P make it now? Do they quarrel as much as ever? How do all get on up there? I should like very much to be with you. Bell talks a great deal about you all. She says tell Grandpa and Grandma that she is going to see them before very long. What has become of Alfred? Why don't he write to us? Tell Jo and Sena I think they ought to come and see us, Oh, you don't know how glad we would be to see any of you. I think Papa and

Mother might come. They could take two days for it and get along very smooth and bring Rant with them. Bell talks about you all a great deal. How is little Mary and Harriet (Jo's daughters)? Oh, I do want to see them very much. We have all been very well ever since you was here. My health is better than it has been for some time. Bell has got almost fat and you know Elias is always well. Do write us. Bell sends lots of kisses to Grandpa and Grandma and all of you. Elias joins me in love to all.

Your sister,
Narcissa

Becker, I would write more but we are out of paper. The Pickensville folks are all pretty well. Ann Briggs has got a little one. It's a gal and they call it Myrna.

John Gill Landrum to Rebecca Whitten—Mt. Zion to Gowensville, South Carolina, 28 Aug. 1845

Dear Miss Rebecca Whitten,

I received your very kind and affectionate letter by the hand of cousin Thomas Earle and I am rejoiced to hear that your mind has been brought to the subject of your soul's salvation. I feel pretty certain from what you say that you have good reason to be comforted in hope of your acceptance with God, your doubt and fear to the contrary notwithstanding. "Afflictions, though they seem severe, in mercy oft are sent," in the sentiment of the poet. Such also is the very correct view taken in your communication to me. God afflicts saints to make them willing to leave the world, and He afflicts sinners to humble the pride of their heart and to make them willing to give up the pleasures of sin. Pray over your case, so will I.

I hope when I come up on the time of my regular appointment you will see your way clear to join the church. Cold weather and bad health have prevented me this time.

With sentiments of high esteem I am yours truly (in haste).

John G. Landrum

Rebecca is under conviction of sin with the hope of acceptance by God. Shortly thereafter she confessed Christ and joined Cross Roads Baptist Church.

In this letter we meet two men who played major roles in the lives of the Whittens, Earles, and upper South Carolina. John Gill Landrum was born in Rutherford, Tennessee, 22 Oct. 1810, and became the dominant Baptist clergyman in northwestern South Carolina from about 1829, the year he was licensed to preach by the Padgetts Creek Baptist Church, until his death 19 Jan. 1882. Known for the quality of his preaching and his leadership in both secular and sacred affairs, Landrum served as pastor of several churches concurrently, traveling from his home to services, not only on the Sabbath but also during the week. He preached in both of the churches frequented by the Whittens, Tiger Creek and Cross Roads. John Landrum and Silas Reagan Whitten were elected delegates to the South Carolina Nullification Convention held in Columbia in 1832. Landrum represented his district at the second such meeting, in 1861, voting with the majority to secede from the United States. He served for a time with the 13th Regiment, South Carolina Volunteers, CSA, as colporter or chaplain, helped to found the Southern Baptist Theological Seminary in Greenville, and was active in support of several other educational institutions. Under his leadership, Baptist churches in Greenville and Spartanburg districts prospered.

After the death of his first wife, John Landrum married, in 1859, Nancy Miller Earle, cousin and longtime friend of the Whittens. We have two of her letters. During his latter years, his home was north of Spartanburg, at Landrum, a village still bearing his name.

The second new face is that of Thomas J. Earle, Nancy Miller Earle's brother, who also grew up with the Whitten children. He began writing letters to Rebecca as he was finishing school at home and preparing to enter the academy at Greenville. She saved twenty-one of them. Tom and Rebecca had a close and treasured relationship. Their correspondence spans the years of his education at Greenville and, later, Mercer College in Penfield, Georgia, where he was preparing to enter the ministry. After graduation, Thomas J. Earle became, like his brother-in-law, a circuit riding Baptist minister and teacher. Though not as well known for secular achievement, Earle's contributions to upland South Carolina Baptists and the Kingdom of his Maker are remembered and respected.

Narcissa to her family—Pickensville to Gowensville, South Carolina, 19 Sept. 1845

My Dear Kin Folks,

I have been expecting a letter from some of you for a week or more. We are very anxious to hear from you all. Papa, I went to Greenville on Tuesday morning, you and Brother had just gone. I was truly sorry that I could not see you. We left there late Wednesday evening. Brewell drew one tooth and put in ten fillings. I can tell you that my teeth fairly shine. There are three to take out yet. I feel pretty well now. Cousin Baylis (Dr. M. B. Earle, son of Theron and Hannah

Miller Earle) thinks my health improves very fast. Since I have been writing Cousin Baylis has passed in going to Pickens CH. Perry (Oliver Perry Earle, his brother) is there sick and he is going after him. He says you are all well up at home. I am very glad to hear from you all.

We will be up the last of next week if nothing happens. How does everything come on at home? Where is Harriet? Oh, how I long to see her. She has done wrong but I love her just as well as I ever did. When I was in Greenville they were all telling me that she was going off soon. Oh, how can we bear to part with her? She is a dear child, but I must stop. I cannot write on such a painful subject. The big tears fill my eyes. We are at Elliott's (brother of husband, Elias) now but we are going to Earle's tomorrow.

How does Jo and Sina come on? Has Jo got well? Bell talks a great deal about Mary and the baby. Bell is broke out just as bad as she was when you saw her.

It is very late and I cannot write much more. The mail goes on pretty soon and Elias wants to write some. Elias sends his love to you all. You must give my love to Jo and Mesina and receive a large share for yourselves.

From your affectionate daughter and sister,
Narcissa

Bell sends kisses to you all. She talks a great deal about you all every day. She says Grandpa and Uncle Alf came to see her once.

I have determined to live in this neighborhood as I find I can hold a school here worth two to three hundred dollars per year. I am building some snug cabins about a mile from Elliott's and will have them ready to move into in two weeks. Cis has left me nothing to write. My love to all.

Yours affectionately,
E. Holcombe

Harriet has married Nathan Alexander Lankford, and they are about to take the long trip west to Pontotoc County, Mississippi, and the wilderness. Cissa does not approve of her leaving the family.

Thomas J. Earle to Rebecca Whitten—Earlesville to Gowensville, South Carolina, 16 Oct. 1845

My dear cousin Rebecca,

You will perhaps be surprised to see this but you need not for it is from a friend. Tis true I never wrote to you before but I have had much pleasure in an intercourse with you and should anticipate much more of a different kind, could I see you often now.

Believe me cousin I feel deeply interested in your situation under two considerations. "I speak the truth in Christ and lie not". I know you are lonely and I know you are, at times, melancholy on account of the departure of your beloved sister (Harriet Earle Whitten and Nathan Alexander Lankford left for Mississippi in early October 1845) and deeply would I sympathize with you if I knew how. I once experienced the loss of a sister very dear to my heart and truly it is very hard to take leave of one whom we love either as a friend or sister. But I feel deeply with you the loss, for a while. You have lost a kind, affectionate, and loving sister. I feel that I have lost a true friend and an able advisor for in all my souls troubles, doubts, fears she would freely advise and point me to Heaven and stay my fainting soul with the promises of God. And I would say this is the only source of comfort to a wounded heart. It is truly a consoling thought that in every extremity when friends have done all in their power and grief weighs heavy on the mind to know we have a friend in Jesus that sticketh closer than a brother, who will hear the cry of the afflicted and support their sinking souls. Then the only thing I can say is, "Cast your cares on Jesus and don't forget to pray."

I rejoice to know that so great a change has taken place in your heart in other respects and I do hope that since you have been truly convicted and brought to see your real situation you will not hesitate in the matter nor wait for too strong manifestations or expect that God will work any great miracle upon you. I know you have doubts in the matter. Though you have long had the plan laid out and though that plan has not been perfected yet there is no one but is disappointed in their expectations. We must not lay the plans but must give up to be saved upon the Lord's plan. And if you are still in doubt I can but point you to "The Lamb of God that taketh away the sin of the world, Believe on the Lord Jesus Christ and be ye saved", and also "Blessed are they that mourn for they shall be comforted".

But I must close. I was at Prospect to Church yesterday and today and saw Mr. Landrum. He asked me about Harriet and yourself and spoke of what she had told him. I then told him I had seen you and that you wished to converse with him very much. And he seems as anxious to see you and others near Cross Roads and bid me say to you that he would preach at Mr. R. L. Goodlets on Tuesday night before he preaches at the Church and that he would like very much to see you there and I do hope that you will go and that it may prove a blessing to your soul, for which, with other blessings you shall have my daily prayers though they are weak.

Cousin, excuse the liberty I have taken of addressing you and accept the best wishes of your best friend and cousin,

Thomas

You need not feel under any obligation to write though I would be happy to hear from you at any time

This is the first of a five-year series of letters from Tom.

Narcissa to Rebecca Whitten—Pickensville to Gowensville, South Carolina, 1 Nov. 1845

My Dear Sister,

I have only time to write you a few lines as the mail will go on pretty soon. I know you all are very anxious to hear from us. I should have written last week but we could not get home and so I thought it would be better to wait until we got home. Bell seems delighted with her new home, and I think myself, when we get everything fixed up it will be quite a pleasant place. Oh, sister, since you saw me I have been very sick. I caught cold that day I left your house coming to Greenville. I suffered a great deal with my jaws and my head, but I feel pretty well now. Rebecca, I do my own work and you must know that I feel a great deal better than common. I am to get Ann in a few days, the girl Mariana had.

How do you all come on? Do you grieve so much about Harriet as usual? I do not think it prudent for us to take on about her as she appears to be perfectly happy. She stayed one night with us as she went on. I never saw her look as well in her life.

We received a letter from brother A last week. He says Lexington is a delightful place and that he enjoys himself finely. I reckon you have received a letter from him before this time. Rebecca, you must come to see us, Bell talks about you all the time. She very often says "oh, Ma, I do love my Aunt Becker." She wants to know now if I am writing to you. We has a show here Wednesday. Bell was delighted with the monkeys, ponies, and everything. I do wish you could have been here. There were a great many animals, bears, leopards, tigers, the Anaconda, and a great many things. They had some beautiful birds; eagles, parrots.

I heard that Uncle Isaac (Isaac Smith Whitten) had come. I should be very glad to see him. Nothing delights me more than to meet my relatives, but Oh, it grieves me to part with them. I hope that he will call on us as he returns.

I must stop. The mail will close. Give my love to Jo and Mesina. Tell them to come and see us. You must all come so soon as you can. Bell sends lots of kisses, Elias joins me in love to you all. Send our bed to Greenville the first chance. We need it.

Your affectionate sister,

Narcissa

Sister Harriet and husband, Nathan Alexander, spent the night with the Holcombes as they journeyed to Mississippi. It was the last time the two sisters were to be together.

Alfred Washington is studying medicine at Transylvania College in Lexington, Kentucky.

Thomas J. Earle to Rebecca Whitten—Home (Earlesville) to Gowensville, South Carolina, 14 Nov. 1845

Dear Cousin,

I have once more laid aside the tiresome pages of Horace to perform one of the most pleasing duties, I may say that I am ever called upon to perform. I hope therefore you will pardon me for again troubling you with my marks.

It is truly a happy season when I can call my mind from the varied scenes of men and things, from the painfully pleasing thoughts of the past and from endeavoring to pierce the thick veil of the distant future to write to as kind a friend as I believe you to be.

I was happy to receive a line from you giving a history of your case, the cause of your serious feelings and was glad to find that you had been so strongly and truly convicted. You fear as is common that your conviction is not of the right kind and say that you have often prayed for convicting grace. Why, my girl, this is itself conviction, strong and pungent. Conviction first made you feel the need of a Savior and of humble prayer to God for assistance. "Twas grace first taught my soul to fear" I tell you I am convinced from your own language that your heart is really softened. We may strive to make ourselves penitent, ponder and sum up all our sins, and strive to believe we are the greatest of all sinners, but the work is not ours. We can't hurry it or direct it but resign ourselves into the hands of Almighty God to be saved alone by the merits of the life in Christ.

Tis said that Mrs. Judson at a very early period of life, having some serious feelings, determined that she would be more serious. She therefore shut herself up in a room, abstained from all lively company, and almost entirely from food, read nothing but her Bible and hymn book. But she could not be more serious. The more she tried the farther it was removed from her. She finally gave it up, returned to her companions and self again.

Soon after, under a very persuasive sermon, her attention was engaged and she found herself believing ere she was aware of it. And thus she found it was not a great labor to be wrought but simply to believe on The Lord Jesus Christ.

And I say to you again, do not wait for some great miracle to be wrought on you. It is not necessary. Set out with determination never to give it up. Go to yourself and in a most solemn manner declare your intention before God. Pray fervently to Him for assistance and support, trusting on His promise that "Whosoever calleth on the name of the Lord shall be saved". Read the conversion of Lydia, of the Eunuch. No great miracle in either nor is it common in the New Testament. Read second Corinthians sixth chapter and second verse.

May God bless you and bring you to Christ is the wish of your unworthy friend and cousin,

Thomas

Harriet to Rebecca Whitten—Pontotoc, Mississippi, to Gowensville, South Carolina, 9 Dec. 1845

My own dear sister,

It is near two months since I left home, and I have not yet received one line from you, not any of my folks, though I heard from home two weeks past through a letter from Father to Aunt Davis (Mariam Whitten), and I can assure you that it afforded me a great deal of satisfaction. I wrote to Father from Mr. Scott's in Alabama. We have just now received a letter from Curren (probably her husband's brother) from which I learn that my letter had not reached you. I am sorry you did not get it for I know your great anxiety to hear from an absent daughter and sister. In that I gave you a full account of my journey, the scenery and on.

I will now give you only a short history of my travels. Our trip to this country was a very pleasant one, and not the slightest accident or misfortune attended us from the time we left home until we arrived in Mississippi. My health has been excellent ever since I left home.

I must now tell the reason why I delayed writing so long since my arrival in this country. I thought I would wait until I got home so that I could tell you just how I was situated at home. As soon as we arrived here Alexander procured a situation for us. He rented an excellent tract of land. It is a beautiful situation, but we had to live in a cabin, though that is fashionable here. The reason why we have not got home is that the house is occupied by a family, and we could not take possession until they moved. We spent about two weeks with Uncle Davis (husband of Aunt Mariam). Since then we have been traveling.

Alexander had some business down in Lowndes (county) collecting some money that was due him there for teaching, (he must have worked in Mississippi before the marriage) so I accompanied him. He said it was such a beautiful country down there that he wanted me to see it. I am much pleased with my trip. We visited several families of wealth, refinement, and taste and were treated with great attention and kindness. We are now at a hotel in Pontotoc on our return home. It is certainly the most splendid tavern I ever saw, superior to Colonel Coleman's.

When I arrived here I was disappointed in not getting letters from home. You can better imagine than I can tell you how very anxious I am to hear directly from home.

We are going home this morning. We have settled 14 miles from Pontotoc, 1 mile and 1/2 from Uncle Davis.

During our stay at Uncle Davis's we were busily engaged in preparing for housekeeping. Alexander was making bedsteads, tables, and so on, while I was preparing comforts, beds, and other things.

Provisions are dear here, but we will be as comfortably situated, and a great deal more so, than I had any idea of. Corn is selling at 50 cts, flour $7-8 per barrel, pork 5 cts, beef 2-3 cts, groceries, a little cheaper than in Carolina, dry goods about the same.

Uncle Davis's family are getting pretty well. He has made upwards of 200 barrels of corn this year. He has a splendid situation. Aunt Mariam received a letter from Uncle Ranson a few days past. They were all well. John Prince (probably Uncle Alfred's first wife's brother) was at Uncle Alfred's and I have been expecting that he would come to see us before he returns. I hope he will. Uncle Alfred, his wife, Mary Jane, Rebecca, and her husband have all joined the Church. I am pleased to hear it.

I learn through Curren's letter that a great many of my young companions around the Cross Roads have joined the Church. My heart exults at such news. I trust that ere long they will all be gathered into the fold. And my own dear family, may they everyone, Father, Mother, brothers, sisters be initiated in the Church of Christ, and ere long may we meet around that blessful throne, never to be separated. I wish to say a great many things on this point, but I have very little time to spare this morning, and can only write a hurried line, and will write all the particulars of home when I get there.

Curren told that dear brother A had written home twice, that was well and in fine spirits. I was rejoiced to hear it and will write to him soon. I was delighted to hear that you were all well and that my dear Mother has not been sick. I wrote to sister N about two weeks past and asked her to write to you all.

And now, with regard to my being pleased with the country, I can tell you truly that I like it very much, and think I shall be perfectly reconciled. Truly, I shall miss the society of my dear parents, brothers, and sisters, but God has wisely ordered it so, and thus it should be. I do not repine nor regret the past. I think my lot a happy one. I do humbly trust that my friends will not forget me, tho I am far away, and I hope that ere long my dear parents, brothers, and sisters will be settled in the same country with me. It would indeed be a happy state of things.

I will write to brother J in about one week. Tell Dr. Mooney I am astonished that he will settle down in that old country, when this is the garden spot of the world. Give him my best respects and tell him to come to see us and bring somebody with him.

I hope to write a great many letters to my friends at home very soon. Remember me affectionately to all my friends, to cousin Thomas, Nancy and all their folks (Earles), to all of Uncle Prince's folks (William Prince, husband of Lydia Maverick Earle, her mother's sister), and kiss cousin Ann, cousin Mary Lizzie and all, to Mary Elizabeth and Virginia, to Lizza Wilkinson, in short, to all my friends. My best respects to Mr. Landrum. He requested me to write to him, and I will very soon. All my brothers and sisters at Cross Roads, I hope they will not forget me. Now is a time of rejoicing with them and I rejoice with them though I am far away.

Give my best love to Jo and Mesina, kiss my sweet Mary and Harriett for me. Do write soon. I can scarcely quit writing and say farewell for a while. Do not be anxious about me, but know that I am reconciled.

And now, my dear Father, Mother, Rebecca, Silas, Ranson, will you all accept the best wishes and warmest love of your affectionate,

Harriet

Do excuse the hurried style in which I have written. I will do better the next time.

Harriet and Alexander arrived in Mississippi in early October 1845, and are living in a log cabin. The Cherokees abandoned that part of Mississippi via the "trail of tears" about ten years earlier.

Uncle Alfred and family have recently joined a church in Fayette, Tennessee. We later learn it was of the Cumberland Presbytery.

Narcissa to Rebecca Whitten—Pickensville to Gowensville, South Carolina, 17 Dec. 1845

My own dear sister,

I received your truly affectionate letter in due time, and, oh, my sister, you don't know how happy I was to hear that you were all well. It really seemed to me as though it had been an age since I heard from home. Home I say because I can never call it anything else. You think I have been very negligent in not writing to you before this time, and so I have, but it was not because I was unmindful of my dear friends at home. No indeed, there is not a day passing but what I think affectionately of my dear parents, brothers, and sisters.

They are all as dear to me as life itself. I received a letter from Harriet last Sunday and one from Alfred to sister, seems to be quite happy and in every respect she is delighted with the country. She said they had quite a pleasant trip. She said a great deal about you all, wants us all to go out there. Alfred seems to go on very well with his studies, thinks that he can get through very well. I have written him once since I saw you but he has never received it. He seems very much insulted because he has not received a letter from us. Sends love to you all.

When are any of you going to visit us? Do come. You won't know how glad we would be. Bell talks about you every day, asks me very often why you don't come. Oh, you would not know her, she has fattened so, I never saw anything grow like she has. Her cheeks are as red as roses, she is the best child I ever saw, she is no trouble at all.

We have moved to where Earl Holcombe used to live, he has moved further down. My health is very good now, I think better than it has been for two years or more, I can just eat anything I can get hold of. I have not had the first mess of turnips this year. Now don't you think that's bad?

Oh, you don't know how glad I would be if I could but see you all. Come, do come to see us.

I am very glad to hear that there is such a revival of religion in the neighborhood of Cross Roads. Oh, my good sisters, pray for us, oh, Rebecca. I know you will tire reading such a letter as I write. I am so wicked, I can't write anything good but perhaps there will be a change for the better some time. It is very late, my sister, and I can't write much more.

You said Pa requested Elias to write something concerning his hogs. He went to Greenville before I received your letter and I don't reckon he will be back in time so I will send this letter to him open so he can write and then put it in the office there. I will write to you again soon. You must all write me soon. Bell sends kisses, give my love to all and receive a large share for yourself.

Your affectionate sister,

Narcissa

Mother, do take care of yourself this cold weather, give my love to Jo and Mesina and kiss them.

P.S. from Elias to Silas Reagan

Dear Sir,

I will try and come up and see you as soon as Christmas is over and bring a wagon with me. Pork is selling in Greenville at 4 cent net. If you can get 5 cents cash you may sell my hogs. Mr. Rener, the shoe merchant has land and I have been engaged this week taking inventory of his stock on hand, otherwise I should have come up this week. Give my love to all the family and friends.

Yours affectionately,

E. Holcombe

Alfred Washington to Rebecca Whitten—Lexington, Kentucky, to Gowensville, South Carolina, 19 Dec. 1845 (mailed from Washington City)

Dear Becca,

I received your very kind letter on the 17th inst. and you know, Becca, that my heart was gladdened. Will you write again? Anything that you may say in a letter, however trivial you may think it, will be interesting to me. I also received a letter from Jo on the 12th inst in which he stated that corn was selling from 75 to 87 cts per barrel which I regard as very cheap for this season. Will you ask him to correct this?

I feel that he errs in his statement. Will you let me know at any rate.

I am anxious to get into a cheap country and if times are so fair in South Carolina I may conclude to return. Jo also stated that hogs and hominy were very plentiful. Please request him to save some for me. I will answer the rest of his letter in a more appropriate manner in a few days.

I regret to hear, as I have from three or four sources, that cousin Mary's family had become so sorely bereaved. I had almost concluded to write to her but after reflection thought it best to say nothing to her as it would do no good and she certainly knows that she, together with all the family and friends have my warmest sympathies. Does she seem to be much depressed in spirits or does she exercise the same Christian fortitude and forbearance that she has always done? You know that she has been well schooled with trials, hardships and sufferings and she might be expected to appear callous and indifferent. But I know that she is not. Is Lizza very sad? I hope not.

In all the letters written me not one word has been said about Aunt Liddy (mother's sister Lydia Maverick Earle), cousin Ann, and Pats. Shall I be under the necessity of addressing the old lady a letter. I will if you don't write about her. Sis, I will do it anyway.

Why won't you tell me how Nancy (Nancy Miller Earle) gets along? You wrote me about others of the girls. I suppose you see her married and never think of letting me know. (She married John Gill Landrum in 1859.) Do you suppose that I have forgotten any of the girls about home? I could repeat more than a dozen of their names.

Now, how are you off for beaux? Are the Tygers and Peobles pretty well supplied to Tryon? What sort of beaux are most acceptable? If Docs will do I'll capture a half dozen and haul them over when I return with me. How much do you think it would take? I'll make it a matter of speculation if you think it well (as I am needy), and they can be bought cheap here, say something like a weeks board per man.

Give my respects to all the girls. Respects, did I say? Love, I mean, and if any one refuses to take it she becomes due me a Christmas gift to be placed in the hands of my sweetest female friend for safekeeping until I return. If you are over bothered to know who that is you have only to ask me about it and I'll make an intimation too plain to be missed, L C.

But Becca, I must quit fun and tell you of the solemnness into which the medical class have been thrown. About three weeks ago,

Mr. Peterson, medical student of Newberry District, South Carolina, who, you recollect, was boarding at the same house that I do, (Mr. Patton's of Greenville) was taken sick with something akin to typhoid fever which prostrated him, and the disease, growing gradually worse, terminated his system on Thursday morning last. Mr. Peterson was a man of ordinary talents. His constitution was much impaired previous to his travels here. Every remedy was used that the concentrated faculty could advise, but to no purpose, only to mitigate his sufferings whilst the disease was wafting him off. The class paid every respect to his remains. His funeral was preached by a member of the class and was attended by the whole school, professors and students, and his body placed in a vault. His friends have truly the sympathies of all.

Becca, continue to write and tell Father to write. I don't get letters from my uncles, tho I write to them. Give love to Father, Mother, and all. Tell the boys to mind their books. Tell Lizzy G to spell baker and Virginia to say three long slim slick saplins.

Alfred

The snow has been between 14 and 16 in deep, pretty deep for a short legged South Carolinian. It is never melted. The winter is so cold the dogs can't bark. I received a letter from Elias, they are well.

Alfred is completing his studies at Transylvania and is soon on his way home to open a practice. I cannot explain the letter having been mailed from Washington, D.C.

Thomas J. Earle to Rebecca Whitten—Earlesville to Pleasant Grove, South Carolina, Saturday evening December 1845

Dear Cousin,

With a dejected mind and a sorrowing spirit I seat myself to write you another something, God only knows what it will be, whether song or sermon. Fain would I see you as a good for I know you are one and pour out some of my temporal afflictions to you, for it is a healing balm to the wound to have a friend to whom we can communicate all, both joy and grief and will, with us, bear a part. It sooths the saddened spirit and unloads the burdened mind.

But enough of this. One of the greatest pleasures I enjoy is to impart pleasure to others, then cousin, excuse me. When I left you yesterday I am sorry to say you seemed somewhat depressed in your feelings. I know not why but knowing that there are many doubts or rather fears that all young Christians labor under I have attempted to write you something on that lead hoping that God will bless the effort and may He pour down His Holy Spirit on every word and accompany it with the word of His grace and drive away all doubts, fears, uncertainties, in short, all troubles and sorrows, whatever name or kind. And O God, may these lines fall unto you in pleasant places, yea may you have a goodly heritage.

Then, cousin, let me give you some of the promises unfolded to us in the Bible, the word of God, for God is our refuge and strength a very present help in the day of trouble, wait on the Lord, be of good courage and He shall strengthen thine heart, wait I say on the Lord. Be of good courage and He shall strengthen your heart all you that hope in the Lord. And the God of peace shall bruise Satin under your feet shortly. And moreover God hath said My Grace is sufficient for thee for my strength is made perfect in weakness.

Long did you doubt and fear to unite yourself with the Church but finally concluded to do so which most assuredly was right for, cousin, you are certainly changed, you have certainly felt the action of the Good Spirit on your mind, that you have been regenerated, in short, you are a Christian, and a good one. But God hath not given us the spirit of fear but of power and blessing of a sound mind. He that believeth and is Baptized shall be saved. And as many of you as have been Baptized into Christ have put on Christ. Then, O my Cousin give not yourself unnecessary pain but trust in the Lord. Cast all your care on Him for He careth for you. We are saved by hope.

I told a young friend to say to you that Mr. L (minister Landrum) bid me say to you that he would be glad to receive a letter from you soon, cousin write. You can send it here via the mail by next Saturday and he will get it Wednesday. You have my prayers. Pray fervently and sometimes think of your cousin.

Thomas

Narcissa to Rebecca Whitten—Greenville to Gowensville, South Carolina, about 1846

Dear Sister,

Cousin Adde (Adeline Foster) is going to send a band box and I will just slip a line in it. We are all very well except Elias. He has had the head ache for two or three days but it's a great deal better this morning. I know you are all anxious to see us but not more anxious than we are to see you. I came from Pickensville yesterday. They are all well. I expect to be at the Baptist church tomorrow. Dr. Curtis and

Mr. Furman will preach. How do you all get on? I hope you are all very well. I look for a letter from home today. I expect to be at home some day next week. I do not know what day. Give my love to Joe's and cousin Mary's folks. Elias and Bell joins me in love to you all. Adde and Sally sends love to all.

Narcissa

Dr. W. A. Mooney to Alfred Washington Whitten—about 1846

I am glad to hear that Mr. Kestler is improving. If he still continues quiet and appears more rational today, the opium may be given at longer intervals. Exercise your own judgement in the case.

I should be glad to accompany Squire Whitten to Greenville, of course, but there is a certain gall who I had rather accompany to church, or see at least, so I cannot go. As to the grape seed, the neighbors will be supplied. I will see to that.

I'm off this morning for White Oaks, alias Mountain Wilds.

Respectfully,
W. A. Mooney

Dr. Mooney was Alfred's teacher and friend. He seems determined to be off on holiday.

Dyer S. Mooney to Silas Reagan Whitten—Greenville Courthouse to Gowensville, South Carolina, 1 Jan. 1846

Dear Sir,

As this is the time for closing and settling out, your son, Alfred Whitten, before he left this fall he stated to us that you would settle out his bill with us. When you come to the village you will please to come and see about it, for we are asettling up our old books of the firm of Dyer S Mooney and at the same time very much in need of money and your early attention to the same will oblige us very much.

Yours respectfully,
Dyer S. Mooney

Narcissa to Rebecca Whitten—Dark Corner to Gowensville, South Carolina, 7 Jan. 1846

Dear Sister,

I have again taken my pen to write you a few lines. Little did I think, my dear sister, when I saw you last that it would be so long before we should meet again, but time has passed off and we hardly know how. When are any of you coming to see us? Oh, we would be delighted to see any of you at our home.

How does my dear Mother do now? Is her health fairly good? You must not let her expose herself. Does Papa have the backache? And now, Becker, you must write to me how all of you get on. We are going to visit you all in the course of 6 to 8 weeks.

Oh, I know you would hardly know Bell. She has grown so much, she is quite fat. She was very sick yesterday but I think she will soon get well. She recollects you all very well, there is not a day passes but what she says something about some of you. Oh, how does little Mary and Harriet (daughters of Jo and Mesina) come on? Do they grow much? I often think of them and would be very glad if Jo and Mesina would visit us. Have you heard Alfred or Harriet lately? I have never heard from them since I wrote to you. How does cousin Mary come on? Lizzie said she would visit us. Give my love to them and tell Liz she must come and see us if she can. Give my love to cousin Nancy when you see her.

Becker, I am very busy making comforts. My health is so good now I can do my work very well. I feel better than I have in two years.

Well sister, it's getting late and I must close. Elias wants to write some. You must give my love to all the family and reserve a large share for yourself.

From your affectionate sister,
Narcissa

Silas Jr. and Ranson came to see us. Mother, if you have any garden seed I wish you would send me some. Send such as mustard and so on and if you have any hops I would be glad of some, rolls would eat very well these cold mornings.

Elias to Silas Reagan

Dear Sir,

I send the bearer, Jack Burdin, for my hogs. I should have come myself but Belle has not been well for a few days and I did not like to leave home and I expect to bring Cis and Belle to see you the first good spell of weather. I want Jack to leave your house on Friday in time to get to Uncle Davis, if possible, so that he can get home on Saturday. I would have sent for the hogs sooner but it has been out of my power as I have been writing at Greenville (quarter page torn off) for the last two or three weeks. If convenient, I wish you to send my books and pamphlets, etc. by Jack. Give my love to all our friends.

Yours,
Elias

Note on back: "the conflict is short-the rest eternal"

Dark Corner is a vaguely defined area in northwestern South Carolina. The term is still in use. These letters frequently refer to being fat as good. Obesity must have been rare and fat meant healthy looking. Not so today. How does one use hops to make rolls?

Narcissa to Rebecca Whitten—Pickensville to Gowensville, South Carolina, 6 Feb. 1846

My dear sister,

Little did I think when I last wrote to you that I should have to write to you again before we met, but disappointments are what we all have to encounter in this life. I know you all feel very anxious about us. We have set two or three times to visit you and every time it would rain or snow, but if it had been pretty weather we could not have gone. We have all had such dreadful colds. Bell had several attacks of the croup and I never had such a cold and cough in my life. At last the cold all settled in my jaws and then you know I suffered, but we are all a great deal better now.

Well, I reckon you will all laugh when I tell you we are going to move again. All the Pickensville lands were sold last Monday. Elliott (brother of Elias) purchased one or two lots so next Monday he is going to move here and we are going to his place. It will be the last move we will make this year. As soon as we get things freed at home, we intend going up to see you which will be the last of next week. If we don't come then it will be a bad chance for I know Elias will not like to stop after he gets to work on his farm, but I think we will come then. If we don't you must all come and see us for it seems to me as if it has been ten years since I saw any of you. How do you all get on at home? Does the boys work as hard as ever? Tell them to take it easy. We'll all get rich when the rail is complete. Have you heard from Harriet or Alfred lately? I received a letter from Brother (Alfred) a week or more ago. Oh, he seems to get on so well it makes me happy to read his letters. I have not received but one letter from sister (Harriet) since she left. How does Jo and Mesina come on? Oh, I do want them all so much. Bell talks a great deal about little Mary and Harriet. There is not a day passes but what she asks me one hundred questions about all of you. She has got a new pair of shoes and says she will never wear them until she goes to her Grandpa's and Grandma's. She wants to know very often why some of you don't come and see us. I have not heard a word from home since you wrote. How is Papa's back? Oh, I hope you all are very well. Sometimes I think about you until I almost imagine me in your company. How does cousin Mary and Lizzy and all of them come on? Tell them they must not forget me. Tell Jo I dreamed the other night of getting a letter from him. I must stop. It is late and the mail closes in a few minutes. Do give my love to all. Tell them to write to me often. I think I shall see you all soon and then we will talk it all over. Bell sends lots of kisses. Do excuse this dreadful scrawl for Bell has been hanging round my chair chattering all the time and saying "now Ma, we are going to Grandpa's, ain't we?" Goodby until I see you.

Your sister,
Narcissa

Elias sends love to all.

Narcissa to Rebecca Whitten—Pickensville to Gowensville, South Carolina, 26 Feb. 1846

My Dear Sister,

I received your kind and truly affectionate letter by Monday's mail and to say I was happy, my dear sister, would be repeating what you already know. I had looked anxiously for a letter for some weeks and still I had very little hopes of receiving one, for I know very well that you all were expecting to see us every day and I do assure you it made my heart ache to be so disappointed but it has been impossible for us to go. You know we have had a great deal of bad weather within the last two months and we have all had dreadful colds. I have had a very bad spell of the jaw ache since I wrote to you by the Doct (Alfred) and Bell has had several attacks of the croup but we have both got entirely well now but Elias has had a very bad cough for several days. I reckon, my sister, you are all still looking for us but we cannot visit you soon I fear. Elias says the roads are real bad now, that it would be disagreeable to go so far. I know you will all be sadly disappointed but you cannot feel worse about it than we do for we really anticipated great pleasure in spending a week or more with you all.

Well Becca, we have moved to Elliott's place on the road. Don't you recollect coming with us on a visit while we lived in Greenville? We have a well of excellent water and everything is very convenient.

Elias has commenced farming and we have sowed a good many seeds in the garden. I am in hopes we will have some vegetables for you know I think much of them. How does Mother come on with her garden? Oh I am delighted to hear that Mother's health is so much better. Does Papa ever have the backache now? I am very sorry to hear that Ranson has had such a bad spell but I hope he is entirely well now. How is brother Joseph now? Does he still have the sore throat? I sincerely hope he has got the better of that. Is Mesina and the children well? Oh I do want to see them so much. Tell Mary she must not forget Aunt Cis.

Rebecca, do some of you come and see us. You don't know how glad we would be to see any of you. Whenever Alfred comes home tell him he must come and see us and as many of you come with him as can.

Becca, Bell is sitting down by me writing to Grandpa and Grandma. She has a pen and it would divert you to see her. She is always jabbering about you all but she never forgets Doct Mooney. She cried a long while that day he left to go with him. She said he would take her to Grandpa and he would give her lots of grapes. Becca I would be delighted to have you come and stay a while with us. Oh I cannot tell you how glad I would be.

Give my love to Cousin Mary and Lizzie. Tell Liz to come to see us and Cousin Nancy, I have not forgotten her, and cousin Pat, I would be glad to see any of them. What's become of Mary and Liz? Are they married yet? Tell the girls they must not forget me. When they get married I shall expect a piece of the cake, at least.

But enough of such nonsense. I reckon you think I am a foolish kind of creature, but I just write it down as I think of it, and Bell is talking to me all the time. It is late Becca and I must stop. Bell sends lots of kisses to you all and says tell Grandpa and Grandma and all of them to come to our house.

Silas, are you and Ranson not going to visit us before you commence farming? Come if you can. Elias joins me in love to you all.

Your affectionate sister,
Narcissa

Thomas J. Earle to Rebecca Whitten—Male Academy, Greenville to Gowensville, South Carolina, 10 March 1846

Dear Cousin,

Again I seat myself to perform the delightful task of saying a word to a friend and thus communing as it were for a few moments with a kindred spirit. But I fear the task will be badly performed for the time is stolen and I have the blues pretty tolerable badly so you need not look for a song.

The first night after I came here I heard some splendid music on the bagpipes. The gentleman performed on 4, viz., the Scotch, the Irish, the Union, and the Northumberland. It was indeed magnificent and I wanted you all here to hear it.

We have preaching in all the Churches now. The Baptist minister Mr Breaker is a talented young man and a good speaker.

I commenced my studies the first week after I arrived, since which time I have made tolerable progress but "constant dropping wears away rocks" so maybe I shall be able to succeed after a while at least in getting part the way up the hill if I do not get to the top. Onward and upward is my motto.

Crawford (brother) is tolerable well satisfied but not pleased. Our school is small yet but better than last year this time and I hope it will be better.

We have had showers of rain every day for 2 months back, i.e., some every day or two but it does seem like we shall never have dry weather again. From what I can hear from the farmers we, it appears, will have to withhold our assistance from the wretched Irish and look at home. I have heard very often from up there and truly can I say that country is inhabited by a wonderful people.

Marrying seems to have become contagious and running away a la mode, so Theron Jr. won't be like the rest for he goes off to D-l-n tomorrow night sure enough. Don't it look like I should be left alone ere long. But "what is to be will be" and "all's well that ends well."

Just tell cousin Jenny that she need entertain no hopes of becoming a Queen because she is about to become a Prince-ess and maybe she is not the only one to attain that grade. But I guess there is nothing doing that way just now.

Well I hope you will all enjoy yourselves finely and I will be with you in spirit but can't in person. Tell Mary that as we did for her all I promised her when she was out here I shall look for a piece of cake worthwhile talking of.

Tell cousin Ann that she did not want to see me worse than I did her but I guess it is alright.

I have seen very few of my acquaintances yet for I have not been as far from the Academy as the river yet but I hope we will have some weather soon. The first robin I heard I thought of the song fest and the rest of you. Oh what a blessing is memory, without man were naught but wretched.

It is now twilight and I must close. O what a delightful hour, what a holy time. Well can I say with the immortal Campbell,

"At the silence of twilight's contemplative hour
I have mused in a sorrowful mood
On wind shaked weeds that emblossom the bower
Where the homes of my forefathers stood"

I was much pleased with the music and especially the note but it was not long enough. All that asks of Tom tell howdye. May God's blessings abide with you and yours.

Your friend in haste,
T. J. Earle

NB if you will hold the last of this letter to the fire you will see something else. You need not have stayed away from N Pacolet till I left but I won't chide as you and I hope you record the other of my message from. I will attend to it for I feel this need. T.

Narcissa to Rebecca Whitten—Pickensville to Gowensville, South Carolina, 19 March 1846

My dear sister,

I must hasten to write to you a few lines as Elias wants to write some to Pa. We have been looking anxiously for some of you all this week and although I am now writing I shall look for you constantly until you come. Has brother Alfred arrived yet? Oh yes, I almost know he has come and you were all so glad to see him. Oh, Becca, you don't know how glad I would be to see you all. It seems to me as if it has been a year since I saw any of you. Oh, how are my dear Father and Mother? I do hope they are well. Becca, it has been a long while since I heard from home. Why don't you write to me often. I received a letter from sister Harriet last week. She has her health very well and seems to be delighted with the country. How are Jo and Sina? Oh, I hope they are well. Becker, Bell talks about you all a great deal. She wants to know why you don't come to see her. She says when Grandpa and Grandma come she is going to kill the turkey and all the chickens. But enough of such nonsense. We are all very well except for colds. Bell has a very bad cold and I have one all winter, but the weather is getting warm now and I think we will get well. I must stop. Do come and all of you. Bell sends lots of kisses. Farewell.

Give love to all and receive the best wishes of your affectionate sister,

Narcissa

Do excuse this dreadful scrawl.

Elias to Silas Reagan

Dear Sir,

I wish you, if possible, to get for me ten bushels of sweet potato seed as it is impossible to get them in this country. I should like to get ten bushels rye if you can get it from 50 to 65 cents per bushel. I want you to write as soon as possible by return mail or before if you can get the above articles. I will come as soon as I hear from you. We are looking for you or some of the family every day.

Yours affectionately,
E. Holcombe

Thomas J. Earle to Rebecca Whitten—Male Academy, Greenville Court House to Gowensville, South Carolina, 5 April 1846

Dear Cousin

You with others of my friends are beginning to think, perhaps, that time, distance, and the town, with all its Sirenic influence, have entirely estranged my mind from the past, that my friendship which once appeared so warm and devoted has withered like a little flower when exposed to the rays of a noon day's sun and that the promise that I made of writing is like a name written in the sand soon spoiled and forgotten. But not so. The moments which we have passed together are too dear to my heart to be forgotten so soon. As we know not how to appreciate a blessing till we are deprived of it so we know not how much we love those who have been our associates until we are denied their society. The mother who watched over my childhood, the sister, brothers and the bosom friends and companions of my youth often appear before as in days gone by when at the hallowed hour of twilight I give myself up to the painfully pleasing recollection of the past.

The excitement of the town, the din of the workman's hammer, the rattling of carriages and the noise of the rabble greatly contrast the quietness of the country where the forest, the flowers, and the merry note of the chirping bird attract the attention of that wondrous creature, man, and point him to the adoration and praise of nature and nature's

God.

Two months have elapsed since I arrived here during which time I have been closely engaged in study in which I have progressed tolerably well. I will not mention what I am reading for you are perhaps unacquainted with the books of this language except that I have just commenced the Greek Testament about which I am able to learn much more than to read it in English. I am perhaps better satisfied than I expected to be. I find many temptations and inducements to draw the youth from the narrow path of duty and the rule of right by which, were it not for the silent monitor, conscience, and the hope of the Gospel, I might be led away and finally wrecked upon the quicksand of vice and lost amid the waves of worldly prosperity and flattered vanity. But by the help of God I trust I shall be able to pass through and ride triumphantly upon the lofty wave of Christian duty.

For some time I roomed with the Dr., but found it a bad place to study on account of the company, but my teacher offered me a room in the Academy where I now stay. It is a still, retired place and oft reminds me of the retreat of Petrarch among the mountains of Europe, i.e., when the boys are gone.

I must hasten to a close for tis getting late. Mr. Landrum has been here twice since I came but I have only seen him a short time. He preached at Berea 2 weeks ago. (ask Lizzie about the trip) and on the same night at this place. Mrs. C. Roberts joined and was baptized next day but the meetings are not like they are at Cross Roads and Prospect. Mr L is expected here tomorrow night. I visit Aunt Betsy (wife of Dr. Joseph Berry Earle, Eleanor Kee's brother) frequently and her only. She is about and is pretty well.

I wrote to Cousin Harriet the first week after I came and that is the only letter I have written except a note to JWD on business. I expected to have written to Theron or the Dr. (his brothers) before this but have not been able to do so for, cousin believe me, I have but little time to spend idly for the studies I have on hand require my whole attention but I hope I shall have more time after a while.

By the by, my teacher is a very learned, modest, moral, and gentlemanly man and I am much pleased with him thus far.

Tell the Esq. (Silas Reagan Whitten) that I expect to write to him sometime and I think it is most time I should receive a letter from some of you. Though it is not far, it would be interesting.

But I must close though there is a long letter yet to come if I had time but this must suffice now. May you be happy and prosperous and live under the direction and smiles of God.

Farewell,
T. J. Earle

Thomas J. Earle to Rebecca Whitten—Male Academy, Greenville, to Gowensville, South Carolina, about 18 April 1846

Cousin,

You must excuse me for not writing sooner. What I have said in the other letter is the truth. I think you might have sent the letter you had written. I met with Cousin Lizzie at the prayer meeting the other night and was glad to hear from you all. I spent some very pleasant moments with her, perhaps more than I shall spend with any of my friends soon. In visiting her I became acquainted with some ladies but beside that I have visited none, but believe me they are very plenty. I have received an invite from the school girls to assist them in the celebration May day but shall decline. Every dog has his day. Mine is over.

Can't you come down at that time? Cousin John is here and has been for 3 weeks and seems to be getting on in both studies pretty well. We had a pleasant night at the falls last Saturday night and, O, it brought with it many a sad regret for the past which has not been so plainly before my view for sometime. O it is painful to think that so much of our lives has been spent, that the many happy hours we have passed are gone forever, yet their recollection is pleasing.

Though I would like to send howdye to all, I cannot forbear to mention Ann. Tell her her request is granted, she wrote me a short but sweet piece of poetry before I left. I promised to write to her but it must be seldom, also Theron and Mr. Golightly. But you all can write. Tell Dr. Mc to write and I have been looking for him out here for some time. All the folks used to come to Greenville oftener than they do. Tell Cousin Lizzie she performed but 1 of her 3 promises and that some of us were much disappointed by her sudden departure. I expected to write to her but she left sooner than was expected. Ask Theron if they have let him go yet.

Let us pray for each other, our Church, and the world and "strive to enter in at the strait gate" and that we may be able to do so is the sincere prayer of your friend and Cousin.

Thomas

Excuse errors and bad writing and be sure to burn this when read.

Thomas J. Earle to Rebecca Whitten—Male Academy, Greenville, to Pleasant Grove, South Carolina, Friday night May 1846

I sit me down once more to write a letter to a friend. I am constrained to attempt to write you again, to thank you for your very sweet letter and because I expect to not have the opportunity long of doing what I so much love to do.

I received yours with a heart full of trouble and read it with a degree of pleasure. Your sentiments of friendship seemed to have been sent to soothe, as it did in part, my wounded spirit. O how consoling it is to a kindred spirit to whom one can go and pour out all the sorrows of his soul, who will weep with us when we weep and rejoice when we rejoice. But alas, such an is seldom found, yet there are some and truly they may be called, as I esteem them, among Heavens richest blessings, and such an one I believe I have found in you. But I need not stop here to talk of friendship. You know I am your friend.

I am truly glad if I have said anything that has been any benefit to you for nothing gives me so much pleasure as to be engaged in the service of others and nothing would give me such a world of pleasure as to know I had been the means of saying a word that would comfort a "mourning soul".

I am glad to see your great penitence and entire devotion to God. I know somewhat the workings of your heart. Well may you exclaim "why am I so lifeless? why not have a livelier hope?" But let me tell you that I believe these doubts, fears, and disappointments are necessary. I know the "heart is desperately wicked and deceitful above all things". And let me tell you this. Coldness oft times is caused by a neglect of duty, ie, not being satisfied with what the Lord is waiting to give and neglecting to "put on the whole armour of God" by doing that which is required of us after the Lord has done His perfect work. And, my cousin, you need not try to be penitent. You can't do it without the help of God. You may desire to believe yourself the greatest sinner in the world but it is all to no purpose. And I believe when one has been regenerated and born again as I believe you have they never can feel so much concern about their sins and so penitent as they may desire or as they once did.

And let me beg of you not to hesitate too long. It is dangerous. You may think it is prudence to wait and see if you are not mistaken. But it is not the voice of prudence. It is the temptation of the wicked one. I need not point you to the promises of God when He says "Come unto me all ye that are weary and heavy laden and I will give you rest" then come with us and we will do the good.

Give me your prayers Rebecca and remember you shall ever have the friendship and prayers of,

Thomas

NB We look to you for a song for the song fest and you must get it. Write much cousin. Good night

Dr. John J. Harris to Alfred Washington Whitten—Cedar Bluff, Cherokee, Alabama, to Gowensville, South Carolina, 18 May 1846

Dear Friend,

I have but little doubt that before this time you have censured me with forgetfulness or a kind of a don't careitiveness about my fellow student, roommate, and bed fellow. But if you have, oh Alf, take it back, for there is none that has thought oftener of his friends of last winter than I have.

It is with pleasing reflection that I look back to the few brief months we passed together at old honored Transylvania where we sat at the feet of a Gamaliel and drank instruction as water from a sweet fountain, that I trust will be of service to us as long as God, in His providence, sees cause to let us have a being in this mortal sphere where people sicken and die.

Alf, you will think it unbecoming in one so young as myself to be giving advice to anyone, but still, I must drop one word of admonition. Viz., still continue in the course you pursued last winter. Be sober, industrious, and persevere. Honor and be an asset to your profession, and when many years shall have been measured out to you, then, as the testimony of all good men agree, you shall have your reward.

I will now, if you admit to it, give you a short history of myself since I left Lexington. I was 14 days come home, and when I reached that humble and beloved place I found my people well and anxiously looking for me. Indeed it was a treat to see them all, but you know better how I felt than I can tell.

I have been getting some little practice, some one or two very important cases of my own and several of the old man's. I have two or three better offers about locations that I anticipate, but Father is not willing now for me to leave his shop, and, indeed, it would not look fair for me to do it. Therefore, I expect to remain with him two or three years yet unless I go to the wars in Mexico. Ben Barton went through here sometime last month on his way to Mexico. He is the only one of the boys I have saw since I left Waterhouse.

Look over all mistakes for you know my careless manner of writing. Give my respects to your people all, tho I never saw them I know you, and accept for yourself the highest regard and esteem of humble and affectionate servant.

John L. Harris

P S We have the appearance of an abundant harvest of wheat. Corn looks well but cotton poorly. The Grogans and Adams are all in good health.

Yours,
J. L. Harris

Dr. John L. Harris was Alfred's Transylvania roommate. Alfred's Uncle Charles Whitten Jr. lived in Cherokee, Alabama, when this was written, as did several of his children. Could Grogan and Adams be husbands of his daughters?

Harriet to Rebecca Whitten—Pleasant Grove, Pontotoc, Mississippi, to Gowensville, South Carolina, 20 May 1846

My own dear sister,

I have been reading your sweet affectionate letter, the last I have received from you, which was written two months past. In looking over your letters, my sister, I find so much of your natural affection, simplicity, and sweetness that I cannot read without dropping a tear, not of regret, my sister, but of gratitude and thankfulness that God has endowed you with such a congenial heart, and that He has united us with the sweetest cords of affection and love.

Though I am far from you and my dear parents, brothers, and sisters all, yet I love to think of you and to hope that I will meet you all ere long, if not in this world, Oh, let me indulge the fond sweet hope of meeting parents, brothers, sisters, and friends in a brighter world than this around the blessed throne where our Heavenly Father dwells. I love to hope that you are doing good, not only by your orderly walk and pious example, but by exerting your all of influence in the cause of our Blest Redeemer.

I received a letter from brother Jo not long since. I was truly glad to get it and will write to him before long. A(lexander) and I are getting on very well. Thus far we have had excellent health and I have been remarkably blessed with everything that is needed for comfort and happiness. The spring has been unusually cold and wet in this country. Consequently the farmers are considerably behind and

Alexander has a very large crop on hand that is not quite done planting. This is the 20th of May and we have had fine Irish potatoes a month past and will soon have beets and tomatoes and so on. I never saw so many strawberries as I have this season. You could walk out at any time and gather as many as you wanted, by the bushel, if you chose, and we have berries and plums in the largest quantities, but not so many peaches and apples.

It seems a very long while since I heard from home but I presume that you hear from me very regularly as I have written often to many of my Carolina friends and you doubly hear from all the letters I send. I want to hear what you all are doing and how you are getting along and how is my dear mother's health. Brother Jo wrote me that Mother was very smart. Tell her she must not be too active. She is too feeble. I hope she will take proper care of herself, Brother said you and Alfred spoke of attending school this summer. I am glad to hear it. If you have a good teacher it will be of great advantage to you. As for brother A, I suppose his practice in his profession would consume most of his time. He had better take care of himself and not go to a sickly clime for I think his constitution is very delicate. I hope that Father is not troubled with the backache now. He must not hoe the garden so much and work so hard as he used to do.

I am glad to hear that Silas has grown so steady. I shall look for him and Ranty to see us before long. Do take care of my dear little Ranty, I think a great deal about him. I know he is feeble and his health is not good. I have never enjoyed such good health as I have since I came to Mississippi. I have not had one hour's sickness. Dr. Ben Barton spent several days with us a few weeks past. He came directly from Carolina and could tell us many things that were interesting. You know not the pleasure it affords us to welcome a friend from home.

Tell Mother I wrote to Aunt Poole (Letitia Sorrell Earle, mother's sister) and have received a letter from her. She expressed a great deal of pleasure in receiving a letter from me and said if it was possible she and her family would visit us, and seemed to think they would ere long. She lives in Philadelphia, a small town about 100 miles from us. She said tell Mother and her other sisters to write to her, that she had been neglected and forgotten.

How does Dr. Mooney get on with his new prairie farm, and has he got anyone to stay with him, to drape, and ornament, or decorate his rooms? And Lou, how does she? Is she married yet? And cousin

Nancy, what is she doing? And Mary Lizza, and Virginia, and Lizza Blasingame, and John? How is cousin Ann? Has she been to see you recently? Is cousin Thomas still at Greenville, and all the folks, how do they all? Does Mr. Landrum still attend Cross Roads? I wrote to him by his request but have not received an answer. I hope when I hear from Cross Roads to hear of a great increase in the church. I imagine that you enjoy a great deal of pleasure in attending there with such a large concourse of brethren, and many of whom have always been your intimate friends. It is a very great blessing. I hope you will duly appreciate it. Alexander and I have attended church almost every Sabbath. Churches are very convenient and we have able ministers of all denominations. We are truly blessed but I often think how happy I would be to sit with my mother and my sisters in my own church at home.

I love all my brethren and sisters and do hope that though absent I am not forgotten. Especially when they intercede at the Throne Of Grace, will they not think, and will you not think of an absent sister. Oh do, Rebecca, pray for me and my dear companion, not only for us but for our dear parents, brothers, sisters, and friends, with our enemies. I have not heard from sister N for a long while, dear sweet sister, I love her much. Kiss Mary and Harriett for me. I hope I shall hear from you soon. Remember us to all our friends who inquire after us.

Give our love to Jo and Mesina, father, mother, brothers and accept the warmest love of your sister,

Harriet

Why does not brother A write to me?

The Texas war has come and the citizens of Pontotoc County are actually summoned to attend at the Village tomorrow for the purpose of calling out volunteers. My husband will attend but I do hope there will be enough without him who can leave their homes, families better than he. (He did not go.)

Uncle Davis's family is well except Aunt M(ariam). Her health is not very good. Tell Mother Aunt says she would write to her if she could but she doesn't write at all. As for Ellen (Nancy Ellen Davis) she is too wild to write to anybody.

The war with Mexico is the focus of national attention. It is mentioned in this letter and the one before it.

Narcissa to Rebecca Whitten—Pickensville to Gowensville, South Carolina,

22 May 1846

My dear Sister,

I reckon you think I am very negligent in not writing you and the others at home but I might say the same by you. I have been expecting a letter ever since I came home. How do you all come on? We here had lots of rain within the last two weeks but it has been clear two whole days now and everything seems to be growing very pretty. Our vegetables look very well but when we came home our garden was almost ruined. The gate had been left open. The chickens got in and ate all our cabbage very near up. I will have a mess of beans in a few days. I have peas.

Becker, our walk is lined with roses and a good many other flowers. Oh how I do wish you were here with us. I want to see you all just as much as I did before I went up home. We did not come all the way home that day we left your house. It was 3 o'clock when we got to Greenville and raining pretty lively so we stopped and stayed with Aunt Betsy (wife of uncle, Dr. Joseph Berry Earle). The old thing seemed very glad to see us. She has fallen off very much. I do not think she will live long.

Bell has been very sick since we came home. I suppose she has a bad cold. We gave her 4 doses of turpentine and oil and she is mending very fast. She is getting fat again. Law, Becker, how time flies. The wedding is drawing so near.

As soon as the wedding is over you must come, every one of you that can. Bell talks about you all every day and says you will everyone come to see our home and see us. Papa, you and Mother must come and see us. The days are so long you can come very easy. Silas, you and Ranson must not forget us. Does Alfred come home to see you often? Tell them to write to me. I am always glad to receive a letter from any one of you.

I have had the jaw ache very bad since I come home but it is a great deal better now. How are Jo and Mesina? I hope they are well. Tell them to come and see us soon. How are cousin Mary, Lizzie, Adaline and all of them? Has Pus got well? Have you any ripe fruit yet? We have had some very nice peaches and some nice May cherries. Oh, it will not be long till we have apples and pears plenty. I wish you were all near us so that you could come over and eat them.

Have you heard from Harriet since I saw you? I have not received a letter since I came home. I must stop. Let me insist on your coming soon, as many of you as can. Bell sends lots of kisses to you all and more to Grandpa and Grandma than any of the rest. Give my love to Jo and Sena. Elias joins me in love to you all.

Your Sister,
Narcissa

Tell Jo my tomatoes are growing very prettily. They are all I know of anywhere in the neighborhood.

Thomas J. Earle to Rebecca Whitten—Greenville Court House to Pleasant Grove, South Carolina, 30 May 1846

Dear Cousin,

Having a leisure moment and a good opportunity to send a note I again take the liberty of addressing you. I speak thus because I do not know whether you expected me to do so or not. But I know your kind and Christian heart will forgive me if I am wrong. "To err is human, to forgive divine" I write not because I have anything interesting to communicate but because it is a pleasure to me to speak as it were a word of tenderness and friendship to a kindred spirit. And especially to receive a line from a friend which it seems I shall not do if I do not write, and perhaps not then. Now I don't allude to you for your letter is the only letter I have received.

But I fear my letter, cousin, will be dull for it cannot be otherwise than my mind at present, yet I must beg you to receive my most sincere and heartfelt thanks for your very kind and affectionate letter. Believe me cousin, it was a blooming and fragrant flower of spring thrown across my path in withering blast of chill December, not to lie unheeded and forgotten, but to be read, remembered and cherished as friendships purest and brightest gift. And I will just say that I will endeavor to follow your good advice. Since I saw you cousin, my spirits have been low and though I am not happy I am as contented and resigned as circumstances permit. But I can not speak of the recent past, only to say "Oh Lord Thy will be done."

Cousin, I hope you will visit Nancy (his sister) and write to her and console her as often and much as you can.

I am getting on tolerably with my studies by close application and hard study and my whole time is given up to that for I have not been to a party since I've been here nor do I visit anywhere. I received a very long, kind letter from Cousin Harriett (Harriet Whitten Lankford) a week since. She says they are well that she enjoys as good health as she ever did in South Carolina, seems still well pleased with the country and her own situation. May God bless them.

Give all the girls my best respects and tell them I am much obliged to them that I am not forgotten when they, at a social meeting, enjoy the sweet communion of youthful friendship. And among the rest don't forget my cousin Ann. Tell Mary G that April and May is past and she has not been Greenville yet, but the great attraction is not here.

Tell the Dr. (Alfred Washington) good bye for I suppose he is rapidly hurrying the downhill road to the city of "Doubling" via the Spring, that I am sorry to give him up but I must submit not to an older, but a better right.

We have had a large meeting going on since Saturday night, but very little interest taken in it, i.e., by unbelievers. Messrs. Landrum and Curtis and other ministers near this place, of all denominations attended, and well might they say "all day long, yea for many days have I stretched out my hands to a wicked and gainsaying people". The meeting closed yesterday at six o'clock and Mr. L left for home after church. He preached a powerful sermon yesterday.

If any curious body shall at anytime enquire for Thomas tell him he is still here and does not expect to go to Mexico, till winter time at least. But I am looking for Doct any moment.

May God protect us from evil. Accept the warmest friendship of your cousin,

T. J. Earle

Rebecca, excuse the errors, in haste, T. J. E.

Narcissa to Rebecca Whitten—Pendleton to Gowensville, South Carolina, 9 Sept. 1846

My own dear sister,

I have at last taken my pen to let you know how we get on. I reckon you think long of the time since you heard from us. I have thought of writing you very often but I have been very much engaged for the last two or three weeks. I have been making some cloth. Winter is coming and we will need something.

How do you all come on at home? It seems as if its been an age since I heard from there. Oh, you don't know how I want to see you all. We have been looking for some of you down for some time. We would have been at your house about this time, but Elias can't leave his corn. We can't visit you until he takes care of his crop, for if we leave home two days the fence is down and the hogs in. I reckon it will be about a month before we can be at your house. You must come to see us as soon as you can. We would be delighted to see any of you. How is my dear mother? I have been so anxious about her health since you wrote me last. You said she was very unwell.

Why don't you, or some of you, write to us often? Elias goes to the office every time the mail comes but it's only to be disappointed. Do write often and let us know how you all are. I received a letter from sister H two weeks past. She was very well and perfectly pleased with the country. She thinks her babe is perfect. I would be delighted to see the little thing for I reckon it's a very sweet child.

Becker, I don't know that you can read this. I have written it in a great hurry. Elias going to Greenville in the morning and thought I would send it there. He gave me his love to Jo and Sina. Tell them to come and see us. Give my love to cousin Mary. Kiss cousin Adeline. Tell Pluck (Silas Jr.) and Rant (Ranson E.) they must write to Cissa. Oh, I would be so glad if some of you would come and see us. What has become of Alf? Why doesn't he write to me? I reckon is very busy. I believe Elias is sorta looking for Papa down here. You all, how I want to see you. Do write often and come as soon as you can. Bell sends lots of kisses to you all. Elias joins me in love to you all. I must stop. Good night, dear sister.

Your affectionate sister,
Narcissa

Thomas J. Earle to Rebecca Whitten—Male Academy, Greenville, to Wilson's Ford, South Carolina, delivered by A. W. Whitten, 27 Sept. 1846

Dear Cousin,

As I have for sometime intended to do I seat myself to drop you a line, not because I have anything of much importance to communicate, but because it is a pleasure to me to communicate, as it were, with a friend of former days and because I think there is much benefit derived from a proper correspondence. I hope there is no impropriety in writing. I was about a week after returning ere I got fairly under way in my studies, since which time I have been and am getting on very well.

We have had quite a crowd of strangers in the village lately and more especially for a week. The dust is from 1 to 2 inches thick all over town and the carriages all the time going. On Monday we had the RR convention, a meeting of some interest, and Tuesday the anniversary of the Agricultural Society in which I saw some beautiful specimens of needlework. But of this, I suppose you have heard. But then Tuesday night the wedding. Yes, the wedding came off and Billy and Jenny were made flesh of one bone and bone of one flesh. There were a great many persons there, house and piazza full, yea, as thick as pig tracks and as hot as Ethiopia. But I believe it all came off without any serious injury even from the affairs which I did not attend though strongly urged.

But I forgot to mention the Fair on Monday night which I suppose was a beautiful thing though I did not attend, but went in preference to hear the Rev. Francis Johnson who will soon start as missionary to China, preach a very good sermon. I have today heard Bishop Capeds, he is a very good speaker and preached a plain and very instructive sermon. JBP stayed with me Monday night and I was glad to hear from you all though he did not tell me a great deal and what he told I have no doubt was true but whether he told the whole truth I know not, he said little of himself. You may congratulate Crawford (brother) upon the good impression he made upon the folks from Greenville down at the affairs. Especially the female portion of them. Mr. Dodd has been here for a week, left last Friday and says he is about as well satisfied as any chap can be. He is not certain whether he will return to school or not.

Aunt Earle (wife of Dr. J. B. Earle) is pretty well. Tell Lizzy howdye that I would be very glad to see her in Greenville and that I have many things to tell her. If she'll come there are some of her acquaintances here yet if the attraction is not so great. Tell Mary I am still looking for her for I heard she was coming. Somebody said so.

I need not send word for any body to write to me for I suppose they would all with one accord begin to make excuses. I know the Dr has married a wife but that no excuse. But who has bought a piece of land or a yoke of oxen I know not. One thing I know, none of them have written to me. I wrote a long letter to cousin Harriet the first week after I came out but have received no answer yet. Tell Ann howdye and anyone that may ask of Tom.

I have been reading the Bible, ie, the Old Testament lately with the greatest interest and can but wonder why more young persons don't read it than do, such beautiful language and ideas. "How Godly are thy tents O Jacob and thy Tabernacles O Israel."

May you be preserved from all the snares of Satan, from all troubles, trials, and vexations of life. God grant you in health and prosperity long to live. "Peaceful sleep out the Sabbath of the tomb and wake to glory in a life to come."

T. J. Earle

Miss R. B. Whitten, cousin, do excuse this bad letter. I've a very bad cold and feel very dull. How does the singing at Cross Roads flourish?

Note by Rebecca: a good letter, R. B. Whitten

Mary and Virginia P. Goodlett to Rebecca Whitten—Nearby to Gowensville, South Carolina, 25 Oct. 1846

Dear Rebecca,

I will just say a word or two to let you know how I am getting along by this time. I am considerably better than when I saw you in one respect, but I do feel very bad today, but not half, half as bad as I did last Sunday. You know that the school was just out. Sunday morning Mary, Mother, Papa, and Alexander all went off and you may depend I had a lonesome day of it, but Beck, I turned back that day. I have got to about a bushel and a half. Beck, have you turned back yet?

Ann said that you said that you was on the old log yet but I think you surely have jumped down by this time. You know I said you would about the middle of the week, but when you do, mind and don't sprain your foot.

Beck, he is just as pretty as ever. He stayed here Thursday night and I never heard him talk so much. The school commences tomorrow at Tyger and he wants us to go very bad. He says that we can go for nothing, and any of the rest of the scholars, for it will be a great help to him and to the rest of the school. He left here to go see you all Friday, and he talked of going to the mountains Saturday, but took another notion and went home. He will be here tonight. Beck, can you work any? I thought I could not but I can. Oh, I want to see you so bad, so come soon.

Well, I will quit for it is late. I don't know whether you can read it or not. My pen is bad and I have got the trembles. Mary and Elizzie send their love to you all. Give my love to all. You are my most humble Rebecca.

Do not thy thoughts oft fondly trace,
Thy native haunts of peace and joy,
And tell thee neither time nor space,

The bond of birth can n'ere destroy.
Virginia P. Goodlett

Please burn it up. Don't let anyone see it.

Dear Rebecca,

I thought I would not write today but I must. I reflected one moment. I thought how long it has been since either of us have wrote. I don't know which wrote last, no difference. If you will write R, do write to me if you please. How do you feel at the present. Are you better or worse?

I feel much the same toward Mr. Parsons. Oh Rebecca, don't you want to see him? I do, but I want to see somebody else worse. He will be here tonight on his way to Tyger. He is very anxious for some of his Cross Roads scholars to go up there. He says some of us shall go whether or not, and that any, or all, may go free. I think that some of us ought to go but I can't go. Alex and some of the rest will go, but I don't know how many yet. I suppose you did not go to Prospect. I wanted to go very much but it was not convenient.

Oh Reb, I want to see you so much. Do come and see,

Mary

Close girl friends who lived nearby, both enamored by Mr. Parsons, a teacher. Virginia, like Rebecca, is involved in her gardening; she writes of turning back the potatoes. Being "on the old log" may have been a crude reference to a regularly occurring female malady.

Alfred Washington to Rebecca Whitten—Philadelphia, Pennsylvania, to Gowensville, South Carolina, 15 Nov. 1846

Dear Rebecca,

Did I not know that you were in possession of a kind and forgiving heart it would be natural to suppose that my neglect in answering your kind sweet letter of the 23rd ult would dampen your affection. I certainly desire and design answering punctually every sweet letter I get but should it so happen that I delay acknowledgement of any kind favor from your hands and those of the friends, I hope it will be attributed to anything else rather than a want of affection.

Were I to write down what springs uppermost in my head I should ask you a thousand questions about home and the scenes around it. I would quiz you till moon up and never get out of the social circle and until moon down, but I know your feelings claim something else, not that I can tell exactly what you want but suffice to say that you would first have a beaux. Well if that handsome, clever, young friend, so much admired, so much sought by all the social girls determined to address you I guess you'll get a beaux and a clever one, indeed. Mind you, catch him if he passes your way. You will not be surprised at my loss of matter on this subject when I inform you that I have already written down nearly as much as has been in my head since I left. Did you discern any before. I guess not.

You perhaps sympathize with me as you may suppose that I am lonesome and low spirited, being so far from home and in a land of strangers. Not so, Rebecca, not so, thanks forever to a merciful and provident God it is not with me as it was last winter. Then I was blind. Then I was dejected and lost. Then I thought of home, the home of the flesh. Now I think of Heaven, the home of the spirit. Blessed be God, I am not desolate here. No, the fervent gushings of old Cross Roads embalm me and my soul exults in thankfulness to the blessed Jesus for the consolations of religion. I feel myself gathered in to the fold of believers, and I find myself seeking their society here, even here, in this great city of wickedness and vice.

The Baptists have four Churches in the city, all large and flourishing. I presume besides these there are about 70 others of all classes that ever have been instituted.

By referring to the early history of this beautiful city you will find that the tract of ground on which it stands, in 1681 was covered by the forests and peopled by the savages. In 1682 William Penn determined on the present site for the location of this city. Many circumstances render it peculiarly fitted for the building of a city, among the most important were its being situated between two rivers which are separated at no great distance. The Delaware sufficient to float vessels of any size and the Schuylkill navigable for vessels of smaller class, besides the greatest abundance of every material necessary for building. From that time forward until the present the city has increased in size and wealth. In 1701 Philadelphia was incorporated into a city. The plan of the city is a parallelogram, the larger sides of which are two miles. The two shorter one mile in length. It is bounded by Vine St. on the North, South or Cedar on the South, by the Delaware on the East and the Schuylkill on the West. The streets cross each other at right angles. Market St. is the center between the northern and the southern limits. The houses are numbered from it both north and south and the streets running north and south are distinguished according as they are on the north and south of Market St. This street is 120 ft. wide. The other principle streets are 40 to 60 ft. in width. The streets south of Market are Chestnut (the most fashionable), Walnut, Spruce, Pine, and Cedar or South. Those north are Mulberry, Arch, Race, and Vine. I board on Race. There are some intermediate streets which do not extend generally from river to river as those already named. The city from N to S is divided by Broad St. which crosses Market at right angles. The portion from Broad St. to the Delaware contains 13 streets running parallel with Broad. These are named numerically as 1st, 2nd, 3rd and so on until it reaches Broad. That part of the city on the west of Broad and to the Schuylkill is laid off in the same way and numbers 7 streets and squares.

Philadelphia is widely celebrated for the number and beauty of its public buildings and this is the case with those I have visited. I hope I can see them all ere I return home. It is far before Washington in beauty and affluence as you are doubtless aware. It would astound a back country lad to see Charleston, Petersburg, Richmond, or Washington but all of them put together would make a city no more than half as large as Philadelphia. But am I not blinding your progress in geography, I might at least venture to surmise that I had almost, or quite, exhausted your patience, but I have not begun to tell you all I might. I have been thus concise in describing my whereabouts with a view to assisting your attention to the contributions I am disposed to make to our little local geographical circle as I believe Mr. Hill did not give us the minutia which I have detailed.

I am boarding in a Quaker family and really like it very well. They seem to be what the name implies, being friendly. You will recollect that that denomination has received the name of Friends, i.e., Family of Friends, and in many places are known only in that way.

In nothing am I so disappointed in as in the weather. I had supposed it was uniformly cold, but it is quite changeable. I have as yet suffered no inconvenience whatever from the climate. I presume I will be able to withstand the greatest extremes. My health has been good all the time since my arrival. I wrote to Father soon after I got here on about the first of the month. I expect a letter from him soon and letters from my cousins, Theron, Lizzy B., and C.

I have joined the class at the University and am decidedly pleased at the school of my choice.

Affectionately,
A. W. Whitten

Alfred is settling into Philadelphia preparing to enter the University of Pennsylvania School of Medicine. That old city remains as Alfred described it nearly 150 years ago. He refers to his conversion to Christianity within the past year.

Alfred Washington to Kindred—Philadelphia, Pennsylvania, to Gowensville, South Carolina, 13 Dec. 1846

My dear Kind(red),

Should I fail to write as often as your kind solicitations demand, I hope I will be able to supply the neglect by the great amount of matter included in each letter. But another question arises. I may not make them sufficiently interesting to pay the trouble of writing them, over this you are to judge of and if it becomes a task to read them, I, at least, hope that my error will be abridged by the imposing a like task in your replies.

Perhaps I had better tell you I received your long delayed but very acceptable letter four days ago. It grieves more sorely to hear of Mother's illness. I hope she is much improved ere this. I am glad to know that you are not afraid to acquaint me with her real condition. You would treat me very unjustly to suppress anything in which I am so deeply concerned. Therefore, I would always expect to hear the worst and that, without delay, I am prepared at all times for this state of things and I thank God for it. However as this is a melancholy state of things it may not be so interesting to you.

I cheerfully participate with you in the return of our little Pickens family (Narcissa, Bell, and Elias Holcombe) to your own fireside. I can anticipate all the pleasures with which it is surrounded, regretting only that I can not be with you in person.

I hope dear Cissa will enjoy better health and that Elias will make the move a profitable one, that sweet little Bell will not be made a plaything, but be made to become the lady, a station for which she is amply capacitated.

I envy Theron and John most heartily for I cannot conceive a more pleasant employment than the one in which they are engaged. I cannot do better for them than to add the wish that their labors be crowned with Virginian success

If I did not think that some of the boys were looking up to things of that sort, I should feel a delicacy in introducing such a thing. From the carelessness of Mesina and Addelin the idea was suggested that they might have thought of awaiting my return. Knowing them to have great confidence in me, and for fear they have come to that conclusion from something I have said or done I must beg you to inform them by hint, if you can, that there is some uncertainty in my being able to suit their convenience without accommodating myself somewhat. And I want them to understand that I will not be offended at them even though they disregarded me in the matter.

My best wishes attend Major Foster wherever he goes, but I hope I will not be regarded as acting illiberally when I express my regret at the move of his choice (I discuss the grocery business) in all its alcoholic forms.

The weather for this climate has been unusually warm and wet. I have suffered no inconvenience from the change in climate. We have had one light snow and one only. There has been a single frozen day, or a single day in which ice remained ice all day long. I have not seen ice more than a half dozen times.

I am comfortably situated about 3 squares from the medical hall. I pay $3.00 per week. I am more likely to pay more than to get it for less. I have bought all the tickets connected with the University, which cost me $140. The whole course, including diploma will be equivalent to $200, though I am by no means certain of getting a sheep skin. Much depends on my examinations this winter. I have bought about $45 worth of books. This I was compelled to do, and clothing to the amount of $20. I am wanting more clothing still. Therefore do not be surprised if I make a draw of about $50 more. If I send for it, it must come.

Be assured I will not spend much money unnecessarily. I would like to get of Mr. Blythe if at all, and I may write to him asking the reserve of the amount above named, more or less. I only name these things to get you used to them.

If I graduate I will not be able to leave before early in April. If I do not take the degree I desire to remain until I can prepare myself for it. The examinations are awfully close here and success very uncertain.

Will you present me in the most affectionate manner to our kindred collectively,

A. W. Whitten

Elias and Narcissa have returned to Gowensville from Pickensville. Alfred warns the family not to spoil Bell. Cousin Theron and friend John opened a store in Greenville. (Theron Earle died soon after the first goods went on its shelves.) He chides Mesina and cousin Addelin for becoming *pregnant while he is not there to care for them. Mesina delivered Baylis Earle Whitten on 31 Dec. 1846. Alf's aside about Major Foster's liquor sales probably did not sit well with his father. As with college students even in this modern day, Alfred warns the family that he may fail and could need more money. We are greatly relieved to learn later that he did need the $50, but he did not fail.*

Harriet to Rebecca Whitten—Pontotoc, Mississippi, to Gowensville, South Carolina, 14 Dec. 1846

My dear Father, Mother, Brothers, and Sisters,

After a silence of several months I have again taken my pen to resume the pleasant task of writing to you. I know that you are anxious to hear from us and I ought to have written sooner but I know you will pardon me. My dear sister Rebecca, last week I received your truly kind sweet letter and the emotions that so many interesting particulars that you communicated excited in my ardent bosom, you can better imagine than I can describe. Oh, how I love to hear from or read letters from those dear friends so fondly beloved by me, my parents, my brothers and sisters. Oh, how ardently I love them, and though, I may never meet them until time shall be no more, still will I love them the same. I'll cherish the fond memory of their affection for me and, oh, how I thank my Heavenly Father that His Spirit hovers round you, "when I am gone."

Twelve months have passed since I left my paternal mansion, and oh, what a change has been wrought in our family. When I refer to the many events that have occurred at Pleasant Grove since I left I am often lost in thought and, oh, how ardently I hope that our Heavenly Father will carry on His work in our dear family, until our dear father, our brothers, and our dear sister will be brought to the knowledge of the truth as it is in Jesus, until we will be a family wholly devoted to God. That it may be so is the earnest prayer of your sister, Harriet.

I must waive the subject awhile and tell you something of our welfare. About one month ago we took a trip to Tennessee, about ninety miles distant from our home. We spent about ten days with our uncles, their families, etc. My stay there was very pleasant. It seemed like I had almost got to Pleasant Grove again. Our relatives were all delighted to see us, and my uncles reminded me so much of my dear father, especially Uncle Alfred. I do not see a great change in their appearance. Uncle Alfred is much changed in his way of living. He is still full of joking, and relates the stories and scenes of his youth with a good deal of humor, but he is certainly one of the most orderly, proud devoted Christians I ever saw. Oh, what emotions did it excite in my bosom to bow with him around the family altar every night, as is his usual custom. He is quite gifted in prayer. His family are all religious except the small children. Uncle A speaks of you all with great affection. He often spoke of Mother and scarcely ever mentioned her name without weeping. He said he loved her so much and I reminded him so much of her. Uncles Alfred and Ranson fondled on me all the time and I sat upon their laps and kissed them as I used to do. Uncle Ranson looks just precisely as he used to. He says I was always his girl. He lives well and seems to be well pleased, says he thinks he is settled for life. Aunt Elizabeth's (wife of Ranson) health is bad. Their children all look well. Edwin is the same bad boy. I was much pleased with Uncle Alfred's wife (third, Nancy Ann Malone). She is a sweet, interesting woman, and seems to be beloved by all who know her. She has two children, Harriett and Alice. Ellen is a very sweet girl, and quite handsome. Father will remember her. Frank came home with us to stay several months. (Sarah Eleanor and James Frank were children of Alfred and his second wife, Bridget Graham.) He is a very smart, interesting boy, reminds me a good deal of my own brother, Ranson. He seems much pleased and says he does not want to go home. He says he wants to catch a deer. Uncle Alfred is coming to see us in a few weeks.

And now I must tell of the wedding. We arrived at Uncle A's just in pudding time. The next day after our arrival Mary Jane (daughter of Alfred and Carolyn Matilda Prince, his first wife) was married to Colonel Anderson (Edward Americus) young gentleman of great worth and with all a pious Christian. I will refer you to cousin John Prince (probably brother of Alfred's first wife) for particulars. He saw him at Uncle Alfred's and he will recollect him. He is a tradesman, makes spinning machines. He appears well informed, intelligent, and interesting. Rebecca Ann (daughter of Alfred and Carolyn Matilda) and her husband get along very well. They had the misfortune to lose their babe a few months ago. Rebecca goes by the name of Bec all the time. Well, now I'll come home again. When we returned home we found all well. Not one thing misplaced during our absence, and here we are at out little, peaceful home, and have I written all this while and nothing of my sweet little babe. She gets the praise wherever we go of being the best and sweetest child that ever lived (Rebecca Eugenia). Oh Sister, I cannot tell you half how sweet she is. She can now sit alone and call Ma and Pa with so much sweetness. Her hair is just beginning to grow prettily. After a while I will cut a nice lock and send it to you. I regret much to hear of my dear mother's ill health. I think of her often with much anxiety. She is a dear, good mother. I rejoice that dear brother A has chosen the good part that cannot be taken away. Religion will fit him for the cares of life. It will strengthen and support him in every difficulty and he is calculated to do so much good. May God be with him wherever he goes. You write to know the names of some of the churches near us. The one to which I belong is Prairie Grove. There is another near us called Smirna and another, Zion.

I have long looked for a letter from cousin Ann, dear girl, I hope she is better, and my own dear Cissa, I want to hear from her. I want to hear of brother Jo and Mesina and all my dear relatives. I love them all. I have not room to mention them individually. Love to them all. My husband joins me in best wishes and love to you all.

Your sister,
Harriet

Harriet's account of her visit to Fayette, Tennessee, where uncles Alfred and Ranson and Aunt Nancy lived with their families identifies aunts, uncles, and cousins. David and Elizabeth Barrett have migrated to South Texas. Harriet is impressed with the piety of Uncle Alfred, who has been converted since she last was with him.

In her June 1847 letter, she tells of his appointment to represent his Presbytery at the General Assembly of the Cumberland Presbyterian Church to be held in Cincinnati. After his move to Texas, Alfred became a Methodist. I wonder if David and Elizabeth told Alfred of their experiences with the Cumberland Presbyterians while traveling to Tennessee.

Harriet sent locks of hair as she promised. Murry Whitten still has them.

Narcissa to Rebecca Whitten—Greenville to Pleasant Grove, South Carolina, about 1847

My dear sister,

I reckon you will be very disappointed in not seeing me this week, and indeed, I fully expected to be at home, but I cannot have it so. I would not have you think, my dear friends, that I have forgotten our meeting. I know my heart will be with you, and I do sincerely hope you will all remember me at a throne of grace. I went to church twice last Sabbath, and in the morning we had an excellent sermon by Mr. Furman. I must tell you how I have enjoyed myself since I came here.

My friends are so kind that I hardly know how to act. Cousin Jim and Adda (James P. and Adeline Foster) won't let me go home. I have not visited much. Just as soon as Mr. Tom Butler heard that I was in the village he sent Mrs. B in the carriage for me and I stayed two nights and one day and I could get off only with a promise to return there and spend some of my time with them. Mrs. B is very much like Dick Stone in her disposition. I felt perfectly at home there. They are so gentle that you would not feel any other way. Mrs. Tuens called to see me. She says that I shall spend a few days with her. She wants to be very kind. I called to see Aunt Betsy (wife of Dr. J. B. Earle, mother's brother). Her health is a great deal better. Cousin Nancy Earle is there. I don't know how long she is going to stay. Mr. Hornbuckle will call on you. His little girl is very interesting.

Rebecca, I want you to send by them when they return, which will be Sunday, I expect, your old straw bonnet. I want to have it dyed black and trimmed for Mother. It will be a few days yet before I can go home. I want to see you all very much indeed and Bell talks a great deal about you all.

If you know when the camp meeting is on at Jackson's Green I wish you would write some of my friends here so I will know when it is. Write when our camp meeting comes on at Prospect, too. I heard Alfred was at the Association.

I must stop. Give my love to cousin Mary's folks. Cousin Addie sends love to you all.

May the Lord's blessings attend you is the prayer of your sister,

Narcissa

Alfred Washington to Rebecca Whitten—Philadelphia, Pennsylvania, to Gowensville, South Carolina, 1 Feb. 1847 (letter badly damaged)

Dear Sister B,

The day after mailing a letter to you on this day two weeks past, I received your letter of the 8th Jan. If you have received the letter to which I allude you will see that I am disposed to think myself rather neglected in the way of getting letters from my friends. Suffer it if you are implicated in my complaints. I take back part of it, Pluck, for your letters are regular and well timed, but always exceedingly interesting to me. I almost envied you the pleasures you enjoyed Christmas. There is more noble giving, more liberality, and manliness, and I might add womanness in the circle of your acquaintances or the social circle there than any other portion of the state or U. S. Now is this downright partiality or is it the truth?

I was glad you know to hear that our Mother was so much better. I feel sure that she will not wantonly expose herself to an attack.

I wonder if any thought of me when on Glassy Rock. Let me know quickly how our sweet cousin Lizzy (Elizabeth Earle, daughter of Theron) makes it. She will not write to me. Tell Sal she is too young to engage in the troubles of love. Tell Jenny to scratch my name off of her pitcher. Ask Mary if she likes Zubbils. Kiss the whole of Ann for me. How comes on Dr. Mooney and lady? I hope they are quite happy. Always remember me to them.

Heartily congratulate our dear kind Mesina (her son, Baylis Earle, was born 31 Dec. 1846) and sister. What a race, what matchless precision. Pity they have not got the house done. Tell Mesina to call him Baylis Earle Jr. I cannot suggest a better name but I presume it will be named.

If Dr. Barton wrote me, his letter has been misplaced or I have not gotten it, nor have I heard from Theron Jr., nor any of them. I am glad to know that Mr. Gibson is supplying Wolf's Creek Church. I hope the members will be blessed. I am disposed to think it fortunate that he has consented to attend them. You know he is a strong and rigid disciplinarian and zealous Christian. They have been split up, their Church discipline and fire, the lack of it. Who knows but what, through Mr. Gibson, all will be made clear and all become reconciled to each other and to their God, Let us pray for it. Does Uncle Billy H preach? I often think of him. Tell me how he is getting on. Does Mr. Burton attend you occasionally? I think he ought to. I can't conceive a more pleasant state of things than that. You should have a protracted union meeting at Cross Roads with Mr. Landrum, Mr. Burton, and others to preach for you. Why don't I hear of some one or more of our dear friends taking up their cross. Do you all pray for it? Becca there is value in religion. Oh there is power in prayer. We have the witness in our own hearts.

Father, I shall complain if you don't write me oftener. If you knew certainly the pleasure it affords me to hear from you and under your own signature you would not neglect me. In a letter I wrote you in December or early January I stated the probability of my wanting more funds. Shortly after that time I wrote Mr. Blythe asking $50 and requesting him to send you my letter. I believe that time in a letter to Rebecca I made a statement of the matter to you asking that the money be remitted by the first or middle of March, that if Blyttes could not furnish it, Jackson, I thought, would. I have not heard from any of you. If you can get it I would be glad to have it as before stated. If you cannot provide the amount desired I might call on the Dr. to part with books, etc. I might do without. I have spent but little money which I could have avoided. You will not have any difficulty believing me. It is so. I ought to have it by the middle of March. I would rather get some earlier I have reason to suspect, am uncertain about my being able to pass the examinations satisfactorily but I shall try and hope to graduate. If I do not pass you shall hear in due season my determination as I do not know whether I would remain and graduate (he graduated two months later) or return and practice. This may be rather contradictory to what I said in a letter two months ago. Don't be uneasy about me in any respect. My health is excellent, my head pretty clear.

Your affectionate son,
Alf

And you Col. (a nickname for brother Silas) and Ranter, you are small fry but if you were to write to me I would answer you. Why don't I hear from you Jo? You ought to regard it as quite a privilege and honor to correspond with an old playmate.

Alfred Washington to Rebecca Whitten—Philadelphia, Pennsylvania, to Gowensville, South Carolina, 10 March 1847

Dear Becca,

I did not intend replying to your letter of the 17th Feb. for a week or more, but it is entirely convenient to send out a letter by Mr. Wilson who called on me today. Should this be mailed at Greenville you will know how to account for it. The day your letter came to hand I got one from Theron's Lizzie, which I answered last Sunday and which, no doubt, you will see.

I am glad to hear that Mother is better and sorry to hear of Cousin M's illness. I hope Lizzie has recovered from her fatigue. Cousin Ann is very kind to inquire so closely about me. I wonder if she supposes that I ever think of her. I think Nancy must be very lonely. Does she have any beaux?

Tell her I inquired of you. That was a curious dream you had. Why did you not interpret it? It has no meaning without. I am glad to hear of the great changes in Patty. She'll be swarmed with boys. Who saved for me any of that wedding cake? Some time or other did Jo get the legacy? I guess he'll need it, and more besides. Tell him I am much obliged to him for writing me.

How did you get along at your protracted meeting? I hope it was a season of rejoicing. I am glad Mr. Gibson attends at Wolf's Creek. I trust there will be a move there.

I congratulate Elias and Cissa on their new home. Do you think if I was to stay here a year that Elias or Jo would write to me during the whole time? Cissa will, is great to do it, but I know it's hard to begin.

I received a tip top letter from Uncle Ranson the other day. The kin in that country are well.

Spring is beginning here this morning and it thunders and rains very much, like a morning shower at home. I will write you again in 2 or 3 weeks.

In haste, your brother,
Alfred

James P. Foster to Silas Reagan Whitten—Greenville to Gowensville, South Carolina, 8 April 1847

Dear Sir,

I went and seen Alexander and he had but little flour on hand but said for me to send down this morning and he would send you what he could spare, which I done and sent you same. There has been none of your whiskey sold as yet. Dr. Hoke says he received a few lines from you yesterday and was going to write you by T. E. Prince, so I made no inquiry of him concerning your business as I thought you might of changed your notions of writing so soon and Hoke said he had to go to where Joseph Emery will be Saturday next and you could see him there.

We arrived here safe in good time and all is well and I expect to go to housekeeping today and hope to see you there before long. My respects to all, in haste.

Yours respectfully,
J. P. Foster

Alfred Washington to Silas Reagan Whitten—Philadelphia, Pennsylvania, to Gowensville, South Carolina, 13 April 1847

My dear Father,

On the 3rd inst I wrote you a letter and told you I was to leave the city of Philadelphia that day, but what do you think. The letter was written on the night of the 4th. I was to start on the morning of the 5th, had everything packed and greased ready for an early tramp, when, to my chagrin, I discovered I had the mumps. Recollecting that it was rather lucky than otherwise I should thus be attacked before I left the city, I laid aside my traveling apparel and began treating my first case. How I have succeeded you will judge when I tell you that I am now entirely well and will be wending my way the next hour to good old South Carolina. From here I shall go to Baltimore, a distance of 98 miles. From Baltimore to Washington City, 46 miles. From Washington homeward there are two routes, one leading by the way of Lynchburg, Natural Bridge, Virginia, by Germantown, Rockford and Morgantown, North Carolina, another passing through Fredericksburg, etc., and Statesville, and Lincolnton, North Carolina. The difference in the distance of the two roads is inconsiderable, each being about 465 miles from Washington home, i.e., according to the best calculation I can make. Each or either will be quite sufficient to give me a long and tiresome journey.

I must again beg of you to pay no attention to my movements. It is impossible for me to say exactly when I will get home, or in what way. That I am anxious to see you all is not doubted. I hope will not be long though my course looks like it. If after trying my feet and legs for a few days, I find that it won't do, I will bounce into some traveling concern and go as far towards home as my money will carry me. When that gives out, I will halt, till you send me some. As I have, thus far, since I left home, been punctual to write home, dealt openly and freely with you, leaving out nothing that you would care to know, I will continue to do so. From what point I should next address you is uncertain.

I expect now that my trunk will arrive before I do. If does you can send for it. It will be found in the possession of Dr. Earle, Greenville. Should you be so curious as to want my diploma you can get by sending to my friend Dr. G. Michall or Dr. Calaway of Rutherford. Either of them can give it to you. With it are my tickets which you will procure likewise. I think Dr. Michall is about getting home now. If you conclude to send for it, but it makes no sort of difference with me, the post boy would carry it safely as it is enclosed in a neat tin case. Ere long I hope to enjoy the long hoped for reality of settling in your midst.

Your son,
Alfred

Alfred graduated from the University of Pennsylvania School of Medicine, and set out to walk home, more than six hundred miles. He arrived, but may not have walked the entire distance. That the diploma was recovered, "neat tin case" and all, there is no doubt. My mother, May Isom Whitten Moore, Alfred's granddaughter, gave it to me and I gave it to my first cousin, Dr. C. W. Merritt, son of Alfred's granddaughter, Lottie Helon. He still has it.

James P. Foster to Silas Reagan Whitten—Greenville to Gowensville, South Carolina, 13 May 1847

Dear Sir,

I made my arrangements to come to your house this day but Adeline was taken sick about a week ago and on yesterday I thought her much better but she was worse again last night so I can't leave home.

I have been looking for you down for some time. I have not been to Charleston yet for a very good reason. I lack some money as Mr. Davenport did not get the money he was to get. We have collected some, but not enough, and I asked Captain Lobeland for some and he said he did not have the money or I could get it and there is no person here that Mr. Sayse is willing to take for security that I would ask except Captain Lobeland and he says he had promised not to do so again and I have placed myself in a situation. I am compelled to go ahead if I can. Had I known before this time that there was any doubts about the money I could have made other arrangements, but persons I could got the money without security has not the money. I seen Mr. Sayse myself a few days ago and he says he had the money that he had kept on purpose for Davenport but he must have good security, and you know I was saying something to you before about security, and you said if WA would, you, perhaps, would and Davenport says he has no doubt but his grandfather there will endorse for him and he is good as any person for the amount we want. I would prefer, if you see proper, to endorse for me and him giving you a mortgage on my land until the money is replaced, for I don't want you losing on my account. There is no danger unless we was to get burnt out and in such a case I would want you safe.

I am to have the contract of the business so I am willing to mortgage property to get money to commence one. I did not expect to have to resort to such measures before but I see no other choice.

Adeline says she wants to see Rant and Rebecca and all neighbors and will look for Rant until she sees his horse. Puss and Sis is well but has suffered very much with colds.

Adeline says tell all howdy for me and Puss and Cissa.

You must not think my document too long for I have a heap to tell you if I could see you.

Say to May Blassingame, Sally is well and satisfied.

Yours respectfully,
James P. Foster

Foster, husband of niece, Adeline, is trying to start a business with a Mr. Davenport, needs financing, and asks Silas Reagan to endorse his paper.

Thomas J. Earle to Rebecca Whitten—Male Academy to Gowensville, South Carolina, June 1847

Ego Sum Nunc Solus

Dear Cousin,

School is just out and I having an opportunity to send it (I suppose) seat myself to write you a short note.

Your kind epistle came to hand for which I am and was much obliged, and here I will just say I did not think your letter came too soon for I thought it not very soon and as you will perceive I have acted on your own principle, i.e., carried it out.

I could not come to the wedding as you know but I will come if possible to the one you alluded to if it comes off any time soon. From what I can learn there will be a wedding at the Well ere long, I don't know though. Cousin Mary told me you had a fine meeting at Cross Roads some times since but I believe there is not much news up there. If there is I want to hear it.

I saw Alfred a short time since but just to say howdye. I wanted to talk a heap but could not and here I'll say that I received a small bundle by him but I know not whence it came yet I am much obliged to the donor whoever she may be.

Just turn over

We, i.e., Crawford (brother) and I, Tom, are well now. I have been troubled with a pain in the head lately but not for 2 days past. We are getting on slowly with our studies and are closely engaged and, cousin, I do think this has been the shortest spring I ever passed, not because it has been so pleasant to me, no no, yet I have had some pleasant moments not like the past but it has been very short.

We have a good deal of preaching such as it is and some of it is pretty good.

Messrs. Green and Drummond commence a protracted meeting here by order of the association. I am a member of P Lyceum and also of a small Bible class which I find most pleasant and instructive. The ladies have also a class of about 20 both taught by the Rev. I. M. C. Breakin. O, the study of the Bible is most delightful task. I had the pleasure of seeing the far famed Mr. West's painting of Christ healing the sick. O, it was a splendid thing. I saw by night and day and have not time to tell you anything to interest you about it but I hope to see you all again and then if think of it I will. There will be a meeting in the Baptist church some time this summer. Some fine ministers are expected, viz., Professor Furman, Edwards, Dr. Curtis, Landrum, and C. Can't you come? Do if you can.

Aunt is quite sick today but not very bad. I saw Lizzie Miller Monday night going to Pendleton with Mr. Camel.

Tell Ann howdye and that I know she can write if she would to her friends. Do write to Nancy and visit her and as you see above I am not tired of your letters.

Cousin, I have not said anything yet but I must close. I have not mentioned Theron and the Dr. (two brothers) and all the rest nor given you any poetry, but I just say give them all my respects and receive for yourself a Benjamin's portion of my best wishes.

Your sincere friend and humble servant,

T. J. Earle

NB this is just the worst pen I've seen today.

O ever thus in childhood's hour
I've seen my fondest hopes decay
I never loved a tree or flower
But 'twas the first to fade away.

Harriet to Rebecca Whitten—Annsville, Pontotoc, Mississippi, to Greenville, South Carolina, 17 June 1847

My dear sister,

It has been several weeks since I received your kind sweet letter. I know you begin to think long of the time since you heard from me. The privilege of corresponding with each other certainly affords us a great deal of pleasure. But, my sister, could we meet on some blest spot and there unfold to each other the inmost recipes of our devoted hearts, oh, what pleasure, what unspeakable joy it would afford us. That blessing once was ours but we scarcely knew how to appreciate its worth. We are now separated by hundreds of miles and rivers and mountains roll between us. Yet that affection and love that was implanted in our bosoms in infancy while we were resting on our fond mother's bosom is still unfading. Yes, my sister, those lessons of love that our dear parents taught us are still cherished in our fond bosoms and neither distance nor time can ever efface from our memories these impressions. I cannot muse on the past without shedding a tear of sympathy, I cannot say of regret, for God had been so kind to me. I ought rather to be grateful and thankful, but it is unpleasant to be deprived of the society of all my dear relatives.

I have been expecting a letter from sister Narcissa and brother Alfred. I am so anxious to hear what Alfred is going to do, whether he is coming to see us and so on. Oh, how glad we would be to have him come. I received a letter from Uncle Alfred a week or two past and also one from Uncle Ranson (Whittens). Uncle (Alfred) wrote me that he rather expected to go to Cincinnati sometime in June or July. It is the time of the meeting of the General Assembly of the Cumberland Presbyterians and he was appointed by his Presbytery to represent them, which is considered a very honorable appointment.

I am very anxious to hear how my dear Mother is getting along this summer, whether she is getting rid of the pleurisy, that dreadful disease. Is Father's health better? I often think how he used to suffer with the backache. I hope he is better ere this, and brother Joseph John, does his throat still distress him? I often feel anxious about sister N. Is she any stouter that she used to be? We have enjoyed fine health all the time.

My sweet little Beck (Rebecca Eugenia) is remarkably healthy. Oh sister, could you but see her, I know you would be delighted with her. She is a little, low, fat, straight, well formed child, a beautiful figure, fair as a lilly and cherry cheeked with eyes beaming with expression and sweetness, the prettiest teeth you ever saw. Her hair is naturally curled all over, a real Sally Blassingame head. She is full of vivacity and life and playful as a kitten. She is running about all over the yard, feeding the chickens, puppies, and cats. When we carry her to church she sits perfectly quiet by my side and listens with great attention. She was one year old last Friday. I baked her a nice birthday cake and I wished you were here to have partook of it.

Two or three weeks ago we had the pleasure of meeting Col. Joel W. Miller, he who married Elizabeth Earle (daughter of Theron), and his lady at Dr. Calhoun's. His present wife is Dr. Calhoun's sister. As soon as they arrived at the Dr.'s and found that we were in the neighborhood they sent for us and seemed to greet us with as much affection as if we had been near relatives. They could tell us many things interesting from Spartanburg. The Colonel said so soon as he returned home he was going up to Mrs. Earle's and would call to see you all and tell you something about us. Dr. Calhoun and family are very kind to us. Mrs. C is quite an accomplished lady. She manifest a great deal of friendship for us and says I feel to her almost as near as a sister, having only one sister and being distantly separated from her as I am from mine.

We donnot find the same kind of friends here as we did at home, tho some of our neighbors are remarkable kind, but the people are generally too selfish. Our churches here seem to be in a very cold state, but I trust that God will, in due time revive His work again, that He will pardon our weakness and much imperfection. I hope, my sister, that you are growing in grace and that God gives you strength according to your day, and that our dear brothers and sisters are enjoying much religion together with all that little band of believers. May God help you all, both in a temporal and spiritual light is the prayer of your sister.

Alexander and Eugenia join me in love to you all,

Harriet

I send you a lock of Eugenia's hair, a sweet little curl. We have a post office now at D. M. Davis (husband of Aunt Mariam) called Annsville. Direct your letters there. It is so much nearer to us. I have never received a letter from Mr. Landrum. My respects to him.

The spring has been unusually cold and it is raining all the time. We have the first vegetables ever, and irish potatoes so large that we cannot use more than two or three at a meal.

Silas Reagan to William A. Atkin—Gowensville, South Carolina, to Asheville, North Carolina, July 1847

Sir,

Last week I received a note from you requesting the payment of four years subscription of the Messenger and in this weeks number of second paper I see a very abusive article addressed to such subscribers.

That I have been receiving, regularly, your paper for a period of three or four years is true, and that I have not remunerated you for it is equally true. But how and by what authority my name was enrolled to your subscription list has always been a mystery to me. In view of the fact that I am not known at Asheville to yourself, your partners, nor to any other persons in any way connected with your paper, I concluded that I was indebted alone to the gratuitous favor of some friend, and having no call from the office for so long a period, the opinion was confirmed.

If you blush to think that S. Whitten will thus act, and are sorry and ashamed that the world should know it, why announce it in the article alluded to?

Sir, I shall not assume the payment of so subscription until I have who authorized it, and will no longer be accountable for numbers addressed to me at Gowensville.

E. P. Jones to Silas Reagan Whitten—Seavers Springs, North Carolina, to Gowensville, South Carolina, 21 July 1847

Dear Sir,

As I passed over to Rutherford I drank some of your whiskey at Dr. Mooney's. It was very fine. Colonel Lynch, a friend of mine from the low country, wants to get some that is fine to bottle up and carry down with him. I wish you to send a ten gallon keg down to the court house to the care of Foster or Brattie and I will pay you for it when I see you. Send it in the course of three weeks. Don't send it unless it is number one. I am over here for a short time, will be at home soon.

Very truly yours,
E. P. Jones

Another hand has written on the letter, "Ranson E. Whitten, Silas R. Whitten Jr., Sulphur Springs, Erwin Jones, 22 July," and the following poem:

Farewell, I ask no pledge of thine,
I feel no foolish fears.
For if thy heart is fond like mine,
For softness and for tears,
Each whisper of the twilight breeze,
Each murmur of the sea,
Will fill it full of thoughts like these,
Will fill it full of me.
Each twinkling o the distant star,
Will tell the tale of one,
Who dwells from thee and thine afar,
Beneath the setting sun.
I long had thought, my youthful friend,
A something to have sent you.

Tho it seem not other and,
Than just a kind memento.
But how the subject, thine may gauge,
Let time and chance determine.
Perhaps it may turn out a song,
Perhaps turn out a sermon.

Throughout the collection, there are letters and envelopes that have been used for doodling, practicing signatures, or recording some poem or comment. On the envelope containing this one, a male hand has several times written Ranson E. Whitten. There has existed confusion between the names Ranson and Ransom in the Whitten family. These letters clear it up. Every reference to the several Whitten Ransons has been spelled with the n, by family and friend alike. Ranson E. was at home in 1847, Alfred and Silas Jr. were away at school. It is, therefore, almost certain that Ranson Edwin Whitten has left us his autograph to erase all doubt about the spelling of his name.

Uncle Ranson to Silas Reagan Whitten—Sommerville, Fayette, Tennessee, to Gowensville, South Carolina, 31 July 1847

My very dear brother,

I duly received your very kind letter of 18th June and was disposed to give it an immediate answer, but some party required me to see brother Alfred before I could do so. Be assured I have not received a letter with more pleasure than yours. Besides telling us of the improvement in sister Ellen's health, and the general good health of our friends, it was evidence of not being entirely forgotten by a beloved brother whose long silence I could not account for. I will not say whose fault it is that our correspondence has been suspended, but in future we must do better.

My own family as well as Alfred's and his sons in laws are all in our usual good health, and there is probably less sickness in our country now than I have ever known it at this time of year. Our prospects for corn and cotton crops are about a fair average, wheat and oats same. My wheat crop is just cleaned out, about 60 bushels.

I have not heard from Mariam and Harriet recently, last account all well. Irvine Sullivan visited us in June and remained about five days, Georgia friends generally well. William Sullivan has been in this country since last January. He is living at brother Alfred's. (Ranson's wife was Elizabeth Sullivan. These Sullivans were probably her brothers.) Mary Dalton (daughter of sister Nancy) is living with me again since last December. I am her guardian again. Her father, her last guardian died insolvent, and I have had considerable trouble to get the business straightened again. By the operation of changing guardians, her estate is lessened by some $130-140.

You ask am I settled, how I am doing, etc. I answer that I have no expectation of moving shortly, though my location is not as good as might be selected in this region of country, and were I to move, I think I would go into North Mississippi somewhere (he did, nine years later). As to how I am doing, I will say I am driving on a meat and bread business, and not much more. When you was here I was smartly in debt. Since then I have worked through, and we are now clear of any indebtedness, and have granted my land, 400 acres.

As to your Forked Deer land, I have not been able to do or know anything about it. I have written several letters to court officers and others on the subject without being answered, and I have never had the opportunity of going to see about it. I showed your letter to Alfred and called his attention to that part of relating to money. He said he could not tell me anything to say to you on the subject.

I am not surprised to hear that the Mexican war has produced great excitement in patriotic South Carolina, and that her sons turn out to prosecute it avidly and promptly, but I am surprised that so clear a head as yours should attribute to the President incapacity and superciliousness in it's prosecution. Does history furnish any parallel to our success thus far? It is conceded on all sides that the Mexicans have never before fought so bravely, yet, in this war, they are uniformly defeated, yet the disparity of forces engaged be ever so great in their favor. Is not the President entitled to some credit for planning our campaigns and selecting and dispatching able commanders to prosecute them? I think he is. Is his sagacity not to be appreciated in permitting Santa Anna to return home at the time he did, thereby putting Paredes out of power, whose policy for calling a Spanish Prince to a throne in Mexico would inevitably have led to European interference. Reflect on these things, dear brother, and forget that you were opposed to Mr Polk's election, and surely you will agree with me in placing him beside Mr Madison as a statesman.

As to General Taylor's presidential pretensions, I have but little to say as yet. As a military commander, he has proved himself competent to every exigency and is deserving the lasting gratitude of the country. But whether he is possessed of the qualifications requisite for exalted civil station is a subject on which people are not yet informed.

Our state elections come off in a few days, and the leaders of each party have used the usual means to produce excitement and party feeling, but, I am glad to perceive, without effect, for among the people there is scarcely anything said on the subject, an indication that they are tired of so much turmoil.

My want of paper admonishes me that I must close. Give my warmest affection to all your family, as well as our friends and acquaintances generally in your country. Tell Alf it has been some time since I received anything from him. Tell Rant he must write to me so I can see how much he has learned. Our children grow finely and are all going to school except the youngest, who is a son named James Lawson.

Adieu,
Ranson Whitten

Postscript, Summerville, 2nd August 1847. I open this to acknowledge the receipt of a very gladly received letter from Alfred this moment which I will answer before long.

I find it remarkable that Ranson, born in the Carolina mountains and living in rural Tennessee, could be as well educated and informed as this letter shows him to be.

Judge Thomas O. Vernon to Silas Reagan Whitten—Spartanburg to Gowensville, South Carolina, 28 Aug. 1847

Dear Friend,

I received your letter informing me of a duty unperformed, as you supposed, in regard to your land. I wrote to W. Black as you requested me shortly after the reception of your letter last fall and advised him, if he was still determined to buy a place, to write you, if he had abandoned all idea of doing so, to write me and I would inform you of the fact. In reply to that letter I have not received a single word. I supposed that he had been negotiating with you for your land until last month when he had not written to you, he said. Thus you will see that I am not censurable for a want of attention to, or subject to criticism in the discharge of my duty. Mr. Black, at the interview referred to, told me he had declined purchasing. I hope you will excuse me therefore as he is to blame and no one else.

I regret very much to hear of and deeply sympathize with you in your late affliction. Feeling the delicacy and force of the ties that bind parents and children I can to some extent, if not fully, realize the anguish and pain of your bereavement and most hardily tender you and your family our warmest sympathies.

We expect to visit you if no unforeseen causes prevent on Tuesday next.

Yours truly,
T. O. Vernon

Judge Vernon was the husband of Harriett Bomer, daughter of Amaryllis Earle, sister of Eleanor Kee Earle Whitten. I can find no evidence of a death or injury to any of the Whitten children or grandchildren to account for the expressions of sympathy. The land is on the market. A move is contemplated.

Thomas J. Earle to Rebecca Whitten—Male Academy, Greenville to Pleasant Grove, South Carolina, Oct. 1847

Ego Sum Nunc Solus

Yours was received Saturday last and I cannot forbear to thank you sincerely for your very good advice. I know God is the only refuge but I often feel the chastening rod, I fear, and can't perform my duty as I ought. I am sorry I gave you any pain in my last note for I would not hurt the feelings of a true friend for all the riches of Croesus. Rebecca, do believe me, it gave me much pleasure to read your sweet note and find that you can sympathize with an unworthy friend. It did sooth my feelings. I could say much to you verbally if it were any benefit and I know it would be a comfort to me to pour out the miseries of my soul to a good friend but you have pain enough of your own. Then let me not trouble others. You perhaps know some things.

My feelings remain in status quo. My heart in one point of view may be compared to the General's hat which time nor the Drs. could cure. I could say much now if I were permitted. I hope I shall see you soon and must stop this nonsense. I was made comparatively happy today by receiving a letter from my particular friends Alexander and Harriet. O, it is pleasant to hear from friends and know that there are a few to whom we can fly from the wintery blasts of grief and the cold world. A and H are well and very happy. It is a sweet letter you shall see it.

Cousin, excuse me for writing so often. I have this opportunity and thought I would write for it is a blessing which I cannot enjoy long. Fate has decreed that my nearest ties of earth shall be riven and I must be resigned. But my dear friend I dread the conflict but "the Lord is my refuge and strength."

Write, cousin, often if you wish. It will be received with pleasure while we can enjoy it. I shall leave soon but must see all you girls together once more, i.e., my friends.

I have a great deal to do, don't spend an idle moment scarcely. I am studying and thinking and writing. I am happy to hear you are composed in your feelings. We have a rough road to travel but if you ask, Mighty God will be our support. Your letter should have reached me one week sooner but was delayed. It shall go the first chance. I receive your pledge of friendship with pleasure. Do pray for me. I shall be happy if I have the prayers of a friend. And remember, cousin, I will never forget Rebecca. I meant to be short but it has turned out as usual a long string of nothing. Tell the girls I am looking for some poetry.

God's blessings rest upon us. Farewell.

Thomas

P. S. Tell cousin L to be careful of Cupid.

Thomas J. Earle to Rebecca Whitten—Penfield, Georgia, to Gowensville, South Carolina, 23 Nov. 1847

Dear Cousin,

At last I seat myself to perform a duty which I owe to you and to myself, a duty which always affords me a pleasure of no common kind, for I know to whom I am writing. When I address you I feel at liberty to dispense with a long exordium which might be used on some occasions. I know that I am communicating with a chosen, with a kindred spirit, a sincere and devoted friend. When I get to writing on the subject of friendship and especially when I write to you I know not when to stop, for fancy plumes her ready wings and visits scenes forever passed which once were well enjoyed and which are yet to memory dear. But before I lead off on such a strain, I will give you some general items.

I left home and the Dark Corner with a sorrowful heart and a deep dread of the future and of the task which lay before me, but with a degree of resignation and a strong trust in God without which I should be amid the storms of adversity and in all my trials "as chaff before the wind." But what were my feelings when I arrived in Greenville and heard the news of the glorious revival then, and especially when I heard that one more member of my family had been brought (as I trust) to a knowledge of divine truth and had manifested that he was not afraid of the Gospel of Christ.

In Greenville I stayed one day and conversed and took leave of some of my young friends individually. I thought it was a farewell yet there was a sweet pleasure in the pain so that I almost wish that it could be protracted. In fact, I did want to stay till after Sunday but I could not, so I took leave of the folks generally in the sunrise prayer meeting on Friday morning and left that day. We traveled from Pendleton through a very poor country. I thought the land worn out and too poor for goobers, the timber all cut down, especially near the roads so that the sun shone very warm. The whole country was very dry, it not having rained for 8 weeks until about 2 weeks ago. We passed but 1 town, Lexington, a very old ugly and declining place.

Penfield is a largely laid out and well built place, the buildings all new but very scattered. As I have said to every body else it is literally a town in the woods for there are a great many fine oaks growing throughout the place. There is 1 store, 2 hotels, 2 printing offices, and the college here. The papers published here are The Christian Index and Temperance Banner. Nearly every person you meet is a Baptist. A majority of the students are members of the Church.

The college chapel is the only Church they have, ie, it answers the double purpose of Chapel and Church. The mode of Worship is rather formal to suit me but similar to what I was accustomed to when I first went to Greenville. It is altogether different from good old Cross Roads and North Prospect where I have so much delighted to be. O how different are my feelings here when I go to Church to what they were when I visited those dearly loved sanctuaries. There, indeed, they worship God in spirit and in truth and there did I delight to sit and hear the unsearchable riches of Christ preached by our plain, unsophisticated, honored, and worthy pastor. I have heard some of the first preachers in the state, the literate, but nothing extraordinary have I heard yet.

I am rooming with a young licentiate from York District, South Carolina, a clever young man. We are the only South Carolinians in college and I assure it pleases me much to have even 1 from South Carolina with whom I can converse. We often talk of our dear native homes and anticipate the almost infinite pleasure that will be ours, if we are ever so fortunate to return to the bosom of our friends.

I have seen but 4 of young ladies of Penfield for there are but few who I am acquainted with now. In fact I never had so little inclination to visit the company of the gentler sex and to form new acquaintances since I first began to go into company.

The weather has been very warm until within a week. We had a glorious frost Saturday morning. We are all as busy as bugs on a spring morning preparing for our examination which commences tomorrow and holds a week, at the close of which we have a vacation, till the 1st of Feb. 1848, which I expect to spend in this place. I mean I shall be here in person, studying and writing letters. There are some that I should have written to but have delayed it till that time.

I have received letters from Crawford and from Mr. Landrum and from Perry (Oliver Perry Earle, brother). The latter informed me of several persons having been added to the Church at Wolf's Creek. O I rejoice to hear that the Lord is visiting His Zion in some places. I saw Ann the day before I left home but had no time to converse with her, although I wanted to very much for she is indeed a good friend. My arrangements are so made as that I could spend 2 or 3 in the neighborhood besides going Church but I was disappointed. Perhaps it was for the best. Under no circumstances could I have left home and gone with greater reluctance. I had just arrived at the point where I could enjoy myself well but Pope says whatever is right so be it.

Permit me to say in answer to your last letter that your letters have been anything else than uninteresting to me. I read them with extreme delight. The only objection is that they are too short. I hope you will write to me and tell me all the little particulars, anything from there and especially from you would be thankfully received. You have no idea how I long to hear the news generally from Greenville and Spartanburg districts.

Accept my warmest thanks for your promise in the close of your last. I feel deeply the need of prayer especially occupying the station I do. I feel my unworthiness. Pray for me Cousin, especially at the present and be assured that I will endeavor to continue to pray for you as I ever have done. Give my respects to the family, to Ann, and any others you think would receive them well.

Your friend and Cousin,
T. J. Earle

Tom says good-bye to home and leaves for Mercer College, a Baptist school in Penfield, Georgia. His description of the countryside, especially the old town of Lexington, is not flattering. Mercer College, now a Baptist university, then recently founded, was becoming the focus of a small city. Apparently he traveled by horse or coach, as he refers to the roads. Letters written later show he also used the train. ✳

CHAPTER SEVEN

1848 to 1851

These were critical years for the Whitten family. Alfred began to practice medicine in Pickensville, then moved to aristocratic Pendleton. Thomas J. Earle completed his final years at Mercer College and graduated, Uncle Alfred moved from Tennessee to Texas, Harriet regularly reports the news from distant Mississippi, little Bell dies, and her parents forsake farming for the world of commerce.

Dominating the thoughts and activities of the family is the desire to move west. Sell the land! Who will go? Who will stay? Where will they settle? Having resolved these issues, they bid their farewells and move to Mississippi to begin new lives.

Thomas J. Earle to Rebecca Whitten—Penfield, Georgia, to Gowensville, South Carolina, 11 Jan. 1848

My Worthy Cousin,

Yours of the 17 Dec. 1847 I received on the 23rd and was the most welcome birthday present I could have received. That was my birthday and it was spent not in the happy company of young friends assembled to celebrate the day nor in the social converse and sweet communion with kindred but in deep and solemn reflection on the time that was past and bitterly did I sigh to think that so much of my life was already passed and I had been so negligent, that I had done so little good to my fellow beings and so little in the cause of my Great Redeemer. But I trust I shall be of some service in this world yet. I'm sure it is my greatest desire. I feel that my life is not my own-that I was created for the service of those around me. As I have often said, nothing affords me so much pleasure as when I am able to, and am engaged in making others happy. I rejoice to see you talk so kindly and encouragingly to me and that your heart is "warmly engaged with me in my present undertakings". I hope and think I am pretty well persuaded that it is the course I ought to pursue. If I were not I am sure I never should have taken such a step. I know the station is an important one and I feel my inability to do anything without the help of the Lord. But I engage with a firm trust in the power of God for support and a faint hope that I may be of some service to someone, that I may do some good in this extensive field which is continually opening to every honest laborer. I can't imagine why you think that is the course I ought to pursue, although it seems to be the opinion of several others of my young friends, and from 1 or 2 I have received great encouragement. It may seem like a pretty wild scheme to some who know me and who can't know any of my feelings on the subject, especially to some old experienced persons. But I trust I have the prayers of all my friends. I know I have yours.

You can not imagine with what pleasure I read the letters of my young friends. It arouses all my feelings and, in fancy, I converse with them as I was wont to do in days gone by. I review the many happy moments I've spent in their company with regret and sigh bitterly over those golden moments that now can live but in memory.

I felt the force of your modest but keen rebuke when you said you were more pleased because my last letter was rather unexpected as well as that of cousin Lizzie in her poetic efference. But I have several correspondents and in fact 1 or 2 more than I expected. I will tell you the joke when I see you and if I think of it.

My time is also now more occupied in term time than it ever was so I write all my letters in a hurry. But cousin none of my corespondents I assure you shall supplant you-nor shall business kindness. I can write sometimes and I hope you will never indulge another thought that your letters are troublesome.

Do beg Lizzie to excuse Tom. He has done the best he could. I certainly did not expect and do not merit your "sincere thanks and lasting gratitude for past kindness." Sufficient the reward for anything I can have done, that you were pleased. You surely can not have been much benefitted from my acquaintance or correspondence. But know that if you have been pleased, I have been delighted. If you have been benefitted I have been more so.

I hope you will not let sociability die entirely, though many of the old song fest are absent. But it is true that when I left it seemed to be at a very low ebb. There is Alfred and Crawford (brother), and two left, and Cis (Narcissa Amaryllis) and the Dr. (Michael Baylis Earle, brother) but he's married a wife and would pray to be excused.

I am very sorry that the mumps have got amongst you all and spoiled all your fun. What a pity, what a pity. I have just heard of the affair in the Wolf's Creek Church about their pastor. It grieves me to see that old Church distracted so and going down but a house divided against itself can't stand.

No doubt but that was a lovely scene you witnessed in Greenville. O how I wished to be there but I could not. I'm sure I never had such feelings at that place as I did during that meeting and I never felt more deeply interested in one than in that after I returned to Greenville from home and the camp meeting at N Prospect.

O cousin, I wish you could have been there the morning I left. I never had such feelings before. I made a short address warming and encouraging but my feelings were such I could not say much. I guess some thought it a poor excuse for an exhortation but I can't help it. I could not leave without it.

Yes I shall return home next summer if nothing prevents. I'm sure you all can't miss me more than I do you, not so much. One word about Penfield. I had a dull Christmas as I expected. We have had 2 or 3 little fandangos, ie, social parties, this vacation and I enjoyed myself pretty well. You know I always do if I can get into company. There are about 15 young ladies here and some of them pretty fair to look upon. They seem to be quite free and familiar. Some of them are perfect parrots to talk so we got along pretty well. But, mind you, I am not captivated yet. I am no ladies man. When the term commences I am done with the ladies and parties. We have had vacation since the last of Nov 1847, but the new term commences 1st Feb.

I wish I could have spent this short rest time with you folks at home but I could not. I had a very polite and pressing invitation to spend it in Greenville and gladly would I have accepted it, ie, to spend part of the time there, but it was not expedient. Don't be surprised now.

Please remember me to your Father and the family all, also Ann if you ever see her and all the girls.

Your letter would have been just as welcome if you had filled up the 4th page. I always fill up all the paper. I could write much more now but will stop, I believe. When I get to talking on some subjects it seems like I never know when to stop. I have written this just as fast as I could, I write to keep up with the train of thought and hence make many mistakes and have to interline. But I can't be particular and nice like some folks. I hate fashion or anything studied.

Accept the best wishes, the esteem, and the strong and lasting friendship of your unworthy friend and cousin,

T. J. Earle

This is to that mountain goddess, no poetess, or rather dark corner muse, which I hope she'll excuse.

Miss Lizzie B
Good morning to your ladyship
May Heaven augment your blisses
And send you health content and peace
Friends, lovers kind, and kisses
My friend, I read your verses through
And Bessie, dear, believe me.
They gave me joy, they pleased me much.
And yet they most did grieve me.
They brought to mind those happy hours
we've spent with one another
When round a neighbors fire our friends
assembled all together
And ore the withered flowers O joy
I sighed with deep regret
To think those scenes forever past
Yet which I can't forget
Yes still within my memories shrine
A thought remains you see.
And past enjoyments are not
Remembered but by thee
Still Cousin Lizzy lend a thought
At eve in prayer most fervent
To him who ever shall remain
Your friend and humble servant

John Lankford to Silas Reagan Whitten—W. Scott's home in Alabama, to Gowensville, South Carolina, 17 Feb. 1848

Dear Sir,

We reached this place two days since without encountering any difficulties whatever. We called to see Albert at Gainesville and left him there. He is doing well. From that we called to see Mother at Gwinnett. From that to this place is 120 miles. We made it in 5 days. From this to the end of our trip will be a little short of 250 miles. From this we shall travel by way of Tuscaloosa, Columbus, Aberdeen, etc.

Curren is with us, at this time in good health. His prospects are very flattering. He says he has books and $175 since 1st January.

I left 2 good cowbells and a good claw hammer at McMakin's. I wish you to get them. We shall leave this in a day or when. W. Scott says if you ever go to Mississippi you must call on him.

My love to you and family,
John Lankford

Jinnet (Harriet's dog) is doing well.

John Lankford is the father of Harriet's husband, Nathan Alexander, and is on his way to Pontotoc, Mississippi, to settle near his son. He gives us his route and says they are covering about 20 miles each day.

Thomas J. Earle to Rebecca Whitten—Penfield, Georgia, to Gowensville, South Carolina, 29 Feb. 1848

Dear Cousin,

It is now 9 o'clock but it has been some time since I had the pleasure of receiving your last welcome letter and duty bids me respond. I yield to the voice of duty because it is imperative, because it should ever be our desire to know our duty and when we know it do it at all hazard. "Be sure you are right then go ahead."

I can truly say I have little to communicate, and less, I fear, that will interest you. News is literally out of the question except little local matters, incidents that occur in town and college which would interest you about as much as the larger catechism in Hebrew. But want of news and push of business says Seneca should never be an excuse for not writing to a friend. And let me say that he was right if he had a friend as devoted, as sincere, and as true as I know you to be. It is always a pleasure to me to receive an epiette from you, breathing as they always do warm friendship and true piety in such pure and elevated strains. I feel like I had been communicating with a kindred spirit and an old associate and it hardly seems absurd to me, at it's close, to take a formal adieu as if you were present in person.

But I must touch upon some of the items in your letter and hasten to a close with 1 or 2 reflections. I rejoice to hear that cousin Ann is still able to visit with her friends. I wish she would do so much oftener. It would be to her interests no doubt. As to the wedding I have only to say I wish them all the happiness and felicity which they anticipated. That is a kind of happiness that I can stand off and see others enjoy without envy. Truly, I have neither part nor lot in that matter now. The future is dark also.

Yes, Cousin, I do rejoice with you and would join the Angelic Choir in rejoicing over the sinners that have repented. It is indeed a season of rejoicing. It is always a source of great pleasure to me to hear of the prosperity of Zion and the advancement of the Redeemers Kingdom, but it is a source of most extreme pleasure to me to hear of the conversion of those whom I love, my friends and associates. You have great encouragement to pray and praise. You may yet see the same change in others. O would to God it were mine to rejoice for the same cause, but alas! I fear I shall not have soon. I wish I could have more faith.

The poets and consequently the pudding I must pass by from necessity and also other things of a like nature.

An uncommon and somewhat remarkable circumstance occurred here on the evening of the 2nd Sabbath which I can't forbear to mention and which I suppose you will not be displeased to hear. Immediately after supper we all assembled for preaching and our old Pastor arose and said he had chosen a text "Seek ye the Lord where He may be found and call upon Him while He is near", and tried to pray over it and prepare a sermon but all his labor was lost. The more he thought on it the farther he was from the subject. He said he could not conceive of a time when the Lord was farther off, that he had asked so much without effect, that he thought he as well quit. But just as the bell rang for Church he was called to pray for a young man under deep conviction of sin. This revived his spirits. It proved to be a young man who is rooming, for a time, with me and my friend from South Carolina. After Church the pastor and 3 young brethren came home with us. We found several persons here and the convict rolling over the bed and sobbing aloud. When we came to the door he arose and threw his arms about my roommate's neck and begged him to pray for him. He did so, several prayers were offered and he became more calm but does not profess a hope yet. The Spirit of God works with power sometimes, nay, at all times.

But I must close. I am very much obliged to you for your remarks concerning my future course and your advice about my health and C. I will try to be careful for you are right. Permit me to correct your supposition that I receive a great many letters from home. I have not received 1 since 19 Jan. except Crawfords. I don't know what they mean. All my correspondents are in my debt and it is now 2 weeks since I received a letter. Shocking, Shocking. I am not complaining of you. I will write home soon anyhow. The measles are in town. I have not taken them yet and its no use to run. My health is good.

I want to tell you something about Penfield, but can't now. You may ask me what you will about my correspondent when I see you.

"Tired nature needs repose." Give my love to any that may chance to inquire about Tom.

God's blessings on your youthful brow. Good night.

T. J. Earle

They have had a great fair in Greenville I see in the paper. I fear they attend more to fairs than they do to their prayers. I hope not. I have seen a copy of the Evening Star.

Alfred Washington to Eleanor Kee Whitten—Pickensville to Gowensville, South Carolina, 17 March 1848

Dear Mother,

This is the first scratch I have made with a pen since I left home. I was truly glad to receive a letter from you, but it was quite unexpected. I doubted that you were inclined to write and supposed you would make the attempt but allowed it would be a failure as usual. Now it is not flattering to say that. You write a first rate letter, one full of interesting and instructive matters. Will you write me again and again.

I was sorry to hear of your illness, hope you are recovered, sorry to hear of Lizza's indisposition, hope she is well ere this. Give my love to her and all the family. Glad Mr. Akins is improving, sorry Mary Vaughn is sick, you had better give the quinine.

Nothing interesting to write. I have been well and hearty. As yet, I do not regret coming to Pickensville. It is the place for me if I can get employment. I have not had a case of much importance, having been treating Minor H for a bad cough, etc. Was called to Mrs. Robinson's (widow). I have not made many new acquaintances. Have attended Church twice and heard good preaching, have been invited to two or three places in the neighborhood. I think I shall get practice after a while, but it's uncertain how soon and how much. If the people don't employ me it will not be my fault, or rather it will not be in consequence of any carelessness or neglect on my part to render myself worthy.

I am kindly treated and feel at home and conduct myself in the same manner that I did when I was at home. I keep things set out in the service style and with the wood frame you would not know any difference. I wish I had supplied myself with socks, etc. for I find them rather scarce here. You will see that I have written in a hurry. The mail passes in a few minutes.

In writing to me your only chance is to write on Friday, but I do not get the letter until Monday morning, i.e., if you write by mail the stage passes by here on the way to Greenville three times a week, and I could write and send to Greenville on Tuesdays, Thursdays, and Sundays. But the only mail that brings me letters from home passes on Monday morning. I stated this to let you know when letters could be mailed to me from Greenville, i.e., on the evenings of Friday, Sunday, and Thursday.

Tell the boys to write to me. Tell Jo to have that bowl of jugware turned and burnt. I need it. When it is finished he must contrive to get it to Greenville and let me know where it is left. Tell Cissa good luck to her kitchens. Kiss Bell and Nancy, Harriet, and Doctor. Love to all the family, etc.,

Your affectionate son,
A. W. Whitten

Tell Becca thanks for her six lines, and thanks to any gal who will write to me from the Dark Corner.

Dr. Alfred Washington Whitten has moved to Pickensville and launched a medical career. Note that brother Jo is the family potter.

Harriet to Alfred Washington Whitten—Annsville, Mississippi, to Pickensville, South Carolina, 24 March 1848

Pleasant Grove

My ever dear brother,

Long, long have I neglected to write to you but I did not forget it, nor have I been less mindful of you, but time passes away and we neglect many duties that we ought to perform. I can assure you that my affection for you, my dear brother, is still the same. I love you in sincerity and truth and though more than two years have elapsed since I enjoyed the heartfelt pleasure of seeing, and conversing personally with, my dear parents, brothers, and sisters, yet I love them just as dearly and fondly as when I used to join the social circle at home.

Imagination often wafts me to the home of my childhood and my heart naturally and fondly clings to those who nourished and cherished me in the days of my infancy, but methinks I view the hand of God placing me in a foreign land and I am astonished that I am so contented as I am. I do not look back with anxiety, only to have the social intercourse of those so dear to me. Oh, I do wish you were all here in this beautiful country. I think that you could do a great deal better here than in Carolina. Our nearest physician, Dr. Calhoun, booked about $6000 last year and is just as good as paid, and he could not attend to near all his calls. It is said that collecting here is not near so difficult as in Carolina. The people are not so poor and make so much produce.

Mr. Lankford's family arrived here safe about three weeks ago and are now living within 1 mile and 1/2 from us. They brought me a great deal of news from home that was interesting to me. They brought me many little presents from my dear Father, Mother, and sisters, for which I tender them my most hardy thanks. Father, the beautiful dress you sent me is admired by all who see it, and my Mother and sisters, the dresses for the children are equally beautiful. They all display the peculiar taste of the donor, and Jeanette, when I saw her my eyes were suffused with tears. Dear little pet, I prize her very highly. I know she was petted on and fondled on at home on my account, and I prize her now because you all were so attached to her. Eugenia and Willa (children, Rebecca Eugenia and William Henry) are delighted with her and she seems to have great care for them. Eugenia feeds her.

I received a letter from sister N a few weeks ago. She said she expected you would leave home soon, but did not say where you would locate. I donnot know where this letter will find you but I will direct it to Gowensville for it will be written to you all. I do think, Brother, that you might write oftener, whether I do or not, but I will try to do better in the future. Sister N told me more good news, two more of our dear family came into the church (Jo and Silas Jr.). Let us thank God, my brother, for His mercy endureth forever. Now all are gathered into the fold but our dear, good father and one dear brother (Ranson E.). Let us never rest till they are brought in. You who are warm hearts, good Christians, pray, pray for them without ceasing. My most earnest petitions shall be offered up for them, but I am so cold and careless and sometimes fear that God will not hear my prayers. Oh, how ecstatic the thought or hope that we will all one day be a family united in Heaven, that blissful place, where parting, and sorrow, and trouble will no more annoy us. I want to write to brother Jo before long but I owe so many letters and fear I shall never write them.

We have preaching within 2 miles of us almost every Sabbath, but the church that I belong to is 5 miles distant. It is the nearest to us of our faith and order, though the Baptists preach in our neighborhood frequently and hope soon to establish a church.

Well, sister R, I think I promised a long time ago that when I got home I would tell you just how we were fixed. I hardly know how to begin but will first tell you that we have a splendid quarter section of land, the richest, I think, that I ever saw. It lies beautifully and will be very easily improved. We have a beautiful situation for our house. It is on a ridge called high for this country. We have a first rate wood log house, remarkably neat, and well put together, a good brick chimney, a door on each side, and one large window. So much for our house. We have the largest and best meat house I ever saw and a fence around the whole is as far as we have got yet. We only have a choice little orchard commenced, paid $3 for a small lot of apple trees. Our house is situated in a beautiful little grove with small flowers in view all around. The winter has been so wet we cannot have a garden plowed in until the crops are laid by. Alexander expects us to get 12 or 15 acres in cultivation. We are getting a fine stock of hogs and cattle around us. I suppose we have near 50 head of hogs. The wolves have destroyed a great many pigs for us but they seem to have left. Our wheat crop looks fine.

And now, of all the sweet creatures on earth, Eugenia and Willa are the sweetest. Little Willa prattles all the time. He is very large, has 2 teeth and can almost sit alone.

Do all of you write to me soon and accept the warmest love of your,

Harriet

Love to all my dear relatives and friends, kiss the sweet little Bell (daughter of Narcissa), Mary, Harriet and the little B (Mary Eleanor, Harriett Earle, and Baylis Earle, children of Jo and Mesina).

21 April, Dear A, after writing the above I see from The Mountaineer that you are located in Pickensville. I will direct my letter there but you will please send it home to let my folks hear from us as I may not write again for a few weeks. Willa did not take the whooping cough. We are all well.

Life in Mississippi in 1848! 160 acres, twelve to fifteen cleared by hand and horse, log house, single room, one window, a smokehouse, orchard, and wolves that eat up the little pigs.

Alfred Washington to Rebecca Whitten—Pickensville to Gowensville, South Carolina, 1 April 1848

Dear Becca,

I got your letter and it is a good one. No apology is necessary for it, but though it is a good letter, yet it is a bad one, bad news. It grieves me to hear that you are all so sick. Wish that I had been with you, hope you are better before this time. How is Mother? How

Father? How are you and the boys, Jo and family? How is cousin Mary and Lizzie, the family all? How is Silas and Cis and Bell, and Cox Goodlett? I received a letter from Margaret Vaughn and answered it.

You want a recipe for making tartar emetic ointment and here it is. Take of tartar emetic finely powdered, two drachms, sand one ounce, rub them together. It may be made weaker but I would not advise you to have it stronger. Some caution is necessary in the use of tartar emet Oint. It should not be rubbed on an abraded surface, none other than sound skins. It should be discontinued on the appearance of a crop of pustules. I am tempted to recommend something for your colds and coughs. Take pills occasionally of salts and sage tea or salts and senna. Don't eat much. Keep your bodies warm. Take one or two teaspoons full of the following mixture every two hours; liquorice ball, three drachms; warm water four ounces; dissolve the liquorice and add spirits of nitre, 2 drachms, antimonial wine, 1 drachm, laudanum 40 or 50 drops. If I am not mistaken you have the articles up there. I hope, however, that you are all well or better at least.

I am in the attitude of moving my office across the street to a room occupied at present as a taylors shop, the rent of which will cost me $15 per year, pretty tough. But I am shut up, not making acquaintances fast enough. When I move I shall tack up a shingle. Can't tell what I will do over here, have not had much encouragement yet, scarcely a case, some sickness in the country too. Looks like a bad chance but maybe it will take after a while. I shall be fixed sorter bachelor like and want to have some flowers around me. Would you send me dahlias? I'll tell you how you can do it. Get the boys to put them in a box and send to Greenville by some wagon. Have them directed to me and have them in the care of Hughes Holcombe at Phillip Rutleges. I can get them from there if you send them. Please bundle up some flower seeds, nasturtiums and the standing cypress and anything but old maids and old bachelors. You may put in some viola too, just anything that you think would suit, if you have it to spare. There is the Pride of America, Mountain Lilly, snowball, the dwarf rose, etc, and the horse radish calemint and not more than 2 or 3 roots of a sort. I want some sunflower seeds, cousin Mary has them, a little bunch of yellow velvet pinks, and 1 dozen grass nuts. If you are sick, or sorry, and can't talk much, or in love and have a beaux, or are too busy, and it's not convenient now to send me some of your herbs and flowers pay no attention to it.

I thank Jo for writing, Tell him so. Hope he'll write me again, tell him so. I don't want to incommode him, tell him so, but I do want my jugging and must have it as soon as it is ready, if possible. Tell the Col. (Silas Reagan Jr.) I want to see what sort of letter he writes. Love to all.

Your brother,
Alf

All's well

Thomas J. Earle to Rebecca Whitten—Penfield, Georgia, to Gowensville, South Carolina, 9 May 1848

I have often tried to write and was unable to say anything to the point, anything worth reading, and I fear I am not far removed from that situation now. I feel quite dull and so you must put up with a short and sorry letter as usual. Your letter should have been answered sooner but, of course, I have been quite busy, for I had several letters on hand to answer when I received yours and besides I have been unwell, ie, I have had a very severe cold and with it a continuous headache for the last week, but I am better now.

I am always glad to get a letter from cousin R for she always talks so plain and familiar, and in that old fashioned interesting style that never fails to interest.

Your excuse is certainly a good one yet unnecessary entirely and hereafter don't take up so much room apologizing. Don't take any for you know they do no good. Those who believe or admit an apology would be satisfied and excuse us without it, whereas those who are hard to please and satisfy would not admit the apology. I don't think you are especially guilty but I say the above because it is the truth and applicable to most persons.

I don't think my letters deserve the complement you paid them. Let me say I wish they were what you seem to think they are, that they deserve the praise they have received. I am truly sorry to hear of so much sickness in the Dark Corner. I heard of it before by Crawford, ie, some of the cases. We have many trials, and afflictions, and sorrows, and temptations without and corruption within. By one man disobedience, sin, entered into the world and brought a long train of evils, mental and physical pain. And what is worse than all, temporal and eternal death, the death that never dies. But we must not, resigning, cry out against fate and fortune and say, like one of old, our punishment is greater than I can bear. No, let us not charge God with injustice, but live so that though our outward man perish, our inward man is renewed day by day, hoping that these light afflictions which last but for a time will work out for us a far more exceeding and eternal weight of glory.

We have very little interest of feeling manifested here in religion though we have precept upon precept, sermon after sermon. We sometimes get up a little excitement in our prayer meetings in which we have a speech, or exhortation rather, almost every evening but the effect seems only to nick the surface and so the interest is not lasting. Wayside hearers, that anon with joy receive the word.

I should have liked extremely well to have been at the dedication of your new Church (Cross Roads' new building), but I could only wish and think. I guess you had a fine meeting. It was a good time and I hope you all dedicated yourselves anew to the service of God. "Consecrate yourselves as living sacrifices, holy and acceptable to God which is your reasonable service."

Our profs (some of them) and many of our citizens have gone to attend the Baptist state convention but it has happened so that I have not been allowed to rest by the trip. There has been some sickness in our village lately but no fatal case except one little girl. I get along very well except that the water don't suit me. It is not generally good. The young man I spoke of in my last has been added to the Church.

You ask if I write much. I answer yes but I write everything in haste. I have much writing to do besides letters. I don't keep a journal, wish I could, but the fact is I have nothing worth recording, and besides I fear I am too lazy. Cousin, what makes you so melancholy? Cheer up and be happy. Christians of all people ought to rejoice and avoid gloom. I know we have some cause to be sad, and that sometimes we will be, but we should resist the inclination. I know at most that you have not so much reason to complain of your coldness and unfruitfulness. God does not require us to be always on our knees before Him. Let us by patient continuance in well doing seek for glory and eternal life.

I have just received a good letter from Bro. Landrum, told me that the Cross Roads Church was dedicated. Cousin, I would say much more but the bell for recitation will ring in a few minutes and I must stop. I write worse and worse every time. But I write too fast. Nobody sent any word to Tom and he sends none back. Only if anyone asks about me tell them howdy for me.

Your sincere and devoted friend,

T. J. Earle

I have not heard from Alfred or Harriet yet. Nothing more. In haste, T.

Alfred Washington to Silas Reagan Whitten—Pickensville to Gowensville, South Carolina, 22 June 1848

I would like to know what disposition has been made of the Liqueur, whether it has been sold, engaged, or delivered. If it sold for it's value there was money enough to pay the $60 note with Smith and pay me some $12 or $15 besides. I left home with about $25 and it has done me along, but its got pretty low now. I must have a little more and that's the way I want to get. I've got the same thing as no money since I came here. I've had some work to do and would have all I could attend to if it was not for my opponent. He is beating me badly, but doing it in a way, I think, in which he cannot be sustained. I have booked, since I came here, about $100, and some of it in pretty good hands.

At the Association last year I subscribed $4.00 to the Domestic Mission. I want the Col. (brother Silas Jr.) to collect the note on Alex Henson with an account on somebody else and discharge that pledge. Send it to the Association.

Miss Jane H (niece of Elias) is a little better but quite low yet. Elias, I think that you and Cis ought to come to see her,

A

Alfred Washington to Eleanor Kee Whitten—Pickensville to Gowensville, South Carolina, 22 June 1848

Mother,

Yours received, thank you for writing, thanks for correcting my negligence toward you. I know I ought to write oftener, but have been pretty busy, and am careless anyhow. Sorry it is so, wish it were otherwise, but stop! Did not you teach it me or where did I get it, wonder if it's natural. What say you?

Sorry to hear of so much sickness amongst you. Glad you're getting better. Glad your own health is improved. Glad you are able to go amongst your children, your neighbors, and to Church. What a blessing to any community to have Brothers Landrum and Gibson to preach for them. If you were away from there for a while you could better appreciate their services. Both those brethren are engaged in the advancement of domestic missions. Would they knew the state of religion in this community and do something for it.

Would be glad to come and see you but can't say when it will be convenient for me. Sorry to hear of cousin Ann's illness, hope she is much improved now. Tell Father if he will come and see me I'll do something for his cold. Sorry Cissa is not well, guess she needs medicine, and Mesina, she ought have those old teeth extracted. Glad Elias and Jo work, don't think they will hurt themselves. Heard from Pluck and Ranty. Wish Col. (Silas Jr.) would come over here and go to school to Kenedy at Dr. Robinson's. Kiss the children for me, every one of them.

Love to all, etc., etc.,
Alf

Becca's love accepted. Blossoms don't look well, too wet and too dry, too troublesome. Still want the evergreen but haven't got the bowl to put it in. Wonder if it would not do well in a tater patch with a little log cabin in the corner of it. Glad the Sunday School is reopened. Hope Becca will pay good attention to it and make the boys help her, and all others who will engage in it. She must always have the taters ready.

Alfred Washington to Elias Holcombe—Pickensville to Greenville, South Carolina, 11 July 1848

Elias,

I received your letter and thank you for it but its lost or torn up and can't be answered in detail. I heard you and Cis were to be over last Saturday, wanted to see you and looked for you. Why didn't you come? I hope you will come soon. If you do not, write to me. I want to know how you're getting on up there, what you're doing, and what you are going to do, etc.

I am advancing in business and prospects seem to be a good deal better for me and so on. It's a leisure time with you now and some of you ought to come over and see us.

I heard Father was at Greenville and stayed a day or two. I reckon he was rather pressed or he would have come to see me.

The Rev. Mr Kenedy gave a temperance lecture here on Saturday, before the 5th Sunday, inst, and presiding Elder Gamewell preaches at this place on Thursday before the third Sunday in August. Yes there is to be preaching in Pickensville and right in the heart of town, too.

Ys etc.,
AWW

R. Elliott Holcombe to Elias, 14 July 1848

Dear Brother,

We are all well except Jane (Elliott's daughter) and she is improving slowly. I am going to take a trip out in Georgia and hunt me a place, and I want to know if you don't want to go with me. I am going in my buggy and your expenses will not be anything, hardly. If you want to go I want you to be certain to come down Monday or Thursday at the outside and see about it and then you can take the buggy up and bring Cis and Bell down to stay with Eliza while we are gone. Be certain to come and let us get ready.

Respects to all yours, in hurry,
R. E. Holcombe

R. P. Goodlett to Silas Reagan Whitten—Greenville to Gowensville, South Carolina, 18 July 1848

S. R. Whitten, Esquire Dear Sir,

I wish you to send me all the law that you have that will be in point in this negro insurrection case. The acts of the legislature of 1835, I find, has an act to amend certain laws in relation to the trial of slaves and free negroes. If you have that act send it by the bearer and you will oblige.

Yours truly,
R. P. Goodlett

Send me the record of the Henson boys case.

Elias Holcombe to Silas Reagan Whitten—Addison's (Elias's brother) Pickensville to Gowensville, South Carolina, 28 July 1848

Dear Sir,

We would have arrived at home today had it not been that Belle was taken very sick on Wednesday morning. (She died 29 August.) She was attacked with inflammation of bowels which has terminated in inflammation of the brain. Alf has been tending on her until today when at his request and my desire I went after Dr. Earle, who has been here for two hours.

Belle has evidently improved but it is hardly perceptible. The Drs.

say it is a very bad case and I would be very glad to see you or some of the family as soon as you can possibly get here as it is very uncertain when we shall get home. I wish you would have my new ground hoed out. Get somebody to do it and I will pay them for it when I come home.

Myself and Cis are as well as we could be under the circumstances. Cis says she can't write a word to save her life. Belle sends no word as she has been out of her head all day.

Yours affectionately,
Elias Holcombe

NB we have just cut Belles hair off short. (Elias spells the name Belle; Narcissa, Bell.)

Bell's illness results in her death one month later. There was much sickness during the nineteenth century. Medical knowledge was limited, causes of yellow fever, malaria, dengue fever unknown, antibiotics a century away. Cures from that time seem strange, almost bizarre, today. Matters of health, and the doctors who dealt with them, were of everyday importance and, therefore, are featured prominently throughout the letters.

Silas Reagan Jr. to Rebecca Whitten—Pickensville to Gowensville, South Carolina, 3 Aug. 1848

My own dear sister,

I have seated myself one more time to write to you. I have been here four weeks and not a single word have I received from home as yet. I must acknowledge I am a little mad with you for you well know the anxiety I have and the interest I feel in the welfare of those with whom I have been raised. I believe I have recovered at last though I had a pretty good spell of it. I would have written last week but I was looking for a letter from home.

The folks are well down here. Mrs. Robinson's folks are just as kind as can be. I reckon you heard of an accident that occurred in this neighborhood about ten days since. Rufus Oats, whose house we live in was blowing rock about 2 1/2 miles below here, at Clyde's tan yard. When packing the powder in the drill it ignited and blew two fingers and his thumb off one hand, the thumb and about half of the wrist off of the other, blew one eye entirely out, and injured the other, I fear, a good deal, burnt nearly all the skin off his face and neck. In fact, he was the most used up man I ever saw though he is recovering as fast as possible.

This is the day appointed by Gen. Taylor as fast day and we have tried to suspend business and observe it as well as we can, believing it to be our indispensable duty.

I believe I am as homesick now as I ever have been since I came here. Tis hard to forget our native home, the place where we were raised, and where we have spent so many happy hours. The thought of being severed from there is more than anyone can bear. If I had anyone to associate with it would be a different matter, but you know it is my nature to seek company, but here I can see no one but the little Robinsons. True enough, they are a good deal of company for me, yet there is something else wanting. There are fewer Baptists here than any place I ever saw, and you know it is our nature to want some one to commune with. That is our way of believing. I have never been to a Baptist meeting since I came to Pickensville, except when I was at home. The nearest church is about 6 miles, the same name as our church has (Cross Roads) but we were not placed on this earth to enjoy happiness all the time, neither can we expect it.

I reckon you are in a great buzz about the Association which comes on the 17th of this month, not much time to go on. I reckon you will have lots of company, be as well fixed for it as you can. I know it is a great trouble but somebody has it to do and I am in hopes the Dark Corner will do it up brown. If Doct (Alfred) is not too much engaged he will come up with me, though you know it is very uncertain about him. I will come if I can get there and if I am well I can do that. I was out to hear Mr. Ready preach last Sabbath and saw them sprinkle one member and administer the Lord's Supper which you know was exciting, a new thing for me as I had never seen it before. There is more form about it than I like yet they seem to be impressed with the right sort of feeling.

I have heard nothing said lately about sending for Jane (daughter of Elliott and Eliza Holcombe), and Alf can't leave home now. Elliott Holcombe starts for Georgia Sunday morning. I don't know whether Eliza is going with him or not. Miss Reese is very well and looks pretty.

Well, you know I am getting on as well as I could expect with my studies though it's very slow business and requires great patience, which you know I am not blessed with. I must close. The stage takes on a short time. When I come home we can talk it all over. Give my love to all the girls and the family.

Your brother,
Silas Reagan Whitten Jr.

Thomas J. Earle to Rebecca Whitten—Penfield, Georgia, to Gowensville, South Carolina, 19 Aug. 1848

Well, dear cousin Rebecca,

I seize this moment to answer your last long and interesting letter. I know that you are surprised that it has lain so long unacknowledged and indeed I am ashamed or rather I am sorry that it is so, yet the circumstances have been such as I thought would justify my silence. They are these. When I received your letter about the 1st July I was closely engaged preparing for our examination and my studies all were hard. Besides which I had to prepare a speech for commencement as one of the junior speakers which engaged my spare time for you know we all have pride enough to make us wish to do as well as others. While on this head I will just say (all that modesty and propriety allows) that I passed through the examination very well and at commencement we all delivered our speeches well. The large and attentive audience seemed to be well pleased and gratified. A short notice of the exercise you saw in the Southern Baptist. I shall not attempt to give a description of the scene until we all meet at our next Christmas frolic next December, both which I hope to do the Lord willing.

But the most interesting part of the apology has yet to come and I know it will do your soul good to hear of. Much more would it to have been with me in the soul churning scenes which it has been my pleasure to witness for the last two weeks. That I may not keep you in suspense, cousin, I have been in the midst of, and one of the actors in, a glorious revival of religion. The circumstances are these. Just after the noise and bustle of commencement was over a meeting commenced in a church a mile from town. I was there on the first day and few persons attended. After two days there was more interest manifested. Several mourners came up desiring an interest in the prayers of the people of God and the Blood of Christ. Thus we continued having preaching day and night while the deepest feeling was manifested for thirteen days. I have never seen more deep feeling at any meeting in my life although I was more interested in the revival at Greenville. It was painfully pleasing to see thirty and oftener forty persons on the anxious seats, some crying for joy and happy enough, and others weeping for sins and crying "pray for us, Oh what shall we do?"

Then did I truly obey Paul's command. I wept with those that wept while I rejoiced with those that did rejoice. At the close seven people joined the Church and were baptized and thirty or forty profess to have a hope in the atonement of Christ, perhaps not more than thirty that may be relied on. Some of the wickedest young men in the institution were converted there.

The pastor of the Church is a student and married man in college. He came to all the young men who are studying theology and asked their earnest cooperation and we all went into it with spirit, determined to do something, and we did it. At the close of the meeting out of town notice was given that there would be preaching at the Chapel in the village and we have had meeting every night since. I have been at church once and more frequently twice every day for eighteen days besides attending on inquiry meeting part of the time.

Besides all this I spent last Thursday and Friday in company with several brethren visiting and praying in every family within the incorporation. It was a new idea for me but I spent the time very pleasantly indeed. When we shall discontinue our meetings I know not. I guess not under three weeks. I tell you, cousin, when Christians go to work with the proper spirit and labor in Faith, Satin's kingdom must fall.

Well, this is a pretty long preface to a letter, and a longer apology than you anticipated, but you see I have been quite busy and I know you won't scold me for working while it was day for the Lord.

I have no news of another kind that will interest. One death in town lately, viz., Mrs Brown, a married daughter of the president of the institution. Not from local disease.

Vacation closes in about a week and then I hope to be able to meet you all again next December, the Lord willing. I have not heard any news from Carolina for a long time. But I must close. Give my respects to all the friends whom you meet and especially to your Ma and Pa. What is cousin Lizzie B up to now a days? Tell her I am just the same. I hope you won't think me unjust in asking you to write soon for really I am so anxious to hear from them that I must ask it. If you delay under the same circumstances that I did I will excuse you of course.

Cousin, I am so nervous that I can't write. I could say more but circumstances forbid. Goodbye till I hear from you.

May God bless you and you will be blessed.

T. J. Earle.

P. S. Do write me a long letter next time and tell me all the news about Crawford and Jo (Joseph John Whitten) and the other children.

Judge T. O. P. Vernon to Silas Reagan Whitten—Spartanburg to South

Pacolet, South Carolina, 11 Sept. 1848

Dear Uncle,

We reached home on Thursday as contemplated without an accident on crossing. Mike (Mike and Charles were slaves) performed his part faithfully. For his use and services I offer you many, very many, thanks. I send Charles this morning with him back to you and hope that you have not been put to any great inconvenience on account of his absence.

Harriett and Mrs. Bomer (Amaryllis Earle Bomar, sister of Eleanor Kee, and her daughter, wife of Judge Vernon), together with myself and little ones write in sending much love to you all and request that you all without exception visit us shortly. We will look for you at Fall Court.

I have no news of importance to communicate. The political discussions terminated without making, so far as I have learned, any conversions.

Yours re,
T. O. P. Vernon

Alfred Washington to Rebecca Whitten—Pickensville to Gowensville, South Carolina, 30 Sept. 1848

My dear sister,

Though I have a bad pen and am without a quill to make another, I will not longer delay answering your letter, which I received in three days after it was written. No excuse on your part is necessary for delay in writing, at least I am not going to complain now, for fear it may be said that I am in arrears myself. You are indeed very kind to write to me and your letters cheer me a great deal. Not the first Monday morning has passed since I came to Pickensville that I did not look for, and hope to get, a letter from some one or more of my dear family or friends in, or around, the Dark Corner.

It always makes one sorrowful to hear of the afflictions of our beloved Mother and Father, and I often desire to be with them, and to be divested of stubborn, distrustful, and deceptive, selfish human nature and to put on the whole garb of duty in its most innocent, abiding, and affectionate bearing.

Oh, my dear sister, carry out in your imagination the subject. I have been touched. It is perhaps better to suppress the gush of feelings with which my bosom swells. I rejoice to hear of the additions to

North Fork and Tyger Churches. What a wonderful work seems to be allotted to our dear Brother S. Truly his labors are blessed.

I am pleased to hear that Aunt Ammy and Uncle Elisha (Eleanor Kee's sister, Amaryllis Earle Bomer, and spouse) had visited. How very affectionate she seems to be toward us.

It is hard to acknowledge that I was tempted to pass over that part of your letter alluding to our own, our bereaved sister. Oh, what shall I say? What can I say? Bell, sweet Bell, she was the crowning bud of the whole rose, the richest and brightest gem in the constellation of the whole circle. But alas, she is gone, gone to that land where there are no chilling winds nor poison's breath, where sickness, sorrow, pain, and death are no more felt, no more feared. With the poet I can, and will say that;

I am weary of straying, oh, fain would I rest,
In the far distant land of the pure and the blest,
Where sin can no longer her blandishments spread,
And tears and temptations forever are fled.
I am weary of hoping where hope is untrue,
So far but as fleeting as mornings bright dew.
I long for that land whose blest promise alone,
Is changeless and sure as eternal throne.
I am weary of sighing ore sorrows of earth,
Ore joys glowing visions that fade at their birth,
Ore pangs of the loved which we cannot expurge,
Ore the blightings of youth and the weakness of age.
I am weary of loving what passes away,
The sweetest, the dearest, alas, may not stay.
I long for that land where those partings are ore,
And death, and the tomb can divide hearts no more.
I am weary, my Saviour, of grieving Thy love,
Oh, when shall I rest in Thy presence above?
I am weary, but, oh, never let me repine,
While Thy word, and Thy love, and Thy promise is mine.

Then Becca, let us lay aside every weight, every grief, and the sins that beset us and press forward to the mark for the prize of the high calling of God as it is in Christ Jesus. And finally, whatsoever things are true, whatsoever things are honest, whatsoever things are just, whatsoever things are pure, whatsoever things are lovely, whatsoever things are of good report, if there be any virtue and if there be any praise, let us think on these things. Excuse the great rush with which I have written. Love to all.

Your brother,
AWW

Bell has died, and a grieving uncle pens a sad and beautiful farewell.

Thomas J. Earle to Rebecca Whitten—Penfield, Georgia, to Gowensville, South Carolina, 19 Oct. 1848

Well cousin, the time has again come that I should respond to your last short letter. I write this time not because I have anything of interest to communicate, not because I have nothing else to do, but because you expect it, that you may not conclude that I would willfully neglect a friend.

It is sometimes pleasant for me to sit down and pen a few thoughts to a friend in a good old fashioned conversational way. My imagination places him or her before me as they were wont to be. It pictures before my mental vision some of those fireside chats and scenes of enjoyment which I engaged in and passed through in my boyhood's bright days and which rapid and relentless time has rolled into the dark oblivions of the past and left no traces of their being save on memories livid pages. "Gone glimmering through the dreams of things that were a schoolboy tales, the wonder of an hour. "But Oh, it is not a pleasure of unmingled sort I feel when vagrant fancy in her backward flight revisits all my old familiar haunts and loved retreats. Long and regretfully do I linger as I pass and gaze wistfully on that little crowd of youth assembled round a cheerful burning fire, or standing in smaller groups in the old and sacred Church yard. For, oh! I know the time is past that I was wont to mingle in their youthful joys, that I can never be what I have been, that although the time is short since these things were so with me, I now am looked upon as a being of another sort, as a friend indeed by most I've left behind, but a friend to whom those gay disports and innocent and boyish amusements are forbidden. Though I am the same Tom yet I am not looked upon as such by but a few.

And then Alas, I miss among those groups of friends the forms of some, who like myself have early learned that this world is all a fleeting show, some who were kindred spirits, or sought for honors in this fading world, I am aspired but to be a friend. And when I break the long and sullen silence by the short interrogation where are they? I find that some have gone to seek for honors in a distant land, that some, yea many, have sought the end and aim of life by linking in the connubial tie their destinies with those whom fortune, or fate threw in way. Some have heard the distant cry of war, and burning with a patriot's love, or wish to win a deathless name have gone with youthful pride and perished mid the din and thunder of the battlefield, and some have gone before me to try the dread realities of a future world.

"How painfully pleasing the fond recollection".

But I waive the subject for one more deeply fraught with sadness. (Bell, daughter of Narcissa, died August 29.) Twas with feelings of deepest sorrow and sympathy that I heard of the loss of your lovely little niece, and yet I joyed to hear of the Christian fortitude with which the Mother stood the shock. Tis all for the best. Twas fitting that she should go before care or grief should flood the soul and drown the peace and innocence of her young heart. Like a fair young plant of heavenly seed she was permitted to bud in this waste desert where thorns and thistles grow but was early transplanted to the upper garden to open its tender petals and bloom in fragrant beauty there. Then bid the Mother mourn not oer the loss for she was too bright for earth and ere the rude polluting blast of sin could touch her spotless purity of soul she has been carried by Angels to the presence of Him who said "Suffer the children to come unto me and forbid them not for such is the Kingdom of Heaven" And when the Mother's spirit shall be called to join the spirits of the just her once loved babe will lead the band of Angelic Host that shall come forth with joy to bid her welcome.

Bless the Lord. There they shall be reunited and engaged in praising Him for redeeming grace and dying love, long after the glaring sun shall have been blocked out by that effulgent blaze of Glory which forever shines around the Throne of God. "I was dumb. I opened not my mouth because thou didst it."

I have nothing of importance to communicate in the line of news except that 2 young ladies lately joined the Church here and are to be Baptized next Sabbath. Twelve months on the 6th inst since I saw Ma (Hannah Miller Earle) and I assure you the time seems long yet, for I want to see you all. I would have answered your letter a little sooner but thought it would be too late anyhow for you to write again before I leave here. So I will not require you to answer this letter this term.

Give my love to your Ma, sister, and cousin Ann and tell her not to scold about my silence about her last time for I have much to think about. And then I had troubled you so often with some messages that I thought I would keep my silence once.

There's Lizzie, and Mary, and Betty, and Sallie,
and Pattie, not less than a score.
If you see them just tell them all howdye for me,
for I have not time now to say any more.

Affectionately yours,
T. J. Earle

Like Alfred, Thomas J. Earle seeks to console the family with a view of heaven as a happier, safer home for little Bell.

Silas Reagan Jr. to Rebecca Whitten—Pickensville to Gowensville, South Carolina, 15 Nov. 1848

My own dear sister,

I have seated myself in this lonely old house to correspond with those who are nearest and dearest by the ties of nature. I think we have been a little negligent in writing to each other, particularly you. I am very lonesome, indeed, have no one to console me, no mother or sisters to sooth my cares and direct me along through this troublesome world.

I have nothing very good to write you. Minor has a pretty severe attack of the fever, has been complaining for the last two weeks, but was not confined until last Wednesday, ie, yesterday a week. Dr. Earle is waiting on him and thinks he is doing very well. He says he wants to see Cis and Elias very much. I think he is not dangerous with care. There are several cases of fever in this country since Dr. (Alfred) left. I am not very well myself, got the backache and the rheumatism, not very bad though.

I must tell you I went to Pendleton with Alfred and stayed from Monday till Thursday, got him pretty well fixed up. He has a very comfortable house to live in and, I think, will do very good business at that place, at least be better satisfied. Earl Holcombe's wife very sick yet, though improving slowly.

I am staying in the room the Dr. occupied when living here and I tell you I want to see Christmas come as bad as you ever saw anybody. I reckon I am getting tolerably well with my studies, as well as I expected. I am devoting my idle hours to settling up the Dr's. accounts. I visit less than anybody you ever saw, very dry times since the Dr. left. Pickensville is almost desolate.

I went into the circus at this place and was very much pleased with their performance. It was said to have been better here than at Greenville. You know it was rather a curiosity to me, the first I had ever seen.

How are things going at the Dark Corner? Reckon you will have a railroad there in the course of time. Make good crops? Done gathering corn? And sowing wheat? What about the wedding? Alf came back and would not tell me anything about it. You must have run him off from up there. He looked very sorrowful about something.

How are you getting along in the church? You have broken up the Sunday School till spring, I suppose, having no stove. Ours has died away to nothing and will remain so I guess as long as it is carried on by those who profess to be Baptists in principle. I have not heard but one sermon since camp meeting and that was preached by Jesse Dean about 8 miles above here. I could sorter get along when the Dr. was with me but since he has gone I am completely lost, have no one to talk to nor commune with. The nearest Baptist is Maj. Arial three miles above and he is ill with fever.

Has Mother been attacked with the pleurisy this fall? I hope she will escape. Alfred told Jo's little boy (Baylis Earle Whitten) was not well. What has become of Liz and Clayton? Are they gone to Columbia as they wrote me they were going to do? And Sallie and the Dr., have they moved home yet?

Alfred told me there was a great revival going on at New Prospect Church. I do hope it may be the means of warming old Cross Roads Church. Surely they will not live so always. I feel there is a want of zeal in the members. If so, that should not be. Go on. If you all do right your efforts will be crowned with success at some time or other though it may be far distant.

I wonder if Jo cares anything for me. Surely he will write me soon. You must kiss all the babies for me and do excuse this badly written letter for I have been in a great hurry and a bad light. Love and kisses to everybody.

Write soon,
Pluck

This is the first news of Alfred's move from Pickensville to the larger, richer, more sophisticated Pendleton. It is, like most of the correspondence between the members of the Silas Reagan Whitten family, filled with thoughts of home. They loved each other and their church, and were unhappy when separated by even a day's journey.

Rev. John Gill Landrum to Silas Reagan Whitten—Mount Zion to Earles Mills P.O., South Carolina, 10 Feb. 1849

Mr. S. R. Whitten, Esquire, Dear Sir,

I drop you these few lines mainly to inform you that I have Sam W. Walker who pledges to give for the use of the Cross Roads Church as much land as she may desire, five acres, at least. So soon as the boundaries are known he will make a deed in trust to some of you. Maj. H. J. Dean (lawyer and legislator) requested me to say that he will pay 10 cts or weatherboarding at cash price, probably the latter, as his sawmill is nearby. Franklin Vernon (son of Judge T. O. P. Vernon) subscribes $5 which he authorized me to have placed in his name on the list.

I will be at Cross Roads on Saturday before the first Sabbath in March to remain over three days, at least. I have an appointment at Pleasant Grove on Friday, the day previous which I did not remember when I appointed to commence the meeting at Cross Roads. But I will be on, on Saturday as above. My family all well. My respects to yours.

Yours truly,
John Gill Landrum

Silas Reagan is raising money for use by the church. Though never a member, he obviously gave Cross Roads a place of honor in his heart.

Harriet to Eleanor Kee Whitten—Pleasant Grove, Pontotoc, Mississippi, to Gowensville, South Carolina, 3 July 1849

My ever dear Mother,

It has been a long, long time since I wrote to you but I have often written home, and when I write I always consider my dear parents the first addressed. Oh, how glad would I be this morning could I meet and embrace that dear mother that watched over my infancy, whose tender care and sweet admonitions I shall always remember and cherish with a grateful heart. Tho fortune has placed me far distant from my native home and my beloved parents, brothers, and sisters, yet I am often with them in my imagination and love them still the same. You know my naturally affectionate disposition. You know how I love. You know my sincerity.

I received a kind, sweet letter from sister R a few weeks past. I was truly sorry to find out that you had been ill. Oh, how sorry I am to hear that you suffered so much. Ah, thought I, how glad would I be to stand round the couch of that dear mother and sooth and comfort her in her afflictions. I love to visit the sick and do all in my power to comfort and console them and especially my mother. Oh, how I would fly to her aid were it in my power and take pleasure in doing anything that would promote her welfare and happiness, but I earnestly hope that long ere this God has restored you to health.

Our family are all very well. I never enjoyed such good health in Carolina as I do here. I have not heard of half the sickness in this part of the country as I have, through letters, in Carolina, tho some of Mrs. Lankford's (mother-in-law) family have been sick. Coatsworth and three of the girls had the chills but their physician said their sickness was produced by their exposure and their coming here so late in the spring, but they are all pretty well now, and, I believe, like the country very well. I do wish you were all here. I do think, Mother, that residence in this country would restore you to health, and then, if I could get to see you once in a while, I should think I was about the happiest creature in the world, for I have a remarkably pleasant family and feel no disposition to murmur at my station in life.

There is a possibility of our settlement here becoming much more valuable. There is a railroad in contemplation from Mobile to Cincinnati. If it is accomplished it will pass very near us, perhaps through our place. Then this neighborhood will have advantages over almost any other and it is here thought certain that it will soon be commenced. We are getting along as well as we can. Our little place is getting to look like home. If we have our health and nothing ill befalls us, in a year or so we will have every comfort about us that is necessary to make life pleasant.

Does my father or any of my brothers think of coming out next fall or winter? Does brother Jo still think of moving west? How does brother A get on? Do his prospects brighten any? If he was here I think he could make a great deal more money than he can at Pickensville. How does sister N get on? I want to write to her soon, and sister R, I will answer her letter soon. Cousin Ben Earle (grandson of Judge Baylis Earle, who moved from South Carolina with father John and family to Pontotoc, Mississippi, and later moved on to Kentucky) called on us a few days since. I like him very much. He seems to be pleasant and plain. He is a nephew of Theron Earle (son of Judge Baylis), deceased, and you know, my second cousin. I told him we would be as close kin as possible, as kin is so scarce here. He says he was in Carolina twelve years ago at Mr. Earles and Uncle

Prince's (William Prince, husband of Lydia Maverick Earle, sister of Eleanor Kee). I have another relative living at Pontotoc who was a Miss Earle and married a Mr. High, clerk of this county. She is one of the Kentucky Earles. She sent me word that she would be certain to visit me this summer.

I heard from our Tennessee kin a few weeks since. They were all well. I reckon you think it strange that I never say anything of Uncle Davis (husband of Aunt Mariam Whitten) folks. I do not like to speak of people unless I could say something good and they have not, nor do not, merit a good name, have not been kind to me, or, at least, their kindness was of short duration, and that is the reason why they are among the unmentionables. Annsville Post Office is moving from their house. They are all well.

My little children grow finely. Eugenia weighs 30 and Willa 20. He is just like his uncles Alf and Rant.

May Heavens best blessings attend you and yours is the prayer of your affectionate daughter,

Harriet

Love to all.

Every letter from Harriet to her family extols the virtue of Pontotoc, Mississippi, for she wants them to resettle near her.

The entire collection contains surprisingly little mention of friction between family members. This one does. Harriet gets along poorly with Aunt Mariam Whitten Davis and her family. Narcissa echoes these sentiments later when writing from Mound Farm, Hancock, Georgia, home of Uncle Isaac Smith Whitten.

Louis H. Dickey to Silas Reagan Whitten—Greenville to Highland Grove, South Carolina, 6 Aug. 1849

S. Reagan Whitten, Esquire, Dear Sir,

I received yours dated today and am sorry to inform you that I have not got a woman to spare that would suit or answer your purpose. All that would do has got young children and some of them sick. I would be very glad to accommodate you if it were in my power to do so.

I am, sir, your humble servant,

Louis H. Dickey

Louis Dickey was a trader in slaves. The early Whittens had slaves, and casual mention of them is interspersed throughout the letters. This cruel institution was deeply embedded in southern culture, and we are reminded, sadly, that it, too, is part of our heritage.

Elnathan Walker to Silas Reagan Whitten—Rutherford, North Carolina, to Gowensville, South Carolina, 15 Aug. 1849

Mr. Silas R. Whitten, Dear Sir,

Your kind letter of the 21st ult. addressed to me from Gowensville reached me some weeks after date but the answer to it has been delayed thru design rather than negligence.

I have been contemplating a visit to Missouri for sometime past and it has not been an easy task to remove the doubts in the way of setting out immediately. I have of consequence needed a little time to consider your invitation.

Mrs. McMakin and an excellent friend residing with her, Miss O'Hear have expressed wishes that I should visit your neighborhood to preach and take charge of a school. To this disposition of my labors I have made some objections without determining anything definitely. I am rather inclined to conceive that a return to teaching would be going out of my calling under any circumstances, and that any step taken which would lead me to supplant ministerial labors with scholastic ones would be wrong.

These apprehensions, I must confess, have been, as yet, scarcely dislodged. I still wait the leadings of Providence with a partially formed purpose, at least, of visiting Missouri. Some three small Churches in this county have offered to present me a call, and seem to be anxious that I should remain. If this call should reach me in an orderly way, I donnot see how I could resist it and be conscientious. But the presentation of it is uncertain. Should I be notified of it at the expiration of two months, I might return to this place. Should this not be the case, I shall resume my purpose of going westward, unless special Providence should prevent. The interval between this and that, I have concluded to spend in your neighborhood in answer, to some degree, to your letter and those of some friends residing also in your community.

Providence permitting, I will leave my present place of lodging, with luggage, about the 20th or the 24th of this month. I shall stop at Mrs. McMakin's residence, and will be happy to make a more particular acquaintance with you there.

With sentiments of respect, etc.,

Elnathan Walker

This attempt by Silas Reagan to bring a teaching minister to the Gowensville community is hardly the work of an agnostic.

Harriet to Silas Reagan Whitten Jr.—Pontotoc, Mississippi, to Pickensville, South Carolina, 25 Aug. 1849

My dear Brother,

Three or four weeks have passed since I received your kind and affectionate letter. I wonder that I let it lie so long unanswered. I was so delighted to get it. I was not only pleased to hear from home but I was pleased with your improvement in letter writing. Oh, I thought it was a great letter to get from my little brother, Pluck. They tell me that you have grown to be a tall man since I left. It seems so strange. It was only yesterday that you were a little boy, but I believe I would know you if you were seven feet high.

You have heard of our disappointment in not going to Carolina. I was very sorry and I know that you all were, but it can not be remedied and it is useless to grieve about it.

You are from home, going to school. Why not come stay with us and go? We generally have excellent schools. We have a very good one now about three miles from us. I sometimes hope that some of my folks will come out here this fall. Why not come see us and look at the country? I would look for Father but he is so crippled up with his back that I fear he is not able to make the trip, but some of my brothers might come. The whole trip would not cost you $20.00.

About this time the Association is going on at Cross Roads. Oh, how I long to be there, and though I am not there in person, yet thanks be to God for the glorious privilege of meeting you all and my dear brethren whom I so much love at the Throne Of Grace, at the feet of Jesus, to offer up our most fervent prayers, our earnest petitions.

How does religion prosper in old Carolina? The Lord is doing great things for us here. For the last two weeks there has been protracted meetings between all denominations and great revivals all the time. I have attended preaching at two churches every day for two weeks and during that time I have seen numbers brought from darkness into light and made to rejoice in our blessed Savior and I have rejoiced with joy unspeakable. I love to see Christians meet together in harmony and love. I care not what their names are if they are true Christians. I never enjoyed more religion in my life than I have of late. I cannot express my happy feelings but you know how Christians feel when they get revived and cheered up. Oh, it is a joyous thing to put your trust in God. Oh, it affords me so much pleasure to think that so many of our family are religious and I would fain hope that ere this our dear father and brother (Ranson E.) have felt the renewing influence of the Holy Spirit. God is good and He will hear the prayers of His children and I am sure that the most earnest petitions are daily being offered up for their conversion. Father is a man of such kind benevolent temper he surely will be a Christian and who is more feeling and compassionate than my little buddy? Oh, what happy thought that we may be a family altogether reunited in Heaven.

I received a letter from sister R last week. I was truly glad to get it and hear that all was well. I wrote to brother A sometime ago but he doesn't write. We have not declined the idea of going to Carolina at some future time. If Father's family remains there and I keep my health I shall surely visit them.

I have not heard from Uncles Alfred or Ranson (Whitten) for some time, tho I rather think some of them will visit us this fall. I think you would enjoy a visit here very much. The country is beautiful. The people are very moral and generally religious. I think at least two thirds of the population are religious. Believe me Brother, I have never seen a drunk man since I left Greenville and I have been in company a good deal.

Well, I have almost finished my sheet and said nothing about my children. Eugenia and Willa are very sweet and interesting. Eugenia can assist me a good deal about domestic affairs. Willa is not two years old. He has learned the alphabet pretty well and speaks very plain and distinctly. Anna is called the greatest beauty in the world and I am sure nothing can be any smarter nor sweeter than she is (Rebecca Eugenia, William Henry, and Anna C).

I hope you will write soon and often. Love to all.

Your affectionate sister,

Harriet

Send this letter home that they may know how we get on. I will write to sister R in a few weeks.

Alfred Whitten to William L. Gilliam—Mount Comfort, Tennessee, to Montgomery, Texas, 7 Sept. 1849

Mr Gilliam, Dear Sir,

It is with pleasure I sit down to write you these lines. In the first place I will inform you that we are all in good health and better spirits than when you left us. I have sold my land and making my arrangements for your country. I am setting my mind for to start the middle of

November tho it may be later, but of the time I will write you again. I wish you and John (John Whitten Barrett, nephew) to make the best arrangements for me and family that you can. I shall want some corn and meat. You can be as good a judge of the quantity as me. I can't now say how much money I will be able to get there with, perhaps some two hundred dollars. I want a shelter for my family, as it would not do for me to go into the woods.

I shall leave that with you and John to make the best arrangement for us you can. I think I should like to settle near Montgomery for many reasons which we talked about.

I will write you again about the first of November.

Your friend,
A. Whitten

We have only this letter written by Uncle Alfred. It was given to me by a Texas relative. Alfred is preparing to move, and does so shortly thereafter. The John mentioned was a son of Alfred's sister Elizabeth, who moved to Texas in 1836 and settled in Madison County in 1840.

Mariah S. Whitten to Silas Reagan Whitten—Leesburg, Cherokee, Alabama, to Gowensville, South Carolina, 5 Oct. 1849

My affectionate cousin,

I have again taken my pen in hand to write to you. I expect you will think that I am quite anxious to write you again. It has been some years since I have had a letter from you. Now, my cousin, my opinion is that you do not want to be pestered in receiving and reading my letters. Do not think that I have felt anything of the kind. I have only formed my opinion from your own conduct in not writing to me. Now, if you want me to quit writing to you, don't answer this and I will assure you that you will not receive any more from me.

The family is well. Father (Charles Whitten Jr.) was 80 years old the 18th of last January. He is quite heavy and stout. We have only tolerable crops owing to the wet summer. Our wheat was almost spoilt with frost. Father made something like 30 bushels, the best crop in the settlement. We have quite a time in religion. There is revivals almost everywhere. I saw Thomas Grogan (son of Orpha Judson Whitten and Col. Thomas M. Grogan) some two weeks ago. He has had a long spell of sickness, has not been able to preach for some months. He is only able to ride about.

My dear cousin, I have never heard that you have made any profession of religion. I do feel, my cousin, if called to Heaven that I shall meet the smiles and approbation of a kind Saviour. Could I hear that from you it would be more pleasure than all the wealth and honor you could accumulate without it.

Excuse short and bad writing. Give my love to cousin Nelly (Eleanor Kee) and all your children and receive the same yourself.

Farewell in love, and prepare to meet me where pleasure never ends,

Mariah S. Whitten

Some Whitten researchers read this signature as Mureal L. Cherokee, Alabama, land records show her as Mariah S. This letter identifies her as a daughter of Charles Jr. and reveals the date of his birth.

Alfred Washington to Eleanor Kee Whitten—Pendleton to Gowensville, South Carolina, 25 Nov. 1849

Dear Mother,

I think it right enough to answer your letter which I received at Pickensville. I have now been in Pendleton only three weeks, and have for that space of time, enjoyed myself well. I find the people quite willing to receive me, and am quite satisfied that I get credit for all I am worth and sometimes, I fear, a great deal more. I have the promise of doing well here, although, as yet, nothing of importance has fallen to my lot, in a professional sense. Pendleton is all it's been represented to be, except less genuine piety than I expected. There are four Churches in this place, Baptist, Methodist, Presbyterian, and Episcopal. All seem to be rather flourishing but the first, which is barely able to stand, having only one male member and he incapacitated for the office of Deacon. A protracted meeting of five days has just been concluded in which an addition of one member only was obtained, i.e., Miss Mary Maxwell, John's daughter.

I have made the acquaintance of Benj. Sloan and shall visit him soon. I have visited Mrs. Mays, Mr. Robert Maxwell, Archer Caruthers, Mrs. James Sloan, Benj. Butler, all of whom received me kindly and politely. I think I have made the right move and made it in the right time.

There are five doctors here but the practice is pretty well consigned to two of them. I think I shall be able to make a pretty liberal division with those two. Of course it is uncertain, but the impression, so far, is decidedly in my favor.

I can't describe the contrast in living here and at Pickensville. I suppose I must feel something like Lot did when he escaped from Sodom into the land of Nod. I know a most excellent Methodist minister who has preached to large congregations in the neighborhood of Pickensville for about four years, has been instrumental in the erection of a church, has received into the membership of the church between 60 and 80 persons, and for all this service he has received in money the precious sum of 75 cents only and perhaps a few bushels of wheat from one or two individuals. The above facts were related to me by the minister himself and in confidence, about the middle of last week.

My much esteemed friend John Aurial caught the fever after I left and employed Folger, and I thought he would almost die before he would do such a thing, and he as good as told me so. So much for Pickensville. Henry Briggs wife was confined and Folger sent for, but before he got there the frolic was over with. There is no moral standard in that community and this Folger would be hissed out of any or almost any respectable company in the neighborhood of Old Cross Roads. He is just anything that the people call for from the witch doctor as high up as the detestable quack and shamos. It insults me to think that the man above named would treat me with so much injustice. While I stayed there I was sustained in the most decided and avowed opposition to him and to think a man having claims to respectability would employ him at all makes me very distrustful of him, let him be saint or sinner, and I regard it as criminal in a Christian to do it. But pardon such a digression. I am over.

Mrs. Holcombe has so far recovered as to make a visit to Pickensville. The Col. (Silas Reagan Jr.) gets on pretty well I think, but suppose he is homesick. I do think you ought to send him to school all next year, and perhaps Mr. Kenedy would be the very best teacher that could be procured. If he could be satisfied I would rather have him with me, and I know that it would be better to send him to a town or village. He eventually needs that sort of training, and will resist it until it is forced upon him. But I would not want him to stay with me unless he was fully satisfied.

I would be glad to have Ranty with me provided he could be spared. He ought to go to school constantly, for one years schooling now would be worth two after a while. But as I have not got the means to take either of them, I will not insist on them coming here.

I spoke to R. Goodlett to make application for my letter. I hope he has done so, and will forward it to me or the Baptist church at Pendleton very soon. If it has not been done, do not let a meeting pass without attending to it. May you continue instant in prayer in season and out of season, fervent in speech, serving the Lord.

Your Son,
A. W. Whitten

Alfred Washington is talented and complex. He writes well and composes some excellent verse. His education was more extensive than that of his siblings, and they look to him for leadership. We will see many facets of his personality and character through what he writes. This letter, written at the onset of his practice in Pendleton, initiates an interesting exchange with his mother and displays the first signs of an infatuation with the social and cultural advantages of the older, more aristocratic city. We will see it develop and evolve in subsequent letters. He makes it clear that he has no respect for Dr. Folger.

Alfred Washington to Silas Reagan Whitten Jr.—Pendleton to Gowensville, South Carolina, 27 Nov. 1849

Col.,

I received your letter 12 November and was glad to hear from you. In the latter part of last winter Finally came to me for a settlement but did not have the money to pay his account, which amounted to about $3.50, if I have not forgotten. He proposed to give his note for it but stated at the same time, that he would undoubtedly pay it in a few days, therefore I refused to take his note. Some time after that he came to Lotzers for medical aid. I met him and he said he had not still got the money but promised it fairly soon. If I have seen him since I don't recollect it, and as to my receiving the money on the day of the circus at Pickensville or at any other time is utterly false. You did not tell me whether you had got any corn from Adkinson or not, and whether you had made the gun trade. I would be glad if you could sell that gun to John for it would not be of much service to me here.

I expect you to write often and hence forward you may without incurring postage as Mr. Campbell has proffered to carry anything I want free of charge. I am sorry to hear that Minor does not mend and shall be quick to hear of more of them getting sick at that house.

I am obliged to you for the caution against becoming S I N (some religious organization). I cannot object to their system and suppose they afford a great deal of good, but I have never had one serious idea of joining them, and I am glad that you have not done so.

I hope that R S will find or not find in the extensive embrace of his ready and officious W P.

Write me soon. All's well as usual.

AWW

W. G. Woodson to Silas Reagan Whitten—Falmouth, Kentucky, to Gowensville, South Carolina, 15 Dec. 1849

My friend S. R. Whitten, Dear Sir,

I have been for some time trying to work myself into a proper mood to answer your very complementary and friendly letter, and I find myself, at last, prepared to do it, only in a rhapsodial and immethodical way. It has been very onerous to me to even to attempt to perpetuate composition. I have imbibed Crockett's notions of brevity, and very seldom write, only on business, and make as few words do as possible, and quit just as soon as I am done. A young gentleman wrote to Crockett in Congress for permission to marry his daughter. The answer was; Dear Sir, I reviewed yours, go ahead. D Crockett. I find myself in the attitude that auld Bobby Burns did once. He said, perhaps his epistle might turn out a song, and perhaps turn out a sermon.

Cousin Mary speaks glowingly of the vast improvements of your mountain regions. I rejoice very much to hear of it; and feel a little wanting in attempting to keep up with what may be the improvements of your day and time. You must not, however, show it or tell it to none but those of the old Copperas britches order such as we all used to wear up to twenty. I have the vanity to think if I could see you all, I could talk mountain talk with you yet, let your improvements be ever so vast.

You were correct in supposing that I had not forgotten the Dills. I recollect old Solomon as distinctly as though I had seen him this afternoon, with his slim legged britches and narrow backed coat, his little straight tin spurs and his small saddle skirts, and ham string stirrup leathers. I also recollect the very complacent guns that Wash Dill was wont to bestow as a kind of an outside ornament to the little groups that assembled at Harris old field to muster under Capt. Carter.

But my recollection has been prompted to some extent on that subject on visiting the painting gallery in Cincinnati. I saw pictures on the monument smiling away at grief and it reminded me very forcibly of Wash's grins. You say that old squire Davy has become defunct in the estimation of all honorable men. I like the old fellow and reckon it is for his flattery and his sense, not for any moral worth, for that he never had.

Cousin Mary expresses a great wish to see me. If I had one of these daguerreo type fellows here I'd send her my likeness, but as that is not convenient, I can tell her exactly who I look like. I think it is about twenty five years since I was passing by Logan's old mill away up in the mountains and I saw standing in the door a very grave, demure, dignified, and sage looking elderly gentleman. Well, I frequently think, when I look into the glass that I am the counterpart of what I there saw. On enquiring the name I learned it, Nicholas Gosling.

I would like very much to visit Greenville once more but I think it hardly probable. My health is rather moderate and laziness rather immoderate. There were three or four of us entered into an agreement to go to the mountains hunting this fall but the proximity of the cholera prevented.

I live thirty miles from Cincinnati and fifty from Lexington and one mile from Falmouth. We have a charter for a railroad connecting these two cities and Falmouth is made a point. If my constitution and bodily health was not such an entire wreck as it is, I would like to go south for repairs, but as it is, I merely patch up on as cheap and easy a place as I can. The old fabric has rotted and cleaned with a great deal more skill and judgement than I expected. I thought about four years ago that my days had dwindled to their shortest span, but Providence has thought fit for some purpose to protract them.

Making money is a great object, said by foreign writers, of nearly all intelligent Americans. The remark is perhaps too true. We have progressed on nearly all the vocations of life but none on happiness and morals, or at least, if there are, they fall stillborn for the press.

The region of the country that I live in grows and fattens a great many hogs, and my own opinion has long been, from my recollections of the thrift of hogs and the production of your country that you could not do a better business than to make your surplus consist of either pork or bacon. I intend to write to Cousin Mary in a few days, and for the benefit of her and her family, I will give her my views on that subject, though, perhaps, I had better delay till you furnish me a data, say what your land is worth per acre, how red clover prospers if at all, how much oats you can raise to the acre, and how much rye and corn. I commenced farming some ten years since on the old Carolina order. I raised corn, rye, wheat, and sold it to the poor, lazy, and worthless. I followed it for a few years and happened to meet with a man of sense, who soon convinced me that I was working for nothing, and finding myself instead now of selling grain, I would vastly profit when grain is cheap and hogs are a good price. A farmer should have some one thing to convert his surplus to money and that should be something that would yield it in mass, and not be like a great many handy dandy jacks of all trades and good at none. I am much inclined to think that hogs would be profitable to raise with you. We feed, down here, fields of oats, fields of rye, and fields of corn, one hundred acre fields at that. Some of our big farmers, they say that it cheapens labor too much to handle food for hogs.

Though I must desist, write to me without fail, and give me your agricultural pursuits and prospects and maybe if the railroad makes my land worth enough I may sell and return to raise hogs.

Yours, etc,
W. G. Woodson

Woodson may have been an old comrade from earlier days when Silas Reagan served as an ensign during the War of 1812. If so, it is the only reference we have to this part of his life.

Isaac Smith Whitten to Alfred Washington Whitten—Sparta, Hancock, Georgia, to Pendleton, South Carolina, 18 Dec. 1849

Dear Alfred,

I received your marked paper today and would much rather have received you. Why don't you come and see me? I want to see what kind of a fellow you are, and so wrote you in my last letter. I have a great attachment to your Father and family and think I could be of some value and satisfaction to some of my kin if you'd give me a chance.

I am now comfortably settled and fixed and want to see some of my close blood connections about me. Can't you spare a few days and come and see me? We are going to have some of our friends together on Thursday evening of Christmas. Come and spend Christmas with us. I live nine miles from Sparta and sixteen from Cummings on the railroad. If you'd come over I'd send for you to either of those places. If you come by public conveyance it is a little over 3 days travel by way of Ellerton, Washington, and here.

We are all well and desire to be remembered to your Father's family.

Yours truly,
I. S. Whitten

Though other writers tell of Uncle Isaac's letters and his interest in the family, this is the only one in the collection. He misses his relatives and wishes to keep in touch with them. As a fellow physician, Alfred must have been of special interest. Dr. Isaac Smith Whitten later admits his disappointment that the sons of Silas Reagan ignored his invitations.

Alfred Washington to Rebecca Whitten—Pendleton to Gowensville, South Carolina, 28 Dec. 1849 (badly damaged)

Dear Becca,

I imagine that you have spent a happy Christmas, surely Christmas at home is a treat. I cannot say that I enjoyed it very well, for just as I was preparing to celebrate it I got a call, and having had one a day or so previous it kept me busy with them. The cases to which I allude were 8 to 12 miles above this. One of them, I lost. The other recovered. The fatal case was my first, with the exception of a nag and 1 or 2 small ponies.

Christmas has passed by almost unnoticed. On last night a dance was given at Mr. Andrew Lewis's which I attended, not to dance exactly, but to see it and to approbate it, which I still do. I cannot see any impropriety in a social dance. Young people will be gay and often frivolous, they will amuse themselves in some way, and the old fashion plays and kisses to me are disgusting. I think that highly censurable and dancing is a pleasant exercise and healthful, too. It is keeping time with the music which all admit is good. Besides it gives grace and beauty to the movement of the body. The nicety of form and gracefulness in a ladies carriage and movement is paramount, and nothing so thoroughly drills her in this as dancing.

So far was writing to be sent last Friday, but just as I was writing a friend stopped in to talk, and I was prevented from finishing until the mail arrived. I send this by Cousin Prince who stopped on their return from Mississippi. I send with cousin a book belonging to the Col. (Silas Jr.) and a bullet mould which goes with a tool in Father's possession. I scarcely know what to say to you, but already I had said that I was engaged to marry two or three different persons. The people here don't seem to think that I can live without a wife, and I verily believe that some of them want me to get one bad enough, but it's rather uncommon to see an old bachelor fix himself up much when he intends to marry, and I have the character of being the best fixed man in town, and indeed, my house embodies as many comforts as any bachelor with whom I am acquainted, except Dr. Earle of Greenville. Tell the Col. since he left I bought a handsome ladies work table, worth $5.00. I received my goods from Pickensville, but not until today. Mr. Camplett said he carried his goods to Greenville and left them at the stage office for which I paid him 30 cents.

I told the Col. to ask you to make me some shirts and so on. Should you do it, make them all for studs of the regular size. I have plain gold studs for the bosom, but will continue the use of buttons on the collars and wristbands. Mr Gibson was here last Sunday. He preached for us. He told me a good many good things about home. What a good friend he is.

Tell the Col. that Mr. Williams who he will remember as the man I loaned the hair glove to will join the church and be Baptized tomorrow. Tell him that Mrs (?) of Pickensville died at today 11 o'clock. Tell him to write to me. I wish Ranty would come to see me and stay with me and go to school, or if he wants, to learn a trade. He could get a good situation here. I would prefer his being a carriage trimmer as it is the most profitable business in which he could engage, and generally healthy. There is a carriage trimmer here now that gets $2.00 a day for every day he works.

I send a letter from Uncle Isaac. Send to the Col. a copy of the pious poetry that Archer Campbell was to publish in the Messenger, but afterward concluded to withdraw it.

In great haste,
A. W. Whitten

Alfred Washington to Rebecca Whitten—Pendleton to Gowensville, South Carolina, 1 Feb. 1850

Dear Becca,

Your kind note and the shirts, no, the drawers were duly received. It would accommodate me to get the shirts, or two or three of them, as soon as they can be made, conveniently made. My present supply are splitting and already very spoiled, i.e., a good many of them. The Givins (chimar) would be gladly received.

The whole time, a day and two nights, that Thomas Earl remained with the friend here John Prince was drunk. So much so that he could scarcely be picked out of the way, and was spewing all over town like a dog. He even slipped into Holcombe's bar and took a gulp of liquor without paying for it.

You ask for particulars. Well, in front of my fireplace is large and handsome litter. On the mantle, at its middle, is a pretty little ladies work box arranged for needles, of which I have a full sack, spools, thread, and thimble. Immediately above the fire is the beautiful housewife which Cissa gave me. On either end of the mantle there sits a plain china looking glass such as is ordinarily used for bedrooms. On the work table to the right is placed my knapsack. On the top of that the family Bible and hymn books, and immediately back of this the glass with a drawer which I brought from Pickensville. My bed is in one corner of the room, wardrobe in the other. In the left hand corner by the fireplace is a door. In the right my wash stand and toilet which is really the best I have seen in Pendleton, and would be respected anywhere.

For want of space the half has not been told. I am treated with respect by everybody and with more than respect by some of the most influential men here, and with the ladies. I am busy. I am thought to be like Dr. J. B. Earle (mother's brother) in manner and appearance and often reminded of my resemblance to the Miss Sue Earle, Uncle Joe's daughter. I have already been employed by some of the most respected families in the whole community. Col. Taylor, one of the wealthiest and most respected men in the neighborhood has spoken to me to take his son as a student of medicine, which I have considered to do, and he will sit in next Tuesday. Besides I have been elected clerk of the Church and superintendent of the Sabbath School.

I hope you will pardon me for saying so much of myself and recollect that it is done to gratify a friend.

AWW

The country doctor is being noticed and employed by the respected and wealthy. He likes it.

Harriet to Alfred Washington Whitten—Pontotoc, Mississippi, to Pendleton, South Carolina, 10 Feb. 1850

My Ever Dear Brother,

Some few weeks past I received a very kind and affectionate letter from you and I did not then think I could neglect writing to you so long, but time passes away so swiftly and I neglect many duties that I ought to perform, but I know you possess a forgiving temper, therefore you will not indulge one hard thought, you will not for one moment think my devoted affection for you and all our dear family the least diminished. No, no, my dear brother, neither distance, time, or anything else can make me forget, or be less mindful of the friends I love so well.

I had a letter from sister R last week. She writes as though she is troubled and very melancholy. I was sorry to find it so. I fear that the family is not getting along well, and I feel very anxious about it. Sister N wrote to me some weeks ago, she seemed anxious to move to this country, she asked me to write to her what the prospects were for Elias as school teacher. I answered her letter and gave her some encouragement. Good teachers can make more money here than almost any other class of persons, but we will not have any but good. There is a gentleman teacher in our neighborhood who got something over $500 for 10 months. School society is good and the morals of the people better than any place I ever knew and I entertained great hopes that Elias would do better here than any other place, but sister R writes me that they are not coming. Perhaps it is all for the best.

I could not tell you how delighted I am that you have left that ugly, bad, dirty place, Pickensville, and to think that you have such a pleasant location as I have always thought Pendleton to be. I hope you will do well there, for the well being of each individual of my family concerns me much. God is all wise and knows what is best for us. May he guide and direct us in the way we should go.

I have not heard from Tennessee very recently. The last time I heard, Uncle Alfred was about to leave for Texas. We are expecting Mary Jane, Uncle Alfred's daughter and her husband, Mr Anderson, very soon, on a visit.

Aunt Mariam Davis received a letter from Uncle Isaac last mail. In that letter he complains a great deal that his relatives have forsaken him, says that he feels the greatest affection for them, says that he is getting old, has a great fortune, and nothing would give him more pleasure than for his relatives to share his fortune, but that when he offers to do them a kindness, they refuse it and insult him, and added that within the last year or two he had received a very insulting letter from one of James sons and one from one of Silas's sons. I cannot think that any of my brothers insulted him intentionally for an offer of kindness. If they did they were certainly wrong, for we should always be grateful for proffered kindness.

Well, I reckon of all the sweet children that ever you saw in your life, mine take the lead. They are really smart and the greatest little beauties that you ever saw. Willa looks a great deal like you and has an extraordinary memory. He is now about two years old and knows all his letters. I tell you, they are an interesting little group.

I will write to sister R in a week or two. She told me that Silas was going to school at Anderson. I am glad to see that he is determined to have a good education. I hope he will be successful.

May Heaven's best blessings attend you is the prayer of your sister,

H. E. Lankford

In an earlier letter, we see Uncle Isaac inviting Alfred to visit him. There is no indication that he made the trip. Perhaps this was the insult he mentioned.

Thomas Goldsmith to Silas Reagan Whitten—Plain to Gowensville, South Carolina, 22 Feb. 1850

Silas Whitten, Esquire, Dear Sir,

As I am deprived of the opportunity of coming to see you at the time appointed, I will say to you that I have declined the idea of buying your land from the fact that I have become very much dissatisfied myself. Also some of my family are very much opposed to it and I do not wish to render them unhappy by moving against their will to any place.

Yours truly,
Thomas Goldsmith

The land has been on the market for many months. Silas wants to move.

Ranson to Silas Reagan Whitten—Fayette, Tennessee, to Gowensville, South Carolina, 4 March 1850

Dear Brother,

I now break a long, yes, a very long, silence that I can render no sufficient reason for on my part. And knowing the family failing I will attribute your remissions to neglect and laziness. The cause of my writing at this particular time is that I have bargained off your interest in our father's land and ask that you make title to the same. It is the first opportunity that I have had to sell it for a fair price and for cash, which sale I hope will be satisfactory to you. If so you will execute a deed according to the form I enclose and have it proven and certified in proper form and send it to me. The money is to be paid, $100 when I can deliver the deed. In the event of your approving the sale instruct me how to remit the proceeds.

As to your Forked Deer land I know nothing. I have written either 2 or 3 letters to different persons but have no answers and it has never been convenient to go to where it lies.

The health of my family is very good, the same may be said of Desbough and Anderson families, (husbands of Rebecca and Mary Jane) Alfred's two sons in law, and of John Boyd's, Mary Dalton's (daughter of sister Nancy) husband, Mary has driven her pigs to a sorry market. Our children grow well. Edwin weighs 128, Harriet 71, Irvine 53, Lawson about 40, and Fidelia about 25 or 30. She was a year old last August. Rebecca has two living children and has lost one. Mary Jane has none living, has lost one. Mary Boyd has a daughter about a year old.

I am living on that same poor hill and keep pretty nigh about even. At all events I do not gain much. The past summer and fall have been unusually healthy about. Memphis cholera has been pretty severe at times and small pox has been there for some two or three months and was scattered through the country some. There was two or three deaths and twelve or fifteen cases in from four to eight miles of me. Care and vaccination, I believe, have stopped it, as I have heard of no new cases for some weeks. Vaccination has been almost universal through our country recently.

As my children grow up I feel more disposed to change my location in consequence of the poor opportunities of education that surround me, but do not know that I shall do so. As you are aware, my inclination has been Mississippi but I have never been far in that state since I moved here. A day or two ago I received a line from Irvine Sullivan (Ranson's brother-in-law) requesting me to visit eastern Alabama this spring in view of settling on the Coosa River, somewhere in the vicinity of where uncle Charles Whitten lived when you were in this country. I don't think I can go this spring if at all. Irvine writes that he expects to settle his father and mother near him this fall. He lives in Rome, Georgia about thirty five miles above the place where he wishes me to look at.

We have had about three or four old fashioned snows this winter, nearly all the balance of the time rain. Consequently farming operations are backward. Notwithstanding, the great opening of new country west of us, lands are rising in value and our town and county improving more rapidly than at any previous time. Memphis now numbers 12 or 14 thousand inhabitants, various manufacturing, steamboat building all are carried on there and the U. S. Navy Yard at that place is quite an establishment.

I see I am running out of paper before I am near done but must close. Give this an early answer. Write to me in detail what your children are doing. Tell Rant I think he ought to write to me, and Alf, where is he and what is he doing, not giving lobelia and cold water, I reckon. I think I owe him a letter and if I knew his whereabouts, I would pay some of these days.

My love to all,
R. Whitten

To S. R. Whitten:

Brother Alfred left here with his family for Texas some time in the latter part of November. He saw he had overpaid all the legatees of our family estate which I suppose will be news to you if you have not been more fortunate than I suppose you have. He was still owing me a balance of $65 on a note that he gave me on the settlement and division that him, James, and myself made which he said he would settle before he left, but some 30 hours before he started he brought up an account as an offset against my note made up principally of what Barrett (husband of sister Elizabeth) had received more than the rest of us in that settlement and interest on the same. My share of which amounted to near as much again as the note I had on him. He did not ask me to refund, but only claimed it as an offset. I first thought he might go scot free, but on reflection I thought it a piece of imprudence to use no harsher term that ought to be rebuked. I therefore sued him and forced him to secure it to me. I will probably get it the last of this year. I don't know that he left any debts unpaid, only those due his brothers and sisters. He went by water, without wagon or horse. His money matters I knew nothing of. He had been very cool to me for a year or two and left hot. Peace to him.

R. W.

Records from Fayette, Tennessee Courthouse, Book P (1850 - 1851), Whitten, S. R. to Joel Harris, State of Mississippi, Tippah County.

I, Silas R. Whitten of County and State aforesaid, sell, etc., to Joel Harris for $100 my distributive share of land on headwaters of Wolf River, belonging to estate of John Whitten, deceased, entered in the name of J. Nichols 142 1/2 acres, which J. Howard sold to J. Whitten in Sec. 2, Range 5. 13 January 1851, R. Whitten, Curtis Harris Appeared Silas R. Whitten 3 February 1851. Reg. 24 February 1851.

Widely circulated among Whitten researchers, Ranson's 1850 letter tells us of his children and those of brother Alfred and sister Nancy. "Mary has driven her pigs to a sorry market," he says, of Nancy's son-in-law. Irvine Sullivan wants Ranson to consider moving to Cherokee County, Alabama. His father lives there. Ranson reminds his brother that Charles Whitten Jr. lived in that county on the Coosa River at the time of a visit to Fayette, Tennessee, by Silas Reagan. It contains the only known reference to this trip, which may have been occasioned by the death of his father in 1837. The reference to the Forked Deer land refers to land left Eleanor Kee by her father. Col. John Earle's estate included land lying on Big Forked Deer River in Tennessee.

That there was widespread use of smallpox vaccine in the backwoods of Fayette County only fifty years after its discovery by Edward Jenner in England indicates that new ideas in health care were being widely accepted. Chickasaw Bluffs has been renamed Memphis and become a city.

Ranson's postscript establishes that Alfred left for Texas in late November 1849, traveling by water. Reference to a dispute with his brother has been interpreted by some Texas descendants as unjust criticism of Alfred. Ranson's comments need not cause resentment. Alfred was respected and admired by those who knew him in South Carolina, Tennessee, and Texas. He served with distinction in positions of trust, was postmaster, official of his church, and died without blemish on his reputation. He had been appointed executor of his father's estate. One of his brothers did not approve of the way he handled it. This was not unusual in those days when the courts did not oversee the work of an executor as closely as they do today. Litigation between family members and executors was fairly common. The families of David Barrett, husband of Elizabeth, and of Alvin Earle, son of Charles Whitten Jr. and Millicent Reagan, went through court battles over the division of estates.

We have only this record of contact between Alfred and the rest of his father's family after he moved to Texas; his sister Mariam moved to Montgomery, Texas, after the death of her husband. Alfred lived there. Surely he also kept up with the Barretts and Whittens of Houston, Madison, and Wharton counties, all close by. We can only hope there was reconciliation between the two brothers.

Harriet to Rebecca Whitten—Pontotoc, Mississippi, to Gowensville, South Carolina, 20 March 1850

My dear sister,

I have now before me your truly kind and affectionate letter and think I cannot spend an hour better than in writing to you for I know you are all anxious to hear from me and I am indeed anxious to hear from you. Oh, it grieves me to think that I hear from home so seldom, for believe me, my sister, I take just as deep an interest in the welfare of my parents, brothers, and sisters as I used to when I was with you. True, we are separated by hundreds of miles. Rivers roll and mountains rise between us. Years have passed since we met and yet I love you all just as dearly as I used to when I associated with you every day, and indeed I am often with you, clinging around you with fondest affection. Oh, what a privilege that our thoughts and affections can visit our friends in distant lands.

April 7, Well, Sister, since I commenced writing the above, I have received a letter from sister Narcissa informing me that Father had sold out and was moving somewhere and I never could tell you how delighted I was to think that Father had succeeded in selling and that you would all, perhaps, be more comfortable, and the hope that you might perhaps come to this country or somewhere nearer to me. The hope of seeing you all again threw me in such excitement that I hardly had any reason for one whole day. But Sis, it is not worthwhile to try to tell you how I felt. You perhaps know something about it. But then, when I reflect, it is a serious matter. Our parents were well settled. They are now old and will have to undergo some difficulties in settling in a new country, but I think Father will be able to buy improved land and that will be a great advantage.

Now Father, I do insist that you come to this beautiful country and see it, at least before you buy elsewhere. I have often heard you speak of going to Holly Springs in Mississippi. This country is said to far surpass that in beauty and excellence and is much more healthy, but Holly Springs is only 60 miles from here. Now if you and some one of my brothers will come out here this summer I am sure you would be well pleased, and as Alexander is well acquainted with the country, he would take pleasure in showing it to you. If you come you had better come as early as possible for it is thought there will be a great rush to this neighborhood for land this summer. If you cannot come on horseback I would suggest the propriety of your coming in a carriage or buggy, but if you do not come here at all I do hope you will have a pleasant home somewhere to your liking, for I do know that my greatest wish is for you all to be settled and satisfied. I want you to be entirely pleased with a home, then I will be reconciled. The welfare of you, everyone, is near and dear to my heart, but I think more about my parents because they are old (father was 56; mother, 58). I hope you will write often and tell me what you expect to do.

My health is good. Our children grow finely and are just as sweet as ever. The two eldest know their letters and Eugenia can sew. She teaches me a great deal about a needle and thread. Anna is the prettiest and sweetest child you ever saw. She can speak some words very plain. We have a pretty good garden, though the spring is rather backward. I have a great many chickens and eggs and make a great deal of butter. Tho it is rather cold, the prairies are covered with the most beautiful wild flowers. Do write soon and tell me everything.

Your sister,
Harriet

My husband joins me in love to you all.

Silas Reagan has sold his land, and Harriett is beside herself. She wants the family to settle near her and is promoting the idea. Scarcely one month before this letter was written, we see the Goldsmith letter declining to buy. Later, during 1851, shortly after the family moved to Mississippi, Silas Reagan returned to Carolina. I can see no reason for this other than a hitch in that all-important land sale.

Thomas J. Earle to Rebecca Whitten—Penfield, Georgia, to Gowensville, South Carolina, 26 April 1850

My much esteemed cousin,

Rather unexpectedly, yet with much pleasure, I received your last affectionate and sweet letter. For it, let me return you my most sincere thanks, though poor the offering or humble the return. And I know you too well to suppose that the offering of gratitude of an honest and unaffecting heart would be by you despised or even not appreciated. I felt really rebuked at the reception of your letter for I could only unbraid myself for my long silence. No apology from you was necessary. I should have been pleased to have heard from you but yet I did not think hard of you for not writing and your silence had not been the cause of mine, i.e., for some months it has not. Tis true I waited some time to have you answer my last letter but have been intending to write you anyhow, especially since I saw you in the winter.

You were right as to my dropping many correspondents but I was candid, and usually am, when I told you I wished you to write to me. Though others might be more talented and educated, which I doubt, yet there were none I esteemed so highly as yourself. None of them were like you, the friend of my youth, a kindred spirit. To me a letter is not valuable on account of its rhetoric and fine language but because I see in it the image of my friends.

But I must let this suffice as a preface and advance to say something of more interest, if I am able. I have just read your letter for the fifth or sixth time and feel every time a painfully pleasing sensation. I know how to sympathize with you in your despondency and know too the need of a friend under such circumstances. But, alas, what you said is but too true about friendship. To many it seems to be a thing to which they are entire strangers. They profess to have it but like the false professor of Godliness that "dureth for a while but when tribulation, etc., ariseth he is offended". As Luke adds he falls away. So false friends stand well in the sunshine but when the black and chilling winds of adversity blow they fall away. Their friendship withers from the obvious reason that "they have not root in themselves" But are there not some who may be trusted, In whose breasts we find a chord which is ever tuned in unison with our own? Who can "Rejoice with those that do rejoice and weep with those that weep"?

When fortune is smiling whole crowds will appear,
Their kindness to offer and friendship sincere.
Yet change but the prospects and point out distress
No longer to court you they eagerly press.

Is friendship indeed but a name, a charm that lulls to sleep? Ah no, it is more than an empty sound. I've seen her heavenly form. I've heard her angelic voice. My soul has been consoled and comforted by her gentle influence. Yes, there is such a thing as friendship.

The thread of our lives would be dark, Heaven knows
If we were not with friendship and love intertwined.
Oh friendship thou balm and rich sweetness of life
Kind parent of ease and composer of strife
Without thee, alas! What are riches and power
But empty delusions, the joy of an hour.

But what shall I say to the part of the letter where you tell me we've taken our last goodbye. It is a melancholy thing for friends to part, even for a short time but it is sad and afflicting to be obliged to take the last adieu. Like the Ephesian elders I "sorrow most for the words that you spake that I should see your face no more".

Little did I think it was so to be when I told you good bye. Then indeed I indulged the fond hope of again meeting with you and many of my friends around the cheerful fire and talk, and sing, and pray, and praise our common Lord. And is it so? Or do I dream? Shall I again return to "the green land of my childhood, my home, and my dead" and find not the friends of former days? Shall I not meet her who has been my best friend, who was wont to greet me with a sister's tender regard? Shall we not again talk of the love of our Jesus and speak of our trials, and sorrows, and hopes, and fears?

Yes I fear it is ever so. Would that it was otherwise.

Will she be missed? Ah, why ask the question? Can an affectionate heart be treacherous? Can a faithful heart forget? When the young friends are with me assembled around the cheerful fire to engage in our innocent sports, and wiles, and cheat dull care out of a moment of joy I shall miss my friend. When we assemble around the family altar and send up our united prayers like sweet incense to the Throne of Our Heavenly Father my thoughts will dwell wearily on the past for I shall not hear the sweet voice of my friend among us. When I rise in the Holy Sanctuary and survey with solemn awe the waiting assembly of dying fellow men one seat will be vacant. My thoughts will delight to linger around scenes of former days and dwell with increased interest on the joys that have "gone glimmering through the dreams of things that were".

Well I believe I might as well stop now for I believe I have not much more to say. I might say much more in anticipation of your new home but I will only say a word or two of encouragement. Tis true you go to a strange land and "know not the things that shall befall you there". But you go sustained by the Faith of the Gospel, knowing in whom you have believed and with full assurance that He is able to keep that which you have committed to his charge. In our hours of despondency we are apt to feel deserted, and think the world ungrateful, friends untrue, and God at a distance. But let us, under such circumstances remember the blessed promise; "They that trust in the Lord shall not be confounded, world without end. Though a good man fall, yet shall he not be utterly cast down for the Lord upholdeth him with His hands." And it is a consolation to know that our Savior was, like us, tempted, tried, distressed, reviled, scorned, mocked, and deserted in the most trying hour.

Let the world despise and ban me
They have left my Saviour too.
Human hearts and looks deceive me.

Thou art not, like them, untrue.
And while Thou shall smile upon me
God of wisdom, love, and might
Foes may hate and friends may scorn me
Show Thy face and all is bright.

I expect to go to Marietta soon. I have been elected a delegate from the Young Men's Missionary Society here to the Georgia Baptist Southern Convention and if I go I shall pass through Atlanta where I hope to have the pleasure of seeing cousin Lizzy.

I have here no news of interest to you. I am getting along pretty well in my studies. Have seen Mr. Cooper's sister, favors you some, light hair, blue eyes, and more clever than her brother C. I hear from home very seldom and consequently get but little news.

Love to all the girls. Tell Cissa (Rebecca's sister, Narcissa Amaryllis) to remember Tom for he has not forgotten her. Love to your Ma especially and all the family. Cousin, I have tried to write but it is a labored effort but maybe I can do better next time. Receive it for it comes from the abundance of the heart. And write to me again, I beg you. Don't delay so long though. I could say more but have filled my sheet and must close, begging you to accept the kind regards and friendship of,

T. J. Earle

Alfred Washington to Eleanor Kee Whitten—Pendleton to Gowensville, South Carolina, 26 April 1850

Dear Mother,

Your kind letter of the 19th was duly received. I am always pleased to get a letter from you but more particularly now, since you have just recovered from a long and painful confinement. I was sorry to learn of Father's indisposition and that of Joe's babe. I hope they are all better by now.

I am fully aware of your great anxiety for me to accompany you west, but I must confess to you that for sometime past I have had an overwhelming presentiment that I shall not be able to do it. I cannot say heartily that I wish to do it. The time of life has long ago arrived for me to throw off the shackles of family affection and submit to whatever offers the greatest amount of good to be accomplished for myself, my family, and my fellow man. Beyond these, I have not a single desire or aspiration, and to accomplish these I am willing to make any sacrifice which the well directed dictates of an honest, conscientious, sincerity may require of me.

The only condition on which I could leave here, i.e., the entire payment of my debts and to give my individual responsibility for them to the family, Father is unable to comply with. He has already done much for me and I doubt not his entire willingness to do more, and do all he can, and more, much more, than he is able to do. But aside from family ties and family gratification, I cannot see the first inducement for me to go with you. The very idea of practising medicine in the west, with my present conception of its awful reality is humiliating and pride stricken. That society which I delight to cultivate and own is not there to be found. The genial aspirations of professional worth and distinction that spring up in my mind now are lost in the forgetful cup of wistful inebriation, of wistful quailing. I write you the worst for you to meet it at once. I have no thought of going with you. I did write to Father, making some propositions to him, not one of which have been answered, although I received an account of their reception through Elias, who had been appointed a committee to reply. They would, i.e., the committee, would have been promptly replied to but at that time I had a very painful fellen on the forefinger of my right hand and was unable to write. Since that, as good fortune would have it, my finger has recovered without deformity or stiffness and any communication from the committee shall be punctually attended to. But more of this at some other time.

I saw Mr. Kenedy yesterday who stated that Silas was well and expressed much regret at his leaving. I hope you will arrange to keep him at school until the expiration of the third quarter. I am getting a fair share of practice and the prospect ahead is encouraging. I send Ranta the Messenger enclosed. You will see a letter from my old friend J. L. Harris, in reply to one I wrote him since I came here. I have had two daguerreotypes taken, one of which I design for you the other for Harriet. Three weddings have just come off, which are announced in the paper.

Affectionately your son,
A. W. Whitten

Alfred doesn't want to move to Mississippi with the others, feeling that to practice medicine in the wilderness would demean him. He is basking in his new-found social status. The next few letters allow us to peer into his mind and heart as he struggles with his not inconsiderable ego and his great love for the family. The remainder of the letter deals with his financial situation. The use of medicalese in word choice and sentence structure tends to veil his meaning. Doctors today remain afflicted with this malady. Alfred simply says he cannot leave Pendleton and go off into the wilderness without paying his debts, and he does not have the money.

Silas Reagan Whitten Jr. to Narcissa Amaryllis—Slabtown to Gowensville, South Carolina, 10 May 1850

My dear sister,

I have seated myself for the first time since I came to Slabtown to write to you, but although I have neglected you, think you not I that am void of those feelings which should ever exist between brother and sister. No, dear Sister, I am just the same that I always was, just as affectionate as I ever was. The last time I heard from home brother Joseph was very ill. I hope before this time that he has entirely recovered. He should take better care of himself anyhow.

By the by, Alfred found me, on his return home, in a pretty bad fix. I was taken with a swelling in the mouth which continued to swell for two days and nights until it was as large as a common piece of chalk. I was detained from school four days on account of it, but I have got pretty well again, at least well enough to make a hand at the table. I am getting along very well indeed with my studies, as also with the folks generally. This place does not suit me very well for you know I am very fond of company and here the chances are very bad indeed. I have never been anywhere but to Dr. Robinson's.

Well, Sis, I reckon you are all fixing up for the contemplated move and I do think we should make every edge cut. Mr. Kenedy (his teacher) is very anxious for me to remain longer than vacation. He is just as kind to me as Father would. I think you can't well do without me in preparing for the move. Therefore I think I had better return at the time appointed. The vacation will come on about the last of June or the first of July. I don't know which yet. Tell Father I will let him know. I will commence reading Greek on Monday morning. It is very hard but a body can't expect to get along in this world without some trouble.

Well, Sis, how do they all get along at old Cross Roads? I often, indeed, think of that place and the interesting sermons I have heard preached there, but it seems that since I left home I have been rather unfortunate in that respect. I have heard some good sermons and some bad ones. I walked to Pendleton the other day, twelve miles, a pretty good walk, too, for one not accustomed to it.

Well, I must, when I come home, give Elias a brushing for not writing to me. How is he getting along with his school? Cis, I don't know where this letter will be mailed. The mails are so inconvenient about here. You must come with Father when he comes for me. You must write me soon and tell the rest of them to do the same. Respects to everybody that wants to hear from me.

Your brother,
Silas R. Whitten Jr.

Silas Jr. to Rebecca Whitten—Dr. M. B. Earle's, Pickensville to Gowensville, South Carolina, Sunday, 2 June 1850

My dear sister,

Knowing that you are anxious to hear from me, I embrace the first opportunity to write. I arrived home on Tuesday evening, safe and sound, found them all well and glad to see me. I am very anxious to hear from home and hope to by tomorrow's mail. I hope you and my dear mother have both recovered. Take good care of your self and make Mother do the same. I am uneasy about her all the time, for I know she is so easy to relapse.

I received a letter from Alfred yesterday, was well as usual. I hear he is getting a good practice, which of course he will get if he attends to his business and be careful.

I hope Ranty got home safe and in good time after I left him. I came to Pickensville and stayed till evening. About one o'clock they had a tremendous wind which blew the louvres out of the store piazzas all about there. After it ceased, I walked home and I tell you it was a pretty rough walk.

Well part of my object in writing was to let you know when the vacation comes on, which takes place on the last Thursday and Friday in June, this month. Tell Father I shall look for him strong and certain, or somebody else, if he can't come to be here for the examination. He must be certain to come on Friday evening and then we can go to Pendleton on Saturday if we wish. Mr. Kenedy requested the boys to invite their friends to the examination, and if I have any that wish to come, you can invite them for me. I shall not stand a good chance with my class, but I guess by hard study I can come it.

Well, I reckon you will all be mightily delighted next week when Lizzie comes. I had almost wished to be with you and enjoy some of the scenes and pleasures of meeting an old and valued friend. It has been a long time since I saw Betty. How is Sally? Hope she has recovered from her attack.

I hope you all will be preparing in some way or other for the contemplated move to the states. If nothing happens, it shan't be very long until you shall have my assistance, weak as it may be. Every edge must be made to cut, and nothing left undone, which should be done. I am just ready to start to meeting, and in fact, I believe I have nearly written out of a subject anyhow.

May the Blessings of the Most High in Heaven rest upon you all.

Your brother,
Silas R. Whitten Jr.

NB The object of having the vacation, or rather the examination, on both days is to examine the smaller classes the first day. Come Thursday evening if you can.

Pluck,
Double Branch, South Carolina.

Harriet to Rebecca Whitten—Coonwah, Pontotoc, Mississippi, to Gowensville, South Carolina, 17 June 1850

Poem surrounded by locks of hair labeled: Alfred, Narcissa, T. E. P., Thomas, R. M., and Harriet.

To My Sister

Repine not dear sister, oh, grieve not for me,
That I dwell in a climate far distant from thee.
At home and abroad on the land, on the sea,
I'll think of thee, Sister, wherever I be.

Farewell my dear Sister, farewell for a while.
Though I leave you in tears, may I meet you in smiles.
Though afflictions and sorrows and troubles may come,
I'll meet you, dear Sister, in Heaven, our home.

Harriet to Rebecca Whitten—Pontotoc City, Mississippi, to Gowensville, South Carolina, 17 June 1850

My dear sister,

By the last mail I received your anxiously and long looked for letter. My anxiety to hear from home was indescribable since I had heard of brother Jo's illness. Then when I read your letter I found that Mother and you both were sick and it was almost more than I could bear. You know that I am naturally very sympathetic and when I hear of so much affliction and distress in my father's family it renders me very uneasy. Could I be with you to aid in waiting on the sick. Oh, it would give me much pleasure to lend a helping hand, but I am far away and can only think of you and sympathize with you. I am astonished to hear of so much sickness in Carolina, and here, let me add, there is no sickness at all in this country. In all the surrounding country the people seem to enjoy perfect health. I do not hear of a single case and the physicians are all idle.

I received my brother's (Alfred) daguerreotype in due time. Oh, I was delighted to get it, and since I hear that Brother is not coming, I prize it so much the more. It is the most perfect likeness I ever saw. Oh, I regard it as a precious gift. I wrote to Alfred last week. I am sorry he is not coming with Father to this country. It would be such a pleasure to have him with you. I do not blame him for remaining at Pendleton. It is such a delightful location. It is sad to think of leaving him alone, and yet, he will not be alone. Let us all, my sister, leave our Brother in the care of an all wise God. He is such a good friend. He will never leave nor forsake him. He will support and strengthen him in sorrow and disappointment and comfort him in affliction. Oh, have you not learned that it is good to depend upon the Lord?

I feel particularly uneasy with regard to our dear mother's bad health. I know she is so delicate. If she should get to this country I hope the change will be very beneficial to her, and to you all. Oh, you know not how anxious I am to see you all and I certainly shall if you come to this country, but why do you not say that you will call at our house and spend some time? It would afford us so much pleasure.

I do hope you will get a home to your liking. When Father settles again, if you are all satisfied I shall be perfectly so, for my most ardent wish is for the welfare of the family. I shall be all anxiety until I hear from home again. You complain of my not writing. Why Sister, I write at least three letters home to where I get one. I hope you will write oftener and tell me what you are all doing.

This has been a very backward spring and cotton crops are not at all promising. Corn crops look pretty well. I have a fine garden, an abundance of vegetables. My health is pretty good, except the rheumatism in my knees. I have made every effort to check the disease but have failed.

You said you heard I had another babe. Who on earth has been telling tales on me? Tell me when you write. Well I do reckon Anna (Anna C., born 14 April 1849) is the sweetest child you ever saw. She is standing round me now, prattling. She can articulate several of the alphabet very plain and whenever Eugenia and Willa come to recite their lessons Anna is as ready to learn as they.

I deeply regret that brother Jo has such bad health. I fear his constitution is so much impaired that he will never be stout again.

I have not heard from Tennessee in a long while because I have neglected to write. Uncle R is generally very punctual to write to me. I received a very good letter from Uncle Isaac a few weeks ago and should have answered him before this time. I have never heard what has become of Uncle Alfred. I should like to know (her father's brothers Ranson, Isaac Smith, and Alfred).

Remember me affectionately to all my friends. Tell them that I love them just as much as I used to do. My husband joins me in best wishes for you all.

Your sister,
Harriet E. Lankford

The daguerreotype Alfred described as having been made for Harriet has arrived in Mississippi. I wonder who has it now. She wishes to have news of Uncle Alfred, who left Tennessee for Texas in late 1849.

Alfred Washington to Eleanor Kee Whitten—Pendleton to Gowensville, South Carolina, 10 Aug. 1850

Dear Mother,

I did not censure you for not writing to me, indeed think I may regard myself as particularly favored to receive a letter from you at all, knowing well that you are not in the habit of writing letters, and that your hand has become somewhat stiffened and unsteady. It was a source of much gratification to me to hear that you seem all so improved in health, that you were cheerful, and had the prospects of living so well and so happily. Pleased was I, too, to hear that you were making preparations to move and that you had already almost consented to be separated from me, conscious it would be better we should part. I submit, and it is deeply an act of submission. The older I get, the longer I live in the literal sense of the word, the more disposed I am, the more I desire and long to be with my parents, my brothers and sisters, my friends, the companions of my youth. This is reality and these things are more binding than all else besides.

I fear you are mistaken in supposing that I do so well. That I make considerable money is not to be disguised. I am blessed with practice and in the midst of being comfortable, but my charity practice equals that of any other here, and I thank God, for it is a blessing to be able, in some way to be charitable, but my expenses are very heavy and upon the whole, I do not look upon the practice of medicine as being profitable.

I had been informed that Ann Prince was permanently afflicted. Sorry her health is not so good and that she falls so short of your desires and expectations in a religious point of view. I hope, however, that the Lord will have mercy upon her and that she yet may become reconciled to Him through the grace of the Blessed Redeemer.

I am well and all others of whom you would inquire. I cannot answer your letter at length. This must suffice now.

Letters from Rebecca and Silas have come.

Your son,
A. W. Whitten

NB I cannot say that I will go to the Association,

AWW

Alfred's love for his family begins to assert itself.

Harriet to Rebecca Whitten—Pontotoc, Mississippi, to Gowensville, South Carolina, 12 Aug. 1850

My dear Sister,

Reckon you will begin to think long of the time since I wrote and yet I am sure that you get letters from me oftener than I do from you. You know not how hard I take it because I do not hear from home more frequently but suppose you are so busy preparing to leave there that you cannot write much, yet I would be glad to often hear these simple words, we are all well, for you have had so much sickness at Father's that it causes me to feel a great deal of anxiety about you all.

I never heard of so much good health as there is through all this country, but it is the most unusual season in every sense of the word that I ever heard of. The cotton crop is very poor and I hear of many neighborhoods where the people will not make as much corn as they planted solely on account of the dry weather, but in our neighborhood the prospects are tolerable fair. Alexander has 10 or 12 acres in cotton and expects to have made at least 1000 bushels of corn, but it is greatly injured with dry weather.

My little children are all very sweet and bad enough. They all grow finely and are very healthy except Anna. She is the greatest little pet you ever saw. She is a little delicate creature and her health is bad. She has the asthma and sometimes the croup. Our physician who waits on her says he very much doubts whether she can be kept alive until she is done teething. He thinks then she will be more healthy. She is the prettiest, smartest little creature you ever saw.

You spoke something in your letter like stopping in Georgia. You need not believe Lizza's (Elizabeth Ann Whitten, daughter of James) fine tales about Georgia. If I could see you I reckon I could make you believe that Mississippi is the greatest place in the world. Atlanta is a great place on account of the railroads, but we are soon to have railroads all around us, but I want you all to be just suited to a home, then I shall be glad in sincerity and truth.

Why don't sister N write to me? And my brothers, they all neglect me. I regret so much that brother A will be so far from his dear family for I know they are very dear to him. I had a letter from him a few weeks since. I do want to know so bad what you are all going to do and where you will settle.

Since I wrote the above we have had a very refreshing rain, a very great blessing, indeed. It will certainly work wonders in the crops throughout the country.

I wonder why Sister N does not write. Will Father, brother Jo, and Elias (Holcombe, husband of Narcissa) all settle together? Is brother Jo's health good? I think Mother's health will greatly improve if she comes to this country.

Well, I have just finished a fine white dress for myself. I just mention to make you think I am as young as I used to be. You will wonder that a married lady with a group of little children would wear a white dress but it is all the fashion here.

I do hope you will write soon and tell me what you are doing. I declare, if postage was not very low I would not send such a paper as this. I cannot call it a letter. You with all the family will accept my warmest wishes for your welfare and happiness.

Your sister,
Harriet

Despite frequent assurances that she is satisfied and happy away from her beloved family, Harriet is homesick and resents her separation from them. All her letters give this impression, this one in particular. She wants continuing news from home, and longs for them to move nearby. I suspect her feelings were typical of thousands of young wives who, during these years, married and followed husbands into the wilderness.

Thomas J. Earle to Rebecca Whitten—Penfield, Georgia, to Gowensville,

South Carolina, 30 Aug. 1850

Well cousin,

After a long silence I seat myself to try and answer your last, or rather give you a few thoughts by way of keeping alive that friendship which has been long cherished as the richest balm for the wounds of life. I would have written to you sooner but just after receiving your letter we entered upon the hurry, confusion, and excitement of our examination and of commencement at the close of which I started immediately up the RR to Uncle's and have not had time to write to anyone since. If you are as anxious to receive my letters as I am yours I know you thought the time long but I must beg you receive my excuse and number me still among your best friends, among those whose friendship "time can not chill, nor change invade, nor poverty impair".

I might here stop and tell you all about my trip up the country but time forbids. Suffice it to say I had a fine ride upon the RR up to Adairsville where I saw many of my old friends and relations. Among them were Porter, Baylis Lewis, E. Graham and family, King, and others. I then went to Uncles and found the friends all well. The old folks are well located now and living pleasantly. Uncle has turned out to hard work and seems more anxious to gain property than ever before. Aunt has broken much, looks thin, but is still cheerful and pleasant, She has lost one eye entirely and the other is a little injured, no known cause.

The old lady is still on her hobby, election, and preaches whenever she gets a crowd, her sort of preaching. She and Uncle are members of an anti-church and cousin Charlotte Dodd is a member of a missionary church. I had a delightful time there conversing with the old folks, etc., saw all of the cousins and there is a lot of them, so many babies that when they all get together they hardly know which little one belongs to them. John Henry has two beautiful boys, Mary Elizabeth (Dodd's oldest daughter) has one daughter, Cousin Charlotte several small ones, the last one a son, and Lizzy Miller a son and daughter. Charlotte Earle has grown to be quite large and fleshy, better looking than when she left and cousin Sophia Dodd is a nice little girl.

The land in that country is low and in winter wet and sloppy. This summer it has been dry, in Cass county the crops are almost ruined. Some larger farms won't make ten barrels of corn. Up there also I saw Miss Jam McEnter of Rome. She is handsome and lively and I had a pleasant time with her. After my return I went over to Eatonville to an association and saw some pleasant folks, saw old friends and heard good preaching. They had a fine meeting and the Lord, I believe, was working by His Spirit in the hearts of all the people. They will protract the meeting till Saturday. I left last Tuesday.

Our term is now commenced so I must go to work again and I don't feel much like it. I now enter upon my last year in the Institution, a few more months, if the Lord wills, I shall leave this hallowed place to bear the burden and heat of the day in harvest of my Master. And though I have been here so long studying yet I feel poorly prepared for the labor. Much will be expected of me and I fear but little received. The Lord do with me what He will.

This evening I am going out to a Church in the country with old Bro. Sanders of this place. I ought to be preparing for the trip but thought I would drop you a line before I left, lest you should conclude I had forgotten you and my duty. But not so. I remain a friend and a warm friend, but an unserviceable and unworthy friend.

Please remember me kindly to your Ma and sister and all the family, Miss Mary and Lizzy also, and anyone else that inquires about Tom. Write to me soon and "return not evil for evil but overcome evil with good" by giving me a long letter shortly.

Affectionately yours,
T. J. Earle

Alfred Washington to Silas Reagan Whitten—Pendleton to Gowensville, South Carolina, 25 Sept. 1850

Dear Father,

I am winding up my business as fast as I can. As far as I have looked into it, and tested it, nobody complained. (The page is torn and unreadable; he mentions collecting receivables.) Notwithstanding my advertisement, I have all the patients I want and have time to attend to. Many, many substantial men seem to write, regretting my leaving. Others are doubtless delighted at it. The poor in many cases are begging me to stay. I honestly believe that if I were to sell it, the practice would be worth at least a thousand dollars, that would be clear of expense.

But I can leave without a murmur. It must surely all be for the best. My removal to this place however was a good one. My knowledge of the profession, the world, and myself is much enlarged. But like the mariner who had been thrown by the relentless water into an unknown sea, I have labored, and toiled, and battled through the society of rich and poor without an object, without one congenial spirit on which to dote and love and live. No disinterested friendship has risen up to rivet me to people or places. All the time looking through vista of a promising futility, I have beheld in the distance, my beloved family and longed to steer toward them, wading through the quagmire and expanse of a bewildering mystery toward contentment. My Father's house abounded with bread. Ofttimes would I have feasted on the husks the swine did eat.

At Pickensville I got John A. Gunter to ride around to all my debtors and collect what money he could, warning every man, with four or five exceptions, that if this note was not redeemed by the first day of October, they would surely be collected if the money could be made. I have time and again solicited and urged them to pay. They have not done it. I shall make the best of my time here and do everything to sell my practice.

(Here the letter is damaged too badly to read. The gist is that if his debtors knew how poor he was, they would pay him.)

Your loving son,
AWW

Love has overcome pride! Alfred wants to go with the family! He likens himself to the Biblical prodigal, returning to home and father. There is no sense of sacrifice in this letter. Being with his beloved family means more to him than a successful, pleasant, career alone in Pendleton. Nothing in the many letters written by Alfred gives us a clearer picture of his character. It is a shame that some portions of it are too badly damaged to be read.

Narcissa Amaryllis to Rebecca Whitten—Mount Farm, Hancock, Georgia, to Gowensville, South Carolina, 4 Nov. 1850

My dear Sister,

I suppose you are all anxious by this time to know where we are, and what we are doing. We arrived in Augusta on Tuesday evening, put up at the United States Hotel and stayed there until 9 o'clock Wednesday evening. Then we got in the cars and had quite a merry ride on the railroad to Warrenton. There we had to ride in the stage 23 miles to Sparta. We found Aunt Martha (Martha Meriwether, wife of Uncle Isaac Smith Whitten) there with her carriage waiting to convey us to her house, and oh, how glad they were to meet us. Uncle Isaac seems very happy indeed to have us visit him. He is very affectionate. His health is very bad. That is the reason he did not meet us in Augusta.

Elias leaves in the morning for Augusta. He commences business immediately. Uncle is going with him. I will remain here for a week or two until Elias gets his business going on smoothly. Then I will take the car and go to Augusta. We will board at a private house.

Oh, Sister, I wish you could see that beautiful city. I know you would love to sit and look on that large river. I have not heard anything from you since we left. I wish you would write and let us know how you get on. Direct your letters to Augusta.

I do hope you have all become reconciled to our separation. It is all for the best and I do assure you that I am well cared for. Mother, I hope you will be able to bear your trip well. (The family left for Mississippi shortly after this was written.)

We have delightful weather now, very dry and warm. It seems very strange to think that I am really in Georgia. Papa, Uncle Isaac's land looks very much like our old place. The large oak trees remind me very much of home. The water here is not like ours but the people generally look very healthy. There is no small pox in Augusta now and the broken bone fever has got entirely through, so I believe the city is entirely healthy. Elias says he will write about the time you get to Pontotoc. Goodby, I must stop. Elias joins me in love to you all.

Your devoted Sister,
Narcissa

Dr. Isaac Smith Whitten, Narcissa's uncle, had prospered in Georgia. He obviously loved his family and sought closer ties with brothers, sisters, nieces, and nephews. References to his many letters and visits often appear. Broken bone fever is dengue, another mosquito-borne disease, not understood in 1850 and seldom seen in the United States today.

From this letter we learn that Narcissa and Elias are not going west with the family. Elias has a new position with the firm of Betts and Marshall of Charleston. The Silas Reagan Whitten family is going to Mississippi, and their first destination is Pontotoc. Harriet must be delighted!

Sadly, Narcissa has seen her beloved father, mother, brothers, and sisters for the last time. ✳

CHAPTER EIGHT

1851 to the Outbreak of the War

Most northern states were experiencing an industrial revolution. Slavery was no longer useful, or tolerated. Southern economy remained tied to agriculture and cotton, the cash cow. Slave labor was considered necessary for its production. Pioneers were crossing the Mississippi River and pouring into Louisiana, Arkansas, Missouri, Kansas, Texas, and beyond. A network of railroads was binding the nation together. The land was becoming settled, but hotheads and harsh rhetoric were drowning out voices of reason. Black clouds of war were gathering. Indeed, in the Missouri-Kansas territories cruel, bloody, relentless fighting had broken out. The Earles and Whittens, with all southern families, are soon to feel the bleak despair of total war.

With the exception of Narcissa Amaryllis, who remained in South Carolina with her husband, Elias Holcombe, the Silas Reagan Whitten family has moved to Mississippi, settling in Tippah County, in the northeastern corner of that state. Silas Reagan bought land near Ripley; Joseph John acquired an adjacent farm. When war finally came, only Ranson Edwin and Rebecca remained unmarried and living at home.

Harriet Harrison Earle Roddy to Eleanor Kee Whitten—Prospect, Texas, to Gowensville, South Carolina, forwarded to Ripley, Tippah, Mississippi, 13 Jan. 1851

My dear Sister,

I have written you repeatedly without receiving any return, until, at last, I despaired of hearing from you again, until I met a Dr. Barton and Mrs. Goodlett, his sister, who knew your family and spoke as if they had been intimate acquaintances with your daughters. Joseph and Harriet, they said, were married. You, my Sister, know something of sorrow since your children are leaving you. Our two oldest daughters are married. One lives forty miles from us. The other is moving near us. Baylis, Ellen, and Joseph live with us. We have been wanderers all our lives and have just built a new place. We have passed through so many vicissitudes in life that I often feel like a weary pilgrim, and that there is no abiding place here. I feel that it is just that we should be cut off from many of the comforts of this life to make us feel more fully our dependance on that Being from whence all good must come and to give us humble and contrite views of ourselves. And His promises are full of comfort, for He has assured us that as our day, so shall our strength be, and no good thing shall be withheld from us. Have we not found His promises faithful? And shall we not trust Him?

I feel, my dear Sister, when I reflect upon the shortness of time and the uncertainty of all earthly good, that the sum and substance of all my wishes here would be that we would be given Grace and made partakers of the Redeeming Love Of Christ in Whom there is fullness, and that our scattered families may meet in that world where separation is unknown, where pain and sorrow cannot enter.

It would be a very great comfort to me to receive a line from my sisters sometimes. We never hear from Mr. Roddy's relations. His parents are dead and all his brothers but one, and although the estate was considerable, we, I suppose, were forgotten. We never received a dime. Mr. Roddy feels neglected and will not write to them. Our brother (Dr. Joseph Berry Earle) never writes to me. I wrote to him until I was tired of writing and he was tired of reading, I presume, as he would not answer them. Sister Poole (Letitia Sorrell Earle Poole) I have not heard from in a long time. Do write to me and let me know something about all your family, if you feel permanently settled, and if your children are settling round you. Say something about all our relations there. I will write sister Prince (Lydia Maverick Earle Prince) soon.

Mr. Roddy joins me in love to Mr. Whitten and all your dear family. We often talk of you.

Ever yours,
Harriet H. Roddy

Direct your letters to Burlison County, String Prairie Post Office.

This letter, written from central Texas by a homesick sister, provides a clue that helps establish the timing of the Silas Reagan family move from South Carolina to Mississippi. It was mailed in mid-January 1851, took at least two weeks to reach South Carolina, and was forwarded to Ripley, Mississippi. The Whittens left well before January 1851.

Narcissa to Alfred Washington Whitten—Mound Farm, Mt. Zion, Hancock, Georgia, to Ripley, Mississippi, 19 Jan. 1851

My own dear brother,

A part of this sacred day shall be directed in writing to you. I received a kind letter from sister R the eighth of this month and I have read it so often that I have almost committed it to memory. Oh, the pleasure we experience in reading letters from one so dear is almost unbearable. I am truly glad to hear that you get on so well. I almost imagine myself with you at your new home and sincerely hope it will prove a pleasant one. Oh how I long to see you all, to meet the hearts of sympathy and affection which once welcomed me and the kind eyes of tenderness beaming upon me.

Recollection is a pleasing visitor and Oh how often does it weave its spell around me. I would not forget if I could all the past and hope there is not one of you that will think me less affectionate for leaving. Yes it is a hard struggle, my Brother, and almost more than I could bear but it is all for the best. God's will be done. I often think that I have been thrown here on purpose to try my faith. Everything seems so cold among strangers. I often wish I could see one familiar face. Have made very few acquaintances since I've been here. Uncle (Dr. Isaac Smith Whitten) lives in two miles of Mt Zion. Its a small village.

There are three churches in it, Baptist, Methodist, and Presbyterian. I have only been to Church twice since I left home. I often think of Mr. Gibson's good sermons. He used to tell us that religion was becoming very fashionable and the longer I live the more I see of it but I will try and do my duty as far as lies in my power. Sometimes I sicken and almost reel to see the wickedness of this vain world but I know it and try to do right. God will assist me. He will never forsake me. He is a friend that sticketh closer than a brother. I hope you have given up the idea of going to California. I suppose you are all together yet. Rebecca did not tell me where you would locate.

I reckon you will be surprised to see I am still in Georgia. Elias has gone to Charleston. He commenced business last Monday. I wanted very much to go with him but Uncle Isaac was very much opposed to my going until Elias could get his business all going on well. I think I will go there in March, stay there a month or so and then return here or go higher up in Georgia and spend the summer and then go to Charleston in the fall and remain if we both live and do well. I think my husband has a fine situation and I do hope he will do well. He boards at Bomar's Rooming House $5.00 per week. That takes money pretty fast.

I have not heard a single word from the Dark Corner since we left although I have written three letters and one of them was to Dr. Earle (M. Baylis, brother of Thomas J. Earle). Would you believe it, he asked me very politely when he bid me farewell to write to him, and so

I did but he has never answered it. Do you think Croup ever called to bid me good-bye? Tell Becca I am here in twenty five miles of Penfield but have not seen Tom (Thomas J. Earle). I don't suppose that he knows that I am here.

Did you stop at Cumming as you moved? Did you see Elias' sisters? If you did, tell me how they are doing. And now my dear brother, I do insist that you all write to me often. Tell Father and Mother to write. I do feel so lonely here. I did not feel so bad when my husband was with me but it does seem that I am alone in every sense of the word, though Uncle is very kind to me. It is not like having my husband, brothers, and sisters with me. I have almost lost my cheerfulness but I hope to regain it when I once more get with my husband and know that I am going to stay with him if I live. You know that I always have been directed to my husband. Elias has become quite temperate. He drinks nothing but cold water and chews very little tobacco.

I am writing this letter to my brother and I can say what I please and know anything that interests me will be interesting to you. Tell Mother I have had worse colds since I came here than I have for many years. Sudden changes in the weather, sometimes it has been warm enough for summer. They have commenced working in farm and garden here. They make a great deal of cotton in this part of the country. The people in this neighborhood are in good circumstances and some of them are very wealthy. One of Aunt Martha's (Martha Meriwether Whitten, wife of Uncle Isaac) sons in law owns two hundred negroes and has a farm large enough for them all to work that's old enough. There are about seventy negroes here, about forty field hands. The rest are house servants and children.

Uncle has a beautiful house. It has eight rooms above the basement and its decidedly the handsomest furnished house I ever was in. All his furniture is of the very best. They use the library for a sitting room. He has a choice selection of books, takes a great many papers, so you see we have reading enough. They are all political except two. They are the American Messenger and Southern Presbyterian. I have not seen a Mountaineer since I left home. How glad I would be to see one. I would be glad to see anything in the world that came from home.

If you have heard anything from Aunt Letty Poole (mother's sister, Letitia Sorrell Earle) since you have been in Mississippi you must tell me when you write. Tell me everything that's new and do write soon.

I have written to sister Harriet since I have been here but she has never answered my letter. Is brother Joseph and Mesina with you? Tell all the children howdy and tell them they must not forget Aunt Cissa. I cannot bear to think they would forget me.

Give my love to Papa and Mother, brothers and sisters all, and do, my dear brother, receive the best wishes and utmost love of your affectionate sister,

Narcissa

Direct your letters to Mount Zion, Hancock County, Georgia.

Since writing this I have received a letter from Dr. Earle (M. Baylis). He enquires very favorably about you. You ought to write to him. He says the smallpox is raging in Hendersonville. There has been 19 cases, 3 or 4 deaths.

Narcissa knew when she wrote this that the family was in Ripley, Mississippi. The trip took two weeks or more. We will learn that they stayed with Harriet in Pontotoc before moving on to Tippah County where they settled. November 1850 is the likely date for their departure from Gowensville.

Narcissa to Alfred Washington Whitten—Charleston, South Carolina, to Ripley, Mississippi, 27 March 1851

My dear Brother,

Your very welcome letter was received in due time and would have been answered ere this but I was expecting daily to come to Charleston and thought I would wait so that I might have more to tell you. I arrived Tuesday in the car. I waited for company until my patience was worn out. I wrote to Elias when I would be in Augusta, so I got on in Greensboro. I came down alone. It was impossible for him to meet me in Augusta so he sent Mr. Betts. I found him quite a pleasant travelling companion. A lady in travelling on the cars under the care of the conductor gets every necessary attention, indeed. They are very polite. I felt perfectly at home though I could not see one familiar face. It is almost a perfect land from Augusta to Charleston. The cars run much smoother than they do on the Georgia railroad and they are much finer.

Well, I must tell you something about how we are situated here. We have a large, pleasant room with windows opening on the street and only two or three doors from the ladies parlor. There is a church at each end of the house and one in front, so you may readily perceive that we are on Church Street. Mr. Bonner and his lady are very kind and I feel perfectly at home. We have everything that is rich and good to eat. It is all done up in the very best style. The house is very large. There are one hundred and thirty or forty here. Now we use cistern water with ice. It is very pure and there is such a pleasant breeze here all the time. I think this climate will suit me. I have only been here three days and feel better than I have since I left home.

I was not happy in Georgia. I was low spirited and, of course, that would affect my health. I could not give up all my friends and my husband too. After he came to Charleston, it seemed to me that I could not bear it. I have fallen off very much but I hope that I will get in better figure now. I am quite lively and I can just run about here and take as much exercise as I choose to. I have not been out of the city any yet. I have an invitation to a picnic down on Sullivans Island Saturday but I don't wish to go so soon. I had rather wait until Elias can go with me. Elias goes to church every Sabbath. He says one of the Baptist ministers here is a fine man and I am going to put my letter in very soon at the Baptist Church number one. Tell Becker that I am a stronger Baptist than I was when I left home. She said she reckoned I would change when I got amongst so many other denominations but not so. I am just the very same only I am not so proud as I used to be. I dress very plain but neat and do just as I please.

I shall stay here as long as I feel safe this summer and then I am going up to Pendleton and stay there until frost, then return here. I think I shall like a city life very much. Elias has a fine situation and I think he will do very well. He is in fine spirits. He looks better than I have seen him in several years. He is very cheerful. I think its better that we did not go to Mississippi for it might have been that he could not have succeeded so well in a new country.

I am truly glad to hear that you are all settled down at home for I know you must feel a great deal better. There are several here from Pendleton, Mrs. Nancy Sloan amongst them, she sends a great deal of word to you, says it distressed her very much because she did not get to tell you good bye, says you must hunt up her son. He lives in Pontotoc County, William Sloan. The old lady seems to think a great deal of you.

Oh how glad I would be to see you all in your new home, but that I cannot do, so I must content myself by writing. I hope you will write to me often. I received Becca's letter and will write to her soon. I am so glad to hear that Pappa and Mother are so well. I was fearful that new country would not agree with them and wonder if Silas and Ranty ever think about me. I will have to stop. My paper is all gone. Elias joins me in love to you all.

May God bless you, my dear Brother, is the prayer of your sister,

Narcissa

You must excuse this badly written letter. I will do better next time. This is all the paper I have in the house. Tell Jo and Mesina I will write to them soon.

Narcissa to Rebecca Whitten—Charleston, South Carolina, to Ripley, Mississippi, 12 April 1851

My dear Sister,

I reckon by this time you have read a letter from me written to Brother. I thought then that I would remain in the city for some months but I have concluded that it would be better for me to go early. It is very trying to leave my husband, but they make us pay twelve dollars a week for our board and we have to put our washing out and pay fifty cents a dozen. Elias' wages this year will not more than pay our expenses. Mr. Betts said he would give him six or seven hundred dollars and perhaps more. It depends on how he is pleased. He knew nothing in the world about him but I have heard from several since I came down that he is doing very well. It's a first rate house and I am very glad that Elias got a start with it. I leave here in the morning and go by way of Columbia, take the stage at Newberry and go to Greenville, and from there, to Pendleton. You see I have got to be quite a traveler. I have found out that all the way to get on in this world is to go on and attend to your own business.

I have formed several acquaintances and some pleasant ones. I have put my letter in at the Baptist Church number one. Mr. Kendrick, our minister, called to see me. He is very pleasant, told me to make myself perfectly at home. Mr. Stone knows that I am here but he has never called to see me. I reckon he has forgotten the hot muffins and toast he used to praise so much.

Oh, my dear Sister, you know nothing about the desert of this world, and God forbid that you ever should from experience. The longer I live the more I learn. There is very few in this world that can be trusted. I have learned more in the short time we have been thrown amongst strangers than I ever expected to know.

I hope to spend my time pleasantly in Pendleton. Elias will leave here the last of June and travel through the upper districts collecting, and he will have to return the first of September. I will stay until November, I reckon. I am anxious to hear from you all. Oh, I should be delighted to be with you when Harriet makes you a visit, but I will have to content myself with thinking of it.

Sister, there are a great many curiosities here I wish you could see, the Atlantic and the beautiful boats. I walked down on the wharf yesterday and saw the Southern Steamer sail for New York. Oh, it looked magnificent. I went all through it and into it. The berths looked so nice I wanted to take a nap. I have been to the island. Oh, its delightful to be rolling on the deep ocean. I know you would like it when the tide runs high. It looks so lively.

Do you get any letters from home? I have received but two since I left. Elias received a letter from Johnny last week. He says William Dunpert has returned and lying at the point of death with consumption. I shall not make any stay at Greenville. There is none, or very few, there that I wish to see, but of all the places I have ever been I dislike Georgia the most. I would not live there for pay.

But I am not lonely, my Sister. Elias is with me at night and there is pleasant company enough in the house, and when I leave here God will go with me and take care of me. He has always watched over me with peculiar care. He will never forsake me. As long as I stick to Him, He will to me. Oh, I feel so thankful that I was raised by such a pious, good mother, and my father is so kind and affectionate. There are few blessed with such parents, brothers, and sisters as I have.

You said that Col. (Silas Jr.) had written to Elias. He has never received the letter. When any of you write to him direct the letters to Elias Holcombe, care of J. B. Betts, Charleston, and write to me at Pendleton. Hoyt and Mely are here but I have not seen them. Mely's income is two hundred and fifty dollars a year. I understand she is going to take a small school. She is of a good family. I have not been able to hear anything of the Allenders. I reckon they are not much. Let me hear from you often. Tell me everything. I want to know it all. If we all live and are well I intend making you a visit some time. Becker, I want you to open that box that has Bell's things in it and give them to any of the children that you choose, Harriet's some. Save the hair. Well, I have filled my paper.

Your sister,
Narcissa

Since writing this Mrs. Dick Sloan and Miss May have called. Do excuse this hurried scrawl. Elias joins me in love to you all. Give my love to brother Alfred when you see him. Cissa

I have just received a letter from Tom (T. J. Earle). He said he was going to write to you soon.

Thomas J. Earle to Rebecca Whitten—Penfield, Georgia, to Ripley, Mississippi, 26 April 1851

Much esteemed friend and cousin,

Your thrice welcome letter came to hand some days since and I must steal time to respond. And I would that I could write what I feel, that my pen were tonight to trace the deep gratitude of my heart and the strong friendship of former days which I still feel for you and yours. I felt that this motto was peculiarly applicable and still I felt that you ought not to lay on so heavily, not that you would not do so, when you heard me.

The last time I had the pleasure to hear from you was when you wrote to cousin Ann. At that time you were at your sister Harriet's (in Pontotoc County, Mississippi) and of course I did not know where to write, for you had not settled at that time. But just before your letter reached me I had the gratification to receive one from cousin Narcissa. She told me where you were, your P. O., etc., and I had just finished an answer to her letter when yours came like good news from a far country. Like a loved and honored friend it cheered my heart because it came dressed in a plain familiar garb speaking the sentiments of the heart in the language of other days.

I perceive that Mississippi has not made any change in my much respected friend and correspondent. She is still the same cousin Rebecca that she was in bygone days in the happy home of early childhood. Well I am to see it for I can fully accept the past language.

Time's changes, Oh time's changes
We can bear to see them come
And crumble down the cottage roof
Or rend the palace dome
Yes, we can lightly smile on all
Time's changes till we find
Some well known voice grown harshly cold
That once was warmly kind
Till hands and eyes that used to be
The first our own to greet
Can calmly take a long farewell

And just as calmly meet
Oh better then to die and give
The grave its kindred dust
Than live to see times bitter changes
In hearts we love and trust.

I did not visit your old homestead when I was in Carolina last winter. It has no attraction for its old visitors. The cheerful smiles that once were there are gone. The old friends that were once wont to greet us with open hearts and hands are away in the western wilds. Alas! that friends should be thus scattered. When I return to the green lands of my childhood, my home, and my dead I feel like some lovebird without a mate. I tread the paths I used to tread. I ramble ore the hills and Carolina of former days. I pause to gaze around me. I see the same heavens smiling above me, the same mountains rise around me, the same streamlets ripple through the glen and the same groves wave over my head. But all else, how changed. I meet some friends but I meet few familiar faces. Some have grown to men and women who were but a few months since but children. Upon some time has made his mark perceptibly and all are much engrossed with the affairs of life. Some have gone, like you, to try their fortunes in more propitious climes. And some are not.

After the first welcome is over I gaze around me on the past and present and O how lonely and sad to what it once was. I call to mind the scenes of joy forever fled and I am sad. The blessing of memory which affords me much pleasure by recalling the scenes while here gives me much pain while there, for I have there the sad reality before me. I move about among the friends and scenes of former joys but I am not happy. I go with the heart of a man and try to find pleasure in the joys of childhood. Of course, I fail. My old associates have engaged in the scenes of real life and have no time or disposition to spend with me in being young again. Perhaps cousin Ann is an exception.

I shall try, if nothing happens, to get through here in July and return to Carolina. I know not where I shall settle. The Lord must decide. I should be much pleased to visit Mississippi this next fall but can't say. All well when I heard from home. Crawford (his brother) was complaining some.

I sympathize with you much in the loss of your Cissa (Narcissa Amaryllis, who did not migrate to Tippah County) and your religious privileges. But I trust you will soon have both restored to you, if not the Good Lord can make you happy. Give my love to your Ma and all the family, etc. It will afford me much pleasure to receive a long letter from you whenever you can write. Do write soon.

Yours in Christian bonds,
T. J. Earle

Narcissa to Eleanor Kee Whitten—Pendleton, South Carolina, to Ripley, Mississippi, 6 May 1851

Pendleton Hotel, My dear Mother,

Your very welcome letter was received in due time and would have been answered ere this but I was quite unwell for several days. I suffered a great deal with headache, high fevers at night. At length I broke out all over just as thick as I could be in little pimples. Indeed, my skin was a cake from head to foot, my face, hands, and feet very much swollen, but my head easy. I did not know what to do and thought I was in a bad way, but not so bad but what it might be worse. I told them to send for a Dr. Jenkins who called, pronounced it nettle rash, gave me cream of tartar. So by the next morning I was cool and pleasant. And now I feel quite well only a little weak. I sat down last Saturday and wrote Dr. Earle (M. Baylis, brother of Thomas J. Earle) a long letter giving him a full dose recitation of my general health so I have received a general bundle of medicines by last mail. He is very kind, begs me to write to him often and tell him how I am and he will send me anything I need. I have told you all about my sickness. Now I will tell you everything else I can think of.

I came by Columbia and on to Greenville. The stage was very much crowded and I was almost worn out. I put up at Long's. There didn't anybody know me. I made myself known and they were very kind. I got Johnny to bring me over. I was so fatigued that I could not come on the stage. Well, I have been here three weeks and all my kinfolks have been to see me, and can assure you it will take me some time to get round to see them all. The most of them seem very clever. I have been out and spent the day with Mrs. Mays today. She sends love to all of you and says tell Dock (Alfred) to write to her. I am going with Mrs. Gilliard to spend the day at Ben Sloan's tomorrow. Tell brother A that everyone asks about him. Everyone treats me with great respect because I am his sister, so you see what it is to have a clever brother. I think that I will spend my time in Pendleton quite pleasantly. I am going over to see Aunt Ammy (Amaryllis Earle

Bomar, mother's sister) if I get an opportunity.

Oh, Mother, you don't know how glad I was to get your letter. It is the first one you ever wrote me and I do tell you I bragged on it some. I am so glad you are pleased with your new home and that your health is so good. I should like to take a peep in and see how you all look. Tell Mesina I am sorry the country had such an affect on her so quick. I reckon this must be something in the water.

I received a letter from brother A and one from Ranty (Ranson E.) which will both be answered very soon. It makes me feel very proud to think you are all so very good to write. I am very sorry brother Jo's health is so bad, but I feel better satisfied to know Alfred is with him. Is any of the boys coming this fall? It is reported here that the Colonel (Silas Jr.) is coming after Annah, but I reckon it must be a joke. Several have asked me about it. Tell him he must let me know for I don't know what to tell them.

Tell Dock that Mr. Jennings is married and lives here, keeps house near the Female Academy. He wants Brother to write to him and give him a full description of the country. He has an idea of moving there. Mrs. Dr. Jenkins has called to see me since I have been writing, says Brother promised to write to her husband but had not done it.

The weather here is as cold as winter time, but the fruit is not killed yet. The trees are loaded with peaches and Elias will be with me in June. He is going to travel in all the upper districts so I can go and see all our old neighbors. I wish to, but I don't feel now that I should care to go, though it is a dear old spot. I should hate to go there and see it so used up. Those memorable old oaks that I have spent so many hours under are all cut down and it would vex me to see it.

Have you sent your letters in the church yet? We have preaching once in two weeks in the Baptist Church and the same way at the Methodist Church. I wish you had preaching near you, but persons going to a new country has to do the best they can. I consider it a great blessing to be able to walk to church and hear good preaching after you get there.

Well Mother, I reckon you will think this is a real mixed up letter. I just write as I think, so fast that I can't keep up with my pen. Why don't Papa write? I am truly glad that his health is so good. Ranty tells me you are making a fine crop. You don't know what a nice letter he did write me. Well my paper is nearly gone. I hope you will favor me with another letter soon. Tell Becker to write me a long letter. Give my love to all the family.

May God watch over you all with peculiar care is the prayer of your daughter,

Narcissa

Becker, did you hear that Nancy Goodlett was married to a Charlestonian? I was invited to the wedding but did not want to go. *Mesina is pregnant with Frank Adams, born 26 July 1851.*

Narcissa to Alfred Washington Whitten—Pendleton, South Carolina, to Ripley, Mississippi, 19 May 1851

My dear Brother,

Yours of April was received and would have been answered ere this but I thought it would be best to wait a week or so after writing to Mother. I am delighted to hear that you all are so much pleased with your new home, but truly sorry to hear that brother Jo has been so ill.

I should not be surprised if we have fires here. The weather is very warm and dry. I am better than I was when I wrote to Mother but not well yet. The Dr. sent me blue pills and some other medicines. I don't know what it is. I take it regular and I hope to get well by the time I am through with it.

Well, Brother, I have just returned from church. Mr. Murry preached an excellent sermon from this text "God is good", and surely He has been good to me. My dear Brother, I do feel so grieved to hear that Harriet has taken her letter from the Baptist Church. What can it mean? Surely she cannot think of joining the Methodist. I would not have her do it for anything. Were I in her place there is nothing that could influence me to bring up my children in any other but the Baptist faith. The longer I live, the more I am convinced that we are right. In Georgia they are looked upon as the lowest class, and wherever I go they are very much persecuted, but I don't mind that. It only makes me stronger. I could not have you think me selfish, dear Brother. I believe there are good Christians in other churches, but I think, to take them generally, the Baptists are the most humble and the best Christians.

You ask where I am going to make my home and who I will visit. I am at Earles, I visit at Tom Sloans, William Gilliards, John Maxwell, Dr. Jenkins, Mr. Stevens, A. Campbells, Sam Maxwells, Mrs. Mays, Bensons, and call on some ladies that are boarding. I had forgotten Maj. Seaborne. All my kin called on me as soon as I came. They ask very often after you. I should be so much pleased to see your nice little shop. I know you have everything in order.

I saw a traveler a few days past that came through Ripley. He thought it a very pretty place, but he did not know you. I reckon you have plenty of berries now. We have not had any yet, but we will have June peaches.

Elias will be with me in a month. The spring business is over now and he will have to travel and collect in Carolina and Georgia. I will go with him sometimes. He will be in a buggy and I reckon it would be good for me. He will have to return the first of September. The business opens there then, but I will remain here until October, the last of it I reckon. Mr. Betts is very much pleased with Elias. He told some of the up country merchants that he was highly pleased with him and, if his business would allow of it, he intended giving him a thousand dollars this year and I don't think Elias expects more than six hundred. I have heard this since I came and got it straight.

All my kin here want me to spend some time with them. Several invited me to spend a week or two, but I only visit them. I find Pendleton more pleasant than expected. Several of the little girls here say they love me because I am your sister. All the folks here tell me I look very much like you. Old Mrs. Sloan has come home. She asked me to give her love to you when I wrote. I think she is an excellent woman. I have not received but one letter from our old home since we left. When I came through Greenville the folks did not know me. I made myself known at Longs and they were particularly kind to me. I got there before dinner and in the afternoon I walked down to the falls thinking to meet some of my old friends. The first I met was Lealand and Dunham. I spoke and called them by names as usual. They merely passed, did not know me. I suppose I have received several apologies from there because the folks did not know I was there.

Do you get any practice now or is that country so healthy they don't get sick? I never hear anything from Silas. I received letters from Becca and Ranty which will be answered soon. I am anxious to hear how you all are, If brother J has got well. I fear some more of you will have fever. I am glad to hear that Father and Mother have such good health. I was fearful that climate would not treat them well. I must stop. I don't know that you can make out to read this letter. I have not got Elias to make me a pen and this is a horrid one. Good bye, dear Brother, May God bless you.

Your sister,
Narcissa

I think I will take cold bath. Give my love to all our folks and write me often.

Harriet has left the Baptist church, which upsets Narcissa, who speaks of it in several letters. Living her life in the towns and cities of South Carolina she may not realize the problem of distance from home to church in the wilderness. Harriet likely selected a church close by. Her description of the Baptist reputation is of interest.

Her letters tell of the wholesale mercantile business of the mid-nineteenth century. Retailers purchased their stocks during the fall and winter, sold them during the summer, and paid for them the next fall.

Narcissa must have been extremely frightened by the prospects of fever and malaria in the summer low country of South Carolina to be separated from her beloved husband for such long periods.

Narcissa to Rebecca Whitten—Pendleton Hotel, South Carolina, to Ripley, Mississippi, 1 June 1851

My dear sister,

Your welcome, thrice welcome, letter was received and I cannot wait long before I write. I reckon you all think that I write very often. I try to write to some one of you every two weeks. Oh you cannot tell how glad I am to hear from you. I read a letter from brother Alfred to Mrs. Holcombe yesterday. I am truly sorry to hear that sister Harriet's health is not good. What is the matter? I suppose some imprudence. Brother said she was with you at the time he wrote. Sometimes I almost imagine myself with you and often sit and think about you for hours, wondering if you look just as you did, and what you are doing.

Becca, I am sorry that you are low spirited at times. You ought not allow yourself to feel badly on my account. You know, my Sister, that we cannot be together always and I am convinced now that its better as it is. I received a letter from Elias yesterday saying that he would be with me on next Friday. The busy season is over in Tennessee. It will not commence again until September. Elias will be here three months in the country and Mr. Betts only requires him to travel 6 weeks.

You said Father wanted to know what wages Elias would get. He has been on trial. Mr. Betts knew nothing about him. They settled last week. Mr. Betts pays all his expenses from the first of last Jan. until the last of May which was yesterday and gives him a thousand dollars for the next year, his salary commencing the first day of June which is this day. I think that is pretty good. What think you? Mr. B expressed himself highly pleased with Elias. I have heard from several that he is thought to be the best accountant in Charleston. Elias looks better and seems to be in better spirits than I ever saw him. I like Pendleton very well but not so well as I did at first.

Becker, I was always taught to love all Christians whether they are members of the Baptist Church or some other, but here they are contentious and selfish. They seem to be prejudiced against the Baptists. I don't like such doings and have been to Church every Sunday since I have been here only when I was sick.

Did you hear of the death of cousin Addeline Foster? I donnot know what was the matter. I did not see the obituary but I know that she is dead. Poor Jim, I am truly sorry for him and his little children. I reckon when Elias comes I will go up there with him. I don't know that I will.

I am glad to hear that you hear such good preaching in Ripley, and by one of my name, too. I would like very much to see him. Mr. Jennings is going to be in Ripley in about 6 weeks. He wants to look him out a situation. I think him and his wife are excellent people. They are, neither of them, very smart though they both have good educations.

You asked if I wrote to Tom (Thomas J. Earle) first. I did. He is coming in July. He wrote me a very affectionate letter. I do believe nearly all of Pendleton is my kin. They keep calling and say they are kin. It keeps me pretty busy.

But of all places, I think Charleston is the most delightful. Everybody attends to their own business. There is more good feelings. The people are plain. I felt properly at home and I think they are better Christians. I know you and anyone else would be pleased. I was more astonished at the plainness of their dress than I was at their sociability. They dress plainer than they do in Pendleton. I want to get back there very much. Though I was there but a short time I formed several very pleasant acquaintances and I think I have some good friends there. We hardly know who to trust nowdays. I have been deceived in some since I saw you that I thought would do anything for me, but I am glad to find them out.

You say I must keep away from the Dr's. (M. Baylis Earle) if I go home. You ought to tell me what they done, Becca. You spoke of Aunt Mariam writing to Uncle (Isaac). You must not tell her anything that you don't want published for she writes everything she knows to him and a little more. I found that out though he did not show me the letters. I tell you what, Becca, we have lots of kin and some of them are awfully mean. I thank God that I was brought up by such parents.

I hope and trust that I will never be guilty of a mean thing, I know I never will as long as I keep my senses, and I hope they will stick to me as long as I live.

I wish I could be with you for a while, and I certainly will visit you at some time if we should all live. I can go there from Charleston as soon as I can come here with but little more expense. Well Becca, my paper is almost gone and I have not told you half. I write a great many letters. I reckon you are in hopes I take more pains with the rest than I do with yours. I always think faster than I can write. I owe Ranty a letter and will write to him next. You must all write me, tell me everything. You know it will interest me if it does you. Give my love to Jo and Sena and don't let the children forget me.

Give my love to Papa and Mother, Silas, and Ranty and receive the best wishes of your sister,

Narcissa

There was, apparently, remarkably little friction between members of the Silas Reagan family. This was not entirely the case with the aunts and uncles of the Whitten children. Harriet has written that Mariam was unkind; Ranson and brother Alfred were at odds over the estate of their father, John; Narcissa is told of a problem with her cousin, Dr. Earle, and responds that Mariam and Isaac Smith are exchanging letters that contain critical references.

Narcissa to Alfred Washington Whitten—Pendleton, South Carolina, to Ripley, Mississippi, 1 June 1851

My dear Brother,

I read a letter from you yesterday to Mrs. H(olcombe) and I am truly glad you wrote to her, Alfred. She is the strongest woman that I ever have known. You know how she talked last summer. We thought she was going to join the Baptist Church. She had not been taken anywhere for six months until I came. She has been twice to the Baptist Church with me but is prejudiced against the Baptists, says now that she likes the Methodists the best, that she never feels at home, only with them. They have a pew in the Episcopal Church. I think, making a long story short, that she is about nothing and will go with the crowd. Mr. Murray called to see her very often last summer by her request, and the last time he called she would not see him. I just tell you this to let you know. Folks asked her if she was not going to answer your letter. She said she was.

Brother, it makes me sorry to look at the children. They are all very intelligent but they do just as they please. I never have seen as badly spoilt children in my life. They have just about everything they ask for. I talked to Lizzy about the way she was bringing up her children and told her what I thought would be the consequences. I don't think she thanked me for it but I thought it was my duty. Brother, all that family are the most deceitful people that I ever saw and Earle is as much a Robbson now as they are. The way to know folks is to find them out.

I tell you, dear Brother, I have learned more in the last nine months than I ever expected to know and I really think its been of great service to me, being thrown amongst strangers. One has to shift for themselves. Mrs. Mays has just told me that she wrote you a long letter this week and told you all the news.

There's a great revival in Greenville in the Methodist and Baptist Churches. There has seventeen joined the Baptist Church, Tom Roberts and his wife amongst them. Brother, you have a great many good friends here. I do like Mr. Billy Sloan. I do think him a good man. We have a singing class meeting Thursday night in the Baptist Church and practice prayer meeting every Friday week. I expect to go in the country when Elias comes. My health has improved very much since I wrote though I weigh only one hundred. I don't want you to say anything about what I told you of Lizzy. She would never speak to me again. My paper is full. Write soon.

Your sister,
Narcissa

Narcissa to Ranson Edwin Whitten—Pickensville, South Carolina, to Ripley, Mississippi, 26 June 1851

At Elliott's (brother of husband, Elias Holcombe)

My dear little Ranty,

I reckon by this time you have come to the conclusion that your letter has been forgotten, but not so, my dear Brother. I have often thought of it but I have a great many correspondents and the most of my time has been taken up in receiving and making calls. I never expected so much attention from the people of Pendleton. Several of them invited me to spend several weeks with them. I felt perfectly at home wherever I went. This is the first time I have been in the country. I came last Thursday. Eliza (her sister-in-law) seems delighted to have me with her, does everything she can to please me. A great many of the neighbors have sent for me to visit them. Those that I am not acquainted with, its all on Dock's account, don't you think? He must be a great fellow. Mrs. Leon Hambleton has a boy named for him.

Well Ranty, Elias has been with me for the last two weeks. Don't you know I have been happy. He left for Abbeville when I came here. He will be in that district and Laurens for two weeks, then he has to go to Ashville, Rutherford, Henderson, etc., and get back to town by the first day of September. He says I must go when he does. I don't know how it will be yet. My health is much better than it has been. I am very thin but my skin looks better than you ever saw it. I would like to see you all about this time but as I cannot do that I must be content with writing. I am going up the country when Elias goes. I will see all our old neighbors. Lou Meeney heard that I was at Pendleton and wrote me a long letter begging me to go up there and spend the summer, said she would do everything in her power to make me happy. She wrote very affectionately, says she thinks very hard of Becca for not writing to her, that none of us has a warmer friend in Greenville than her. I received one from Annah last week. She is in the neighborhood of Nazreth teaching music. She has a large class and gets on finely. She told me she had to leave home because Elve treated her so badly. She wrote me a long and quite an affectionate letter. Bob is in Newberry serving on the railroad doing better than he ever did and more steady. Mac sent me word to go up there and stay with them.

Ranty, I did not know that I had so many friends. Tell the Col. (Silas Jr.) I received his letter and will answer it soon. I am truly sorry that he hurt himself at work. There is no use in killing yourselves in any such a way. I am so glad to hear that you are all pleased with the country. You must not grieve because we are not with you, for I am sure Elias could not have done so well there. Mr. Betts is so much pleased with him, says he wants Elias to stay with him as long as they both live. He would have given him twelve hundred dollars this year if he had asked for it, says he will give him his own price. He is a member of the Presbyterian Church and an excellent man. He has everything done in order. Elias looks better than you ever saw him. He dresses very neatly, keeps shaved, and, by the by, a very fine looking gentleman.

Tell the Col. (Silas Reagan Jr.) Mr. Hill is teaching at Statetown, has a fine school. Martha Hendricks has a school near here. They like her very much. I have been invited to spend some time at Statetown.

You all owe me letters now. Father never writes. I would be glad to get letters often. Tell Jo and Sena and the little ones that I have not forgotten them.

Give my love to all and receive the best wishes of your sister,

Narcissa

PS NB tell Dock I am looking for a letter. Eliza and Mary send their love to all and particularly the Doctor.

Thomas J. Earle to Rebecca Whitten—Mercer College, Penfield, Georgia, to Ripley, Mississippi, 2 July 1851

Dear Cousin Rebecca,

I have at last found leisure to answer your fine letter. I was much pleased to hear from you but your letter came just in the heat of our final service and in about a week I stood my final examination, the last one that I shall ever stand in college, I guess. Truly it looked like a long road five years ago but to look back now it is not so long.

My stay here has been like life generally, checkered. But I think rather more sunshine than cloud. In fact I have been so happy generally that I am not inclined to leave. I know I must go. The calls of my Master and my neighbors are imperative and not to be disregarded. But my heart would linger long to tell the strong deep feelings that it cherishes for the scenes and associations of my college life.

I received a letter from Baylis (Dr. M. B., brother) Tuesday saying that all was well. I also received a letter from cousin Narcissa Holcombe some times since. She was in Pendleton and will remain through this summer. I hope to see her on my return home. I shall leave for South Carolina immediately after commencement, i.e., the first of August. And you can scarcely imagine the feelings with which I go back, a mingling of joy and grief. I shall be much pleased to see my friends, but there are so many of my old associates who have gone that I feel solitary and alone.

Then there are so many responsibilities resting on my weakness, so much expected of me and so little ability to perform the duties and I almost instinctively draw back.

But the difficulties in the road of the profession I have chosen are so numerous and great that I should long since have given up in despair if my strength had not been in the Lord. I greatly desire more strength and more confidence in the character of God and in His promises.

Atlanta, Georgia, 5 July 1851, You perceive I have travelled a little, came off in a great hurry from Penfield and brought this with to finish it. You will excuse all of this badly written letter. I am almost tired to death from traveling, walking about yesterday (fourth), hearing the speeches, have a bad cold, am not very well myself.

I am stopping at Dr. A. M. Spalding's, seeing much of Atlanta, am going to Stone Mountain, saw cousin Lizzy Clayton, all well, seemed quite pleasant for a few moments while I saw her, shall see her again today, am going to see Miss Duncan (alias Mrs. Brown) formerly of Prospect, South Carolina. She lives 2 doors from Dr. Spalding and is very well, I learn. James B looks very well.

I have a great many things on my mind now and am unfit to write to anyone, but I am ashamed to delay longer.

Give my love to your Ma and all the rest of the family.

I must stop. When you write again direct to Earlesville.

Goodbye cousin, may the Lord bless and keep you,

T. J. Earle

Thomas has graduated from Mercer and is on his way home. This is the last of his letters. We do know, from other sources, that he became an active and productive Baptist minister and educator in South Carolina and married a Miss Kenedy from Georgia. Perhaps she was a college sweetheart. If so, he did not share that information with Rebecca.

Narcissa to Silas Reagan Whitten Jr.—Pendleton, South Carolina, to Ripley, Mississippi, 29 Aug. 1851

Pendleton Hotel, My dear Brother,

I reckon you all begin to think by this time that I have concluded not to write again. It has been a long while since I have heard anything from you. Since you heard from me I have made a visit to South Pacolet, spent a week there quite pleasantly with some of our old friends. The most of them seemed delighted to see me. Elias had business with Mo (the man who bought the old home place) so we went there first, to Dr. Mooney's next and then to John Dickey's, intending to spend several days with the Goodlett's as we come on to Greenville, but Elias went to the Major election alone. Alice and Bob were both there and they told him howdy but never asked one word about me and never invited him to call on them so he did not go. I met Mary and Lizzy in the road. They were as cold as cucumbers. I do not know what is the matter, nor am I sure.

We came back by Chief Springs, spent two days and nights and from there to Greenville and there we remained for another ten days and, I assure, the time passed off quite pleasantly. They keep a very good house at Long's now and there are a great many boarders there indeed. Greenville never has been so crowded. Its very gay now.

There are a good many new buildings going up there. I think in a few years it will be a very handsome place.

Well, Elias has gone to Charleston, left yesterday morning. I feel quite lonely indeed and I almost have the blues. He wanted me to go with him but I thought perhaps it would be better to wait until the first of October. You know one month will soon pass off. The weather has been excessively hot this summer but now for a few days its quite pleasant.

Well, Col., how do all come on? I do feel so anxious to hear from you and I think some of you should have written before this, although I have received three letters from Mississippi since I have written. I was grieved to hear of the affliction that has befallen our brothers family, but I am sure it is all for the best. God's will be done. We ought to rejoice rather than weep to think he was taken so young from this corrupt and wicked world (death of Walter Wood, son of Jo and Mesina, born 25 April 1849, died 15 June 1851).

Tell Becca I saw Tom (T. J. Earle) in Greenville. He seemed very glad to meet me. He thinks of coming here to supply this church. I think Mr. John Sloan wants him for a teacher. He asked me to remember him to you all in my next letter. Silas, why don't you and Becca take a school? It looks to me like you might do better at that than anything else if that country is thickly settled.

I hear that you have all had chills and fever. I am truly sorry but still I don't believe it. I hear that Father has fallen off very much and I reckon it must be a mistake or some of you would write me about it. My health is excellent, now better than it has been since I have been married. They say that I have grown tall but that cannot be so. There is some of my friends that I know that would pass me in the streets at Greenville and never speak. Some of them told me I might have gone there and lived for years and they would not have known me. Elias weighs two hundred and two pounds, his skin is quite fair and his hair almost white, I never saw anyone turn grey so fast in my life.

Jimmy Blassingame passed here this week on his way home. He looks very badly, By the by, I did not see cousin Mary when I was in Pacolet. She had gone to see Sally, she has a fine daughter. Mr. and Mrs. Allendes seemed as glad to see us. Maj. Lester takes it very hard, I mean the death of his wife. I did not see the children. I met him twice at Greenville. Tell brother Alfred I spent all day last week at Mr. Lem Hambleton's, they seemed very glad to have me visit them. They talked nearly all the time of the Dr. They have a pretty little black eyed boy four months old. His name is Alfred Whitten. They call him Whitten all the time. He is a very pretty child. Mrs. H says she is almost broke up without the Dr. Mrs. Andy Hambleton is going into consumption very fast and I received a letter from sister Harriet not long since. She said her health is bad. I hope it is nothing serious. Tell Dock Jim Thompson has married last week to a lady from Charleston, Miss Scott. I don't know anything about her. They board with us. There has none of the Dark Corner girls married. Martha Wilkensen has a very nice little baby without any Daddy. Don't you think its a bad chance?

Well, I do reckon you will think that I am crazy for just write whatever come into my mind first. I reckon Mother won't write me anymore since I have been looking for a letter some time. I reckon some of you will be in soon, perhaps before I go to town.

Give my love to all the family and receive the best wishes of your sister,

Narcissa

If you will excuse this dreadful scrawl I will do better hereafter.

In an earlier letter Narcissa mentions being invited to a Goodlett wedding in Charleston. She did not attend. Could this explain the coldness of that family to her?

Not to go with her husband to Charleston when he urges her to do so reinforces the impression that her fear of lowland disease may be excessive. That her only child is gone, her family far distant, and her husband away from her most of the time must be oppressive to Cissa. She seems overly sensitive, and has lost weight. The thought that some of the distant family might show up before she leaves for Charleston seems strange. Did she know of the trip her father was to make to South Carolina that very month?

Narcissa to Alfred Washington Whitten—Pendleton Hotel, South Carolina, to Ripley, Mississippi 12 Sept. 1851

My dear Brother,

Will you pardon me for so long neglecting to write to you. Little did I think when I received your last kind letter that so many weeks would pass before I should write, but time has passed so rapidly. Oh Brother, we hardly think one month has come before it is gone, yes, gone to never return. I was very glad to hear from you all. Through Mrs. Mays I had become a little uneasy. I had not heard since the first of July. I wrote to Brother Silas last week but did it in a great hurry. It has been reported here that you all had chills and fever. It made me feel very bad though I do sincerely hope it may not be so. Surely it would go very hard with Father and Mother. My general health is better than it has been in years although I look thin. My skin is clear. I am going to try and see if I can't recoup my health. I think bathing in the salt water, moderate exercise, sea breeze will do something for me.

Elias has been gone to Charleston near three weeks. I did not think of going until the first of October but he says the city is quite healthy and wants me to go the first chance. Mr. Sloan is going on Monday next so I am going with him. By the time you get this letter, if nothing providential presents, I shall be with my husband. How delighted I would be to see you all. I thought Father would come before I left but I suppose not now. I leave so soon. I expect Elias will be in Ripley in December. He will go on business though and make a very short stay. He is not positive yet of going but Mr. Betts wants him to go.

How do you get on? I hope you have practice enough. I don't wish the folks to get sick, but if they do I should like for you to be called. Do you recollect Mrs. Williamson, Elias' sister? She died last Thursday. She has been suffering for several months with her eyes. One of them seemed to be growing, the ball bursted. I don't know of any other deaths among your acquaintances. Brother, your friends here make a great many inquiries about you. They all seem to take great interest in your welfare.

But old Pendleton seems to be drying up. Greenville is improving rapidly. It will be a city in a few years. There has been more people there this summer than ever has been known at one time. The private houses are, a great many of them, filled with boarders. Capt. Long has sold his hotel to Rutledge so they will retire to private life. Politicks are as high here now as they were in days of nullification. They fight duels and even go so far as to have street fights and all for politicks. I don't mean in Pendleton. Dr. Whitehead and Dr. Jones had a fight in the street in Hendersonville a short time since. I don't know which got the best of it. They were both very much hurt.

The members of the Church here have more quarrels than any place I ever saw. Mr. Murry's congregation has got so very small that he is going to quit. I don't know who they will get. Thomas J. Earle has been over and stayed several days amongst them, preached four or five times but they don't like him atall. I don't know who they will get next year. I don't think they really desire anybody. A great many of the members think this church will go to nothing. There has got a bad spirit amongst them.

How does your little Church come on in Ripley? I hope it is flourishing. Oh how I would like to be with you sometimes, but if we all live, and we will, I will make you a visit in the course of a year or so. I answered a letter from sister Harriet not long since. They were all pretty well. Tell Becca and Ranty I will write to them soon. I am truly sorry that Sister R is not pleased with the country. I hope that she is better satisfied by this time. Tell her she had better get married and move to Charleston. I am sure she would be pleased with that beautiful city. I hope to see you there.

I don't know whether we will board at Bonner's this year or not, but I reckon we will. We think of keeping house next year if we live and do well. Give my love to all the family. Tell them to write to me. Tell Mary, Hatty, and Baylis (children of Jo and Mesina) that they must not forget Aunt Cis. Write to me often.

May God watch over and protect you is the prayer of your affectionate Sister,

Narcissa

Since I've been writing Mrs. Mays called to see me. She sends her love to all and says tell you she will write soon.

Narcissa to Rebecca Whitten—Charleston, South Carolina, to Ripley, Mississippi, 25 Sept. 1851

My dear Sister,

Your kind letter was received just as I was ready to leave Pendleton so I had to wait until I got here before I could answer it. I was really glad to hear from you all for it had been a long while that I have heard nothing. It grieves me, Becca, to know that you are not entirely satisfied but I hope you will like the country better when you become more acquainted with it.

Well, in the first place, I will give you a description of my trip down. Well, I left Pendleton on Wednesday and got to Abbeville that evening at sundown, stopped there until around twelve that night. The moon shone beautifully and we had not gone far before we found that the driver was beastly drunk. He done better than I expected, never stalled but once, and then we were not detained more than an hour. I was the only lady in company and I felt very small. The gentlemen were very kind to me and the driver made a great many apologies for being drunk. We got to Hamburg safe, stopped there all night, got on the express train at ten o'clock and got here at three. How would you like to travel thirty miles almost equal to the birds?

I reckon you are all often asked to think I would risk my health in Charleston in September. I assure you I think it quite as healthy here as is possible. It is true Elias has fallen off five or six pounds since he came down but that working hard. The weather is not any warmer here than up home, though not so warm for we have the breeze.

Becca, you ask to know how the old place looks. I did not go there. Oh no, I could not think of such a thing. I should have felt dreadfully. Mo (the new owner) has stopped up the road, there is no way to pass. He has cut down all those beautiful trees in the bottom between cousin Mary's and our house. They said cousin Mary was getting on as usual, just makes what does them and no more. I was too much fatigued to visit Aunt Lydia (her mother's sister Lydia Maverick Earle Prince) and I don't think they cared much to see me. Theron (brother of Thomas J. Earle) passed by me and knew we were there and never called to see us. Uncle drinks more than he used to. Lou seems to think very hard of you for not writing to her. Mr. and Mrs. Allander were marked in their attentions to us. They are coming down to spend the winter, Anna is coming too.

Oh, I would be delighted to have some of you here with me, I know you would be pleased here. It is a pleasant place. I have a good many acquaintances here, and there is one thing very pleasant. I can attend church every Sabbath and hear a good sermon. Oh, I do wish you could be here. We are going to have Baptist Convention in November. There will be a great many able ministers here. Well Becca, Tom (Thomas J. Earle) came to Pendleton before I left and preached several times. The people did not like him much nor they don't seem to like anyone. I think the church will go down.

I am very sorry Father could not come before I left Pendleton but it was not convenient for me to stay any longer. I am very sorry Harriet left the church, rather she should never have joined it. She wrote me that. I never should have thought of anything so silly. I am a full blood Baptist and I don't care who knows it, and I am not selfish in it either. I could not have the Bible before me and be anything else. I read more than I used to. My opportunities are better and my mind is free and easy. I can read and understand it better.

If nothing happens I expect to do a great deal of work this winter. There is no chance to stop here until late and you know winter nights are very long. A person must do something. The time passes off very rapidly here. The winters are dreary, so I've been told.

Ask Ranty what made him quit writing to me. Tell Mother I've been looking for a letter from her for a long time. Tell Brother Jo that Bert and Thompson have sold the Messenger to the Anderson folks. Don't you reckon old Pendleton is drying up? Now they speak of starting another paper. They have dancing school there. They want to try their best awhile. You must write to me often. It is a great thrill to hear from you all. What Mesina named the little one? (Frank Adams.) Give my love to her and go tell them its time to stop. I wrote to the Dr. a few days before I left Pendleton. Tell him I am looking for a letter. I hope the Col. (Silas Reagan Jr.) has got his horse ere this. Tell him I am looking for a letter from him. Elias joins me in love to you all,

May God bless you is the prayer of your Sister,

Narcissa A. Holcombe

These two letters establish that Silas Reagan returned from Mississippi to South Carolina during September 1851. That lonesome Narcissa, boarding at the Pendleton Hotel, did not wait to see her Father is beyond my comprehension. No letter contains a clue. Her need to be with Elias was stronger than that to see Silas Reagan. In later letters she expresses grief for not having seen him. It turned out to be her last opportunity to do so.

She remains disturbed, almost bitter, at Harriet for changing churches. Her letters indicate to me that she was not happy with her life and resented being so often alone.

The following article appeared in *The Flag Of The Union,* Jackson, Mississippi, 7 Nov. 1851, quoting the *South Carolina Patriot.* The writer had just seen Silas Reagan Whitten, in South Carolina, back from Mississippi where he moved in late 1850. It confirms that he did return to his home state after the move and suggests he was opposed to succession.

Gen. Foote (Henry S. Foote, who, a few days after this appeared, was elected governor of Mississippi on a Union Party ticket, defeating Southern Rights candidate Jefferson Davis.) This gallant and noble Mississippian, who has done more for his state, and as much for the South and the Union, as any statesman now living, in presenting the true issues before the country, and in defending those issues, has recently come out with an address to his constituents in reply to certain questions propounded to him. In this address he tells the people of Mississippi that a state has no right to secede from the Union: that in the language of Mr Madison, the Constitution "required an adoption in toto and forever." and that the Mississippi Convention of 1834 declared that a constitutional right of secession from the Union, on the part of any State, was utterly unsanctioned by the Federal Constitution. He says that he has ever agreed with General Washington that "it was of infinite moment that we should properly estimate the immense value of our national Union." and that he concurs with General Jackson when speaking of the Federal Constitution, he says: "we have hitherto relied on it as the perpetual bond of our Union."

We have just seen Silas R. Whitten, Esq., who left Mississippi a few days since, where he now resides, and who informs us that General Foote will be elected by an overwhelming majority (he was). Our friend Whitten thinks that Colonel Jefferson Davis will not receive the vote Quitman would have got had he continued in the canvass. As to disunion or secession, in Mississippi, it is repudiated by almost the whole of the Southern Rights Party. If they were to come out there, that is, the politicians, as they have in South Carolina, and declare themselves disunionists, per se, they would not have a corporal's guard to rally around them and defend their treason.—*South Carolina Patriot.*

Elizabeth Ann Whitten to Ranson E. Whitten—Columbus, Georgia, to Ripley, Mississippi, 12 Oct. 1851

Father is fat and hearty and seems very happy. Our city is in great political excitement at this time. Politics is all we hear or see. Father (James Whitten, elder brother of Silas Reagan) is head and heels for Buchanan, brother Tom (Calvin Thompson Whitten) is worse for Fillmore, and between them we understand all the virtues and faults of the candidates.

I had a letter from Uncle Isaac (Dr. Isaac Smith Whitten, another brother) not long since. All well. Three of cousin Alvin's (Alvin Earle Whitten, son of Charles Whitten Jr.) children from Texas are traveling through Georgia visiting their relations. They have been to Uncle Dr. (Isaac), a Mrs. Foster, her husband, and a brother and sister. I reckon they will call on us on their return. Perhaps her name was Julia Whitten (daughter of Alvin Earle Whitten who married W. C. Foster). I have heard of her but don't know anything of them.

Father is away at an association but told me to send his love to all. We still hope to visit you at some time not far distant.

Uncle Dr. wants me to stay all the winter with him but I don't reckon I shall, but expect to stay a portion of the time if nothing happens. Brother Tom starts to New York tomorrow. I was going with him that far but got disappointed.

You must give my love to all, especially Uncle and Aunt and Cousin Beck, also Uncle Ranson and family and write me soon.

Affectionately yours,
Eliza A. Whitten

Eliza is a good source of information. She often wrote Ranson E., with whom she had a close relationship. This letter is important because it is the only proof known to Whitten researchers that ties Alvin Earle Whitten to Charles Whitten Jr. The letter seems to indicate that Calvin Thompson Whitten, her brother, had not yet moved to Guntown, Mississippi.

Narcissa to Alfred Washington Whitten—Charleston, South Carolina, to Ripley, Mississippi, 2 Dec. 1851

My own dear Brother,

Forgive my long silence. I know that I should have answered your kind letter ere this but I did not feel well. I never had such violent cold in my life. Three days I was quite sick. We did not call in a physician. I doctored myself. There are a great many good doctors here but, oh, they are so extravagant in their bills, takes a little fortune to pay them. I am quite well but very lonely. Elias has gone to the country collecting. He has gone as far as Ashville, North Carolina but will stop at different places between here and there, be gone six weeks. That's a good long time to be alone.

It is true I have a great many acquaintances in Charleston, and some of them very agreeable, but still we can't tell who our friends are now a days. Oh my dear Brother, this world is full of corruption. They don't seem to notice a death here. There is rarely a day that I don't see a funeral train pass, either black or white.

But I dare say my dear Brother, you feel sad enough without hearing such sad things. Oh, how I longed to be with you in your troubles, but it was impossible. Oh, it is such a hard thing to think of, those dear little ones being left. But you did not tell me how Brother bore it (Mesina, wife of brother Jo, died 17 Oct. 1851). I never had anything bear so heavily on me, but I know it is not right for me to grieve. She was a Christian. No doubt her soul is at rest. God knows what is best for us all. He has to afflict us very severely sometimes to make us more humble.

It grieves me, dear Brother to know that you are not satisfied. I know that you are not from the way you write. I cannot be content and know that any of you are in trouble. I often imagine myself with you all. Oh, it grieves me to know that Father was home and I did not see him. I have seen a great many that have seen him and they say he is quite thin but still very lively. I am glad to hear that for I think it is much the best. I am not so cheerful as I used to be. You never saw me so thin, but I am not displeased with my situation. I don't express a wish but I get it. Elias is very indulgent. He is generally liked by all that know him. He has had a dreadful cold. It was bad when he left yesterday. I shall be very anxious until I hear from him.

Look here, I think some of you ought to write more frequently. Silas and Ranty never write. Becca does when she can. I hope she does not work so hard as she used to. I do think it is wrong though. I work just as hard as I ever did but it is all sewing. I can get as much as I can do but they pay me little for it.

I am so sorry to hear that you don't get much practice. I am so anxious for you to get something to do for I know you need it. But do not despair, you will prosper, I am sure of it. It would be such a blessing if I only had you near me. But I am content. If we all live we will meet. I am determined to make you a visit if you remain there or don't go to California.

I received a letter from Lizz Clayton a short time since, wanting us to spend Christmas with her, and indeed, she wanted me to stay all winter but I think I had better stay at home. There will be a good many of the Pendleton folks down this winter, amongst them Mrs. Mays and Maria Louisa Maxwell.

I am truly sorry that Dr. Earle (Dr. M. Baylis Earle, brother of Thomas J. Earle) is so much hurt with me. I am sure he has no cause. I stayed in Greenville ten days at one time and thought he knew it and would call whenever it was convenient. Tom (Thomas J. Earle) came in the night before I left, heard I was there, and called immediately. He told me the Dr. was very much mortified. Harriet (Maxwell, Dr. Earle's wife) had known all the week that I was there and never told him. I left next morning before sunrise so I never got to see him. I wrote to him after I went home. They say he is almost crazy about his baby. It is so pretty. Babies are so common nowadays its hardly worthwhile to notice them.

I suppose you have heard of the death of Mrs. Andy Hambleton and her brother. His parents are in great distress, but I think it is wrong to grieve for the death of a Christian. But enough, I must stop, my paper is nearly gone. I have not heard from sister Harriet in a long while. Aunt Ammy (Amaryllis Earl Bomar, her mother's sister) will be here in January to spend a week or two.

Now I hope you will write to me soon and often. Do tell me all the particulars. Tell me how Mother is and how the children and Jo get on, and how Father was pleased with his trip home, everything and all. Give my love to all the family and receive the assurance of my best wishes for your prosperity and happiness. You, my Brother, have passed over a rough sea, but I have a hope that it will be smoother in time to come.

Your devoted Sister,
Narcissa

Elias has begun a six-week business trip that will keep him away from Narcissa during Christmas. She is alone in a Charleston boarding house, grieving over the death of Jo's wife, Mesina. She herself is ill and will in a few short weeks succumb to measles and its complications. This is the last of her letters in Rebecca's collection.

Elias Holcombe to Alfred Washington Whitten—Charleston, South Carolina, to Ripley, Mississippi, 22 Jan. 1852

Dear Alfred,

Yours and Rebecca's letters were duly received and would have been answered earlier but from the fact that Cis was very sick at the time and I concluded not to write until I saw the result of her disease, and, as I then anticipated, it has resulted fatally. Our dear Cis died this morning at one o'clock, and I can now say emphatically that I am alone in the world, and I feel almost as if the last link were broken. First my sweet little Belle was taken from me, and now my dear Cis has gone to meet her in Heaven.

I left the city on the first of December and went on a business excursion through the country. On Christmas day Cis was taken sick with measles. They broke out on her finely and she neglected, or thought it unnecessary, to call a physician until they struck, affecting her bowels, causing dysentery with inflammation of the bowels. Capt. Betts then wrote for me to come home immediately, which I did, arriving here on Sunday the 11th instant, found Cis very low, unable to turn over in the bed. She, however, commenced to improve immediately and continued to improve slowly until last Sunday, by which time Dr. Robertson had got her bowels thoroughly regulated. On Monday morning she commenced growing weaker and continued to waste away until her death. She suffered greatly from twelve to three quarters past when she became quiet and died at five minutes past without a struggle, and I humbly hope, she died as she lived, a Christian, and that our loss is her eternal gain.

We buried her this evening at four o'clock in the Church Yard of the First Baptist Church. Rev. Mr. Cuthbert of the Second Baptist Church preached a very feeling funeral. Mrs. Mays was with us last night and today and has been very kind.

I write to you so that you can break the news to your mother, fearing that if she should hear the news suddenly, it might affect her too seriously. Give my best love to all the family and write to me immediately.

Your affectionate brother,
E. Holcombe

Write me how to direct a box to you and to whose care as I want to box up Cis trunks, clothes, etc. and send to her mother.

The Whittens had known grief. Silas and Eleanor Kee lost their first born a month after birth in 1816, Bell died in 1848, and Walter Wood in June 1851. That beloved daughter, Narcissa, and daughter-in-law, Mesina, were lost to the family within just three months had a devastating effect on them. They understood Christian death to be instant transformation from flawed earth to perfect heaven, as described in Aunt Harriett Roddy's next letter to Rebecca. This belief served to comfort all who mourned the lost sisters.

Now all of Silas and Eleanor's family live in Mississippi.

Harriet Harrison Earle Roddy to Rebecca Whitten—String Prairie, Texas, to Ripley, Mississippi, 10 April 1852

My dear Rebecca,

I received your very affectionate letter and acknowledge that I have been remiss in not answering it sooner. I truly sympathize in your affliction, but I rejoice to believe that you have found the pearl of great price and know from whence to draw comfort (Rebecca's sister, Narcissa, and sister-in-law Mesina, died during the past few months), a peace the world knows not, and yet all earthly good compared with this is of little value. For all that delights and gives pleasure here will soon pass off as a tale that is told (with regard to us). But the joys of eternity will be ever new, ever increasing, where the tear of sorrow will never flow, sickness and death will be there unknown. Our friends cannot return to us but we shall soon follow them. May we there meet and, with the redeemed, join in the praises of the Redeemer.

You wish to know what church or denomination I am attached to. Myself and two of my daughters are members of the Presbyterian

Church, but unless our names are written in The Book Of Life it will avail us nothing. Our settlement is new. We therefore have a small society and a very excellent preacher, one of the best of men and a charming family. They live in less than half a mile from us.

You wish also to know where we are situated in Texas. We are settled between the Brazos and Colorado rivers, some forty or fifty miles of Austin, the capital of our state. Here is a great deal of rich land and beautifully situated, producing abundant crops when at all seasonable, but we have had no rain since last summer and crops were cut off and, of course, there is great scarcity of produce and very extravagant prices.

We had a letter from South Carolina recently. Our friends there were in good health generally. Sister Amaryllis' (Earle Bomar) health was improving and I suppose she has given out her trip to the south.

There has been a good deal of sickness and a number of deaths here this winter and spring. Our family has been blessed above many in that respect. My health has not been good for many years. I have a disease of the lungs from which I have suffered occasionally. I am sorry to learn that your dear Mother has suffered so much, but I suppose that there is few could so submissively submit to bear it so patiently, and then to have such an affectionate, good daughter to solace her declining days and minister to her wants, a treasure greatly to be prized. I know how to value such a treasure, for I, too, am blessed with such a one. We have one dear daughter with us, our third daughter. We called her for your Mother, and she represents herein all that is amiable and affectionate. May you both be blessed with better days.

I have not heard from sister Poole (Letitia Sorrell Earle Poole) for a long time, only what you wrote me. I have several times written to her and my brother but, not receiving any returns, I had to quit writing. Sister Bomar has not written to me, I suppose, in two years. I was pleased to hear she intended to visit the south. No doubt it would improve her health.

I fear I am not to be so fortunate as to meet with any of my near and dear relatives again in time. Whether we shall be permitted to know each other in Eternity is a mystery that cannot be solved. Yet our great concern should be to meet the approbation of the Judge and be received with the Blessed and we shall be happy.

Give me all the information you can about the relations, I so seldom hear from them. Say something about your brothers and sisters and those dear little children you have the care of (brother Jo's). I truly wish you were all near us. I cannot see to write well and my letter is full of blots and errors. Do excuse. Give my love to your father and my dear sister Elen, all your brothers and sisters and little ones. I love them all.

Adieu, dear Rebecca. May Heavens most choice blessings ever be yours is the wish of your affectionate aunt,

Harriet H. Roddy

Elias Holcombe to Alfred Washington Whitten—Charleston, South Carolina, to Ripley, Mississippi, 1 June 1852

Dear Alfred,

I wrote you some time since but, as I have received no reply, I presume you never received my letter. I received a letter from our mother some time since, but I hardly know what to write to her. I have continued putting it off until I am almost ashamed to write to her. Say to her, however, that I have not forgotten her but, on the contrary, that I have for her the highest regard it is possible for a son to feel toward a mother. My feeling toward the rest of the family is the same. It has always been that of the kindest regard and most brotherly affection.

On tomorrow morning I leave this city for the mountains, and when I arrive at sweet little Belle's grave, I will write to your mother. I have this day shipped her Bng. George S. Abbott, one box with the following direction, A. W. Whitten, Ripley, Mississippi, care of Pickett Perkins Company, New Orleans, A. O. Harris Company, Memphis, Tennessee. I have paid freight on the box to New Orleans. The agent will not receive freight to Memphis so that you will have to see to getting the box home and paying the freight from New Orleans. The box contains all the clothes, etc. of our lost and dearly beloved Cis.

I am getting along finely in a business point of view. I commence today on a salary of $1500 in the large establishment now opening in this city of Bancroft, Betts, and Marshall. I will send you a full description of the house and business one of these days.

When your friend, Mr. Rucker, was here last spring I sold him five hundred and sixty nine dollars worth of goods. His note has been due sometimes but remains unpaid. I wish you would inquire about him and write me what his standing is at the present and what it is likely to be. Give my warmest love and best wishes to all the family and accept for yourself my best wishes and kindest regard.

Very affectionately yours,
Elias Holcombe

Write me immediately and direct to Greenville CH, South Carolina.

Elliott Ann Ray Whitten to Rebecca Whitten—Chalybeate to Ripley, Mississippi, 23 Dec. 1853

My own dear Rebecca,

We all enjoy a reasonable portion of good health. I am mending fast enough, I reckon. I am so much better that I have been since I last saw you that I do not feel to complain in the least. The bed gets only one visit in the day from me and that is a short one, as I don't like it much. The Doctor is quite well, poor fellow, he has had a hard time. He and I have cut out one coat and one pair of pantaloons this week. I made a part of the coat and knit some. We are on the gaining ground, I think, and if we remain so we will be there soon as we intend paying you about the first visit.

Jim (probably a slave) got home, and if he has told any stories, I don't know it. He caught a bull this morning and hurt his hand, and the way he grunted. The cake you sent was thankfully received. Give Joe and Mary Jane (Mary Jane White, Joe's second wife) my doubled and twisted complements and tell them to come and see us.

I want to see you all the very first kind. Pluck (Silas Jr.) did not talk much when he was here. Where does Frank (Frank Adams, Jo's son) sleep and how does he navigate in our days? Does Joe kiss Mary Jane much and how does he behave himself anyhow?

Write to me, Becker, you know I am an inquisitive little wretch. Make all the reasonable allowances for this Mrs. and come to see us whenever you can. Our friends and relatives are well as far as I know. The Doct. has one case only, it is mending. Papa (Rev. Ambrose Ray) started down in the neighborhood of Canaan Church last Wednesday to marry a Mr. Brown and Miss Arnett.

My love to all,
Elliott

We have a new correspondent, Elliott Ann Ray, who married Alfred Washington in February 1853. Her father, the Rev. Ambrose Ray, lived in Alcorn County near Jonesborough and Chalybeate. Alfred and Elliott have settled close to the Rays, and he has opened his practice.

Jo married his second wife, Mary Jane White, on 15 Dec. 1853.

Alfred Washington to Rebecca Whitten—Jonesborough to Ripley, Mississippi, about 1854

Dear Becca,

I am pained to hear of your sickness and Fathers. I cannot now consistently come; 1st for these 3 days, busy in the practice, and 2nd today I was stricken with pleurisy I suppose, and cannot comfortably ride, though I doubt not that in a day or two it will all be right with me again.

I guess for the great weakness and the chills into which you have been thrown that your last monthly sickness was unusually profuse and the chills and fever, being unrelieved kept up and increased. The weakness has resulted in still more fever and weakening. Lucorshal on which as it may be found in any domestic doctor book (which see if one convenient).

Treatment. 1st break up the chill and fever and for you I would prescribe 10 gms Davispound, 10 gms blue mass, 20 gms quinine, and a few drops oil black pepper made into 10 pills. Allow yourself 20 hours before the chill expected and take one pill every two hours. This will break the chills and fever the 1st trial. After the chill time has passed take a dose of oil and work the medicine off. After breaking chill and fever (without which you will get no relief) the bark bitters prescribed for Silas taken regularly so as to just keep the bowels right will do very well, but I would add an occasional blue mass pill. In your present distress, as I understand it, warm hip washing and still more local baths of milk and water made warm and even springing with the same will give great comfort. The warm foot bath should be used too.

Under this treatment I should expect a decrease in the discharge which would otherwise be prolonged, indicating steady improvement. Then the greatest possible benefit would be derived from a change to cold hip bath taken twice a day and kept up until the period for nature to appear singularly again. Then the bathing should again be warm comfortably with warm sweating teas and c.

Write me soon and be sure to speak fully, in the case I cannot go I may be of service this way. For Father, equal parts in bulk of Gum Guaiacum and Sulphur, pulverized together and taken a teaspoon full 3 times a day.

Your brother
AWW

Harriet Harrison Earle Roddy to Eleanor Kee Whitten—Lexington, Texas, to Ripley, Mississippi, 8 Jan. 1855

My dear Sister Elen,

I am at a loss to account for your long silence. I have written several times to you and cousin Rebecca but have failed to get an answer from either of you. I have thought that Rebecca perhaps has married and left you, but then, my Sister, some others of the family would write. Yet still I cannot divine the cause of so long silence. I once more beg for an answer. I am very anxious to hear from you.

I am truly sorry that Mr. Whitten did not get on to Texas when he was moving. Why did he stop so soon? The emigrants here from that state think this much preferable and I should have been so much delighted to have had you near us. It would give me great pleasure to have our children associate. Only two of mine have families. Three are single and live with us, Baylis, Elen, and Joseph.

Mr. Woodlief, who married our eldest daughter moved, last winter, to Galveston City, where every contagious disease prevails, lost three of his sons, one fifteen years old, one ten, the other two, the most lovely children I ever saw. The yellow fever swept the city of all that were not acclimated. And what are the treasures of this life that we would take in exchange for our children? The wealth of this world would not recompense in any degree. I mourn the loss of those dear children and lament that I cannot induce the father to bring his family out of danger. I would write many things to my sister but I will write again when I am in better spirits.

Should any of your children come to Texas I hope they will not stop until they reach us. Tell Rebecca, please, to write to me, and do, my Sister, write soon.

Give my love to Mr. Whitten and the family, dear Sister, and receive the warmest affection of your sister,

Harriet H. Roddy

How many thousands of letters like this one were written during this period as families moved on and left loved ones behind? Letter writing was a difficult and time-consuming undertaking, news from home all too scarce.

Elliott Ann to Silas Reagan Whitten—Jonesborough to Ripley, Mississippi, 31 Jan. 1855

Dear Father and Mother,

Without having anything very interesting to write, I seat myself for that purpose. Myself and family are well and have been ever since you saw us. My better half was boasting yesterday that he weighed more now than he has before in several years. There is very little sickness within our bounds. The measles have been pretty thick in Pleasant Hill neighborhood and two that we have heard of died with them.

We received a letter from Pluck (Silas Jr.) Saturday, was very glad to hear from you all. I should think we might move down now as you have your room chimneyed. We have a new smokehouse as well as you and can lock every bit of our meat when we go to see you. It is hung up and drying very prettily. The Doct. works like he loved to. He is now building a very large shelter over his well. He intends using a part of it for milk and I reckon he will build a summer seat of the remaining part. He has it finished with the exception of covering. When that is complete we contemplate moving our wagon shelter from before the house door so that people passing can see our signboard. We have an elegant ash hopper and intend putting up a henhouse as soon as it is convenient.

Ann Greer has been with us about a month. She left last Thursday morning to go to Pontotoc to school. Mr. and Mrs. Greer have been to see us since they moved to Tippah. James McCray ate dinner with us a few days before he left for Panola. Robert (Ray) and family are well. He, James Moor, and Lafayette Norman have bought Abbett Rucker out. James is the clerk. Bob is going to teach school this year.

Pa's (the Rev. Ambrose Ray) family are only tolerable well. He will go to Memphis today, I suppose. Aunt Elizabeth Garrett (Elliott's mother was a Garrett) has almost recovered from her long illness. Uncle was sick last week but seemed well enough yesterday. Uncle John Garrett and wife have got home. They went to Alabama after a legacy coming to her from her father's estate. They lost their youngest child while gone. Mr. Gatlin, our neighbor, got home from Arkansas yesterday evening.

I am sorry Becca and Ranty did not come down. We want to see you all, and if some of you do not come to see us pretty soon we will go and see you. Father, which had on the nicest cape, Mother, or Granny White? I want to see Jo and Mary Jane and the babe (William Andrew Whitten, born 15 Dec. 1854). Tell them to come.

Mr. Greer has been to see us since he returned from Pontotoc. He says Duck (Medora Frances, Elliott's sister) is well and pleased with her school but says she will come home at the close of this session. If she has to take the stage and come to Ripley, she intends making her visit short, then will stay a week or ten days, I reckon. We were sorry to hear that cousin William was confined to his room again. Hope you all will go and see him.

We have had some pretty cold weather this week. I think you might come and see us once in a long while anyhow. We have lots of plates now, and nice ones, at that. Give our love to all the family. Tell Frank I shall claim the babe when I come and ask Hat if she does what I said she must (Frank Adams and Harriett Earle, children of Jo and Mesina). Excuse errors for there are many.

Yours affectionately,
E. Ann Whitten

Here we meet Duck, Elliott's sister, who later will marry Pluck, Silas Reagan Whitten Jr.

Elizabeth Ann Whitten to Silas Reagan Whitten—Columbus, Georgia, to Ripley, Mississippi, 14 April 1855

Dear Uncle,

I am very sorry that it falls to my lot to write you a letter of disappointment, but a circumstance has occurred in our family this week that will detain us at least a week, if not longer. We have had the scarlet fever in our city a good while, but our family has escaped until this day a week ago. One of sister's little boys, about eight years old was taken with it in its most violent form, and it has been, the Doctor says, one of the most critical cases it has ever fell to his lot to attend. With great care we think him out of danger. We hope none of the others will have it but you know it will be something remarkable if they don't. We don't feel willing, at least, to leave until we are satisfied, and the Doctor says I might have it perhaps, and I had better stay a few days longer to try the affect.

If possible we will leave Monday week. I know you cannot be more disappointed than we are but duty, you know, always before pleasure. If convenient, please let Brother (Calvin Thompson Whitten) and Aunt Mariam know what detains us and give our love to all, and accept the affection of your niece,

Elizabeth A. Whitten

I received your kind letter and will abide by your directions as a guide. E. A. W.

The youngest daughter of the Rev. James Whitten of Columbus, Georgia, corresponded frequently with the Mississippi branch. She and her father did make the visit she mentions, arriving at Ripley about May 7. James and Eliza

next visited brother Calvin Thompson in Guntown, Lee County, traveling on to Pontotoc to the homes of Aunt Mariam and cousin Harriet.

Ranson E. Whitten to Luther White (husband of Harriet Whitten, daughter of Uncle Ranson)—Ripley to Hudsonville, Mississippi, 19 May 1855

My Uncle (James Whitten) and his daughter (Elizabeth Ann) from Columbus, Georgia, have been with us ten or twelve days. They left us on Tuesday last for Pontotoc. Uncle is a Missionary Baptist preacher. He went up to Antioc to hear the Antis last Sabbath week and on last Sabbath he preached at our house and I reckon he gave the hardshells the hardest rub that you ever heard of on the subject of Sabbath Schools, Bible Societies, Temperance Societies, etc.

His daughter is a very intelligent and accomplished lady. I found her very interesting and was loth to part from her for you know I am fond of female society.

Elizabeth Ann Whitten to Ranson E. Whitten—Palmetto to Ripley, Mississippi, 1 June 1855

We got to Calvin's (Calvin Thompson Whitten, her brother) safe, found him and family well and left them well. We got a hack there and came down here last Thursday, the 24th. We found Aunt's (Mariam Whitten Davis) family well. They sent for all the children that was away and we had quite a jolly time of it. I have spent one night with Cousin Harriet and will see her again before I leave. I love her very much indeed. I will see her as much as I can. We will leave here the time appointed if nothing happens, June the 4th. We are to take stage at Okolona about fourteen miles from here. Uncle Davis is to carry us that far.

Alfred Washington to Silas Reagan Whitten—Peach Orchard (Jonesborough) to Ripley, Mississippi, 8 June 1855

Dear Father,

I have no news, general, but fine seasons, promising crops, good health, too.

Elliott commenced making ugly faces yesterday evening and I soon found out what to fix for and accordingly summoned all the Grannies around and about 8 o'clock last night she gave birth to a gal baby and her name is Mary (Dora) in memory of Mrs. Ray (Mary Garrett, Elliott's mother) and Grandmother Whitten (Mary Reagan). If it had been a boy, I should have called it John for Grandfather, or for yourself. While on this subject I will say that if it were my fortune to have 20 I should not go out of the family for a name.

The child is of medium size and naturally formed and although ugly looks quite healthy and growing. Elliott suffered a good deal, but has passed the night pretty comfortably, and her and the babe seem quiet and cheerful this morning. Elliott says you must come, tell Mother to come etc.

Affectionately,
A. W. Whitten

Alfred and Elliott have their firstborn, Mary Dora. Even doctors used midwives.

William Blassingame to Ranson E. Whitten—Hendersonville, North Carolina, to Ripley, Mississippi, 16 July 1855

You inquired if (Elias) Holcombe is married or where he is. He is not married that I know of. He still remains with Betts and Marshall. I think he is enjoying himself finely. Nothing to trouble his mind. "Eat, drink, and grow merry"

Elizabeth Ann Whitten to Ranson E. Whitten—Columbus, Georgia, to Ripley, Mississippi, 4 Aug. 1855

Dear Cousin Rantie,

Your very kind letter has been received and you have no idea how glad I was to hear from you all. I have been looking for some time for a letter from Uncle and Cousin Pluck, but Father received one from Uncle this evening and I know that they both have good excuses for I can't believe they have forgotten me. I was getting the blues when yours came for I thought I had been home long enough for one to reach me. I received one from Cousin Martha (Meriwether, stepdaughter of Uncle Isaac Smith Whitten) at the same time, which was joy number two.

I have nothing very interesting to write you. Our city is very dull always at this season of the year. We are having excitement enough politically speaking, but you know I can't participate in that if I am a know nothing. They won't let me vote. I hear nothing else talked of scarcely. Brother Tom (Calvin Thompson) is a full blooded American. Father is very mum, but I believe he is opposed to them. They had a large barbecue here yesterday and everything passed off very pleasantly.

We had a tremendous excitement in our city last night. We have three prisoners in our jail convicted of murder and tomorrow the sentence of death is to be passed upon them. One of them has made his escape once but they caught him and he has been in irons ever since. Last night he attempted to get loose again. Someone had carried him a saw and he had almost sawed his chains in part. He was then to fire his bed clothes and when the jailer came in to put them out he was to break loose and, they suppose, kill him and get away. But, poor fellow, he made a bad calculation. After he set fire to his bed clothes and they had got to burning pretty well, he commenced crying fire, murder, etc. I bet he was in the habit of cutting up so many tricks that the jailer did not pay any attention to him until some of the other prisoners found it out and commenced screaming, but before they could get to him and get him out, he was dead, smothered to death. He was a wretched man. He called to some of the prisoners after he found he was bound to burn up and told them to meet him in hell. He is to be buried this afternoon at four o'clock.

The health of the family is very good. Father is looking reasonably well. I have just got home from my brothers. His family are in fine health. The crops in this country are splendid. Everybody can have aplenty to eat. The health of the city is very good. We have had a great deal of rain but not too much so far.

I have never written to Cousin Alfred (Alfred Washington Whitten) but think I will in a few days. Tell Uncle (Silas Reagan) and Cousin Pluck (Silas Jr.) to write me as soon as it is convenient, and, dear Cousin Ranson, write me soon and I promise you to always answer them forthwith. You don't know how much good it does me to get a letter from that country.

Tell Cousin Beck (Rebecca) I often think of her and wonder how her and Luther are getting along, and dear old Aunt Ellie (Eleanor Kee Whitten), she knows that I love her like a mother. I can't help for the life of me associating her with my mother in feeling. She remembers I forgot and called her Mother several times while I was there. I never knew a mother's love, but with hers I feel satisfied. Give my love to all the relatives. Father joins me in love to you all, Uncle Ranson and family, Cousin Jo and family, in fact, all. Write to me who you allude as being the old bachelor I spoke of. I shall look for an answer soon. Good bye Cousin. God bless you.

Affectionately yours,

Eliza

Is Eliza something of a feminist? She comments with sarcasm about not being allowed to vote. We men continued to control things for another sixty-five years or so. Her comment on brother Tom's preference for the American Party sounds as though he lived nearby. Having visited Calvin Thompson in Guntown just two months prior, I believe she spoke of what she learned of him then. We have no reason to believe this family left Lee County, Mississippi, until about 1863. She has heard from Cousin Martha, stepdaughter of Isaac Smith, and has visited her other brother, the Reverend Arphax Whitten, in nearby Lee County, Alabama.

Alfred Washington to Silas Reagan Whitten—Jonesborough to Ripley, Mississippi, 3 Nov. 1855

My Dearly Beloved Father,

I rise out of bed to discharge what I perceive to be a paternal duty to you. It has just occurred to me from some conversation you had with Elliott the other day that possibly I have incurred your censure, thru some misrepresentation of my real feelings in relation to your election. That I have given some cause for censure I do not pretend to deny. For I said long before I had thought of your becoming a candidate for any office that I would not support my father on the KK ticket. I think I have heard you say, and I thought I knew, that you would not have any office in the gift of the county. I was wrong to make such expression and I did not know how I would feel until I saw your name announced when I wept. I felt committed to my pledge though I never thought of voting against you. You may have heard that I am making harsh expressions against you. If you have, it's a lie. There is more lies than truth told.

We may differ politically and I suppose we do, and in this I may be wrong for I do not claim to be perfect on any subject. It is hardly probable that any changes would be made or any good effected by our talking politics, and I offer this compromise, that in future we say but little about it. Although I do not wish to be understood as desiring to preclude your fatherly advice and guidance on any subject, however refractory I may have been at times that have gone by, I have in reality always desired to be dutiful and kind to you, and God forbid that I should ever be activated by any colder feelings.

I have always delighted to honor you, and if I am spared to get to the polls and permitted to vote when I get there, I shall cast my vote for you. And that you may know that I intend especially to honor you by thus voting I assure you that unless my mind changes, I shall not vote for another man on the Know Knothing ticket.

With an anxious desire for your general welfare, and for your triumphant election, I remain your affectionate son,

A. W. Whitten

Silas Reagan's decision to run for office on the Know Knothing Party surprises and disappoints Alfred, who is opposed to them. His reaction to the news, and the manner in which he communicates his thoughts is further proof of his devotion. I would be honored to receive such a letter from my son. I hope Silas Reagan was also.

Elizabeth Ann Whitten to Rebecca Whitten—Columbus, Georgia, to Ripley, Mississippi, 6 Jan. 1856

Dear Cousin Rebecca,

I determined to write you the first letter this year and though I have nothing of interest for your care I still will feel that I have discharged my duty. You know you told me when I was in your country that you scarcely done any writing and that is the reason for not writing you long since. It is not, my dear Cousin, for want of affection for you. I now shall have you in debt to me for one letter, at least.

I received Cousin Ranson's a few days ago with your post script enclosed and for which I am much obliged. I will write to him soon. I was glad to hear of Pluck's marriage.

I would be pleased to hear of a few more of the same sort. As soon as you get old enough (Rebecca was thirty at this time) I shall expect to hear of yours. I think my lot in life is single blessedness. I have been so disappointed in my calculations that I feel very indifferent about it. I cannot marry those I want and, of course, I shall marry for no one's accommodation. I wish I could have been in that part of the world when Cousin was given in wedlock. I know I should have enjoyed myself so well, but we must be content to do as we can, not as we please.

How did you enjoy Christmas? It commenced raining here on Christmas morning and rained almost incessantly for almost a week, so we had nothing but mud. I was out to a dining on New Years Day and to a party that night that comprised of frolicking.

Our family is all in excellent health. Father (James Whitten) is looking as well as ever I saw him and often expresses a wish to visit you all again. I hear from Pontotoc but seldom. I had a letter from Martha (Meriwether, stepdaughter of Uncle Isaac Smith Whitten) last week. I have not heard from Uncle Isaac very lately. At last accounts he was well. I believe I have nothing else worth writing. I shall expect an answer soon.

Give my love to Uncle Ranson and family, Uncle Silas, Aunt Eleanor, and all the family and Father wishes to be remembered to all. Do excuse my writing. I have a poor pen and pale ink. I will close by wishing you a happy new year, dear Cousin, may it bring more happiness to you than the past did to me, hoping you may all enjoy it.

I remain your affectionate cousin,
Eliza

Eliza is the first to mention the marriage 12 Oct. 1855 of Silas Reagan Whitten Jr. (Pluck) to Madora Frances Ray (Duck), sister of Elliott Ann. She also sends love to Uncle Ranson and family, who have moved from Fayette, Tennessee, to the Shady Grove community in Tippah County, Mississippi. Since she made no mention of them in the spring and summer of 1855, they must have arrived from Fayette after June of that year.

Harriett to Rebecca Whitten—Coonwah to Ripley, Mississippi, 20 Jan. 1856

My very dear Sister,

I have been intending for weeks to write to you but first one thing and then another has deferred it and now it is so cold I can only sit by the fire and write on my lap. We have had the coldest winter I have ever known in this country, four weeks severe weather without one pleasant day, but it surely will change soon. I am anxious to hear how Mother has come through this winter. I am afraid it is hard on her.

I believe I have no news to write. I am disappointed, oh so sadly, in not seeing some of you this winter. Allen Cotes came home and told that Ranson was not coming. I took me a hearty cry. I had so surely expected him and had promised myself so much pleasure with him. I was not prepared to meet the disappointment and then when I thought that he might marry that little Ann, for he would forget me then, I was more puzzled than ever. Alex laughed at me and remarked that if the young lady was so amiable as represented that he would advise R to pitch in by all means, but if he does marry before I see him I'll pull his ears well.

And right here I will remind you that you misunderstood me, Sister, when I alluded to brother Silas being at home with his dearie. My meaning was that you could be happy for the time for you would all be together. But well do I know the sorrow of parting with a brother or a sister on any account whatever. I remember when it used to be the greatest trial I ever endured to bid farewell to a brother or sister for a length of time and I know it is a great trial to give up our dear brother, especially to Father and yourself, but I trust that God will support you in this as in all other trials.

I received a very interesting and affectionate letter from Cousin Eliza (Elizabeth Ann Whitten, daughter of Uncle James). She said they were all well. She says she receives letters from Ripley at least once a month and spoke of you all very affectionately. She said she had never received but two letters from Palmetto and one of them was mine. She said she had been disappointed in getting married but that every dog has his day and she knows hers would come along some day. I have commenced a letter to Brother and sister E (Alfred and wife, Elliott Ann) and it will go sometime. I am ashamed of my neglect.

We have no school convenient. I believe I will be my own teacher this year. I will give them lessons every day if I can do no better.

I have some garden seeds for Mother and some other little things I would have sent by Cotes but he left suddenly and I was sure that Ranson would be here but disappointments such is life. I want to hear particularly about you all, Jo's, Alfred's, Silas's, and Uncle Ranson's families.

Do excuse this letter for all the children are playing around me and once in a while they fall against me and you will see my letter is blotted. My health is good and I am always on foot. Your acquaintances and friends are well as far as I know.

Harriet

Silas Jr. has married and moved to Academy, near brother Alfred and his wife's Rays. Though he is close by, Rebecca grieves.

Silas Reagan Jr. to Ranson E. Whitten—Academy to Ripley, Mississippi, 22 May 1856

My dear Brother and all the rest,

I received your very interesting letter last Saturday and you may be certain I had become somewhat anxious to hear from you. I feared something was the matter. The reason I have not written sooner is because I have been looking for Papa and Mother every day for the last two weeks. I was glad to see in the latter part of your letter that you were all well.

Tell Mary Jane I think she and Jo had better leave for a fresh country. I don't think this country will support them if they continue to continue such a course of conduct. Eleven and three quarter pounds, What! Why it's plenty big enough for two children (birth of Narcissa Amaryllis Whitten 8 May 1856). Well, I would like to know what is the matter with the women. Bob Ray's wife gave birth to a fine daughter last night and I don't know how large.

Well, you want to know something about my eyes. I hardly know what to say, but I will say one thing. They are not well. I believe they are some better than when I was down, yet I am not able to either read or write. I thought for a few days that the soap was doing me some good, but now I am disposed to think it did me no good. I don't think anything will cure them but a rest from my labors.

I suppose you would like to know how we all get on. Well, we are all tolerably well. I left Madora (Madora Frances "Duck" Ray, his new wife) complaining this morning, hope not much the matter. Elliott was sick last week, well now. Molly (Alfred's daughter, Mary Dora Whitten) is well and lively as a cricket. We are all drowned out in this country. It looks like they will never get their crops clean, yet we now have fine weather. My potatoes are not doing very well. I got a few for an early setting from the Doctor (Alfred). I think he has planted about 1700 slips. I think I shall have enough for our patch. My corn looks tolerably well. Pretty fowl. We live very well, well enough, at least.

I bought a cow from Grannie Garrett, a heifer, paid twelve dollars in cash. I think she will make an excellent cow but we have no churn. That bothers me. I want some butter. The Doctor has commenced his house a few days since. I enclose a slip on which are made the calculations in the settlement between Alfred and Father. He gave it to me to hand to him when I was down. I forgot it.

I have no news of importance to write. The evening I came home from Papa's, a man whose name was Crum was stabbed. He lived until last week. Carter and Murray came up and performed an operation that they knew would kill him in ten minutes.

Love to all the folks. Madora says tell you she does wish some of you would come to see her, she gets lonesome sometimes. I wonder if Jo could write a letter, and El and Harriett, (Mary Eleanor and Harriett Earle, Jo's eldest children) have they fled?

I reckon I shall not come down until about July 1st. I expect to have an examination about that time. Can't you come down? I would like for you to see what sort of teacher I am. I have from twenty five to thirty one scholars and, I'll tell you, with my eyes sore, I have as much as I can do, take my crop, school and all.

Write often,
Pluck

Pluck is teaching near home, and farming. What can we think of the stabbed Mr. Crum, whom Carter and Murray killed in ten minutes?

R. Clayton to Silas Reagan Whitten—Batesville, Arkansas, to Ripley, Mississippi, 24 July 1856

S. R. Whitten, Esquire, Dear Sir,

I am at quite a loss to introduce myself to you as a correspondent but will blunder at it the best I can, although I have been thinking of writing you for some time, but since I came into this state I have been traveling all the time but have concluded to remain at this point for several weeks or, at least, until I hear from you. I left South Carolina about the 20th of May last. I left Lizzie (friend of the Whitten children) and the children there until I went or sent for them. I am now ready to send for them.

On the way from South Carolina to Atlanta I made Hancock County, Georgia, on my way and had the pleasure of seeing your brother, Dr. Whitten (Isaac Smith Whitten), who lives near Mount Zion. When I first saw him I was satisfied that I knew him but could not place him until he told me who he was. I then knew that it was his resemblance of you that I saw. I never saw two men so much alike in their manner as you two, only that I believe he can beat you telling a joke.

Yours very respectfully,
R. Clayton

The second half of this letter was damaged and unreadable. He must have been telling the Whittens that he and family would visit. That they did so is confirmed in the next letter from Pluck to his father.

Silas Reagan Jr. to Silas Reagan Whitten—Jonesborough to Ripley, Mississippi, 3 Sept. 1856

My dear Father,

Knowing that you feel a great anxiety to hear from us at all times and particularly at this time, I seat myself to the desk and you may not be surprised if there is a dignity not common with me. Last Saturday morning, about light, Miss Madora presented me with a very fine daughter (Carrie Isabel, born 30 Aug. 1856), as fine and plump a child as you ever saw. She and the babe have been doing fine ever since. She is complaining some this morning of her breasts. We came very near being caught in a snap. We were not looking for a thing of the sort for two weeks. We have been two weeks smarter than common and I got the Dr. in good time. He, with another lady near us, Mary, and I made the company. I am very much in hopes Madora will improve rapidly.

Surely Mother will come to see us again. We want to see her very much. Molly (Mary Dora, daughter of Alfred) was taken on Thursday evening after Rant (Uncle Ranson) and down with the flux. She was very low. I thought Sunday and Monday she would die. She is much better but looks very poorly. Elliott has not been very well for several days.

I can hardly hold my eyes open. I have lost some sleep, and teaching, have no chance to catch up. I have an old Nancy W of a woman with Madora. Preaching at the Church today. I was not there. There were four more added to the Church. We have preaching Saturday and Sunday next, looking for brother Holcombe. He was up this week and preached old Grannie Garretts funeral.

I suppose Lizzie and Clayton stayed at the Dr's last night. I have not seen them. Clayton took the stage this morning, would liked to have seen him. Nancy seems to be very well pleased, likes to go to school. I kept her at home yesterday with her Aunt. I have been very much bothered to get someone to stay with Madora.

My eyes are about to give out and I will have to stop. I don't know whether you can read these scrawls or not. Madora sends love to all, wants to see you all very much, particularly the children. I have not received anything from South Carolina yet. I don't understand it.

Write to us and come along and see the best looking grandchild you ever had,

Pluck

Alfred Washington to Ranson E. Whitten—Jonesborough to Ripley, Mississippi, 11 Dec. 1856

Dear Rantie,

Your letter of the 7th received. Sorry to hear of your extreme cold. Know well how to sympathize with you, tho I am now better than when you were here. I would be highly pleased to have some of your workmanship next week and the week or two following if it suits. As I told you I have made no effort and do not expect to get anybody to do the work of which I was speaking.

Your trip to Pontotoc is doubtless unnecessary for it appears from authoritative declarations that there is no probability of your seeing her during the holidays. I would not hesitate to say that if you will wait awhile you may job here in Tippah until you are tired of it. Dunkin is down with the rheumatism and does not contemplate taking Blake's job. Garrett still calculates to build. I should not advise a man of your cloth and such to betake to the towns and cities. But more of this anon. We are well and Plucks and all generally.

Your Brother,
A. W. Whitten

Elliott remains rather on the quiet. Should she recruit up and the weather open I mean to come tween this and 1st Jan.

Pluck (Silas Jr.) to Ranson E. (on the back of Alfred's letter)

Well Ranta,

I shall have to fill the sheet with some sort of stuff. We have been on a visit since last Saturday. You know we have been cramped at home for some time. We are now on our way home, get there tomorrow. I guess I shall stay there for a week at least. I have been trying to work some but make a poor showing. Shall go to mill tomorrow, not collected much money. The Dr. and I went to Pocahontas last week, bought our groceries. The Dr's amounted to about $30 mine $25, more than I expected, paid 13 cents for coffee, 12 for sugar, molasses 70 cents. Cotton is now worth $11.40 per bale.

The Dr. has swapped off his mare (Jinny) for a mustang pony, got $25 boot, the horse will suit him best. I came near letting Sen go the other day, was offered $35 to boot.

I received a letter today from Miss Ann H. Greer. She seems to be very anxious to come home Christmas, but I think her Grandpa intends for her to remain at the college. We shall look for you next week.

Love to all,
Pluckey

Carrie says tell Grandpa to come and walk her. She does much better than when we were down, sleeps all night.

Elizabeth Ann Whitten to Ranson E. Whitten—Columbus, Georgia, to Ripley, Mississippi, 24 Jan. 1857

Father (James Whitten) and I are home about two weeks from Uncle Isaac's. We found him and whole family well. He seems to be getting along admirably so far at this world is concerned but, I think, cares less for the future than he did when we was there before. He certainly has the strangest notions of any person that I ever met with. He did every thing he could to make us comfortable. We stayed two weeks with him. I wanted to stay longer. He speaks of going to Cuba this winter. His wife and Mrs. Grimes, his stepdaughter, will accompany him. They think of returning by New Orleans and going up to Memphis. In fact, if they could settle up Mrs. Grimes estate in Georgia, they would like to move to Memphis and settle on their plantations in Arkansas, but they never can affect a move of that kind, I don't think.

Uncle and Aunt (Martha Meriwether, Isaac's second wife) want to be remembered to you all. Auntie made a great many inquiries after you all, especially Aunt Nelly (Eleanor Kee Whitten). She seems to love her very much. They have one of James Park's sons of Tennessee with them going to school.

Affectionately your Cousin,
Eliza A. Whitten

Silas Reagan Jr. to Rebecca Whitten—Jonesborough to Ripley, Mississippi, 1 May 1857

My dear Sister,

I intended to have written you last week but Jo came up and obviated the necessity of it and besides that some of us were sick and I thought best not to write till there was a change. Sallie (Sarah Kee, daughter of Alfred) was sick when Jo was here, we thought not seriously so. The night he left she was taken with croup. The Dr. and Elliott thought she was dying but, by using active means she was relieved. She is improving. On Friday night last the Dr. was up with Sally. While standing by the bedside he was taken with pleurisy in the back, The pain was very acute for a while. By scarifying and cupping very severely we succeeded in relieving him in two or three days. He is now up and riding but not well.

He has had a great deal of practice lately and exposed himself too much. The rest of us have kept up, all sorta puny. Carrie (daughter Carrie Isabel) has been unwell for several days. I think perhaps she is teething.

The weather has moderated at last and we have plenty of rain. It looks like we shall have nothing in the garden, however, my irish potatoes are coming up and Madora tells me that one bean has dared to peek thru with a little corn up. We had some fine cabbage plants but the weather ruined them.

We have no news to interest you. The great railroad jubilee comes off in Memphis today. It will be the most sublime affair that has ever occurred in the west. The trains passed on yesterday from Georgia and Charleston, the Governor of South Carolina in company. I should like to be in Memphis to enjoy the fun.

Becca, say to Jo that I received a letter a few days since from Ware Garrett, who is now going to school in Canaan. He intends to quit school sometime in June and wants to get a school for the rest of the year. He asked me to let him know if he could get a school in that neighborhood. I can't tell him anything about it, not knowing myself. Tell Jo to write me immediately and let me know what the prospect is, how many scholars could be obtained, etc. I will leave the rest to Miss Duckey to finish.

Pluck

Dear Rebecca,

I, for the first time, will attempt to write a few lines to you. News is very scarce in these diggings, in fact, we do not have any. We have no garden or chickens but are in hopes that we will improve as the weather is moderating. The Doct sent us some very pretty cabbage plants this morning. He has a great many plants. I have but thirteen chickens, have had a great many and the hogs got all of them while we were staying at the Doctor's.

Ma (Mary Garrett Ray) was very sick last Saturday night down at Canaan, thought she had congestive chill. She came home Monday, is now well. Bob's family have all been sick, pneumonia and croup. Cooper Hilbanks babe died with croup few days back. Mr. Bridges babe is very bad with it now. The Doct was with it two nights this week. Carrie is fat and pretty, can almost walk.

I will have to quit now,

Madora

Tell Father and Mother we will look for them soon, you with them, give our love to Jo's and Uncle Ranson's family.

Dora Whitten

Eleanor Kee Earle Whitten died 18 Aug. 1857 between these two letters. If this tragic event was recorded, Rebecca did not save the letters.

Elliott Ann to Rebecca and Silas Reagan Whitten—Jonesborough to Ripley, Mississippi, 4 March 1858

Dear Father and Sister,

It really seems like we are not going to get to go to see you soon so I have concluded, without having much news of importance, to write to you. We are all tolerable well. I have been suffering several days with a sore breast. It is better now. There is not much sickness in the neighborhood. The Doct, when not employed, is busy fencing. Our young man is getting rails, seems to be pretty well satisfied. Pluck was here yesterday evening, all well. Little Carrie (Carrie Isabel) is not walking yet but is improving fast enough, I think.

Mary Greer died two weeks since, disease, child bed fever. She left an infant daughter about two weeks old. Aunt Sally Burk has it. Mr. Greer has gone to a plantation about twelve miles from Memphis to oversee for Mr. Vernon. He carried his two eldest daughters with him with the intention of keeping house. I think Ann can do very well if she will try. Her little sister is large enough to keep her company. None of us visited Mary during her illness, as she was at Uncle Levi's, but Uncle Henry. He was there when she died. They treated him very kind. Uncle has moved over to his new house. His house is not complete yet.

Billy Garrett has gone to Canaan to school this year, brother Brooks (Joseph Brooks Ray) is speaking of going. I do not know whether Pa (the Rev. Ambrose Ray) can spare him as he is the main stake when Pa is gone. Hosea and Thomas have not started to school yet. I do not know whether Pa intends sending them this year or not. He is very busy now cutting saw logs. He also supplies four churches this year, namely, Bethlehem, Canaan, Pleasant Hill, and Union, so you see he has his hands full.

We have had no additions to our Church lately, but at our last meeting excluded one and gave two letters and have another under charge that I expect will result in his exclusion. There was four received into full fellowship at the Campground last Sunday as they had served their probation, to wit, Briggs and John Burk and two of Mrs. Gatlin's children.

Pluck and the Doct have not bought their groceries yet. They now speak of buying at Salsbury. Money is quite a scarce vegetable in these diggins at present, though I am in hopes it will be more plentiful in a short time as there is being more cotton carried to market, at least than has been heretofore.

Father, I wrote you some time since and have expected an answer but never received it. Now I don't say I think hard of you at all, I only want you to write or come to see us soon. The Doct's negro case has not come off yet. Now don't you think it is surely a failure? If not Providentially hindered, I do think we will be at your house the first week in March as the Doct is supposed to attend court then. Pluck speaks of going down to your next meeting.

Becca, how do you do? I do wish I could be with you and Father often for I know I would enjoy it. I sewed as steadily as I could well today and only made the bosom for a shirt and nearly put it in, so you can see, I get along slowly. I have a great big new ash hopper and am making very good ashes, so I expect I'll have a powerful soap making time after little.

We have not gardened any yet. I want to sow out cabbage seed and kale and lettuce seed the fourteenth of this month. Aunt Betsy sowed peas, beets, and cabbage seeds two weeks since but I think they will feel right chilly tonight if they have made their appearance as the ground is covered with snow that fell yesterday evening and last night. I think we have about the coldest weather now we have had this winter, but we have charming fires.

The Doct has traded his riding horse for a young unbroken mule. He is much pleased with his trade and would be much more pleased if he had his mule well broke. We get milk and butter in abundance for our family, have six young, pretty pigs, and the best meat we have ever had, I think, corn plenty and to spare. Now do not think I am bragging. I only want to fill my sheet and I have not much news to write and, of course, must exaggerate a little. The Doct has built him a stable and lot, made two large gates, and is making preparation to rail in his yard soon.

They have all gone to bed but Beck and myself. She is carding. The Doct has both of the babes. It makes him feel very proud for Sallie to lie with him. The children are very well and the worst brats to their size I almost ever saw, they don't cry very much but are so mischievous. They are so bad about climbing on the beds and tables. I have to keep all the chairs in the other room save the one I use. Sallie gets on top of the highest bed we have, goes where she pleases, can talk a little, and sings a great deal of her kind of singing. There is not a day I reckon but what Mollie talks of going to see Grandpa, and Beckah, and Aunt Jane a Mary (Mary Jane, Jo's second wife). She says Carrie gets in the bugget and comes to see her.

I wrote to Rantie (Ranson E. has moved to work in Holly Springs) the first of the week, had not heard from him but once since he left, was well then. What have you heard from Harriet (Lankford) and Lizzie (Elizabeth Ann, daughter of James Whitten)? Give my best love to Jo and all his folks. Tell him Christmas has come and passed and he has not come to see us yet. We was mighty glad of Uncle Rant's visit to us, hope he got home safe and sound.

I now think of nothing else that would interest you at all and it is bedtime and I had a great deal that I would rather talk out with you when we come down. I will close by asking you to write to me soon, come to see us when you can, and excuse a hastily written letter.

Give our love to Uncle (Ranson) and family, and believe me to be your devoted,

E. Ann Whitten

Alfred Washington to Silas Reagan Whitten—Jonesborough to Ripley, Mississippi, 20 Dec. 1858

Dear Father,

I shall offer no apology for writing to you except the good fortune which has lately befallen us. On the night of the 9th inst. Elliott gave birth to a fine boy, no skinny scrap, but a great big, fine looking, well formed child named (John) Graves Whitten without the Jr. The child seems to be doing well and is more quiet than any of our babies. Elliott, too, is stouter and recovering faster than usual after such seasons.

The little girls are growing very fast and soon they will be beyond your recollection unless you see them more frequently. They are as mischievous as their Daddy ever was and frequently asking about Grandpa and Aunt Becca.

Pluck and Duck have been with us a good deal for the last two weeks. They are well and their children quite a match for ours. Their Effie (Berry) is very cross but as fat as a pig and Pluck says the prettiest child he ever looked at. Of Carrie (Isabel) he says at times she frets him and then again he loves her so that he would not take a world of gold for her. By express invitation I have just returned from looking over the Col's (Silas Jr.) land and pronounce fine land but little sale timber and sorry fences. He has a mountain of work to do and as yet has made no permanent engagement for help.

I have had less practice this year than at any one year since I have been at it. I made a sorry crop, between 30 and 40 bushels of corn and about 85 dollars worth of cotton, 20 bu wheat, 11 hams, fine pork but somewhat queasy about keeping it. I sold a shoat of this years raising for $20 gold. I sold my little mare for $78, some of it met Christmas. My mule colt, that cost me $80 would now, being mature, bring $125. I have an excellent match in strength and action and size. My two horse surrey cost me about $130, and cheap at that, i.e. harness and all. I should have returned your buggy in good time with many thanks but the Col. speaks of wanting it and now the weather is unfavorable for dropping it off. I have it well sheltered but have not been using it for two months.

There is but little news, in fact I have been confined pretty much at home for a long time but think of stretching out pretty soon and it may be, if the weather suits, that we will visit you before long. Pluck speaks of coming next week. I will now leave space for Elliott if she feels like writing.

Affectionately,
A. W. Whitten

Dear Father and Sister,

I scarcely know how to commence writing as my better half has given you the news. We have quite gloomy weather. It commenced raining yesterday and is still at it. This being Monday night, we are pretty well prepared for it, wheat sowed and up beautifully, hogs killed, and a right nice wood and light wood pile. We killed our hogs Thursday was a week or so and before midnight Graves was born. Now don't you think that is doing up matters in style? It fell to the Docks lot to render up the lard and nurse the babes and I do think he was as busy a man as I ever saw. We had so much new lard that he went post haste and bought a new can to help hold it. I tell you we have greasy times now. He did not get his sausage meat seasoned high enough for me but it does first rate.

Pluck finished sowing wheat last Friday, has killed two of his hogs. Rantie just called on us as he returned, staying with Pluck that night, and he carried him to Pocahontas the next day. I feel very much like he ought to come back Christmas. Will not some of you come and see us very soon? I know we wish you would. I will sorter look for some of the last of this week if it is pretty weather.

We have a new stove in our church and I suppose you know that we have a new preacher just moved in our midst by the name of Lancaster. There was a wedding in the neighborhood on the night of the 9th inst., Mr. Wilson and Miss Ragan.

Do come soon and write very often,
Elliott

P S Fredonia Spencer was at Union last Sunday.

Note that Alfred wrote that their first son was named John Graves without the Jr. This must mean that some relatives bore that name. Earlier he wrote that he would name a boy after his Whitten grandfather, John. We do not know John Whitten's other name. It may well have been Graves.

Alfred Washington to Ranson E. Whitten—Jonesborough to Holly Springs, Mississippi, 21 Aug. 1859

Dear Ranson,

Your letter of last week received with thanks, and as I am in the notion, I conclude to answer. Several things of some interest to you have taken place lately, i.e., I conclude that you will be interested in what concerns me. We have had very serious sickness in our family. Just a week ago, in my absence, Beck (perhaps a slave woman) was taken down with congestions, the brain mostly, and for several days I had well nigh despaired of saving her, say two days. The treatment, however, brought on reaction and she is now able to sit up and seems to be improving daily. Elliott has been complaining two months with cold, gets mainly well then takes it afresh. Now she is tolerably well only. The children are all suffering from cold, or it may be whooping cough. Maryann is bloated with filth and worms, and I am and have been troubled with pain in my back. So you see, we are only sorter well.

Old man Ray (Ambrose, father of Elliott) has returned and brought his brother and two cousins to look at the country and with a view of moving to it and they seem to like. Brother Holcombe (Hosea Holcombe Ray) is on the eve of buying Matthew Miller's place. Several talk of moving. Others will come in and fill up, so we are stirred up on the subject.

The Union (church) meeting passed off pretty well, plenty to eat and a goodly crowd all the time to eat it. They had some sparring on brother Holcombe's essay (the scriptural view of missions) but it passed before the body by a clear majority. Brother Ball was infuriated and left the meeting as this movement dug into his agency. He got as far as my infirmary and was taken down with bilious fever. He remains, is much better now, although he has been about as bad as he could be.

Jo came, delegate, and I caused him to leave his little mare. She broke out one night and my mules with her. I could not leave home to pursue far. On the second day Jo found them all at Dr. Waites, and on the day following he brought my mules home, left all well, as usual.

Old David Ray is making ready, I think, to marry a widow lady of

45, 2 children and 12 negroes in his old neighborhood. It may not be so. Brother Ball opines me that he is worth $50,000, has, I think, 7 children, a daughter, 3 married, 2 single and they mostly educated, young, handsome, etc. He has one in her 16th year that surpasses all the others in intelligence, beauty, learning, and fine body form. Don't tell it, but would not this be a great deal better than going to Arkansaw? I think so. Poverty is no objection with him. The association meets at Mt. Pleasant, 14 miles north of Pontotoc, 3rd Sabbath in September. Go go go go go go go go go go go,

A. W. Whitten

What do you want to ramble on about Arkansaw for? You will only spend money and become the more dissatisfied. If you are master of your trade (he was a cotton gin wright) you can make it fast enough. To settle either here, or in Arkansaw, your ultimate destiny is a wife. Then get one and be sure to get a good one and get one that can help you in these low grounds of sorrow. The one I suggest may not suit but there are others, and not a few of them just ready and willing to make the leap. I would rather see you properly married than to know that you would realize a thousand dollars a year for your labor in the single state. If you had a wife and a half dozen children, you would know how to select a good country and what you were living for. You would want good health and good society and a good solid foundation to build up your own character on and that of your family and whenever you get strong enough to colonize a settlement in Arkansaw, to suit you, go there and anywhere else you want to.

Lord deliver me from the rambling pioneer, but give me sobriety, civilization, education, morality, temperance, religion, and all things else to increase the civil and religious enjoyment of man while here and prepare him here for Heaven and Eternal Glory.

I must close,
A. W. Whitten

Advising his younger brother, Alfred reveals his own values. The war delayed any marriage plans Ranson might have had.

Elliott Ann to Silas Reagan and Rebecca Whitten—Jonesborough to Ripley, Mississippi, 13 Nov. 1859

Dear Father and Sister,

We just came in from supper and I asked the Doct how long it had been since you were to see us and he made it out about eighteen months, a long time. Then I proposed that we should write to you tonight and he said he did wish that I would, and after picking my teeth and studying a little I commenced. So here goes.

Our family is all well except our precious little Graves. He has been quite fretful today, teething, we think. Our neighbors and friends well so far as we know, except little Effie (Effie Berry, daughter of Silas Jr.). She has the thrash. Pluck was here this morning. He is engaged helping Pa (the Rev. Ambrose Ray) haul cotton to market, has carried two bales for himself, got 10 1/2 cts per pound.

There is a powerful stir in our settlement now, some moving off, some moving in. In fact everybody, nearly, seems to be in a stir. We have been for the last month as we are having our house ceiled. Uncle Henry is having his painted. The Doct has purchased a quarter of land which corners with this for eight hundred dollars, payments as follows; third cash, the balance in two payments with eight percent interest, one and two years. So you see we are settled if we can ever pay for the land and we are going to do that if we live. Cousin William (William Hosea Ray) has commenced moving among us and our Carolina friends are on the road, and now, if we could just have you and Jo's family with us I do think we would have a capital neighborhood.

The first trip the Doct made to Holly Springs, he spent part of a night with Rantie (Ranson E.). He was well and gave the Doct a very nice hat. We received a letter from him yesterday morning. Hope he is now at home, shall look for him here in a few days and I don't want to be disappointed for I want to see the scamp.

How are you all? I know I want to see you. It really seems a long time between drams lately, and if some or all of you don't come to see us soon I do think you will be losers for I intend to go and see you. So far as Mary Jane and Jo are concerned I don't much look for them but I do think the rest of you might come once in a while. Father, I verily believe you would have come before this but you have already stayed at home until you think it would not do at all to leave. We excuse you but are extremely anxious that you should come and see us.

We have so many children it looks like we can't possibly visit you as often as we have been doing, or at least until some of them get large enough to leave at home. Beckah, come again and maybe we won't be in such a bustle. Can't some of you come with Rantie and be at meeting Saturday or Sabbath?

We made 35 barrels of corn at home this year and have had the use of the pea and corn field for some time. Our killing hogs are improving rapidly, we think, will make plenty meat to do us. Our potatoes turned out much better than we anticipated, made 40 bushels of sweet and 8 of the fall irish potato, our cabbage not worth pulling up for the cows, hardly, turnips a failure, but our neighbors are very kind. We have been frequently invited to use all we wished of two or three patches. Now, as to the chicken matter, I have but little to say, but I do wish the owls and opossums would let what few I have got alone.

Pluck made a fine crop of corn, will have nearly 3 bales cotton, potatoes plenty and meat plenty, I reckon, and he said this morning that he believed his hogs looked better than ours, but I know it isn't so. Duck (Madora Francis, wife of Silas Jr. and Elliott's sister) has quilted three quilts lately and Elliott has been doing pretty much after the same old sort, however she is pretty hardy generally lately. Is Uncle Rant still with you? Give him my love.

The children can sing the do, re, mis, and beat time right ahead and think it is high time their Grandpa would come and sing the bell cow for them. Now I am out of news but you have found that out, but Beckah, if you will come with Rantie this week, I can talk you down, I expect. The Doct has gone to bed, sends his love to you all, would write but has a very sore finger, is very anxious you should visit us, children all asleep. We had a rain and sleet last evening and night, very cold now. Was it not a very sudden change?

Excuse bad spelling and writing. I have not attempted to write a letter for month before. Love to all inquiring friends, Jo and family in particular, and accept quite a reasonable share yourselves. Do hope you are enjoying good health.

I remain yours in love,
Elliott Ann Whitten

This letter and several earlier ones seem to indicate that Uncle Ranson lived for several years in the Silas Reagan home. Ranson's first wife died shortly after their move to Tippah County and he did not marry again until 18 Dec. 1862. Perhaps at this time he moved into the nearby Shady Grove community.

Jabal Faulkner to Rebecca Whitten—Anvil, Sumpter, Alabama, to Ripley, Mississippi, 19 June 1860

Dear Cousin,

Yours of the 5th of May came to hand yesterday, gladly received, and the contents read, and I am at a loss to know how to answer it. It is true we met as strangers and parted as friends and relations in a two fold sense, and yours has confirmed it. The scriptures plainly tell us why it is so "by this ye may know that we have passed from death unto life because we love the Brethren and because we are taught by the same Spirit" which I trust is the case and that God would lead all our friends by the same unerring Spirit if it is His will. Cousin, I could say many things how the Lord has led me and preserved for, low, these many years, and I hope His goodness will keep me to the end.

I got home the last day of March, found all well, getting on finely. My folks was done planting corn, some of the leaves grown, there was great difference in vegetation. Crops look flattering at present although we had no rain for five weeks. It gave us a chance to clean our crops. The tenth of this month we had a good season. If you were down here you could have roasting ears for dinner. Corn worth $1.25 per bushel, I will not have to buy any. I have plenty and if I have success will make a fine crop without some disaster.

You stated that you waited for me to write. I know there is apology due. When I get home thought I would write next week. I have been closely engaged all this spring it is true and hadn't worked much but my time was needed. This is the third letter that I have written since returning. Your father states he would write. Tell him not to forget. I was sorry to hear of his bad health. I want the Lord to bless him with length of days to visit me. Give my love to your father, Jo and family, cousin Ranson and family. Tell them to write and as you opened correspondence I want you to keep it up as returned. I had no chance to call and see Harriet (Lankford). We got to the Davis's (Aunt Mariam and husband) late in the evening and left the next morning. Whitten (no males in Davis family with Whitten in their name) took us to Okolona and he was in a hurry to get back to your cousin.

In bonds of love to Rebecca B. Whitten,
Jabal Faulkner

Herein lies a mystery that cries out for solution. Jabal Faulkner was a cousin. He says so in two letters, written in the worst hand and containing the poorest spelling in the collection. Portions of his letters are difficult to understand. He is more familiar with the older Whittens, and visited them in Mississippi, perhaps with his wife, at least once. A second letter, written after the war, tells us he was born in 1797, his wife, Anna, in 1798, both in South Carolina. They have children, including a son named Silas. Jabal was a veteran of the 1812 war with England.

Faulkner's slaves must have been well treated, for at least fifteen stayed with him after emancipation. Old man Whitten attends them once a month. This sounds like a doctor or a circuit riding preacher. Who was he? Who was Jabal? He is too old to have been a son of Charles Jr.'s daughter. Could he be the son of an, as yet, unidentified daughter of Charles Sr. and Nancy Smith Whitten? ✳

CHAPTER NINE

The War Years

The South went to war with reluctance. A majority, like our Whittens, were small farmers, not dependent upon slave labor. The most aggressive and bellicose southern leadership prevailed, and the Confederate states withdrew, one by one, from the Union. Many southerners were opposed to war and would have accepted compromise if offered the opportunity. Most who fought and died for the South had few if any slaves, produced very little cotton, and had nothing to gain from Confederate victory. They went, and few turned back, feeling their honor and their homes threatened, believing they had no choice. The nation suffered damage from which it has never recovered. A half million of the country's very best perished; the South was impoverished. The well of bitterness is only now beginning to run dry.

The Whittens suffered along with their neighbors.

Alfred Washington to Silas Reagan Whitten—Jonesborough to Ripley, Mississippi, 2 Sept. 1861

Dear Father,

We are all well and all together at my house tonight. The children all have, for the past 2 weeks, suffered much from colds but they are much better now.

I received the enclosed letter from Ranson last Wednesday. I send it to you because it locates the ill fated 17th Regt. better that anything else I have seen, i.e., in the glorious action of the 21st July on Manassas plains. It might be well enough to publish an extract of this letter in justice to Col. Featherstone and his gallant Regt. You will, of course, exercise your own discretion about it. At any rate I should like were read in locations where this foul scandal has been circulated. It is true that Ranson does not say that the Regt. did not run, but it must be noticed that he was entirely ignorant of my object in making the enquiry, and did not have the slightest knowledge of the base report to which he is replying.

You can tell Mary Jane (Jo's second wife) that the meetings continued until Monday and closed with the addition of 16 by Baptism, and several others are expected to come in. We have a quiet time now.

The Valantines are gone to Iuka. We fitted them off pretty comfortably and the friends are very busy getting up material for winter party home, shirts and so on. Silas is taking fodder. I am not ready, think the frost will take part of mine. I fear that our low ground will not be as good as was expected but the uplands are the best I ever saw.

The war news from all quarters seems to look more encouraging for the South. The health of the troops in Virginia seems to be greatly improved. The health of our own country seems never to have been better. This backache has driven me to the necessity of gathering up roots etc. I think I shall be able to stand through with the aid of a little lobelia and steam.

We have been looking for you for some time and hope that you have not given up the idea of coming to see us. I am engaged in building a shed room and do not know when we will come up. Elliott has just put up a barrel of kraut and I guess the soldiers will have to eat it. All send love.

Your affectionate son,

A. W. Whitten

The Civil War has begun. Ranson volunteered and is with the 17th Mississippi Regiment, Longstreet's Corps, Army of Northern Virginia. It was rumored in Tippah that the 17th broke during the first battle of Bull Run. Alfred refutes this with evidence from his brother, who was on the scene.

He also mentions a barrel of kraut. Most researchers believe our Whittens were of English stock. No one yet knows. Is sauerkraut a taste acquired in the mountains of Carolina or a tradition handed down from German ancestors?

Silas Reagan Jr. to Rebecca Whitten—Jonesborough to Ripley, Mississippi, 28 Oct. 1861

My dear Sister,

I have nothing interesting to write, yet I think it is time to let you know how we get on at home, if nothing else. We are all tolerable well now, have nearly all been sorter puny, nothing but colds, etc. We are having fine weather for gathering our crops. Mine is not so hard to gather as it was to cultivate. I find my cotton is very shabby, my corn pretty good. I have not gathered my corn yet, intended to commence this morning, but was unexpectedly called on to attend the funeral services of two young friends, brother Horton's sons, who had volunteered in Capt. Holcombe's company.

One of them, John, died in Hopkinsville, Kentucky, the 20th, the other, James, at Clarkesville, Tennessee, on the 25th. Brother H was with them when they died and brought them home. They both professed to die in the Faith. The occasion was indeed melancholy beyond description, yet brother and sister Horton seemed to manifest much Christian fortitude. This makes eight of that company died since they left, all with measles and there are several more quite dangerous. Brooks Garrett (cousin of Elliott Ann and Madora Frances) has been very low, is now said to be some better. His Ma and Pa are with him. It has produced a great gloom over the community, and all agree, I believe, that there has been awful mismanagement out somewhere. I, myself, think it perfectly ridiculous. The officers of the Regiment, or the surgeon, or somebody else will have to answer for it, yet, I have no doubt that the boys themselves conducted very imprudently.

We have not yet received the particulars of the battle of Leesburg. I have no doubt Rantie (Ranson E.) was in it and I am extremely anxious to hear something from him. They had to contend a greatly superior force but from what I can learn they fought as only true southerners can fight. If my brother has been slain he has fallen with his face to the enemy, and as I humbly hope, and believe, in the arms of his Blessed Savior. It is very probable that in a short time I, too, will enter the field and lay my life upon the altar of my country. We have not heard from Rantie since the 8th of this month. He had not then received his clothes but thought they were in Manassas.

I intended to come down next Saturday but am summoned to appear as a juror in Jonesborough to try a negro for an attempt to assault a white man. Tell Jo I think his month is rather long, and you, I thought you were coming up, and Father said he would come soon again, and Mary Jane, Mary, and Hat (Mary Jane White, Jo's second wife; Mary Eleanor, and Harriett Earle, Jo's daughters by his first wife) and all the balance, come up. We just as well go to see each other and try to enjoy ourselves.

I'll be down sometime soon,

Pluck

The children send love to Aunt Becca. Billy (William Pendleton, Pluck's son) can walk anywhere he pleases and is getting very fat. We hear that Hosea Ray has relapsed with measles (brother of Elliott Ann and Madora). We are right uneasy to hear something from him. Old man Ray (the Rev. Ambrose) has been very sick since he was in Ripley but is now up.

More men died during this war from disease and lack of care than were killed in battle. The loss of so many young men from the Jonesborough community to measles was not an isolated incident. That the parents were with their dying sons suggests the civilian population worked closely with the armies of the South.

Pluck was wrong about the battle of Leesburg, which occurred on 21 Oct. 1861. A small detachment of Union soldiers blundered into the main body of Confederates under the command of Gen. Shanks Evans. They were severely mauled, losing two hundred dead, seven hundred captured. Their commander, a Colonel Baker, was shot through the head. Ranson was there. His service record places him in the battles of Leesburg, Savage Station, Malvern Hill, Fredericksburg, Chickamauga, Wilderness, Belle Grove (where he was wounded), Petersburg, and Appomattox. I believe Silas Jr. here confirms that Ranson has been converted, leaving only Silas Reagan Sr. out of the church.

Pluck's prediction that shortly he would lay his life on the altar of his country, sadly, proved all too true. He died in less than two years while serving with the army defending Vicksburg.

Alfred Washington to Silas Reagan Whitten—Jonesborough to Ripley, Mississippi, 24 Dec. 1861

My dear Father,

I have no news of interest to communicate in regard to the war. It is stated, however, that our forces have been defeated at Fairfax, CH, i.e., some three thousand of the Confederates attacking a very large force of the enemy through mistake, fighting valiantly for several hours and then retreating with the loss of thirty killed. The enemy's losses are unknown. The last call for volunteers swept off all the Rays and many other substantial citizens. These troops, the most rusty of raw militia are near Bowling Green in Kentucky, armed with double barreled shotguns and in daily expectation of a fight.

We have had one letter from Ranson more than two weeks ago. He was well, had received the clothing sent, and sent the overcoat taken at Leesburg to Holly Springs for you and had been required to give up the rifle intended for me. This was the amount of his letter. The overcoat was to have been in Holly Springs more than three weeks ago and you ought to make inquiry for it. I suppose he sent it to Cunningham or Manuel. He did not state. We have been looking for you up. Madora is still on foot, all well as usual.

But I write to inform you that I have no money. I have managed to lay in a supply of sugar and molasses for myself and a supply for you besides, i.e., if you want it, say ten gallons of molasses and thirty to seventy five pounds sugar. These I bought with a cargo for eight of us who sent to Memphis, all bearing an equal share of expenses, on borrowed capital at ten percent. I state this to show you the utter dirth of money in this neighborhood.

Elliott thinks long of the time between your visits and wants you reminded of the promise. Silas Jr. and I have made our first killing of hogs, good meat and a fine turn out. We will both have some pork to spare and if you lack any let me know. My next killing, I guess, will be about the middle of January. The cold chills my hand so that I fear you cannot read the letter. If you do not come up soon let us hear as I see no prospects of being able to come down for some time yet.

Your affectionate son,

A. W. Whitten

Southern troops are furnishing their own weapons and clothing. Cotton can't be sold, so there is no money. Our Whittens, like all southerners, are feeling the effects of war and blockade.

Silas Reagan Jr. to Silas Reagan Whitten—Jonesborough to Ripley, Mississippi, 21 April 1862

My dear Father,

You have doubtless looked for a letter from some of us before this time. Well, really, I hardly know how to apologize. We have been considerably stirred up lately on the war question, and it seems to absorb everything else. Besides this, we have been looking for some of you up to see us for the last six weeks, and certainly expected some of you to write. You have now learned that we now get the mail but once a week, i.e., it goes to Pocahontas on Monday and Ripley Tuesday. It is pretty smart sham on us in the way of news.

We have been generally pretty well. Madora is complaining a good deal today, has something, cholisa morbus. I hope she will be better tomorrow. The children have bad colds and we are looking for them to take the mumps every day. The Dr.'s (brother Alfred) folks have all had them but John and Sallie, and ours were with them.

Right here I'll tell you Elliott has another boy, born about ten days ago (Hosea Ranson, born 10 April 1862). I reckon she is doing very well.

We received a letter from brother Rant (Ranson E.) today, the first time we have heard from him since 12th February. I assure you we were glad to hear from him. He had very bad cold when he wrote, the 26th March. He is at Gordonsville, Virginia, but said there was some talk of their coming to the West. He says it don't matter much where he is. He has given himself to his country.

We all have our hands pretty full just now. Just after, or rather, during the battle of Shiloh, i.e., on Tuesday, some 8 or 10 of us concluded we would go up and see if we could render some assistance. We prepared a quantity of provisions such as are suitable for wounded men. Off we put with four wagons. We reached there Tuesday night. You will recollect the weather was cold and wet. I must say to you, I never beheld such a spectacle. I had not before anticipated the horrors of war. I will say hundreds, and perhaps thousands, of wounded men were to be seen, begging to be noticed, perished for food, and their wounds then undressed. I suppose the surgeons did all they could, but could not keep up. We, at once made application for some to bring home with us, which was granted. We started with 23 but some of them found they could go home, and did so. We have now 15. They are all doing well but one. I think he will die. They are all Kentuckians. I have 2 of them, both shot through the thigh. One of them is up, the other is doing well, but it will be a long time before he gets well.

We are awfully behind with our work, not more than half done planting, and it's now very cold enough to snow. Do some of you come up and see us. I reckon if I can get some money I shall be down to pay my tax before long.

Pluck

Shiloh Church is in Tennessee some 40 miles northeast of Pluck's home. Beginning Sunday morning, April 6, the battle of Shiloh lasted two days. The Confederates, commanded by Gen. Albert Sidney Johnston, surprising a much larger Union Army commanded by generals Grant and Sherman, carried the first day. On Monday, heavily reinforced federal forces drove the southerners back toward Corinth. Albert Sidney Johnston was shot, and died in the saddle.

Shiloh ranks with Antietam for ferocity and carnage. Federal losses were 13,000; Confederate, 10,000. Pluck and his friends arrived on the field on Tuesday, April 8. Wounded men still lay on the ground, hungry and unattended. They did what they could.

Ranson E. to Silas Reagan Whitten—Camp near Culpepper CH, Virginia, to Ripley, Mississippi, 1 Aug. 1863

My dear Father,

I spent a week with Sister Harriet, leaving there on Sabbath after I left home. I arrived at Richmond on the 6th day being the 18th of the month. Nothing of any interest occurred on the way except that some scoundrel stole my hat off the cars between Bristol and Lynchburg which put me to some inconvenience. I had to go from there to Richmond bareheaded. I was not allowed to travel the southern route as I desired, but had to go from Atlanta by Knoxville. It was a very pleasant trip though. The cars were not often crowded. When I arrived at Richmond I found that the army had fallen back on this side of the Potomac and was near Winchester. I obtained transportation and started for the army. I was compelled to go by Staunton and, of course, would be compelled to walk to Winchester. But when I got to Staunton the fact was known there that the army was south of the Blue Ridge mountains, consequently we were all ordered to Gordonsville, and the cars being so thronged with sick and wounded from the army that it was impossible to get transportation on the train back to Gordonsville so three or four of us got together and made our way thru the mountains, a distance of about eighty miles. We made it in five days, arriving at Gordonsville in time to take the train for this place. I found my regiment badly used up by the late Gettysburg fight, the loss being upwards of two hundred. The loss in my company was twenty seven wounded and eight killed in the field.

Our Army was greatly worsted by that movement into Pennsylvania but it is by no means demoralized. All that I have conversed with seem to be in the very best of spirits and feel sure of success whenever attacked on their own soil. The ranks are being swollen every day by those returning from hospitals and from furlough.

We can't tell whether it is Mr. Lee's intentions to make a stand here or not. It seems that Meade has sent a portion of his army down to Stafford County opposite Fredericksburg and a part of Gen. Lee's army has gone in that direction. The yankees crossed the Rappahannock River yesterday in small force at Kelly's Ford. They advanced on the cavalry who, knowing how to take care of number one, retreated. A. P. Hill's corps of infantry, the never failing infantry, went out and met them, the yankees, and they, in turn, retreated. Our brigade was thrown out into line of battle and slept near their arms. This morning we were marched back to our quarters. I forgot to mention in the proper place that our brigade general, Barksdale, was killed at Gettysburg. Nearly every officer in the brigade was killed or wounded. Humphreys, the former colonel of the 21st Mississippi Rifles is our brigidier. The colonel of our regiment was badly wounded, so was our lt. colonel. Our major was wounded at the last Fredericksburg fight so the regiment is now in the command of one of two captains that were left.

My health continues first rate up to day before yesterday. I took a slight chill as I thought, had some fever after it, and headache, felt badly all yesterday, but today I have missed the chill and am much better, feel very well. I am exceedingly anxious to hear from you all. My fears for you are much greater since the fall of Vicksburg. I fear the whole country may be overrun by the enemy.

This is a gloomy time with us, but I still believe our cause is a good one and that our Heavenly Father will, in His own good time and way, save us as a nation.

We can hear nothing from Johnston (Gen. Joseph E., commander of the Confederate Army of The Tennessee). We have news that Grant has left Jackson and gone back to Vicksburg. I have never heard one single word from Pluck. (Silas Jr. died of pneumonia at Newton Station, Mississippi, in July 1863.)

I found on reaching Guntown that Calvin (Calvin Thompson Whitten, son of James) has scattered his family. His wife and youngest daughter (Malinda Catherine Kinsey and Sarah Rebecca Whitten) are near Birmingham at Mr. Kinsey's (wife's father). His eldest daughter (Mary Clifford Whitten) is at Columbus, Georgia, and he is at Okolona. I didn't see any of them except Calvin. I did not go by Mr. Caruth's (Mary Eleanor, daughter of Jo and Mesina Whitten and husband Dr. Adrian Brown Caruth) as I intended from the fact that the creeks were all up and I had to go down by Harrisburg to affect a crossing.

I don't know that this will reach you but, if it does, let me beseech you to write to me often. You don't know how anxious I am to hear from you. Give my love to Jo and family. Tell Mary and Hattie to kiss Hester (Jo's children). Becca, you must write to me for all the pleasure I will have will be in getting letters from home.

Your affectionate son,
R. E. Whitten

P. S. Aug. 3. If you should have an opportunity of sending word to Jonesborough tell them that I went to Hosea's (Hosea Holcombe Ray, brother of Elliott and Madora) regiment as soon as I arrived in camp and found that he and his cousin (Robert Leland Ray) were both wounded in the Gettysburg. Hosea had a wound in one of his arms and was then gone off on furlough. We don't know whether he was gone to South Carolina, Georgia, or Mississippi. Bob was very slightly wounded about the head and was in a hospital in Richmond.

On yesterday we took up the line of march towards Gordonsville and arrived at the Rapidan River about dark, some two to six miles below where the RR running from Gordonsville to Culpepper crosses. We crossed the river and struck camp on the heights where we are now resting quietly. I can write now. The forces are distributed, but I think they are pretty much upon the old line from this to Fredericksburg.

I have not been able to visit Daniel White's (probably a relative of Luther White, first husband of Harriett M. Whitten, daughter of Uncle Ranson) regiment, nor to hear from him, but I was able to send my letters by hand so that he would get them.

Let me ask you again to write me every possible chance. When I write to one of you it is for all.

Affectionately,
R. E. W.

Ranson E. Whitten to David E. Cannon—Camp near Rapidan River in Virginia to Holly Springs, Mississippi, 9 Aug. 1863

Dear Dave,

Lt. Jolly of Co H starts this morning for Mississippi and says he intends going to Holly Springs, so I thought I would write you a few lines. I fully intended to have gone to Holly Springs myself while I was in Mississippi, but I found it very unsafe to stay at home, letting alone travelling the highways. I was very much disappointed in not getting to see you all. I left Fredericksburg about the 20th of March on furlough of thirty days, but my health continued bad. I stayed there three months. I spent the time very pleasantly except that I was constantly in danger of being captured.

My health being restored I returned to my company, arriving here about the 25th of July. I found that our ranks were sadly thinned. Some of our best men fell at the battle of Gettysburg, amongst them Leut. Crawford and Sergt. I. L. Smith. Our loss was eight killed and twenty seven wounded in our company. Notwithstanding this, the boys are in good spirits and seem sanguine of success in an engagement on our own soil.

There have been a great many changes in the company since you left us. There is a few of the old veterans left yet, but you would hardly know any of us. Daniel Rather came in from home on yesterday. I expected he would have a letter or two for me, but not a scratch did he bring. I heard from Pitts Daniel yesterday. He was wounded at Gettysburg, is improving rapidly. I hear that great changes have taken place at Marshal since I left, a great many have moved off, and those that remained at home have been used up, all their property destroyed, etc. I have not time to write any more. Give my regards to Aunt Jane and also to Uncle Ike. My respects, etc, to enquiring friends.

Your friend, etc.,
R. E. Whitten

Write to me every chance you get.

Ranson E. to Silas Reagan Whitten—Camp near Chattanooga, Tennessee, to Ripley, Mississippi, 29 Sept. 1863

My dear Father,

Thanks be to the Lord, He has preserved my life through another hard fought battle. We, that is our division, left Richmond on Thursday the 10th inst. and arrived near this place on Saturday the 19th inst. We came by way of Petersburg, Weldon, Charlotte, Columbia, to Branchville, and thence, by Atlanta, to Dalton, and from Dalton to Ringold, at which place the cars stopped at that time. We marched on foot then a distance of some fifteen or twenty miles towards Chattanooga, arriving, as I said before, near the front (Chickamauga) on Saturday night 19th.

The enemy was attacked on that day by Walker's and Hood's Divisions and driven about one and one half miles with considerable loss of life and property on the part of the enemy. On Sunday morning our Division was moved forward and participated in the struggle. The engagement was not a general one, though we drove them several miles, capturing thirty eight pieces of artillery, twenty five thousand stand of small arms, forty stand of colors and between seven and ten thousand prisoners, what I call a nice victory. The enemy fell back on Chattanooga which is splendedly fortified, and now occupy that place, and I tell you, the prospect of dislodging him is very gloomy, in fact, I don't think it can be done, unless he can be flanked out.

We occupy the heights on the south side, and our line of battle extends from the foot of Lookout Mountain, which butts up to Chattanooga from the southwest, for several miles up the river. We have a strong position and so do they, and the attacking party will be sure to suffer. The loss in our regiment was near one hundred, and our company about fifteen. Our company lost two officers and one private killed. The company is now commanded by the second sgt.

Gen. Longstreet says he is not going to charge the works in front of us. I suppose that is the object of Gen. Bragg, to dislodge the enemy by strategic movement.

I visited the 34th Mississippi regiment today. I saw Bratten, John Bills, Ragaan, John Shepard, and some others that I knew. Bob White is guarding the supply train, I did not see him. Others tell me Bob's health is not good. I have not seen many of my old friends yet. Bob Ray's (brother of Elliott and Madora) regiment is near here but I have not seen him yet.

In passing through Marietta, Georgia, we stopped some two or three hours and a nice looking boy of twelve or thirteen years (Judson J. Thomason), hearing my name called, stepped up to me and asked if my name was Whitten. I told him it was. He said that was his mother's maiden name, and invited me to go down town and see his mother, that we certainly must be some kin. I went with him and found one of your old cousins that I guess you had lost sight of. Her name is Nancy Thomason (daughter of Charles Whitten Jr.), her husband (James Thomason) has been dead about a year (he died 10 Jan. 1863). Her family now consists of herself and son. She has a daughter living with her whose husband is in the army. The old lady said she had been trying to find some of her relatives for a long time. Her brother, Silas R. (Silas Reagan Whitten, born 1815) lives at Louisville, Mississippi, and she has another brother, John, somewhere in Mississippi, but she don't know whereabouts. She is poor just like all the rest of the Whittens and seemed just as glad to see me as if she had found a brother or a son and begged me to visit her again and to write you about her, and she wants you to write to her and give her as much information as you can about her kinfolks. I told her all I could but you know that was not much.

The health of the army is very good, but fare is mighty rough, raw midlin meat, and cornbread three days old, the meal not sifted at that. Our Virginia boys call the cornbread Mr. Bragg's biscuit and have a good deal of sport over it. I hope, though, it will soon be better.

I am very anxious to hear from home. Can't some of you write to me? I get letters from Columbus (Georgia, probably from cousin Elizabeth Ann) occasionally and they make a great many inquiries about you. Excuse me for not writing more. I expect to have to work on the fortifications directly. Love to Jo's family and respect to friends. Write to me very soon and often. May the Lord bless you in your old age and finally save you is the prayer of your affectionate son,

R. E. Whitten

The last three letters tell a continuing story. Ill with pneumonia, Ranson was allowed to leave Fredericksburg on 20 March for recovery at home, remaining about three months. The first letter describes his stay and return to the Army of Northern Virginia. He was forced to travel via Atlanta rather than directly through Chattanooga, since units of the Union Army threatened much of that route. Ranson supplies information about the war and several friends and relatives. He has missed the battle of Gettysburg and reports its devastating effect on Lee's army. Rejoining his unit in Gordonsville, after walking eighty miles across the mountains, he is camped north of the Rapidan River, expecting a Union attack.

Also in this letter is found our last news of the family of Calvin Thompson Whitten, son of Uncle James. After fleeing from Guntown, Mississippi, to avoid Union soldiers, they later moved to Texas.

Ranson did not know of the July death of his brother in an Army hospital at Newton, Mississippi.

Meade did not try to cross the Rapidan. Instead he sent crack divisions south to assist Sherman and Rosecrans. Informed of this, Jefferson Davis detached Longstreet's Corps, and sent them in September to reinforce Braxton Bragg's army located southeast of Chattanooga. Ranson left the Rapidan on Sept. 8, returning to Atlanta, then turning north to Ringold, Georgia, stopping along the way at Marietta and Dalton, and writing on 29 Sept. 1863 from camp near Chattanooga of the trip.

His regiment arrived in time to actively participate in the battle of Chickamauga, a resounding victory for the South. The letter ends with Ranson and his Confederates on the crests of Lookout Mountain and Missionary Ridge with Longstreet, characteristically, vowing to await attack rather than leave his strong defensive positions. General Longstreet was not allowed to make that choice. Instead he was detached and sent with most of his corps to drive General Burnside from Knoxville.

The months spent in Tennessee away from Robert E. Lee were not kind to Gen. James Longstreet. Though contributing heavily to the victory at Chickamauga, his performance thereafter left much to be desired. There was indecision, insubordination, alienation from Jefferson Davis, and premature abortion of his attack on Knoxville. The corps was finally ordered to return via Charlottesville to the Army of Northern Virginia. By this time, Longstreet is said by his biographers to have been a changed man. Most units of his corps remained with Lee for the rest of the war. However, in August 1864, some of Longstreet's veterans, under Richard Anderson, were sent to reinforce Jubal Early in the Shenandoah Valley.

No more is said in the letters we have about Ranson's role in the war. From his service record, we learn he was among those veterans transferred to Early, for he was wounded during the battle of Belle Grove. This engagement is also called the battle of Cedar Creek, during which, after being surprised by an early morning attack, most Union forces fled north. The crack VI Corps broke, but rallied and formed a line across the Valley Pike between Middletown and Winchester. Stubbornly refusing to be driven further, they became an anchor for the rest of the army, reorganized and inspired by Gen. Phillip Sheridan during his famous ride. Early Confederate victory turned to defeat, and southern resistance in Virginia's breadbasket came to an end.

Ranson was taken to the Chimborazo Hospital in Richmond, where he recovered. Rejoining the army, he was present at Appomattox when General Lee surrendered the Army of Northern Virginia to Gen. U. S. Grant.

The letters confirm that Ranson Edwin had been converted and was a believer.

Alfred Washington to Silas Reagan Whitten—Jonesborough to Ripley, Mississippi, 13 Aug. 1863

Dear Father,

Silas was a brother dearly beloved and his loss to me is inexpressible. The last account we had of him he had been cut off in the retreat of the 23rd from (the battle of) the Big Black and was left alone, or found alone, by the Yankees in their pursuit. They very kindly offered to take him into better quarters. He accepted, and while they left him alone and went away for a conveyance, to get him on, he ran off, and by some means, made his escape to Jackson. He was taken from Jackson to the second station hospital in the south of Meridian and there passed through a severe sickness, and at the date of all this news, say 3 or 4 weeks ago, was fast improving and would soon report himself in camp for duty again. Had I known his situation I would have gone to him at all hazard. We do not know the nature of his sickness. I presume chronic diarrhea after measles. (His service record says he died of pneumonia 22 Aug. 1863 at Newton Station, Mississippi; the more likely date is 22 July.)

I have had every opportunity to study the character of Silas for years, and can say with feelings of delight, that a better young man I never knew. Strictly honest and just in all his dealings with men, he constantly sought opportunity to be charitable and kind. As a gentleman, and Christian, and patriot he had no superior on God's earth. His patriotic bearing and his form and physiognomy was indeed noble and it will ever be a source of deep sorrow to me that one so meritorious for position as he, should be permitted to wither and die unobserved in such a struggle for liberty as we are now enduring.

He was a perfect model of industry, economy, sobriety, and Christianity. In his family his soul flowed with the purest morals, the most loving affection, and the most tender forbearance. In the Church, the Sabbath School, the common interest of his neighborhood, and in the councils of his country, his place will not be filled.

We are bereft, but he has left an inheritance of patriotism for his children who are all bright images of himself. This war is truly afflicting, but our fathers paid dear for liberty, and although I can but take it hard to give up this beloved one, yet I confess that I have nothing I will not try, sacrifice, of myself, in this glorious struggle for liberty.

Medora and Elliott are very disconsolate and I would be glad if you could make some way to console with Medora. A letter from you would doubtless help her much and some of the family to visit her.

There has been but little said how we will manage, but you may rest assured that we will try to do for the best.

Our families are all well, the children growing rapidly. Madora will make corn to do. She has 25 bu wheat, meat, milk, etc. I have plenty of wheat and rye, but I cannot properly make half, no not 1/4th corn to do on, and all for the lack of 10 day plowing at the time it was needed. I could neither buy, or borrow, team from my neighbors, who had voluntarily gone up and taken the oath of allegiance.

Ambrose Ray has lost everything that could be taken away (i.e., almost) by either theft or violence, besides 23 likely negroes, all he had. His negroes and mine went off together about 6 weeks ago. We have suffered some from scouts but have not been foraged on yet. How soon we may lose all I cannot say. I can say we have but little left now save our principles. They are constantly besieged but remain till yet as impregnable as the course of Southern Rights.

MHH, (the Rev. Holcombe) after the loss of more than half his negroes, went up voluntarily and took the oath. Since the oath his blacksmith in freedom, sends word to him to send his wife, or he will have him put in the guard house. The Parson complied. And since all this he and another parson are said to be making strong talk of reconstruction and reunion.

We have no news to write. I guess you can hear particulars from the neighborhoods by soldiers, but be careful whom you believe.

Affectionately,

A.W.W.

We all feel that he is much better off than we, and do not mourn as those that have no hope. Poor Duck, she feels bereft of all, says there is no future happiness for her here,

Elliott

Writing several weeks after Pluck's death at the Newton Station Army Hospital, Alfred tells of his brother's capture and escape immediately following the battle of the Big Black, about 17 May 1863. Silas Jr. was among the defenders of Vicksburg. When Pluck was captured, he seems to have been sick or wounded. Alfred writes beautifully of his brother's life and character, and expresses continued hope for the southern cause.

Though the war is to grind on for twenty more awful months, the outcome is no longer in doubt. Vicksburg fell, and the battle of Gettysburg was lost by General Lee's army. Signs of defeat abound. Slaves have run away and demand release of their loved ones still in bondage, neighbors are taking the oath of allegiance to the United States, Union scouts and foragers are operating nearby. Two local ministers are talking of reconstruction and reunion. This must have been the low point in the life of Silas Reagan Whitten and his family. ✳

CHAPTER TEN

The Torch Passes and Dies

The half century after the Civil War were bitter, hard, and hungry years in the old Confederacy. There was little money, and for a time, little hope. These were the recontruction years, and old orders were changing. What has been called the "Revolt of the Rednecks" took place during this period. The conservative, aristocratic, prewar southern leadership gave way to antiestablishment, race baiting, frequently corrupt demagogues whose main agenda was to disenfranchise blacks and line their own pockets. By the turn of the century, through intimidation and Jim Crow laws, they had succeeded. White supremacy became the major topic for political oratory and commentary. In the process, hearts were hardened and racial barriers arose that have not yet been completely demolished. And our letter writers died or moved on, passing their torch to a new generation.

Three letters between Silas Reagan Whitten and Rev. M. P. Lowrey—Ripley, Mississippi, beginning 12 July 1866

To Col. Silas Reagan,
Dear Sir,

Yours of the 7th inst. is before me and its contents considered. As to the course pursued by your daughter, Rebecca, it was, of course, unexpected to me, but I cannot find it in my heart to entertain for her the least unkind feelings, for I suppose she acted conscientiously and in the fear of God.

I have a good degree of respect for the Church she joined and would have favored the giving of a letter from the Ripley Church if she had have asked for one. I regard the Old Side Baptists as, in the main, correct in doctrine and discipline, and their Churches, Gospel Churches. I think, however, that they have gone into some extremes and reject a good deal of the practical part of Christianity, but from these errors, I think they are slowly emerging.

As to the action of the Ripley Church, I feel quite sure that it will be taken in mildness and Christian forbearance for I think all the members have a high regard for Sister Rebecca.

With kindest regards for yourself and family I am, as ever, truly your friend,

M. P. Lowrey

To Mr. M. L. Lowrey 21 Aug. 1869

My dear Sir,

I have been informed that the church record at Ripley in the exclusion of my daughter is simply "excluded". Do I ask too much of the Church, if so recorded, to amend the entry to show for what cause she was excluded?

I don't complain but simply to ask that the offence for which she was excluded may be recorded.

Truly your friend,
Silas R. Whitten

To Col. S. R. Whitten 21 Aug. 1869

Dear Friend,

The record in the case of the exclusion of your daughter is precisely as follows; "Sister Rebecca Whitten was excluded from the Baptist Church for joining another church without the consent of this church" sixty sixth page of church book, minutes of October meeting 1866.

Excuse brevity and writing on this letter as I have no other paper and am in haste.

With kindest regards, your friend as ever,
M. P. Lowery

The Baptists continued their feuding in 1866. Rebecca left the Missionary Baptists for the more fundamental "Old Side" Baptists. For this, the Missionary Church expelled her and her father, now addressed as Colonel, though he never held that rank, and made sure the record was consistent with the facts.

Elliott Ann to Rebecca Whitten—Jonesborough to Ripley, Mississippi, 21 June 1868

My dear Beccah,

I am glad you determined in your heart and did write to me once more, and equally as much so to hear how you all were and how getting along. Do hope Father will not make himself sick at work. You said not one word about Rantie but we supposed he was well and suspect almost killing himself at work. If so, he ought not so to do.

He surely can live by working moderately and taking care of himself, and I am much inclined to the opinion that that is his duty, as well as to visit his brother and sister who love him much. How is Frank (Frank Adams Whitten, son of Jo and Mesina) and all of dear Jo's family? Does he ever say a word about coming to see us? Would love to see Hat (Harriett Earl, daughter of Jo and Mesina) as well as her new saddle and hat.

Beck, I do believe it would revive our spirits mightily if you would just come and stay one week with us. Don't you think they could do without you that long? We know they would miss you but think they would be willing to make the sacrifice for our sakes. Bring little Nelly (Mary Eleanor, daughter of Jo and Mesina) with you. Dora (Maggie Madora Davis Doyle, Jo's third wife) won't come and bring her.

I judge you will conclude I am in a great fever about some of you visiting us and, to be candid, I would be proud for any of you to come, and Father most especially. Oh, that our dear little ones could see and know more of him.

We are all up except Darlin (Alfred), he is quite unwell today, not able to sit up. From the time of his visit to you last his health was as good as has been for the last year until two weeks since he has been quite puny. Last week he worked at his rye and has been worse ever since, has a bad cough and general aching and some fever. I gave him salts and senna this morning and hoped he would be better after its action but he still seems quite poorly, can't get him to eat anything this morning, has been eating very little for two weeks. It seems to be a very deep seated cold and I do hope will work off without getting any worse, for truly I am sad when Darlin is sick, and don't know what I should do were he to get very sick, but I am going to hope for better things.

All of the children have gone to preaching except little Mattie (Martha Earle). She loves her Mommie so well she would kiss and hug me half the time, almost. We went to conference yesterday and I do think heard some of the best preaching on the subject of pure religion by Pa (the Rev. Ambrose Ray) that I ever did hear and I thought Ma (Mary Garrett Ray), at the close, offered one of the best prayers. We were both delighted with the meeting. We send our children to Sabbath School every Sabbath. They are much pleased, have singing after school and, sometimes, prayer meeting, cousin Jim Ray, superintendent, Hosea and Wiley assistant, good deal of interest exhibited. Do hope will prove a blessing to the children and neighborhood generally.

We have plenty milk and butter to do very well, scarcely expect to have as much as we could consume. Have vegetables plenty, chickens enough coming on, and all but Darlin with good strong appetites. What a blessing.

Duck (her sister and widow of Silas Reagan Whitten Jr.) and little ones all well and getting along fine, I think. Children have been going to school at home now. The health of the neighborhood generally good. John Mc's wife in bad health. I have made sixty yards of cloth this year. Don't expect to make any more soon. Excuse all errors. I am not in the habit of writing.

Love to all, write soon,
Elliott

Rebecca Eugenia Lankford to Ranson E. Whitten—Happy Home, Pontotoc County, to Ripley, Mississippi, 22 June 1868

Dear Uncle Rantie,

As I have written all my Ripley kin two or three times and received no answer, I have concluded to write you again, hoping that you may reply, but it is only a faint shot, I cherish. Indeed, I have no reason to hope at all, judging the future by the past, but have been taught to live in hope, if I die in despair. I have not had one line from Ripley since Mr. Joe (Uncle Joseph John Whitten) was here and then only a short note from Mary (Mary Eleanor, daughter of Jo and Mesina). Ah! It is a sad, sad thing to be forsaken and forgotten by those we so tenderly love. But why do I complain when I know that it is alright and that I am loved a great deal more than I deserve to be.

The health of our family is very good now, though we have had a little sickness, such as chills and fever. Pa has come in from the fields three or four times worked down and would be in bed several days, and then back to work again. (He died four years later at age fifty-three.) He is behind with his crops this year, will be a week yet before he is done laying by. The crops are generally very good in this neighborhood, but the farmers are wanting rain badly now, and no prospects for it soon. We have a very fine garden, have vegetables of all kinds, as much as we can use. We have a good deal of fruit though not near as much as we could consume.

Ma has not had neuralgia for some time now. She seems to be in very good health and is worse than Anna (sister Anna C.) and I to run on with nonsense and have fun. She has had bad luck with her chickens this year, has not more than a hundred, I think.

We have a very fine school now, increasing every once and a while. Anna, Sallie, Kee, and Tommie (siblings Anna C., Sallie Florence, Mary Kee, and Thomas Earle) are going. Will is and Charles (brothers William Henry and Charles Alexander) will start at the beginning of next session which will be about a month from tomorrow. Pa and Ma were very anxious for me to go this summer but I knew it would be folly for me to undertake it. I have tried it a long long time and know that whenever I start to school chills are my certain home. I may go again this fall but it is very uncertain about my ever going to school again, and sad, sad thought it is to me though it may not be so for everyone.

What has become of my old Grandpa? Ah! What would I give to see his dear old face once more, but I fear many a long, long day will pass before I see him again. How is Aunt Becca, too? Well, I hope, and still making e'latty. Tell her she is laying a bad example before me, that of living an old maid, and I fear I am so easily led astray that I will follow her.

Aunt Dora and that darling little Nellie (Pocahontas Madora Rogers, wife of Ranson E. and daughter Eleanor Kee), how are they and what are they doing? You promised to bring them down to see us this fall and, dear Uncle, we still hold you to your promise, so do not forget it. How are Uncle Jo's family and what are they doing? Hat (Jo's daughter, Harriett Earle) talking about marrying now or how does she stand on that subject? When have you heard from our relatives in Jonesborough?

Dear Uncle, it is so late that I will have to close and go to bed. Do forgive all mistakes and bad writing for I can't half write tonight. All join me in sending much love to you and all your dear ones.

Goodnight with a kiss.

Lovingly yours,
Eugenia

Mary is very well. We heard from Tren last week. Ann has been in our neighborhood three weeks, don't know when she will go home. I had a letter yesterday from cousin Myra Jackson. She inquired a great deal about the Whitten family. She wrote a very interesting letter, but more so to Pa and Ma than myself.

E

The next generation begins to write. Rebecca Eugenia, daughter of Nathan Alexander and Harriett Earle Whitten Lankford, is twenty-two years old.

Jabal Faulkner to Rebecca Whitten—Sumpter County, Alabama, to Ripley, Mississippi, 8 Aug. 1868

Dear Cousin Rebecca,

Yours of June today was gladly received. Was glad to hear of Cousin Silas' health and all the friends. Rest assured the name Whitten attached to a letter cheers me, and one from you, particularly. Cousin Rebecca, if you knew how I prize a line from you would write often, but I am so trembly it pesters me so to write. Anna and myself enjoy good health generally, the rest of the connection all well. My youngest son is married and lives with us this year.

Corn sorry this year owing to a heavy drought. I hope we will make plenty, we have a good deal planted. My freedmen all with me but five, and I have as many as I want, about fifteen. The freedmen in this section doing well. I made a fine crop of corn last year. We have had a great deal of rain here lately but too late for our corn, cotton crops.

Well, Cousin Rebecca, you stated you thought you had the Gospel preached in that section. That is one of the great blessings, to have the Gospel delivered in it's verity and truth for it is seldom heard. I am often sad to fear, if I be allowed to judge, by their fruits we are to know them. Cousin Rebecca, we are all cold and indifferent in this section of the country, and men that I thought firm seem to give way, but one thing consoles me. The Scripture says it should be so and the truth of it ought to confound us and pray God to keep us from being led away for if God don't keep me and you and all His children, we would be worshiping strange Gods. But to console His children He tells them He will deliver out of all temptation. He will be with you in the six and not forsake you in the seven. Cousin Rebecca, that consoles me sometimes when I'm tottering over my staff. A man my age can't count many more, but God knows when.

My health for a man of 71 (born 1797), is very good and Anna is good tho has become quite fleshy, seventy (born 1798), in November. Old man Whitten attends us once a month. I never saw religion at a lower ebb that is what I call pure. Cousin Rebecca, my mind is be-clouded and dark and I am very nervous, excuse. Do write to me. I am old and you are young. Don't wait for me. Give my love to Cousin

Silas and Ranson and all the friends and a due portion to yourself.

Farewell from your devoted cousin,
Jabal Faulkner

Alfred Washington to Ranson E. Whitten—Jonesborough to Ripley, Mississippi, 1 Feb. 1869

Dear Bro,

Madora (widow of Silas Whitten Jr.) is willing for you to take the old buggy at $75. It is not worth it, of course. The running gear and springs, so far as I can see, are unhurt save one broken shaft. The seat is broken down on one side. The shaft and seat behind were broken down by Brooks Ray (Madora's brother) and he says tell you to assess the damage and he will pay, etc. Now if you will take it let me know by letter, and when I come after mine, I will bring yours.

I had forgotten to tell you that I have a good set of springs off my old babonok and if the old back springs turn out to be too weak for my load I can double spring without much cost. So make my body large enough. Go over if you choose, I will not say, but do not, unless already commenced, come under eight feet in length, three and one half in breadth to chamber a twelve inch plank or more. All well as usual except myself. I am up.

Your Bro,
A. W. Whitten

Mary Dora to Silas Reagan Whitten—Jonesborough to Ripley, Mississippi, 22 June 1869

The longest day in the year, Dear dear Grandpa,

We are all well, I believe, except Hosea and I. We have been having chills and fever. I hope they are stopped now, tho my studies have been disturbed by my having to stop so often from school. In all, I have stopped about a month from school. I think it very hard but luck will have its way sometime and so it will me. Gladly received a letter from Uncle Jo, last Thursday, I believe.

Tell Aunt Rebecca that Ma and I made up new garments last week and Aunt Duck made me a dress besides. Ma got out twenty five yards of cloth the other week. Made Pa a black coat and pants and tell Uncle Rantie that the rye he gave us is not gone. We have had some eight or ten batches of pancakes and its not gone yet. Has he got his bed done, or not? I reckon its nice. Dr. (her father) said it was.

Aunt Duck and her little ones are well. They have had the whooping cough but I believe they are better now. How are Aunt Dora (wife of Ranson E.) and her little ones? Oh how I long to see Ellie (Eleanor Kee, daughter of Ranson E.). Tell cousins Harriett and Frank (Jo's children by Mesina) that we were mistaken about what day we would have our celebration. It will be the 9th of July instead of the 4th. We will have to have all kinds of speeches. The examination is about the cross and all the go. Tell Glear I think it's time she was coming up if she intends to, Grandpa Ray (the Rev. Ambrose) has got leg splints, was very bad off, but we heard today that he was better. Over here Irish potatoes and onions look very well but are backwards.

I reckon you will laugh when you see this badly written letter, but I don't want you to when I tell you that this is the second one I ever wrote. You must excuse this bad writing and spelling. My studies are these; first grammar, arithmetic, fifth reader, and diction. My studies are before me. I must close. May God help and bless you all for ever and ever more, goodby.

Your Granddaughter,
Molly Whitten

Another young writer, Alfred's eldest, begins her letters. She will be among our best sources of Whitten lore, and one of the most refreshing people we will get to know.

Mary Dora to Silas Reagan Whitten—Jonesborough to Ripley, Mississippi, 15 Sept. 1869

My dear Grandfather and family,

We are all pretty well at the present time. Little Joe (Joseph Brooks, her brother) was very sick a short time since. He was cutting teeth. He has eight teeth. He is the funniest little thing I ever saw. Sally and Carrie (sister, Sarah Kee and cousin Carrie Isabel, daughter of Pluck and Duck) are both in grammar, they said tell you without fail. Effie (Effie Berry, sister of Carrie Isabel) says tell Uncle Rantie this and that and I don't know what to do. Perhaps you don't know what I mean by this and that. I mean first one thing and then another.

Grandpa, we had our examinations. Sure enough, Sally got the prize. John and Silas (Silas Ray and John Graves, her brothers) are going to school now, they learn very fast, I think. Willy and Rantie (William Pendleton and Ranson Hosea, sons of Pluck and Duck) are going, too. Grandpa Ray and Grandma are well. Aunt Duck and her children are well also.

Ma thought, and so did I, that Uncle Joe was coming up very soon, or that's what he said when she was there. Uncle Rantie and Aunt Dora said they were coming, too. Uncle Rantie was intending coming up for the Association when Ma was there. Mattie (sister Martha Earle) is quite a pest. She thinks I must close for this evening.

Give my love to all, one due portion for yourself,

Molly D. Whitten

Grandpa, I didn't finish my letter exactly. This is Tuesday night. Ma and myself are all that's up, the rest of the family are asleep. Pa's not here, he was called off about three o'clock. I want Uncle Rantie and Aunt Dora to come without fail and Uncle Joe, too. Effie can't get satisfied. Kiss Nellie (Ranson's daughter, Eleanor Kee) and that little baby (Joseph Earle, born 15 May 1869). She says Aunt Dora for me.

Perhaps you want to know how I am getting along in grammar, very well, I reckon. Our teacher wants to get Moore's Grammar. I don't know whether Ma will do so or not. Tell Cousin Harriett (Joe's daughter, Harriett Earle) that Ma is fixing her wool for cards, or trying to at least. Pa has not come home yet, he had his hands full. I must close now and go to bed.

Give my love to all and a due portion for yourself. Tell Aunt Rebecca howdy for me,

Molly

We are all up this morning, not very well. Silas can't walk a step, rheumatism, we think, Hosea and the babe, puny, the Dr. is never well, suffers a great deal with his back since our visit to you. How are you all? Why don't some of you come? I have been looking for Joe.

Write soon.

Elliott Ann Whitten

Doleska Fitzallen Whitten to Silas Reagan Whitten—Lee Station, Lee, Alabama, to Ripley, Mississippi, about 1875

(Only the last page survived.)

We have a little town around us and good neighbors, have two sisters and three families in Columbus, Georgia that are a great pleasure to us. The Hogan children (of Orpha Judson, daughter of James Whitten, and her husband, Col. Thomas Hogan) live in Atlanta, Georgia.

My health has been my load for years but I am able to manage our affairs and get along very well. My dear love to Cousin Rebecca and all my relatives, yourself included.

Yours affectionately,
D. F. Whitten

The family called her Dolly. She was the daughter of Arphax, well-known Baptist preacher, and son of Uncle James.

Mary Dora to Rebecca Whitten—Jonesborough to Ripley, Mississippi, 26 Dec. 1875

Dear Aunt Rebecca,

It has been a long time since I wrote to you. While silently meditating tonight I thought 'twould do me as much good to try to write to you as it would to Uncle Joe's folks. They are so pushed over there that they make it a matter of convenience altogether about answering my letters. Our folks came driving in safe and well about sunset yesterday evening, found us all well and in good spirits, generally speaking.

We have been having lots of rain, had a considerably storm late this evening, not so much wind as usual, but a terrible rain. Pa and Ma were not home and haven't come yet, I can't help but feel uneasy. Uncle Hosea (Hosea Holcombe Ray, mother's brother) sent for them this morning. The calculation was for Ma to stay, Pa come home, and for me to go tonight, but I haven't heard from them yet. We got along finely while the better part of our family were in our midst. I became somewhat frightened before day Friday morning, thought we were going to have a storm, and did have a light one.

I haven't been off this place visiting since I came home from Blue Mountain but twice and not one single time since Ma has been sick. I'm very well contented, though, have lots of work and a good will to do it. I intend to stay right here for a week yet unless I visit you about fourth Sunday in next month, which I should be pleased to do, but don't make any promises. Have fourteen yards of janes, want to weave next week, then it will be to make up.

Sallie misrepresented me at your house. She told that I was working on quilts altogether, when I had a blanket and a pair of pillow slips already and other things I could mention. I mean to make a sheet piece soon. Ma said she enjoyed her visit much better than expected. June (brother Jesse June) fell mightily in love with his Aunt Harriet (Harriet Whitten Lankford). Sis and Kee (Narcissa Amaryllis and Elliott Kee, daughters of Jo and Mary Jane) didn't exactly wean Maude

(Maude Elliott, her youngest sister) away from her old maidish black sister. The little thing knew me and began hollering and laughing as soon as she saw me. And Sam married to get somebody to help Mother. I'd be like Kee, believe I'da got a negro.

Rantie Whitten (son of Silas Jr.) took dinner with us today. The child looked like he was lost, Billie (William Pendleton Whitten, son of Silas Jr.) has just returned from Blue Mountain, didn't find out anything about his trip, Rantie didn't seem disposed to talk and I asked but few questions. Saw Aunt D (Madora Frances Ray, widow of Silas Jr. and sister of Molly's mother) Wednesday. She treated me cooly.

I think it does look like living to wind a whole bank of coppas filling around a bunch of peppers, and the peppers also, tho must confess that would be hot living. I've gone to bed, more snow.

Monday night, The children have had a powerful time tonight, pulling candy. Rantie Whitten, William Jones, and Uncle Hosea's two oldest boys (Hugh Edwin and Claud Simpson Ray) happened in and that was the crowd. Our boys have all been hunting Christmas today. Aunt Duck's at Uncle Hosea's, Effie and Billie out hunting Christmas, R (Rantie) here, believe all our folks have been abroad for enjoyment except myself, and, if they don't mind, my enjoyment will excel theirs.

Uncle Hosea has a fine boy (Charles Lamb Ray), two days old. The rain kept Pa and Ma from redeeming their pledge yesterday eve. Pa speaks of visiting you last of this week or first of next. Must answer Cis's (Narcissa) note, letter I must call it. My very best love to Grandpa and all, Would appreciate a letter from you but don't claim it.

Affectionately,
Mary Dora

Molly has matured. She is a worker of great talent and energy, weaving, sewing, and caring for the family. Her letters are full of many projects. I wish we could understand the business of the peppers. Ranson Hosea is a sickly son of Duck and Pluck. He died early. There will be later references to his condition. Why would Aunt Duck treat Mollie coolly?

Elliott Ann to Rebecca Whitten—Jonesborough to Ripley, Mississippi, about January 1876

Dear Beckah,

The thought occurred a few minutes ago that I would make the attempt to write to you. I don't do this to grieve you, but, believing you to be one of my very best friends, and one, too, that would comfort me if it was in your power. I am still surely, surely, one of the most miserable beings in existence. Indeed, I can't believe there ever was one more miserable in this life. It is true, I get along a little better than I once did. I can read some, know that the Bible teaches that "blessed is he that hungereth and thirsteth after righteousness" and David says "the wicked, because of the pride of his countenance will not seek after God, God is not in his thoughts". And now I verily believe I have lived in a delusion, and am without excuse, for I ought to have known. I have never been made to do this thing willfully, I mean knowingly, to dishonor God. If I am not deceived in heart, I feel that I would want to love and serve Him, if it was only for this life, but, O, I can't ever thank Him for the many blessings He has already bestowed upon me, and is still bestowing. O, what a wretch I am. Do you believe there ever was one so vile?

I want you to answer candidly, and I believe you will, if at all. Why, Beckah, I feel to be without natural affection, and why I should be blessed with such a husband, and kind children, and a host of friends, for I verily believe I have many good and true earthly friends I don't know. Now I verily believe, if I could feel that God had forgiven me that I would be one of the happiest mortals you ever saw, for I know that I would love Him, and His children here.

I shall not think hard of you if you should not answer this, but if you feel at all inclined, please answer, for I believe you to be one of the best Christians, and one that is able to instruct me, and I know I believe you would comfort me if it was in your power. It seems to me that I could scarcely live were it not for hope. Why Beckah, I would willingly die if I could know that would secure my acceptance with God. Need I ask your prayers? I know I desire them, and of all other Christians. Don't the Bible teach that where two or three are gathered together in My Name, and ask anything they will in faith it shall be granted.

Beckah, can't you sit down and write me a long letter, and I would be glad how soon. Don't be at all afraid to write your very feeling, for that is what I want, need not be the least afraid of hurting. I don't think that is in your power. Reckon this will seem very strange to you. I have tried to write the truth.

Elliott

This strange letter was not dated by the writer, and I have assigned it to 1876, speculating that it is connected to the condition Mary Dora mentions in her 26 Dec. 1875 letter to Rebecca and the 2 Jan. 1876 letter to her grandfather. Elliott is under severe conviction, though she has been a dedi-

cated Christian most of her life. She believes she is guilty of some unpardonable sin, but gives no inkling of its nature. Perhaps she has concluded that her original conversion experience was not real. Mary Dora simply states that her mother can't be consoled about it and has not been her usual happy self for some time. Elliott was 42 years old in 1876 and lived until 1920. She had ten children, the last in January 1875. We have no more of her letters, nor does she add notes to those written by others after this time. Mary Dora, in a letter dated 8 Feb. 1882, tells of receiving a good, long letter from her. She is mentioned frequently, and there is nothing to convince us that this condition continued until the end of her life. Perhaps she was experiencing the emotional instability of an early menopause, after which she regained her happy disposition. Let us hope so.

Mary Dora to Silas Reagan Whitten—Jonesborough to Ripley, Mississippi, 2 Jan. 1876

Dear Grandpa,

It is with a felt sense of neglected duty that prompts me to begin a letter to you at this late hour. All have gone to bed except Sallie and myself, so I have a good chance, if I but improve the opportunity. We are in usual health. Pa suffers all the time, more or less, with rheumatism, though no worse than usual that I am aware of. We think Ma is decidedly better since her return home from your house, but she don't seem willing to admit the change. When she talks, which is not a common thing as in the past, her subject is "the unpardonable sin". We can't pacify her on that at all, so she says, and yet we know her condition is much better than it was two months ago, bound to be so.

Well, I am going to rattle on and tell you what I have been doing and what I expect will come next. Last week I spun and wove six yards of janes, cut it out of the loom, colored, cut coat, pants, and vest for Pa. Ma and I made the coat yesterday morning, had everything cleaned up and ready to go to work by sunup, scoured two of the seams, ironed all, kept in a good humor, and made a coat. Isn't that a pretty good new years start? Providence permitting, I shall begin spinning again tomorrow. When I get the cloth out and made up I shall try to go and see you.

Silas, Hosea, and Bedford (brothers Silas Ray, Hosea Ranson, and Bedford Forrest) have been going to school, Mr. George Holbrook, teacher. Reckon Mattie, Joe, and maybe June (siblings Martha Earle, Joseph Brooks, and Jesse June) will start in the morning. No more tonight.

I wrote to Aunt Beck last week, also to Miss N. A. Whitten (Narcissa Amaryllis, daughter of Jo). Haven't had a word from you since our folks came home, reckon they are out of paper at Uncle Joe's. If I knew that was the cause of their silence I'd send them some. Wish you would jog their memory and see if that can account for their high appreciation for my scribbles. Cousin Frank (Frank Adams, son of Joe) said once, a joke, I thought, that he made tapers of my letters to light his pipe. If the young man don't mind he can get out and buy paper as well as matches. Oh, they do appreciate my scrawls over there so they say and I believe it for actions speak louder than words.

Ma and I went to Uncle Hosea's yesterday. Aunt Sallie's baby (Charles Lamb Ray, one week old) is nearly as large as Maude. I saw Mrs. Adkins, she seems gayly as ever. Her daughter, single, is in delicate health and has been for months. She was so absent minded, one might walk in and she wouldn't notice that anybody was about. Mrs. A's son got drunk, so I've been informed, one night last week at a candy pulling, and yet the old lady appears to be cheerful enough for one of her age. Uncle Brooks (Joe Brooks Ray) and family are in the enjoyment of good health.

Wonder if Uncle Joe had thought about its being a providential occurrence that our folks went down just when they did. He, no doubt, would have killed his meat if it had not been for company and a late rise in the morning, and again, if Pa hadn't been fixing for the trip he likely would have killed the same day and it would have been spoiled. Neither of them are able to lose it. Lots of meat spoiled in this neighborhood. Mrs. Glover, and others, says fifteen thousand pounds already.

All gone to nappy's house and I must shortly go. Our very best love to all. Would appreciate a letter from you at any time and any of the rest that feel disposed to write. Please excuse the haste and bad writing.

Affectionately yours,
M. D. Whitten

P. S. Enclosed please find a sheet of paper which I send to Cousin Harriett (Joe's daughter). I want her to put something on it and send back to me, if not any more than her name. Tell her I will commence it for her. "Molly Whitten, not Simpson yet."

P S again, Pa will visit you this week if not hindered.

Molly spins, weaves, colors, sews, and coyly mentions her cousin Frank Adams Whitten, whom she marries about sixteen months later. Aren't we glad that a visit kept her family and Uncle Jo's from slaughtering hogs on a day before the warm spell? Who was the Simpson she mentioned to Cousin Harriett?

Mary Dora to Rebecca and Silas Reagan Whitten—Poplar Springs to Ripley, Mississippi, 8 Feb. 1882

Dear Grandpa and Aunt Beck,

It has long been my intention to write to you but first one thing and then another has prevented. It has been cold and raining some, and the children have kept up such a racket all day and got me so completely out of sorts, don't know how I'll make it, but I'll attempt it. We are all well, as usual all have bad colds. I've had the worst this winter that I ever had in my life and it holds on the longest. Last week I could hardly sleep at night. Frank's cold is better but he still has headache a good deal. The children are not looking well. Nat (son, Nathaniel Carter) has looked peaked and pale all day but I reckon its so much damp, cool weather. He eats hardy.

We miss Hester (Joe's daughter Hester Virginia) a great deal. I get lonesome and catch myself thinking, she'll soon be home from school, but she don't come. I get right sorry for Mesina (daughter, Mesina Elliott). She often asks me where Hetty is, and frequently cries when the school children pass of evening and Hetty don't come. Nat says hush trying (for crying) baby, I'll take Foy and dit Powell's buddy (for buggy) and go after Hetty. She'll hush crying and join in with to talk about it. She's a great hand to talk but you can't understand much of it. She calls Frank Nappy and Dappy oftener than she says Pappy and calls me Nanny. We received Cis's (Narcissa, Joe's daughter) card Wednesday. Glad to hear that Will (William Andrew, Joe's son) and Hester made it home alright.

We had cold supper here tonight. Frank's been growling about it several times. Now he says his supper's give out and he is going to bed, says he can't eat enough cold vittles to keep him up til twelve o'clock. Tis only a little after nine.

Have you gardened any yet? We've done a good deal of work in our garden but some of it, I think, will be to do over, think we will have to plant Irish potatoes again if we have any and I don't want to make a failure this year. Our cabbage bed looks nice, so do the onions, peas are coming up. Frank broke up and planted his little patch of corn last Friday and Saturday. He's powerful scared about it now, afraid it will snow or continue to rain and his corn will rot and he'll have to plant over and, of course, that will keep him from the store awhile. He speaks of renting three or four acres of land from Pick Norman, our town mayor, and planting corn, don't know yet whether he will or not.

Had a good long letter from Ma week or so since. I believe it was before Hester left. Have you any hens setting? I have one. There was still another hen that wanted the job but I couldn't find eggs for her and had to convince her of the fact by putting her under a tub for a few days. Our hens are not doing as well these days as common. I don't get half the amount of eggs that I did this time last year. We are getting some milk and butter now, have churned three or four times within the last ten days.

Frank went to see old Mrs. Dillard yesterday. She is up, going all over the place. She has been sick since early in the fall. She's the lady Hester and I sent the blister salve to when Frank was gone to Ripley. On Tuesday after Hester left I put my Linsey quilt in the frames, would have got it out today but have picked my fingers till I have to go slow. I've quilted three since Christmas and want to quilt one more, then I will rest awhile. I have no cloth to make new clothes and, I expect, I'll get powerful tired mending old ones. I made a fine pot of soap before Hester left. I put up the balance of my ashes the other day, want to finish making this week.

There's no sickness in the country now, nor hasn't been lately. Dr. Carruth (Adrian Brown, husband of Joe's daughter Mary Eleanor) was here awhile yesterday. He stayed at Jasper Davis's Sunday night. He said they were all well and Mary was nearly crazy to come here. Lee got home from Nashville and was mighty pleased with his trip, stood a fine examination and so on. I shall look for him here next stop. I sent Mary part of the flower seeds. Tell the girls to write to the Dr. (husband, Frank Adams Whitten) by first mail and tell him whether or not the tacks have to be planted in a box. There was a great bundle of tacks rolled up with the seeds that Cis (Jo's daughter, Narcissa Amaryllis) brought. I knew about it but humored the joke and we had a good laugh over it.

Well, Frank and the children are all asleep. Now that I have a good chance to write I can't think of anything to write about. Frank went to New Albany one day last week, more, I suppose, to be going than any other cause and says he didn't do any good for himself nor anybody else but was worn out and nearly sick when he got home.

I went to Mrs. Powell's on a visit one day last week, Mrs. P sashaying along as usual. Mr. Powell was working on his garden then but his general occupation is swapping horses. Sometimes he has as many as four or five pretty good ones and all of a sudden he'll dwindle down to one stack of bones. Jim Simpson and family well. I was there one day last week, helping his wife quilt. Tell Hester that Mrs. Simmons wants the trimming.

Mrs. Milt Caldwell is still a cripple and, I'm afraid always will be. The last news Esquire John Caldwell had of his son Johnny, who ran away five or six weeks since, he was in Texas, finally pleased and inviting all the boys here to go to him, and some of them are plenty good to do it, if they had the chance.

The school continues full, Austin mightily beset about Hester going home. He, Austin, disappointed them at Chesterville again last Saturday and Sunday. Must quit for tonight, may add a P S in the morning.

Wednesday morning, all well, F was called off last night about twelve o'clock, just now got in. It's still cool and raining. Write soon. Love to all.

Affectionately,
Molly W.

Tell Harriett that Doc Brown is married and she can give Frank the glory for I had nothing to do with it. I don't meddle in such matters myself.

Frank (Frank Adams Whitten, son of Jo and Mesina) and Mary Dora have married, moved to Poplar Springs, and have two children. They were first cousins. She is carrying the third, Frank Adams Jr., born that summer. Frank is farming and practicing medicine as an apprentice to Dr. Adrian Brown Caruth, husband of his sister Mary Eleanor Whitten. Now Molly gardens, raises chickens, churns, quilts, mends, and makes soap.

Mary Dora to Rebecca Whitten—Poplar Springs to Ripley, Mississippi, 23 April 1882

Dear Aunt Beck,

Your letter came to me Tuesday, we were very glad to hear from you, and it does seem like the letters we get from any and all of our kin are few and far between. Hester has only written to me once since she went home. She certainly won't study as much about us as we study about her.

We are all well as common. I do most of the grumbling but keep up and busy all the time. Frank has headache, backache, neuralgia, and so on, but eats hardy most of the time. The children are all well enough, I reckon. They have a puny spell now and then but get over it in a day or two.

We are having sorter strange weather for a week or so. Week before last was cold, last week warm until yesterday. After the big rain and a good deal of wind it began to turn cold and seems now like we would have frost, we covered some of the plants in the garden. Our garden don't look as well as it did before the cool spell, though if it would turn warm we would soon have good many vegetables, have already had a nice chance of radishes, and onions, and mustard till we are tired of it, even old fashion six week red beans are very pretty, have runners on them, and need to be stuck, and must be done, will soon be blooming. Have more than a hundred cabbage plants set out and more coming on, a nice bed of sweet potato slips soon be ready to set out, Irish potatoes almost a failure, didn't get a stand. What I have are nice.

Frank's woman corn is very pretty, he plowed it week before last. His patch here at home is coming up the second time. When he planted I followed the corn with beans, watermelons, muskmelons, and cucumbers and see they are all coming up now. My dread is these interested chickens, ready to go for the young plants, yes, and ready for every bloom. I'm having the worst luck with chickens that ever did. My oldest, thirteen very pretty little chickens, all but three went in two nights, don't know what went with them. I had a hen setting on seventeen eggs, had set the best sort, would hatched tomorrow, and one day last week another hen flew up on the box, knocked it down, and broke every egg. My old Henalgeon hen is setting now, tho I don't pay her much attention. I've lost all hope of raising chickens and quit taking an interest, having turned my attention to housekeeping princi-pally, though I do a good deal of jobbing in and out. I cook food for the cow once a day and sometimes twice. We get milk and butter, do very well, have butter three times a day and milk twice, could use half gallon more milk a day if we had it.

I keep up with my washing pretty well, Frank helps me wash nearly every week. I've not made many new clothes but have patched and remodeled many old ones, am about through with, too, have been telling Frank a good while how we needed some cloth, but he hasn't got the money and I can't insist on straining the credit. He got some cloth yesterday evening to make Nat some pants, think maybe I can get him two pair. Tis the first pants goods that has ever been bought for Nat, have always made his pants out of his Papa's old ones, but Papa's old ones are getting about as scarce as Nat's.

Friday night. Well, Aunt Beck, I began my letter first of the week but felt so bad didn't finish it, don't feel like I could write a whole letter tonight so will add a little to the old one.

Well, I must tell the news. Frank didn't want me to tell it, thought maybe some of you would come down and be taken by surprise, but if Will should happen to come, or if Mary (both children of Jo) ever gets to come I know it will be spread, but to the point. Last week Frank tore down that beautiful meat house that stood in one corner of the yard and put us up a room. It extends clear across the back end of the house, then he run a partition across the shed from the west wall of main building making a long cook and eating room, the back end of which is our smoke house. The shed is eight feet wide inside, will chamber two beds besides several trunks and boxes. I'm certainly very proud of it. I don't know how I did turn around or keep anything to its place or even have a place for everything. I've been straightening up at odd times for two or three week, every trunk and box neatly packed, a place for everything and everything in its place.

We washed this morning but didn't hang out the clothes. It has been raining and has been raining nearly all day. I'm nearly out of work now, told Frank today that if I lived till Monday would have to get out my quilt scraps again and I'm tired of that for one time in my life, have pieced about six since Christmas and quilted three, besides pieced two for Mrs. Simpson. Tell Hester that I've got my little star done and set together. I pieced a square for a quilt for Austin (the school teacher) this week. The Liberty Ladies pieced him one and, of course, we Poplarites couldn't stand to be behind. I reckon Chester will be next as he has been there twice.

Last account we had from Dr.'s (her father, Alfred Washington Whitten) folks they were well. Florence (Sallie Florence Lankford, daughter of Harriet) had been there the week before, right sick. Miss Clara humbled herself enough to call a few minutes one evening on her way to Mrs. Caldwell's to see Bill Brown. Mrs. Caldwell is getting well, doesn't limp any scarcely. Esq. John Caldwell's son Johnnie made his way home last Sunday. He says his last trip has broke him from sucking eggs if they will let him stay at home. They took him back, of course, and seem proud of him.

I'm very tired and sleepy. I know this is a badly written, badly composed letter, but about the best job I can make of it now. Do write as oft as you can. Much love to Grandpa and all the family.

Affectionately,

Molly

Son Nathaniel Carter gets his first new pair of pants and Frank remodels the house. Molly complains that she has nothing to do.

Mary Dora to Rebecca Whitten—Poplar Springs to Ripley, Mississippi, 30 Aug. 1882

Dear Aunt Beck,

I've been due you a letter two months, but in first place, couldn't see to write, and since then have been out of stamps. We are all on foot this morning and all sorta puny, but nothing serious, I am in hopes. Frank's health has been remarkably good this year, better than I ever knew it. The children have been blessed, too, have had some chills and light fevers, but yet up in a few days.

But, let me tell you, I was, on last Sunday, an eye witness to a scene most pleasant of any for my erring body to behold, and that was to see Frank buried with Christ in Baptism. None can imagine my joy and surprise when he told me, on Thursday night, of his intention. I couldn't work. I couldn't eat or sleep, but could see him in my imagination just as plain as I did at the Church and at the pool. Brother Austin says I saw part of it. They had their happy time out in the woods. Frank says he don't know what kept him out of the Church so long, says he had had a hope seventeen years and had been all this time trying to brighten his hope and get better. Do wish all of you could have been here. I intended writing for Mary but Carruth (Frank's sister and her husband, Dr. Adrian Caruth) was here on Friday and said she couldn't come.

There has been a good deal of sickness for a few weeks, last week, and week before. Frank was riding almost day and night. Hasn't lost a case yet and has had some of the worst he ever had, bad bilious fevers, congestion of the stomach and bowels, and inflammation of the stomach and bowels, some bilious colic, and one child of spasms caused by an over gorge of fruit. I've been afraid we would be visited by some of those dangerous complaints but thus far we have escaped. I haven't seen a well day since Christmas, but am able to do my house work, but do it lots of times when I don't feel like it. I'm by myself so much it keeps me weak and nervous to think about.

But, changing the subject, Aunt Beck, I can show boys with anybody, I think, here about. He's (Frank Adams Whitten, born 21

June 1882) about the largest two month child ever saw, I'm satisfied. He's the best and healthiest one we've ever had. Of course, he takes up some time but I don't mind. He just lies and sleeps from morning till night, and from night till morning, the first light. Night has yet to be made for him. He likes to be talked to and bragged on and can hold up his head and laugh as big as anybody. Frank thinks Papa's little boy is of almost as much importance as Papa's big boy. Mesina grows and fattens and the most mischievous child I know, full of laughter, but cries loud enough when disposed. If you could stop in some day and see the house you would say, well, I didn't know that Molly was so trifling. But honestly, Aunt Beck, I can't help it. She goes into the dirty clothes box, gets my shoes and stockings, puts them on, puts on Nat's breeches, gets into her Papa's undershirt and drawers sometimes and squalls for me to come and take her out. She's on top of the beds, into safe, into my dried fruit, throws everything out of the cradle. She don't think she's got a pallet till she gets a quilt spread full length and breadth on the floor.

I don't pretend, today, any kind of study work. I can't. Have been visiting the sick a little while I'm at home, keeps me busy minding children and chickens and doing around trying to keep straight. Have big meetings for six weeks. I haven't attended any except Sunday and Sunday night. Have looked for Ma until I'm almost sick.

I dried about a bushel of fruit, mostly apples. Frank bought a bushel of peaches, green fruit, about gone. I have but few chickens, have good many cabbage, but about out of meat. First sowing of turnips up, sweet potatoes very good.

Received letters from Harriett and Hester (daughters of Joe) last week, will answer soon. All well at Caruth's last Friday. We are anxious to visit you but can't promise. Excuse bad writing for I can't hold the pen steady. Write to us often and come to see us if you can.

Love to all,

Molly

Frank's conversion after a hope for salvation of seventeen years illustrates the concept of selection by God held by these Baptists. Molly rejoices with her husband and dries fruit.

Mary Dora to Rebecca Whitten—Poplar Springs to Ripley, Mississippi, 13 March 1883

Dear Aunt Beck,

I have been trying to write to you since Christmas but first one hindrance and then another has prevented. And now I am rocking the cradle with one foot so you needn't judge by this writing that I'm always so nervous. We are all on foot and generally eat at mealtime but not with the desired relish that I like to see in working folks. Frank had spell last week brought on by overwork. He got over it, however, in a few days and looks better than common, and, I believe, would get stout if he would work moderately and take quinine.

He bought a piece of land from Mr. Ray, a ten acre lot, and is trying to get five or six acres cleared, has three or four cleared now, has been trying to get men who owed him to work but succeeds slowly in that line. Don't anybody want to work who have received value in medicine, but them chaps require more medicine than those who expect to pay for it.

We had a rail splitting last Friday, got rails enough to fence in what he intends clearing, had seventeen hands for dinner and supper. Everything went off decently and in order throughout the day. The men all seemed to enjoy their dinner and supper.

There is little sickness in the country. Frank saw Professor Lee yesterday. He said there was a great deal of sick at Chesterfield and he was getting all the practice. That's powerful close to us to be no closer, don't you think? The old Dr. is improving some but very feeble, not able to ride yet.

Has Silas and his lady (Molly's brother, Silas Ray, and new wife, Ruth Sawyer Burt) been to see you? I received a letter from him last week stating that they intended visiting you this month. I think that when they make that trip they might afford to try this end of the road and see if they can find some kin. Have you gardened any yet? We planted Irish potatoes, English peas, onions, tomatoes, radishes, cabbage seeds and so on, bedded our sweet potatoes this week. Frank bought a bushel on debt last week for half dollar.

Mrs. Caldwell had another bad spell week or so since, is up now. She was worse this time than I have ever seen her, don't think she can stand many more such spells. Have you any little chickens? I took off mine, eight, a month ago but an old hawk got five of them, then run afoul of Mrs. Caldwell's geese. They caught it on one. It killed two and crippled another. Something has been after one of mine but didn't succeed in getting it, only have three. Have three goose eggs and tomorrow is lay day. Have twenty seven on hens and pullets, two setting, have sold eighteen dozen eggs in two or three weeks, want to sell more this week, bought Irish potatoes and all our garden seeds with eggs.

Am now knitting some cotton socks for sale. Don't know how they will sell, but if I can't get a quarter or thirty cents, Frank can wear them. Mrs. Caldwell went to the patch and picked some cotton for me to finger pick and knit stockings. I've knit two pairs of stockings, three strands, and two pairs of socks, and there is fully a third of it to pick. I was very anxious to quilt some but I don't get any nearer ready than I was last fall. House is so small and weather been so bad, can't put up a quilt until the spring opens and then Frank says I have to work the garden and this patch here at the house. He is going to plant cotton enough for a bale so he can pay for his land. It only calls for fifty three dollars and some cents.

I haven't heard from home for nearly a month. Reckon they are fixing to go to Blue Mountain. Every time I hear they are going or have just been. I really think they treat me shabby about writing and visiting, too. The children grow fast and are full of their mischief.

Mrs. Caldwell gave me a turkey and told Nat that we would get it fat and maybe his Grandpapa would come. He says he wishes his Grandpapa would come on. He wants some turkey, and he wants his pigs. Mesina is just as fat as can be. Messy is a good name for her. She slipped out some dirty clothes this evening to a tub of rain water. She'd stoop over the tub of rain water and rub awhile, then throw them out on the ground and bottle awhile. Tonight, after it got dark, she went out on the entry and saw the moon. She came running back to tell me, she says, Oh, Mama, ain't that the prettiest buzzard? The baby grows fast, is going to be just like Nat, I think. He has a bad, bad cold now, so have all the children.

Well, I've been soap making yesterday and today, made my kettle full of good soap, plenty to do me. I have another barrel of good ashes but no soap grease. Why don't Harriett (Joe's daughter) answer my letters? I wrote her a long letter a few weeks since. When are you coming down, any of you? I must quit. I haven't seen Mary (Caruth) but once since we came home, her quilt and fruit still here. Love to all, write soon.

Affectionately,
Molly

Nat talks a great deal about his old Grandpapa and I thought I would have written to him before now, but my chance for writing is bad enough. Our very best love to him.

Frank bought ten acres and is clearing it for farming. Like most of the land east of the Mississippi River, it was covered with virgin timber. During the years spanned by these letters, millions of acres were cleared for this purpose. To realize that they did it without chain saws or bulldozers is to understand what a mammoth undertaking it was. Fell the trees with axs and hand saws, grub out the stumps, pull them up by man and animal power. Break up the ground with horse- or mule-drawn plows.

And now Molly finger picks (removes the seeds) cotton and knits stockings and socks, makes more soap, and wants to start quilting if she can find time away from the garden.

This is our last letter from her. Rebecca moved to Poplar Springs the following month and lived with Frank, Mary Dora, and family until her death 2 May 1919. Ranson and his children had come to live with Rebecca and her father in January of 1878 when his first wife, Pocahontas Medora Rogers, died. He married Mrs. Sallie Rowland 17 April 1883 and they remained with Silas Reagan. Rebecca moved from her father's home for the first time in fifty-seven years during the month of this marriage. I wonder why.

Grandchildren of Frank and Molly tell of the tragic death of a son, named for his grandfather, Alfred Washington. Born 26 Feb. 1885, he was killed in an accident involving the big wash kettle on 19 July 1887. What a shame that we have no letters from Molly describing this and later events.

Harriet Earle Whitten Lankford to a daughter of Joseph John or Ranson E. Whitten—Belton, Texas, to Ripley, Mississippi, 2 Oct. 1884

My dear Niece,

It has been so long since your last letter that I am really not sure whether I answered it or not, but I would write all the same. You have been very kind to write to me and, rest assured, I appreciate it. Sometimes I think I have to wait a long time without hearing from your dear old Grandpa, especially since he has been so sorely afflicted. Glad he was so much better when Ammy (Narcissa Amaryllis, Joe's daughter) wrote that he could wear his shoes and walk about, and poor Aunt Becca, that cough is so weakening to her. I am sure tis some liver affliction and wish she could be relieved.

Are you at home or at school? Do you write darling Dwight (James Dwight Lankford, her son)? Oh, how I long to see him. He wrote me he would come to see me before long. He seemed very well pleased, is in good business in Atoka (Tennessee) but I have never liked for him and John (her son, John Silas Lankford) to live there. I think tis a kind of fast society, there's not enough religion there to suit me. Kee (daughter Mary Kee Lankford) lives one hundred eighty miles from us at Albany, Shackleford County. She is delighted with that country. She says she is among the best and kindest people in the world. Charles (Charles Alexander Lankford), her brother, went up to see her not long since. He says the people are all wealthy and make a perfect pet out of Kee. She is so pleasant and entertaining. She is coming to Belton in about ten days to spend a month with us.

Our little ones keep us very busy. They are very bright little children and I try to teach them all the good I know. Juanita and Rennie (Mollie Juanita and Maurine Earle, daughters of Anna C. Lankford and James Sample) are going to school to their Aunt Sallie (daughter, Sallie Florence Lankford). She has a small school in her own house and, by the way, there is one of your Ripley girls teaching at the public school. I think her name is Alma. I have not met her but Sissie has met her and says she is very pleasant. She came here with Peter Haynes Smith, her rich Uncle. Do you know her?

Tell John Whitten (John Dayton Whitten, son of Joseph John) when you see him we are living near the Post Office in a very pleasant part of town. Tell him I wrote to him and his Pa long, long ago and have been impatient for an answer, would like so much to have letters from you all often.

Tell your Grandpa I will write to him soon. I write a great deal, having so many children so far away. They write to me often and it keeps me busy to answer. Write often to Dwight in a merry, pleasant style and cheer him. I wished to write you a long, long letter but baby (Dora Eugenia Sample, daughter of Anna C.) is here and I am hurried to send it to the office. Sissie (Anna C.) says I wrote you last so you must write twice now. I wrote to Father two or three weeks ago. Will write right soon to him. Love all most tenderly.

Heaven bless you is the prayer of your most affectionate Aunt,

Harriet

Fewer letters survive as the years go by. Sources are older, some dead, Rebecca is no longer in Ripley where her Father, Ranson, and Jo live and where more letters are received. We catch up with Harriet in this one. She and several of her children moved to Bell County, Texas, after the death, 16 May 1872, of her husband, Nathan Alexander Lankford. Harriet is still filled with love for her family and her God.

Doleska Fitzallen Whitten to Silas Reagan Whitten—Smith's Station, Lee,

Alabama, to Ripley, Mississippi, 4 March 1885

My dear Uncle Silas,

I heard through a sister of mine living in Cameron, Texas that you had a daughter there, Cousin Harriet Lankford, and that you were living at the great age of ninety four years. I wrote to Cousin Harriet and she wrote me a beautiful letter telling me all about her own family, and yours, and gave me your address. I think it wonderful that you have attained such an age, and I feel very proud that I have a relative so favored, and Aunt Mariam, too, is living, she says. If my beloved and honored grandfather (James Whitten), your brother, had lived he would have been one hundred years old the 26th of last January.

I was devotedly attached to my grandfather, and I thought him, all my life, to be the best man I ever knew. When I was young I spent much of my time with him after his second wife (Sarah Little Hogan Whitten) died, and we two being alone he had to talk to me, and many is the hours I'd sit listening to him talk of his father's family. That is the way I came to know so much of his family. Yourself and Aunt Mariam seemed to have been favorites with him. I never saw any of the family, except Uncle Isaac (Isaac Smith Whitten). He came to see Grandpa just before he died. He was a very aristocratic looking old gentleman and was very kind and pleasant. He and Grandpa did not look very much alike. He has since died himself, but I do not know in what year.

You remember Aunt Eliza (Elizabeth Ann Whitten, daughter of James) went with Grandpa when he visited you. Of course you have heard of her death which occurred twenty years ago. The brother-in-law who raised her, Col. T. M. Hogan, was my uncle by marriage, having married Orpha, Grandpa's oldest daughter. She is dead, his children scattered over the country and he lives with me. He is seventy-six years old, a boy compared to you, but he is helpless, cannot walk one step. We have a rolly chair, made expressly for invalids and he, in the morning, when taken out of bed, sits in that chair, and there he has to sit until he is taken out and put to bed. He is so heavy and helpless that it takes two good strong people to handle him. His mind has been a very fine one, but is somewhat impaired by his confinement and he frets and harries some, but beings his troubles, as rule, are better than most men faced.

From having been associated with my old Grandfather and then with him I am in more sympathy with old people perhaps than most people of my age, but I am getting old. I will be forty eight the 22nd of this month. My father was Arphax Whitten, the oldest son of two of his father. He had eight daughters by his first wife (Matilda Bennett Whitten) and two and one son by his second (Aurelia Priddy Whitten). His widow and their children are in Tyler, Texas. My oldest sister (Julia Ann Elizabeth Whitten) died at thirty two years of age, unmarried, and one married sister dead (Orpha Judson Whitten Lamb) who left one son. I have five married sisters living, one in Texas, two in Stewart County, Georgia, one widowed sister near me and one with me.

I live at the old homestead, on it, and manage my own business. Our place is a little village. I am the Postmistress and have a comfortable living.

Dear Uncle, if you feel like it, get someone to answer this letter and tell me all about yourself, how you enjoy living, living at such an age, and do you take much interest in your Sundays now? Give my love to Cousin Ranson if he is near you. I shall always remember his visit to us with pleasure.

With love to your family I am your affectionate niece,

Miss D. F. Whitten

Dolly sends family news to her great-uncle. His sister, Mariam Davis, still lives, and is in Texas. She has heard from Harriet. Dolly's Whittens are scattered over Georgia, Alabama, and Texas. She mentions that Ranson E. had once visited her family. Although we don't know when he did this, it is worth speculating that he went to see Eliza, who had visited the Silas Reagan family many years before, and with whom Ranson had exchanged several friendly letters. Dolly asked for an answer. I suspect her letter was sent to Rebecca for that purpose, and she complied and saved it for us.

Alfred Washington to Ranson E. Whitten—Jonesborough to Ripley, Mississippi, 10 July 1885

Dear Rant,

Your letter just received is comforting indeed, from the fact that we were fearful that Jo would not recover. His wisdom in seeking a good Samaritan home is to be highly praised. Adrian and Mary (Adrian and Mary Eleanor Whitten Carruth, daughter of Joe) deserve the kindest regards, the lasting gratitude of every kinsman. Adrian, to me, is a dearly cherished type of the grand old heros of our mother country. Long may he live and the full fruition of a happy life and a useful Providence attend him. His affectionate regard for Father has long ago brought me in close sympathy with his interest and his marked attention to the visit of my wife deserves more than the ordinary congratulations of friendly intercourse. If you should ever see him again tell him that I mean no harm in speaking this feeling on his behalf and his better half.

We are all up. Elliott and I improved since the weather softened down. Business growing and increasing every day and not a stick of preparation for spring work, absolutely no work done with mumps all about and measles approaching rapidly. Bedford (son, Bedford Forrest Whitten) and family, I suppose, have measles. Hosea (son, Hosea Ranson) is dodging the disease. Silas and family well last week and Sallie trying to make herself useful with them (son, Silas Ray and daughter, Sarah Kee).

Old Andy Drury died last with bronchitis, I suppose, and old Mrs. Rutherford, across the Hatchie (a river nearby) died, some chronic disease. Let me hear from Jo again. I am fearful you left him too soon.

Give love to Father and tell I am waiting only for a better time to visit him. Rant (Ranson Hosea, son of Pluck and Duck) is about as usual, probably not so well as he had certainly retrograded since the holy days.

Affectionately,
A. W. Whitten

June (son, Jesse June) waited with Rant last night. For three days he has been reported improving.

Jo is ill and now lives with daughter Mary Eleanor and her husband, Dr. Adrian Caruth. Jo died 18 November of that year. Mary Eleanor died the following month. All three of Jo's wives were dead by 1885. His younger children became wards of brother Ranson E.

Alfred Washington to Ranson E. Whitten—Jonesborough to Ripley, Mississippi, 23 June 1887

Dear Rant,

We are much gratified to hear of Father's improvement and recovery, although he may say "shough, shough", I reckon I know. We are tolerably well at home except Elliott who is threatened with bowel trouble, better this morning.

I think the oat crop which was poorly sowed is short, but enough to meet and early corn and have seed left. The corn is extra fine and the peas but the ever failing cotton is short and unpromising.

There has been bowel complaint but it yields, largely, to domestic treatment. The weather has been so extremely hot that we may look out for some stroke north and the cholera to follow. I think it a good plan to use quinine freely in all sickness approaching, particularly at its inception. The rain with us was a light shower, better however, on other side.

Our protracted meeting this year begins on 2nd Sunday and continues to the 3rd. We would like to have you with us. Just eight inches of table to write on this morning without support to the arms.

Affectionately,
A. W. Whitten

Alfred Washington to Ranson E. Whitten—Jonesborough to Ripley, Mississippi, 18 Dec. 1887

Dear Rant,

Your kind letter along with the blunt reminds me that I should reply. It is truly painful to hear of Father's afflictive imbecility. I should have gone to see him but the children took my time, then I thought I would go in a week but was taken down with my back, all the back part of my body, so severe that had to be confined to my bed and my room. Now I am up and out as usual, feeling as well as I did before I was taken sick. I think of coming but it depends on the weather and the possibility of relapse.

Effie's (Effie Berry, daughter of Pluck and Duck) fall on the visit took a turn and threatened to be serious but she is up and not complaining much. Rant (Ranson Hosea, Effie's brother) is about the same, probably better, takes an opium pill at night, tannic acid, English Rosin, and quinine in day time.

My building work gets up slowly but the whole thing would please you. I have half the house nearly ready for use. Nine young fattening hogs sinks my corn rapidly, but they meat so fast I must bear the shrinkage longer. We have a fine chance of milk and butter. Have gotten tired of beef and have others that should be slaughtered.

Our friend Brooks Garrett and the block adjourning was burnt out last week at Pocahontas. Garrett lost several thousand dollars but saved enough to be up and selling goods next day. Silas, I suppose, has returned, Hosea and Bedford well. Our preacher has finished his year and W. T. Lowrey takes his place, has an appointment for the 1st Sunday in June 1888. Thanks for the seed.

Your Brother,
A. W. Whitten

Afflictive imbecility is a harsh label for the loss of mental faculty due to old age, or disease, or both. Silas Reagan was suffering from a condition that seems inherited by many Whittens I have known. Today we refer to the condition in gentler terms. This does nothing to reduce the pain it brings to loved ones. Mercifully, Silas Reagan Whitten died ten months after this letter and was buried in the Ripley Cemetery, where he lies with Eleanor Kee Earle, Joseph John and his three wives, and the Carruth family.

THE OBITUARY OF SILAS REAGAN WHITTEN FROM THE *SOUTHERN SENTINEL*

8 November 1888

An Old Soldier Dead

Silas R. Whitten, deceased, was born in Greenville District, South Carolina, on the 19th day of February 1794, and died in Tippah County, Mississippi, on the 27th day of October 1888. He was married at the age of 18 to Eleanor K. Earle, daughter of Col. John Earle, of the American Revolution.

Early in life, he became a prominent, useful, and leading man in every avocation of good citizenship. He was a close and constant reader, particularly of the Bible. His political acquaintance and culture was large. His influence was decisive and strong; although not a professor of Christianity, he revered and honored it before all men, and devoutly gave it a voluntary support of his time, talent, and substance.

Being a direct descendant, and one of the first born after the revolutionary war, he imbibed the early manhood of civil and religious liberty as the paternal fathers taught it, and to this he adhered throughout his long life. He was a volunteer soldier in the second decisive war with Great Briton, which secured for him a pension from the general government, which was a merciful help to him in his extreme old age. At age 40, he was a self-made, well read, well educated, leader of the Whig party in his own county. His clear conception of truth, firm conviction of duty, and fearless address gave him a popular bearing before the people, and he was elected to the nullifying convention of South Carolina in 1832, as a Union delegate. The result of this meeting is a matter of governmental history.

Assuredly he was a good man. In the last months of his extreme debility and affliction, the angels of mercy continued unceasingly to console and strengthen his pillow, by day and by night. At the great age of 95, he was taken away from us, to join the grand old army of his day and generation. As we revere and honor the century which has made us a great and wonderful people, let us not forget the individual heroes, who gave us constitutional liberty, and who have perpetuated its civil and sacred institutions to the American people.

Rest patriot, rest from affliction and strife,
Sepulchered beside thy dutiful wife,
From the toil of a century given to time,
Rest patient, rest in hallow sublime.
Rest patient, rest till the dead shall arise
To mingle in praise, with the Lord in the skies,
Till the dead and the living, caught up in the air
That the happy reward, immortality wear.

Martha Earle Whitten to Rebecca Whitten—Jonesborough to Poplar Springs, Mississippi, 1 Jan. 1889

My dear Aunt,

Your unexpected, but welcomely received letter was received several days ago, but for want of an opportunity I have neglected writing until this time. This is the first night of the new year, 1889 and to admit that it is a pleasure for me to converse with you tonight is only half way expressing my feelings. We have been a little lonely today as we have had to part with our boys this morning. June has gone back to school and Joe has gone to learn the art of typesetting. Maude will stay with us a few days for company (brothers Jesse June and Joseph Brooks and sister Maude Elliott Whitten).

It seems real strange not to have even one boy on the place. It puts so much responsibility on me. I have to see to everything around the place and do all the necessary bossing. Maude and I went over to see our little nephew today and I must acknowledge that he is a right fair specimen of humanity, and Artelia (Artelia Clara and Alfred Washington, children of brother John Graves and Sally Worsham Whitten) is growing very fast in her own estimation, though she is right sweet, I think. No late word from Silas (Silas Ray Whitten, her brother).

Everybody seems to be doing very well now in way of financial business. We spent an extremely dull Christmas up here. Everything was more quiet than usual.

How did you enjoy yourself? I learned through Hosea and Joe that you had donned your new corset and bustle, and of course, ere this you have purchased a fashionable bonnet. I would be more than delighted to be there and assist you in arranging your toilet for the many entertainments that, of course, you attend. I guess that Molly takes a late magazine and it will not be necessary for me to describe the latest mode of dress.

And Aunt Beck, they tell me you have started to school. How do you like the PSNC? Are you taking music and art? Aunt Beck, you must not fail to subscribe for the Pocahontas Normal Index, as I expect to contribute to its interest almost weekly.

We enjoyed a visit from Uncle Rant and Frank (Ranson E. and daughter Frank Alma) not long since. Joe Earle (son of Ranson E.), after a visit home returned to Pocahontas Saturday. Effie (Effie Berry, daughter of Pluck and Duck) is now on a visit to Blue Mountain, Carrie (Carrie Isabelle Whitten Richardson, daughter of Pluck and Duck) and children well. We were glad to see Flora (Flora Lee Bennett, wife of brother Bedford Forrest) but they did not stay near long enough. It seems too much like a dream.

We made very good success of our Christmas dinner. We has a small, but select crowd, a large quantity of dinner, and of the very best variety, and three nice complementary speeches, clearing $13.85. Our society is, I trust, in at least a gentle current of prosperity. Well, Aunt Beck, I did intend to write a long letter to you but I have a chance to post it and I must close in for this time. Tell Molly (sister Mary Dora) that her letters should have been answered this time but Pa is waiting on me and I must not keep him is suspense. Give my love to all my relatives and friends and accept a portion for yourself. Write often, Aunt Beck. We appreciate your communication.

Affectionately your niece,
Mattie Whitten

Another correspondent, Mattie (Martha Earle), age 22, sends Rebecca family news and sounds like she has taken over the running of the household.

Rev. T. T. Weatherly (Primitive Baptist Minister) to Rebecca Whitten—Ripley to Poplar Springs, Mississippi, 21 Dec. 1890

Miss Whitten, Dear sister,

I hope a sister in Christ. With Christian love and fellowship toward you I thought I would try in my weakness to drop you a few lines in answer to your letter that I received of late. I was glad to hear from you and that you had not forgotten us as tho we were dead. I feel gratitude to know that your faith and trust in Christ is ever the same. Know confidence in the flesh when the storms of persecution arise as a trial of the Christian's faith, to try him, to see if he will deny his Lord and Master as Peter did, and pierce themselves through with many sorrows causes them to weep bitterly and then they have to deny themselves and look to Jesus alone for life and for Salvation, for Jesus says "I am the way, the truth, and the life and there is no other name given under Heaven nor among men whereby we may be saved in and thru the Lord and Savior Jesus Christ." Jesus said "No man can come to me except the Father which sent me draw him, and I will raise him up the last day." Jesus is the way and it is by Grace we are saved thru Faith and not of ourselves. It is the gift of God, not of works, lest any man should boast. We see it is by the imputed righteousness of Jesus that we are saved thru His Mercies, then as poor pilgrims in the midst of the furnace of affliction we plead with Him for mercy, waiting for the Redemption of our bodies when thou shall rise in the likeness of Jesus a glorified body with all the glorified Angels and sing His praise forever.

My dear Sister I heard you are back to the Association and joined New Salem Church. I went and asked advice of the Association and I went back. We had been falsely represented to the Association and they acted too hastily. I saw the Church at Antioc was dead and I could not live in that condition. I saw that we did wrong in drawing off from the Association at the time and place when we did. I saw it. I was willing to acknowledge our wrong and go back. I could not do anything for the Church. I had no authority and don't know what the Church will do.

I must close. May the Lord bless you and save is my prayer for Christ sake,

T. T. Weatherly

I hope Rebecca understood what Reverend Weatherly tried to tell her in this letter. It leaves me confused. This much I did grasp; Baptist churches are known for their democracy, autonomy, and freedom from clerical authority. Reverend Weatherly seems to have run afoul of this characteristic.

Joseph Earle Whitten to Rebecca Whitten—Slope #2, Pratt City, Alabama, to Poplar Springs, Mississippi, 26 Nov. 1894

Dear Aunt,

I suppose you will be somewhat surprised at receiving a letter from me, but it is frequently the unlooked for that happens, you know. While I have not been in direct correspondence with you I have heard of you very regularly through Dayton's (John Dayton, son of Joe and Mary Jane Whitten) folks.

I learn that you are in great deal better health than you used to be, or at least, you are relieved of the cough you used to be so bothered with. Tis a pleasure to know that you are so situated that you may spend your declining years pleasantly. It has been my intention to stop at Poplar on my way to Tippah but my visits have been few and far between. I was home last summer but only for two or three days. I was home about ten days but spent eight of them in Memphis with Pa (Ranson E. Whitten). I learn that he is greatly improved of late and I'm truly thankful for I don't think I ever saw anybody suffer as he was suffering when I got home.

I rarely ever hear from Nellie (Eleanor Kee, his sister) but I suppose she is getting along about as usual. Frank (sister Frank Alma) is with friends at Grand Junction, Tennessee, and has been for a month or six weeks. I don't know how long she intends staying. If it wasn't for Pa, I wouldn't care if she ever went back or not. I don't intend she shall stay long when she does go back.

I'm making a living but there isn't much satisfaction in it. I'm just staying here. I'm not living much. I came to the prison and got a job on the 10th of May and I have not lost a day since, except when I was gone home. The Tennessee Coal, Iron, and Railroad Company work about twelve hundred prisoners here and near here. They were just opening a new mine when I came and there is where I have worked all the while. I was promoted on the 12th of this month to engineer and general outside boss, so I'm better pleased than I was before, you may be sure. It doesn't pay very much but there is a good deal of satisfaction in being boss, you know.

Well, my regards to Frank and family (Frank Adams and Mary Dora Whitten). I must close,

J. E. Whitten

It is heartwarming to think that these young nieces and nephews thought enough of their old aunt to write and keep in touch. He gives her news and describes a unique business where prisoners are employed in mining coal for a private company. I wonder who was paid, the prisoner or the state of Alabama? It is unusual to see sibling conflict in these Whittens. What could have come between Joseph Earle and his sister, Frank Alma?

Alfred Washington to Rebecca Whitten—Burgess to Poplar Springs, Mississippi, 27 March 1895

Dear Rebecca,

Last week I received a letter from you, and one Harriet (Lankford, his sister) and one from Ranson. Well, I answered the one from Rant (Ranson E.), the one from Harriet, and thought I had answered yours. I was, indeed glad to hear from Ranson and Harriet through you but more so to get a letter from Rant by his own hand. He is greatly improved and says he will not be operated on again and hopes by time and care to be restored to health again. Harriet, though not well, seems to be on a continual feast with her wide spread children in the big state of Texas and the Indian Territory. How kind and considerate her children seem to be to her.

I made a great sacrifice to huddle with the greater part of mine, and as I thought, make a living easier, and although I will not complain, it was a mistake, and I expect to return to the old farm this summer. Rents here are so high that I long to get where all this will be free with meat and bread at home. My health has been frail indeed, this past winter. I now go on two sticks and cannot stand long, with weakness and pain in hips, and besides this, I have frequent threatenings of the old heart trouble, this I attribute largely to the severe winter and spring.

Did you ever see such a time? I did not. Merchandise is here but no money to buy with, but little preparation for farm work, inattention and idleness, discredit and financial pressure seem to rule. How cold and inhuman it all appears.

The school here so large, say two hundred and more and seems to breast every temptation and trial with severity and firmness. This week will close the third term and the walls are vocal with debate and recitation and it seems the whole place is in it.

Elliott is much worse but bears her part of our paper sack hotel with determination true as steel. All work hard with but little rest and with eight dollars per month can pay with nothing left for rents. We have four boarders only.

I often think of Cross Roads Church, the Glossy Rock, the Hog-back, and Pacolett, yes North Pacolett, and South Pacolett.

Adieu,

A. W. W.

Late in life, Alfred and Elliott Ann moved to Burgess, Mississippi, near Oxford, where several of their children worked and taught in Burgess Normal Institute. Son Hosea Ranson was principal, his wife's father operated a store nearby, daughter Maude Elliott taught art. Hosea's wife, Agnes Durham, was the music teacher, her sister Laeta taught English and physiology. Son Joseph Brooks taught history and ran another store. Son Silas, my grandfather, was business manager. Silas built a large house for his family, which also served to board students and teachers. My Aunt Lucille told of boarding there at age six and having a charge account at Uncle Joe's store. My mother was born nearby just two years after this letter was written.

Alfred said he and Elliott moved to assist his children and make an easier living practicing medicine. They were disappointed and returned to Jonesborough that summer. Costs were too high, living quarters not comfortable. He sounds like those of us who today have grown old and feel the world has changed for the worse, no one works, no one cares, everything is too costly.

Speaking of sister Harriet in Texas, he praises the way her children love and care for her. Having read many of her love-filled letters written over fifty years, I am not surprised.

Alfred recalls, with yearning, the shrines of his youth in Carolina, his Cross Roads Church, Glossy Rock, Hogback Mountain on whose slopes he was born, and the nearby rivers, North and South Pacolett.

Ranson E. to Rebecca Whitten—Ripley to Poplar Springs, Mississippi, 19 July 1896

Dear Sister,

I send you a letter from Dolly Whitten (Doleska Fitzallen Whitten, daughter of Arphax, granddaughter of James) asking for information in regard to our ancestors. If you can give me this desired information I will send it to her with pleasure.

I made a visit to Jonesborough three weeks ago, found all well except our Brother (Alfred Washington Whitten). His health is fading rapidly. He had a light stroke of paralysis in one side of his face recently and it is difficult for him to talk, his articulation is imperfect. He spends much of his time sleeping in his chair and I would not be surprised at any time should he pass off in that way. I did not allow him to sleep much while I was there. He was jolly and pleasant all the while.

My health has been better this spring and summer than for two years past. I have, however, been quite feeble for a week past, indigestion is the trouble. I have not had a severe pain in my face since the first of February but threatening snaps every day. Frank (daughter, Frank Alma) is at home now and Silas (son, Silas Reagan) has been with me all year and has a splendid crop. We haven't suffered a day for rain so far and everything is fully a month in advance of the season.

Dayton has a fine crop. Hester looks thin but is lively. Harriett spends most of her time with Maggie (John Dayton, Hester Virginia,

Harriett Earle, and Maggie Madora were children of Joseph John). Our garden has been good but the fruit crop a failure except pears and a few wormy peaches. Love to Molly and the children.

Your affectionate Brother,
R. E. Whitten

Haven't heard from Sister Harriet in a year or more, would write to her if I knew her PO.

This is the last news we have of Alfred. He has suffered a stroke, and sits most of the time. He died 9 March 1897, eight months later. The facial pain that plagued Ranson almost certainly was tic de la rue. Ranson's son, Alfred Tennyson Whitten, was also afflicted with it.

This is the obituary of Dr. Alfred Washington Whitten:

Alfred Washington Whitten was born in Greenville District, SC, March 1 1822. In early life he made choice of the medical profession, and, so soon as he had procured a literary fitness for his Herculean task, he began professional study under Drs. Wm. A. Moony and M. B. Earle, both of whom were honored physicians of that country. For three years he plied himself under their trusted supervision and then entered study in the medical department of Transylvania University, Lexington, Ky., where he took two full courses of lectures. He next matriculated at University Pennsylvania, Philadelphia, and on April 3, 1847, graduated with full honors from that distinguished school. His first three years of professional work was in his native state, but in 1850 he moved to Ripley, Tippah, Mississippi, where he formed professional partnership with Dr. W. D. Carter, thus entering upon an extensive work immediately. On the 26th of January, 1853, he was married to Elliott Ann Ray, daughter of the lamented Ambrose Ray. This union seems to have been one where "God had joined together," for until death severed the sacred ties they walked together over the rugged paths of this eventful life. The disappointments, anxieties, cares, and toils of this changeful state were matters of mutual concern, while the comfort and cheer of one was the gladness and joy of the other. With reciprocal affection, congenial minds, and hearts fettered by each other's love, they braved the storms of this tempestuous sea. Shortly after his marriage he settled near Jonesborough, in the northern portion of the same county, where he spent the remainder of his life. He was a devotee to his profession, and enjoyed an extensive

Dr. Alfred Washington Whitten
1822-1897
near the end of his life

practice, the appreciation of which was fully attested by the shadows that gathered about the brow of rich and poor, black and white, when it was announced that his life had ended. Early in life he professed faith in Christ, and in his own peculiarly humble way exerted an extensive and intense influence over the circle in which he moved. The secret of his success must have nestled in his relation to God, for the Lord was his counciling physician. He was fond of reading, and aside from secular matter and professional study, he searched the Scriptures often, and left his marks of pencil and tears as a commentary for his children. He cultivated the habit of often writing his thoughts, and sometimes found himself in a poetical mood. His thoughts were always pure and lofty, and many of his writings are worth a place in the archives of American literature. In his home life he was cheerfulness personified, and while under a cloud was always looking for a rift through which the streams of sunshine might come. His smiles could chase the shadows from the home circle and his hope could inspire every latent energy of his associates. While he had faults, yet it was hard for those who had known him longest, and loved him best, to discover the blemish upon that character which was wrought with an unsurpassed energy and in Godly fear. On the morning of March 9 1897, he fell asleep in Jesus, and his spirit took its flight to God who gave it, where it will await the redemption of the body on the morning of the resurrection. He left a wife and ten children, all of whom cherish his memory and are striving to emulate his example.

Harriet Whitten Lankford to Rebecca Whitten—Columbus Street, Waco, Texas, to Poplar Springs, Mississippi, 18 Dec. 1901

My dear Sister,

I received your kind letter promptly and hasten to write you a short note to tell you the genealogical papers the girls sent you are for you to keep and dispose of as you wish. We have the original copy. They were compiled at the city of Washington by the Seniors Club of Daughters of Revolution which is located there and from them you can obtain any revolutionary history you wish, which is a great convenience. Sallie (daughter, Sallie Florence) gets the American Monthly Magazine. On the papers you have you will see our father's and mother's names and our aunts and uncles.

There are many of the Earle kin here who are an honor to the grand old name. One of Uncle Baylis, or Gen. Earle's (John Baylis Earle,

1771–1836, half-brother of her mother) granddaughters who speaks of our mother as Aunt Nelly Kee, says she was her grandfather's favorite sister.

I am very sorry you are so afflicted with a dreadful cough. If you will drink strong Mullen tea at night, made very sweet with honey, it will help you. Sorry our dear brother (Ranson E.) suffers so dreadfully, but I know he is patient and his reward will be in Heaven. I am tolerable well and blessed with innumerable comforts, kind friends. My Heavenly Father careth for me.

Love to all, remember your sister loves you,

H. E. Lankford

Having become interested in family history, Harriet is well aware of the good name earned by her mother's family, the Earles of Virginia and South Carolina. She knew that her grandfather, John Whitten, was a veteran of the Revolution and she became an early member of the DAR.

Annie Ard to Rebecca Whitten—Lumpkin, Georgia, to Poplar Springs, Mississippi, 6 April 1909

My dear Miss Whitten,

I recently saw the name of your nephew, Mr. Silas Ray Whitten (son of Alfred Washington Whitten) in the Christian Index, our Baptist paper, and wrote him, supposing that he was a relative, and a letter that he wrote to me tells me that we are related.

His grandfather, Silas Reagan Whitten and my great grandfather, Rev. James Whitten, were brothers. I have made a tree of James Whitten's branch of the family, and have the names of a few of the other branches. I will be so glad if you will help me to complete it with such information as you have, either from your family records, or, if you have not records that extend back very many years, will you please tell me what you know about the family through hearing your father speak of its various members and its history? I will send you a copy of my tree if I hear from you, and I hope this letter will reach you.

Yours very truly,

Annie Ard

Rebecca saved many letters proving that the two branches of the Whitten family kept in close touch, especially through the efforts of Eliza and Doleska Fitzallen Whitten, daughter and granddaughter of James. Rebecca's reply to Miss Ard's letter would be so interesting to us.

Martha Earle (Mattie) Whitten Flinn to May Isom Whitten Moore—Olive

Branch to Jackson, Mississippi, 21 Feb. 1940

Dear May Isom (daughter of Silas Ray Whitten and the author's mother),

If that is Homer Whitten, and I am sure it is, he is a son of Dr. Will Whitten (William Andrew, son of Joseph John), who was our first cousin. Sister Ellen and Agnes both better. I am so glad Mr. Moore went to see brother June (sister Maude Elliott, Sarah Agnes Durham wife of brother Hosea Ranson, and brother Jesse June). It rains and snows here all the time. Brother Bedford some better. Cousin Effie (daughter of Silas Reagan Jr.) not so well.

In love,

Aunt Mattie (daughter of Alfred Washington Whitten)

Aubra Burford Whitten (wife of Joseph Brooks, son of Alfred Washington) to May Isom Whitten Moore (daughter of Silas Ray, also son of Alfred Washington)—Memphis, Tennessee, to Jackson, Mississippi, about 1942

Dear May Isom,

Your sweet note received several days past. I want you to know that we all appreciate your visit so much. I have always wanted to know more about Brother Silas's family. We all loved him and fell so in love with Lottie (Lottie Helon, daughter of Silas Ray). You remember she brought her father to see Mr. Whitten a short while before he left us. It did him so much good.

Lourelia and her husband surprised us with a visit last week end. They could only be away a week, so, of course she had to go with him to meet his people. They live in Pine Bluff, Arkansas. However she came back here on Tuesday and remained till Saturday. She likes Buffalo very well. Corinne and baby doing very nicely. (Lourelia and Corinne were her daughters.)

Since you were here DeWitt has joined the Navy and is to leave the 9th of March. I don't see how I can spare him, yet I have to. That will leave me here alone unless Joseph Burford and Maggie Lee decide to move over. I wrote Woodrow about your nephew being in San Francisco. He is very anxious to meet him. So if you have his address please send it to Woodrow at 2435 Bancroft Way Berkeley, California. (Aubrey Dewitt, Joseph Burford, and Woodrow Carlton were her sons.)

Now, when you and Mr. Moore come to town again, come around to see us. We will always be delighted to have you.

J. B. and Maggie Lee are to go to see Sister Mattie (Martha Earle

Flinn) tomorrow night. They often spend the weekend with her. The last I heard from her she was feeling as well as usual.

Aunt Aubra

Martha Earle (Mattie) Whitten Flinn to Lottie Helon Whitten Merritt—Olive Branch to Boyle, Mississippi, 15 Feb. 1951

Dear Lottie,

Ethel wanted me to send her dates of my father and mother's birth but she failed to give me her address so I am sending it to you. I enjoyed your little visit so much and wish you could have stayed longer. I show my apron to ever body who comes in. I am so proud of it. I went through this awful cold spell far better than I expected. Three white children right near here froze to death. Can you imagine anything more awful? I have had a lot of company since you were here. I rather think they thought I would not stand it.

I like my new people just fine. They are really good to me. I am sleeping better and eating better than I have been doing. The other family had nine dogs and they kept me awake.

Sunbram and baby came to see me Tuesday, Leon (son of brother Bedford) Sunday, Hubert and wife (son of brother John Graves) Tuesday, J. B. and Maggie Lee (son of brother Joseph Brooks) Wednesday. I love my people and always glad to see them. I hope you can come back and stay longer. Give all the children my love.

Truly,

Aunt Mattie

Father borned 1 March 1822, mother borned 22 Nov. 1834.
Father died 9 March 1897, mother died 31 Aug. 1920

Cora Mae Whitten to Alfred Tennyson Whitten (son of Ranson E.)—Rt. 3 New Albany to Jackson, Mississippi, 7 Feb. 1957

Dear Sir,

My father, Dr. William Andrew Whitten (son of Joseph John and Mesina Whitten) married May Tate. There were four of us children (Harriet Beaulah, Harvey Earle, William Homer, and Cora Mae). Earle and Homer both are dead. They died with heart attacks about three months difference in their deaths. Father died in 1924 and mother in 1948.

We are living at the old home here in Keonville where my father lived. Hattie married Carl Hines. He died in 1932, left her with four children, two boys and two girls. The boys have a nice little country store here in Keonville.

Now, I don't know anything about my father's people but I would like to know. I knew all of his brothers and sisters, but know more of Aunt Ammie and Maggie (Narcissa Amaryllis, daughter of Joseph John and Mary Jane, and Maggie Madora, daughter of Joseph John and Maggie Davis Doyle) than the rest because they died when I was small. I know cousin Nellie Rucker and Joe (Eleanor Kee and Joseph Earle, children of Ranson E. and Pocahontas R. Whitten). I have been in cousin Joe's home when he lived in Cullman, Alabama. He married Lulu Tate. He was a wonderful man. He was so good to mother and me. Mother lived to be eighty-six years old.

Well, I am an old maid, never did marry.

Lots of love,
Cora Mae Whitten
Hattie Hines

The older generation is gone, Rebecca died 2 May 1909, Ranson in 1906. The younger Whittens are scattered over the South. Some tried to stay in touch, to preserve family history and retain family ties. A few efforts succeeded, most failed. Families are mobile, life is complex. They lost each other in one generation!

Account of a trip written by Silas Ray Whitten (son of Alfred Washington) for his children—Summer 1936

Feeling a little weary and in need of a vacation, my daughter Lottie and I decided to do some trotting around through Mississippi, visiting our relatives and friends. We got together our best "bib and tuck" and put out on the morning of the 5th of August for Boyle, Mississippi, where we spent the first night in my daughter's home. We enjoyed the beautiful cotton fields all along the route from Jackson, also the corn fields which were full of corn, the sloping hills, the spacious Delta. It was a three hour drive. We stopped only once in route, and that was to see some interesting scenes in Yazoo City, where I had spent many hours years ago when in the life insurance business.

Having arrived at Boyle, we rested and had a wonderful night of sleep. We arose the next morning to find it a beautiful day. We left at eight o'clock, drove through cotton section again, and beautiful little towns, to Marks, Mississippi, now a thriving little city of three thousand. There we stopped to speak to an old friend, Mr. P. M. B. Self. Mr. Self is one of the leading men of the town. We were glad

Silas Ray Whitten
1860-1940
who traveled into his past

to visit with him for an hour and talk over the old times had back when he and I were young. I was glad, indeed, to hear that Mr. Self is now a wealthy man.

From Marks, we journeyed to Batesville, where we struck highway 51 for Coldwater. We enjoyed the new concrete highway through Sardis, Como, and Senatobia. We had lunch at Sardis and did a little politicking there for my good friend Pat Harrison. At two o'clock we arrived at Coldwater, a pretty little town with nice residences, spacious lawns, and beautiful trees. There we found the home of one of my brothers, Bedford Forrest Whitten.

Finding them all at home we went in to enjoy a nice afternoon visit with them. They were all very happy, just celebrating their 50th anniversary. They had with them for a visit their daughter Laeta and granddaughter. Laeta is now Mrs. Lipscomb from Albany, Texas. Also visiting them was their son's wife, Mrs. Leon Whitten, from Memphis. Their son, Steadman, lives with them. This formed a very congenial party, so after many jokes and talking of old times, a watermelon cutting, etc., we left, after spending a very happy three hours with them. We were glad to see that they own a lovely little home and everything around them for comfort and happiness.

We bade them goodbye at four o'clock and headed for Olive Branch, over a poor dirt road, but it was an experience, for we went through a section that is as old as time, men still sit and whittle, veritable Rip Van Winkle towns. We lost our way once or twice as there were no road signs, but all was peaceful and quiet, and friendly people to straighten us out on our route.

At six o'clock we drove up to the home of my sister, Mrs. L. Flinn, (Martha Earle) to tarry for a few days. I had not seen this sister, Mattie, for fourteen years, so it was not strange that, when I asked to get lodging, she refused me entrance, saying the man of the house was away, and she could not take me in. But finally, after being insistent, she recognized me and gave me a great big hug and a most cordial welcome.

Three days we tarried there at Olive Branch, and they were happy days. We talked, we sang, we ate, we slept. Cousin Effie Perkins (Effie Berry, daughter of Silas Reagan Whitten Jr.) was there, a dear sweet cousin of mine, looking so young, yet so old, old in years but young in spirit. We saw Hosea Ranson, my brother, who lives there with Mattie.

Mattie was not well, but oh, what a good time we had talking.

Never have I seen so many good things to eat. There was gladness mixed with sadness, for at this home my mother (Elliott Ann Ray Whitten) passed away fourteen years ago and just one month ago my sister, Sallie (Sarah Kee) was called home, so Mattie was the guardian angel that waited on them and made their remaining days happy. Olive Branch is a busy little town, good schools, nice homes, and a large cheese factory. It is located in a good farming section.

We had the pleasure while visiting Mattie to take her and cousin Effie to Memphis and spend the day with Joseph Brooks, my youngest brother. Joe has a wonderful wife (Aubra Burford) and seven sweet fine children. Two sons are married and live at home. We found Joe quite sick with cancer, but so hopeful of recovery. They entertained us royally and seemed so glad to see us, and we certainly enjoyed the day. Joe has a nice home and has done well financially. It was with reluctance that we said goodbye for it was the end of a perfect day.

On returning to Olive Branch, we passed through Mineral Mills, where we visited an old girl of mine, Miss Leota, found her young looking and well, and also enjoyed seeing Agnes (Sarah Agnes Durham), Hosea's wife. She is still bright as a dollar, though her health has been very bad. She has two children grown and out in the world making a good living. Miss Leota has one daughter, Mary, and one grandchild.

We also visited a lovely little resort nearby and saw the summer cottage of Naomi Bradley, Maude's (sister, Maude Elliott) youngest daughter. She married a sportsman and wealthy man. They are now travelling in South America. We had the pleasure of seeing Louise Elverta Bradley, Maude's oldest daughter, who holds a position in Memphis. The two sons of Maude (Frank Herman and Ed Farmer Bradley) are away, one in Kansas City, the other in Los Angeles.

One night while we were in Olive Branch, Bedford and his family came up and visited with us, and we had a good old singing bee near Memphis. We hated to leave Olive Branch but time was passing fast and we had many more places to visit farther on. We journeyed over Highway 78 to Holly Springs, a distance of thirty eight miles, pretty scenery. We made brief stops at Byhalia and Potts Camp for me to say a good word for Pat Harrison, thence on to Holly Springs where we looked up Isabelle Tyson (family friend). We enjoyed seeing her and she took us to an antique shop which Lottie enjoyed very much. It was noon then, so we hastened on to New Albany, ate dinner, and went up to our rooms for a nap.

It was Saturday, and never have we seen so many people on the streets. They say New Albany banks have more money in them than in any other town on North Mississippi, and we were fully prepared to believe that. New Albany is a pretty place, pretty trees, homes, etc. Many substantial, lovely people live in that town.

We rested for several hours, then drove around to see Mesina Elliott (daughter of sister Molly, Mary Dora), a niece of mine. Mesina married Mr. Varda Smith, City Clerk. They have a nice home and two daughters are living at home, the other married and living in Kansas City. Mesina and her family were so sweet and lovely to us. We went with them to Sunday School and Church the next day, and I made a talk at Sunday School for Mesina. Lottie says I am still pretty good at speech making. We heard a good sermon by Mr. Kirkwood, Baptist minister, and then enjoyed a fine dinner at the hotel. Mesina and family carried us out to see Molly that afternoon and we spent several very happy hours with her. The children all came by to see us, Nat (Nathaniel Carter Whitten) and his family and some of his children and family and then Frank Adams Whitten Jr. who lives with Molly (Nat and Frank Jr. were sons of Molly).

Molly is eighty two years of age, just as spry as a cricket, and keeps house and cans everything in sight. Frank is a fine man and looks after everything for Molly. We certainly had a very happy time together. Molly was so glad to see me and I to see her. They have everything around them to make life worth living. Tis the same home she has lived in for years there in Blue Springs. We enjoyed the fruit very much, figs, peaches, watermelons.

We drove back to New Albany late, very tired but glad indeed to have visited with so many of my family. The next morning bright and early we left for Blue Mountain. That was a very happy visit for me, for it brought to my mind so many happy memories of courting days and our first housekeeping. We did not see Love Rock but passed near it, but we did go and see the home I built and we occupied as newlyweds. The house still stands in good preservation, and to me it was a mansion of memories. We visited Mrs. Palmer Cossett, found her in good health. She didn't know me but I didn't know her. Years have passed since we met before. We drove around to see the College. Many fine buildings have been built since I last saw it. We enjoyed such a happy time with Cousin Lucinda Ray and Nora Lee (cousins of his mother, Elliott Ann Ray Whitten). They keep house, have a cozy little place, and nothing would do but we must lunch with them. We did and a lovely meal they served us. We talked of old times and heard about many of my old friends who have passed away. Cousin Lucinda and Nora Lee are so interesting, and looking as young as they did thirty years ago. Nora Lee still teaches English at the College. Blue Mountain is still a beautiful and sacred spot for me.

Ripley was our next stop, a distance of only six miles from Blue Mountain. We spent the night there and saw many dear ones I haven't seen in years. Cousins Ammy and Maggie (Narcissa Amaryllis and Maggie Madora) Whitten, daughters of Uncle Joe (Joseph John) Whitten, are still beautiful women, white hair and lovely complexions. They live with a niece and daughter. Cousin Amaryllis is eighty years old, but oh, so young. We visited cousin Susie Garrett's two daughters, Ethyl and another. They both have nice homes there. They were all so glad to see me looking so well. I sent around to see Marshall Bennett who used to work for me, and found him in fine shape physically and financially. He said that Bedford Forrest and part of his family were visiting them, so we drove by to say hello. Bedford, Flora, Laeta, husband and child were there and persuaded us to join them for the day.

Brother Bedford got in our car to show us over the country. We enjoyed the scenery, tis beautiful country up through there. We ate dinner at the Tom Bennett's and after dinner went to the old Bennett home. It was like a visit to an old home in Natchez. It was a beautiful old one story house, green shutters, lovely old shrubbery. Never have we enjoyed such hospitality, not since I was a boy have I seen a table so laden with good things, side table full of cakes, pies, and all kinds of desserts.

Mrs. Tom Bennett is Corinne Garrett, a cousin of ours. (The mother of Elliott Ann Ray Whitten, his mother, was a Garrett.) She welcomed us and certainly entertained us royally. Tom Bennett is a very prosperous farmer, has seven children, one in Washington, one away at Marks teaching. We were having such a good time, visiting, exchanging jokes, etc. that we hated to leave such a comfortable place.

Accompanied still by Bedford and family we drove to Chalybeate, but the place was so changed, and not knowing anyone, we just visited the old Union Church grave yard. There we found the graves of my father and mother, a nice large monument marks their resting place. In looking around there were many names familiar to me, Hollis, Willbanks, Perkins, Rays, etc. The old Union Church where I worshipped as a boy has gone, but I heard that soon a new church would be built on the same spot as the other one.

We drove three miles to the old home place. The lane leading up to it has changed so little. The trees are still on each side of the lane. The house still stands as of old, though beaten considerably. We went in and looked over it, all rooms standing, the windows as they were when Mattie (sister, Martha Earle) painted them, the kitchen and dining room off from the house. We saw the same hoops that held my Father's guns, the room which was called the apple room. The same well stands and we could not refrain from drinking from the oaken bucket. All scenes were still familiar. The Hardins own the home, having lived there since we sold it years ago. Lottie brought back with her some of the old flowers out of my mother's yard. The old cedars still stand but have grown to such large trees. We did not visit the old orchard but we did eat some of the fine yellow apples that were planted by my father, and tasted of the plums from the plum trees. We were sorry that we did not have a Kodak to take some pictures of the old home, but some day we will return again and do so. My father practiced medicine in the community for fifty years. He was a wonderful doctor, graduated at Philadelphia, Pennsylvania, and took a course in Baltimore. (It was Lexington, Kentucky, not Baltimore.)

We did not go to Jonesborough, but many were the incidents we recalled of our trips over there to get the mail and visit with Aunt Duck (Madora Frances, wife of Silas Reagan Whitten Jr. and sister of mother, Elliott Ann Ray). Negroes occupy the home once owned by my Aunt, but nearby live the John Hollis family. We wanted to drive over but the roads forbade. Going back to the highway we stopped to bid goodbye to Bedford and his family, for we were leaving them and going in another direction. They went back to Coldwater and we over to Corinth.

We drove twenty miles, by the old home of my Uncle Hosea Ray (mother's brother) on toward Corinth, but as we got within a mile of Corinth we turned and went to Tupelo, as the infantile paralysis was so bad around in that section. We wanted so much to go to Iuka to see Brother Jesse June, but had to forego that pleasure until a later date.

In route to Tupelo we passed through Baldwyn, not a bad little town, and on to Tupelo for the night. We got a suite of rooms and bath in the Tupelo Hotel, a good supper, and then to bed, but, being overtired, did not sleep very well. But next morning, getting a nice bath and shave, I was greatly refreshed by going out and going through a shirt factory. It was very interesting, indeed. Fifteen hundred young women are employed in this factory making nothing but work shirts. Tupelo boasts of several large factories. It is a wide-awake town. We drove all over the residential section and saw one new home after another being built up since the dreadful storm of April of this year. Tupelo people are still sad over their misfortune, but soon things will be cleared away, new trees growing, and years will blot out all traces of the storm.

We had a nice lunch and left for Oxford. We enjoyed this drive of fifty miles. Many times in years past I have driven it in carriage. It reminded us in spots of North Carolina, so beautifully hilly and the valleys so green with vegetation. There is a concrete road the entire distance. I recalled many old friends living along the way. Many of them have passed beyond.

It was just sunset as we rolled into Oxford. We went to the hotel and got a room and it was the same room that my bride (Ruth Sawyer Burt) and I occupied the first night we were married, just fifty six years ago. I recalled many happy experiences and scenes. One was the reception held at the Hotel the night of our wedding. It's a quaint old place, but good rooms and nice food. After supper we walked around the square reading familiar names on the business houses, such as Rowland, Chilton, etc. The next morning we drove into University Street, saw Mamie Burt's old home, visited the University grounds, to the hospital to see Hattie Mae Burt (wife's cousin). She was glad to see us and to hear from the family. Hattie May is even more beautiful than since we've seen her and she is happy with her fine husband. We looked up cousins Garner Owen and Nona Beanland and sat with them an hour in their home. They were so glad to see us and told us many things about our old friends. Lottie visited Mary Vick Rowland whom she had not seen since she left Coffeeville. We drove past the Childress home and it is one of the prettiest old homes of Oxford.

It was getting late and we were anxious to spend the night at Boyle. The weather was getting very hot and we were getting anxious for cooler weather. We turned our faces toward Coffeeville. It was a nice drive through Water Valley, then to Coffeeville. We intended to surprise the Bryants (family friends), but not so. They had some mail for us, so they were watching out for us. It was a happy meeting. They gave us a cordial welcome and we had lunch with them and a happy good visit. We drove around town, by our old home, and on to

Oakland.

We spent an hour with Mr. Moore (Green H. Moore, my grandfather), enjoyed seeing him and talking over the times, etc. He was in fine spirits and sent us on our way much refreshed. It was eighty miles to Boyle, the western sun beaming down on us very heavily, but we made it by five o'clock over very dusty roads through Charleston, Webb, Drew, and, finally, Boyle. Lottie's place looked good to us for we knew that here we could rest for a few days before going to Jackson.

So this ended the trip. We agreed that never had we spent such happy times in travelling together.

S.R.Whitten

What better way to end a study of family letters than to read of a trip into the past. Silas Ray Whitten and his daughter Lottie Merritt, who I called Aunt Nannie, visited several brothers, sisters, aunts, and cousins still living in north Mississippi. There were brothers Bedford Forrest, Hosea Ranson, and Joseph Brooks, sister Mattie, at whose home mother Elliott Ann Ray and sister Sallie Kee had died, and cousin Effie, the beautiful child of Pluck and Duck. Then on to Poplar Springs to see one of our favorite letter writers, sister Mary Dora, eighty-two and still working in the house. With her were some of her children: Mesina Elliott and her daughter, Frank Adams Jr., and Nathaniel Carter and some of his children. I like to think that Nat's son, Murry, who loaned me Rebecca's letters was there. Would Nat have been embarrassed at our laughter while reading of his first pair of new britches?

Next, they drove to Ripley, where Silas Reagan and Eleanor Kee, Jo, Mesina, Mary Jane, and Maggie, Ranson E., Medora and Sallie, Rebecca and so many children lived for so long. All are buried there save Rebecca, who lies in the Baptist churchyard near Frank and Molly's home, where she died. Only two of Jo's daughters were there to greet them, Narcissa and Maggie Medora.

They visited the old home between Jonesborough and Chalybeate. There, Elliott bore all ten of her children, and letters were written by Alfred, Elliott, Molly, and Mattie.

The last stop of interest to us was at Oxford-Burgess, where many of the family labored at the Burgess Normal Institute, and Alfred remembered Cross Roads, Hogback, Glossy Rock, and the Pacolett, North and South.

I have no more letters, but stories of real families never end and ours is no exception. Children are born, others die. Our Whittens and Earles are spread over the country, too numerous to treat as one family, many not knowing they descend from these letter writers.

This book was assembled because my mother wanted me to learn about her people. It has consumed years of my life, and I have no regrets. There is little to apologize for and much to be proud of in mother's family. Some still show traces of Alfred Washington's creativity, the stubborn strength of Silas Reagan, the pure love of Harriet and Pluck, the versatility of Mary Dora. There are physicians and ministers. A few write poetry and books, sing songs, and paint pictures. They farm and run for public office. Many have served, with Ranson's courage and dedication, in the armed forces of our country.

Our ancestors all shared an abiding and deeply felt faith in God. Their lives centered around Him and His Church. We have seen that He cared for them, and held them up in times of trouble. I have met many of the modern-day members of the Charles Whitten family, and find that most have stayed true to that faith. This makes me glad. ✳

INDEX

Letters, Articles, Illustrations, and Obituaries

Chapter Seven

INDEX

Names

www.ingramcontent.com/pod-product-compliance
Lightning Source LLC
Chambersburg PA
CBHW070543270326
41926CB00013B/2189
9780788403040